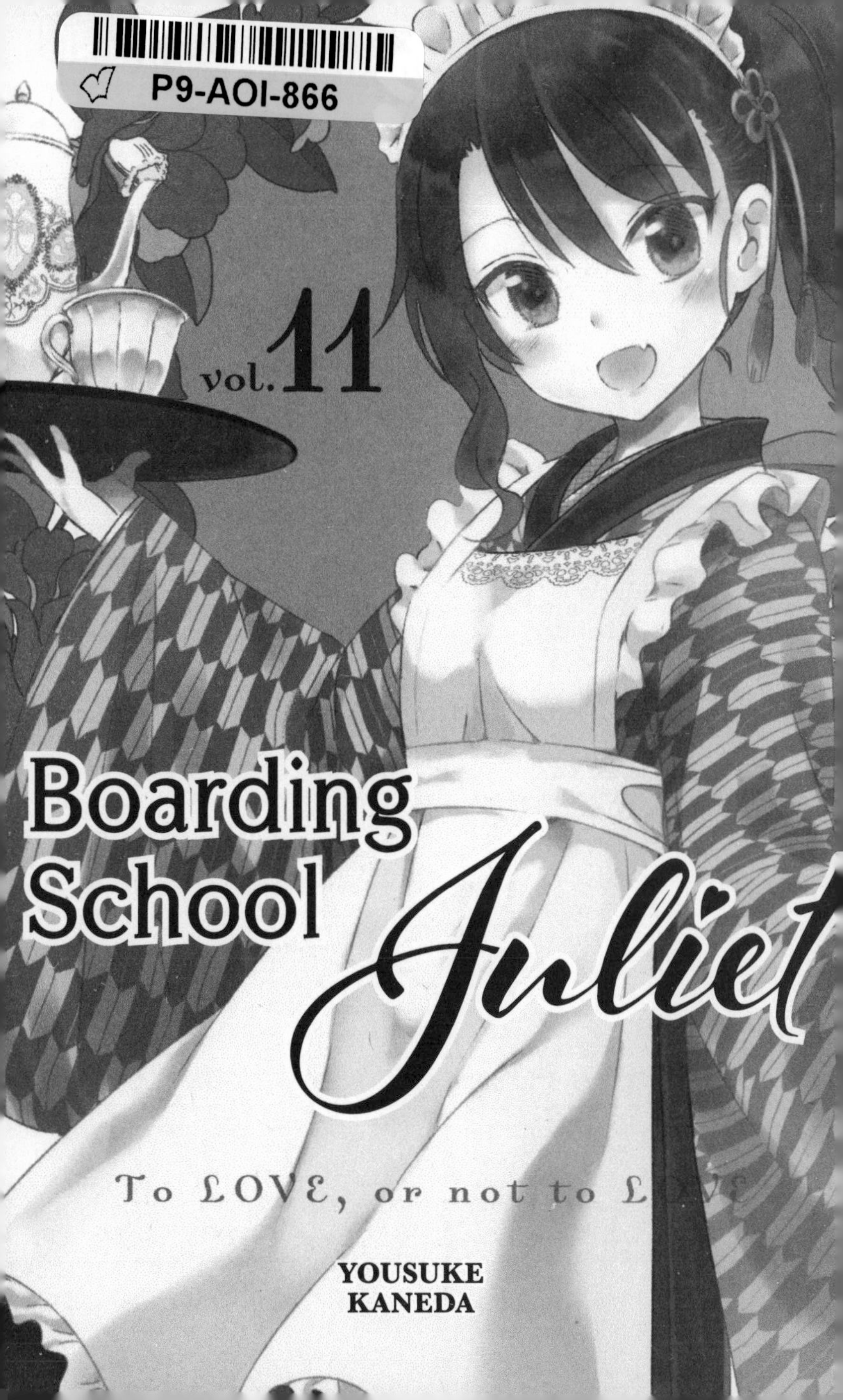
vol. 11
Boarding School
Juliet
To LOVE, or not to
YOUSUKE
KANEDA

THE PLAYERS

character

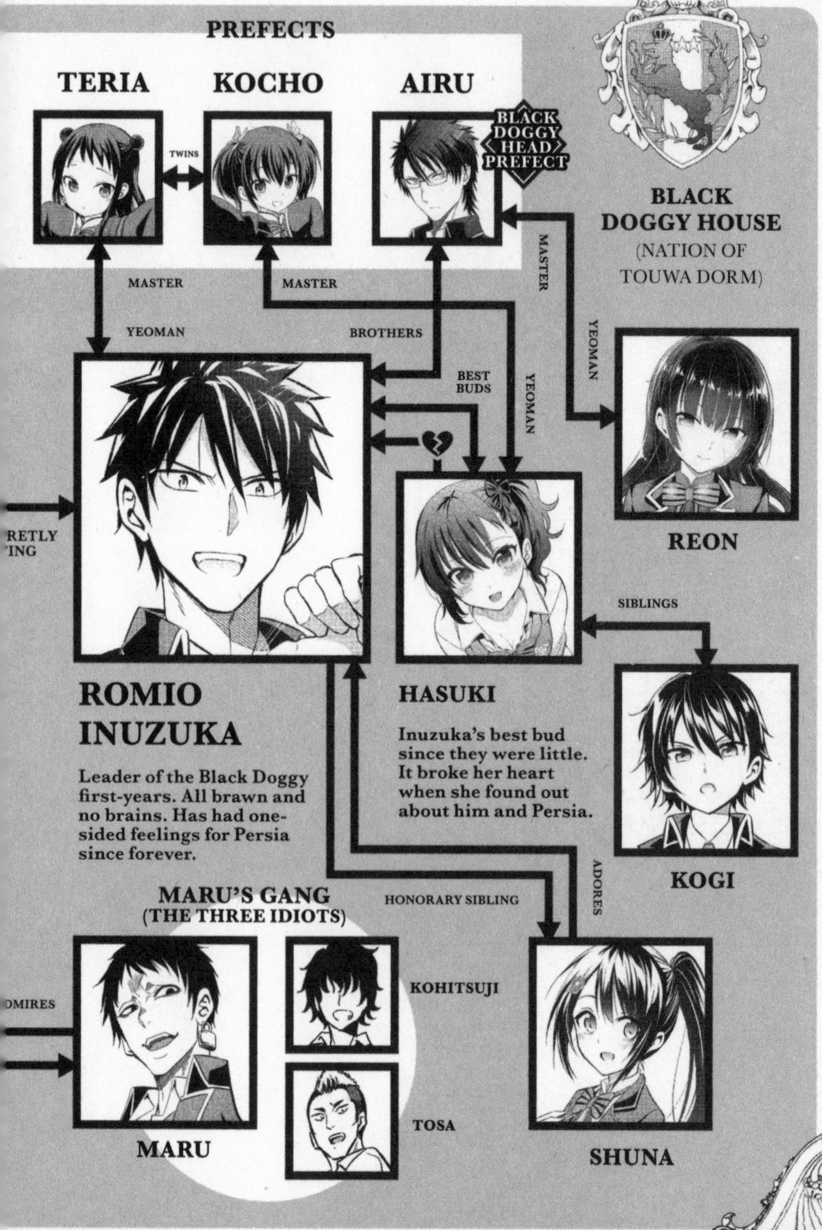
PREFECTS
TERIA
KOCHO
AIRU
TWINS
BLACK DOGGY HEAD PREFECT
BLACK DOGGY HOUSE (NATION OF TOUWA DORM)
MASTER
MASTER
MASTER
YEOMAN
BROTHERS
YEOMAN
BEST BUDS
YEOMAN
REON
RETLY
ING
ROMIO INUZUKA
Leader of the Black Doggy first-years. All brawn and no brains. Has had one-sided feelings for Persia since forever.
HASUKI
Inuzuka's best bud since they were little. It broke her heart when she found out about him and Persia.
SIBLINGS
KOGI
ADORES
HONORARY SIBLING
MARU'S GANG (THE THREE IDIOTS)
OMIRES
MARU
KOHITSUJI
TOSA
SHUNA

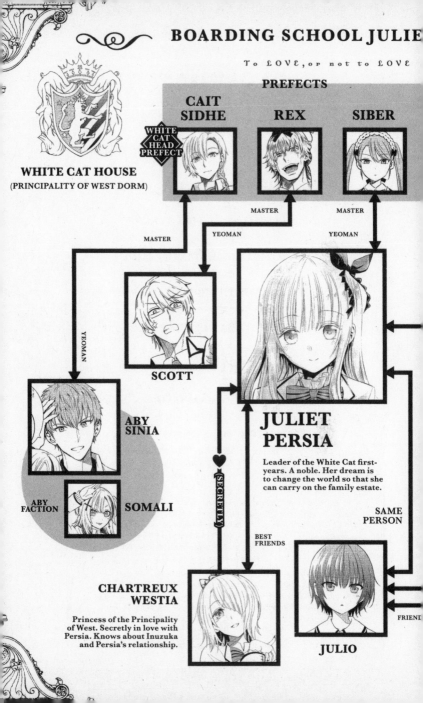

BOARDING SCHOOL JULIE

To £OVE, or not to £OVE

PREFECTS

CAIT SIDHE

REX

SIBER

WHITE CAT HEAD PREFECT

WHITE CAT HOUSE
(PRINCIPALITY OF WEST DORM)

MASTER

MASTER

MASTER

YEOMAN

YEOMAN

MASTER

YEOMAN

SCOTT

ABY SINIA

ABY FACTION

SOMALI

JULIET PERSIA

Leader of the White Cat first-years. A noble. Her dream is to change the world so that she can carry on the family estate.

(SECRETLY)

BEST FRIENDS

SAME PERSON

CHARTREUX WESTIA

Princess of the Principality of West. Secretly in love with Persia. Knows about Inuzuka and Persia's relationship.

FRIEND

JULIO

contents

story

At boarding school Dahlia Academy, attended by students from two feuding countries, one first-year longs for a forbidden love. His name: Romio Inuzuka, leader of the Black Doggy House first-years. The apple of his eye: Juliet Persia, leader of the White Cat House first-years. It all begins when Inuzuka confesses his feelings to her. This is Inuzuka and Persia's star-crossed, secret love story...

In preparation for the prefect election to be held in May, the current prefects' yeomen all came face-to-face at the Prefect Assembly, where Reon's fierce hostility toward the White Cats manifested in a declaration to become a Head Prefect and crush the rival dorm. Inuzuka and Persia, too, threw their hats into the ring for the Head Prefect positions. They're all vying for their own dreams...

ACT 68:

ROMIO & REON & AFTER-SCHOOL DUTIES

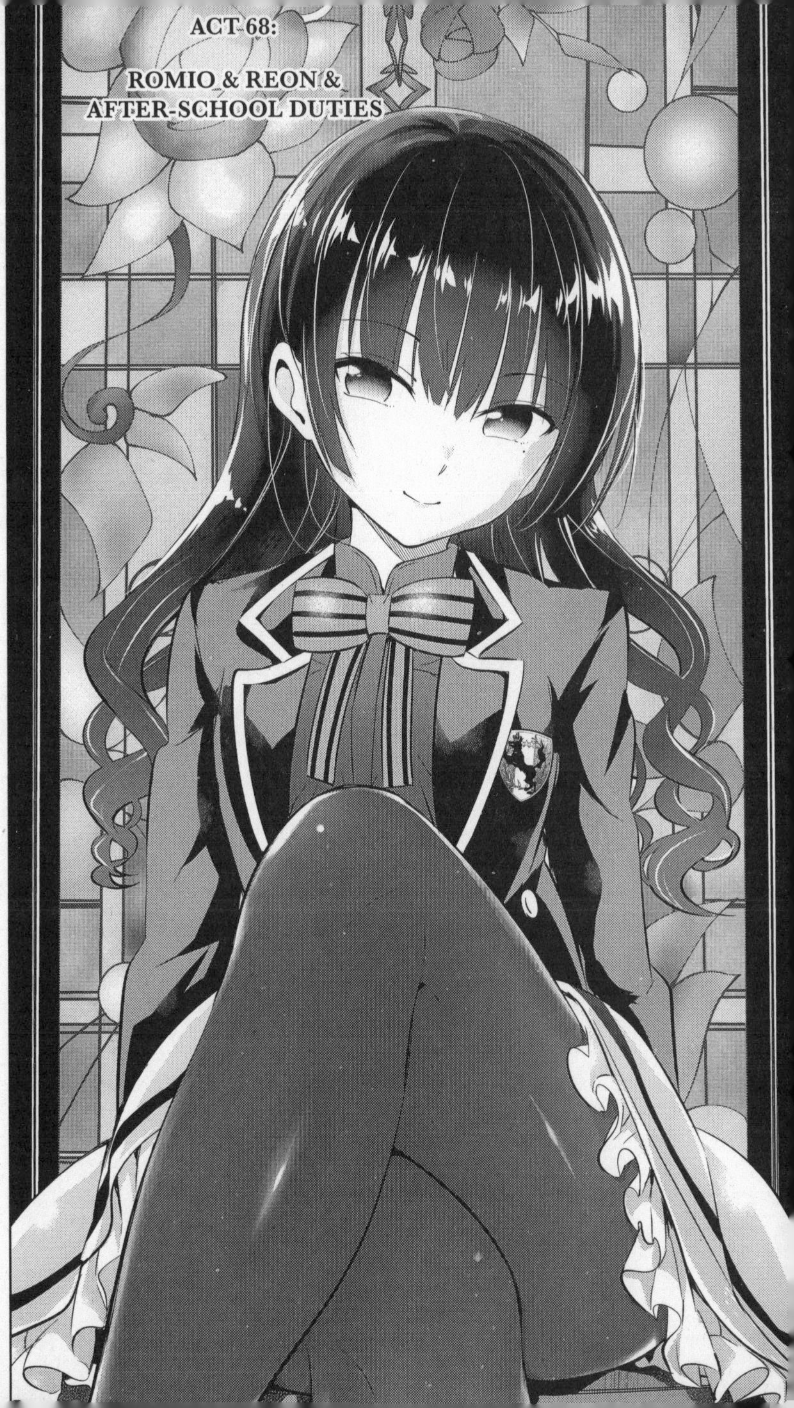

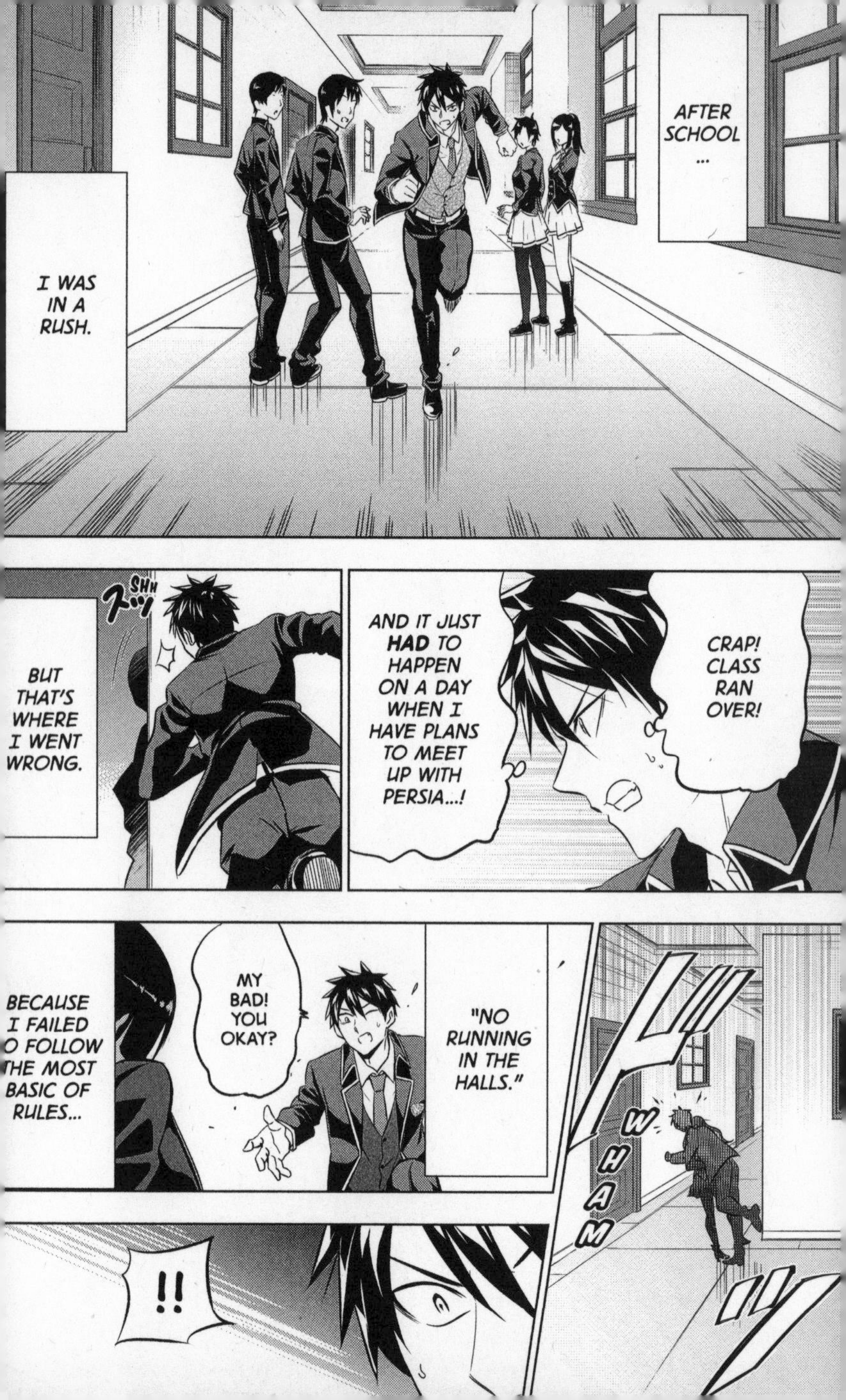
AFTER SCHOOL ...
I WAS IN A RUSH.
CRAP! CLASS RAN OVER!
AND IT JUST **HAD** TO HAPPEN ON A DAY WHEN I HAVE PLANS TO MEET UP WITH PERSIA...!
スッ SHH
BUT THAT'S WHERE I WENT WRONG.
WHAM
"NO RUNNING IN THE HALLS."
MY BAD! YOU OKAY?
BECAUSE I FAILED O FOLLOW THE MOST BASIC OF RULES...
!!

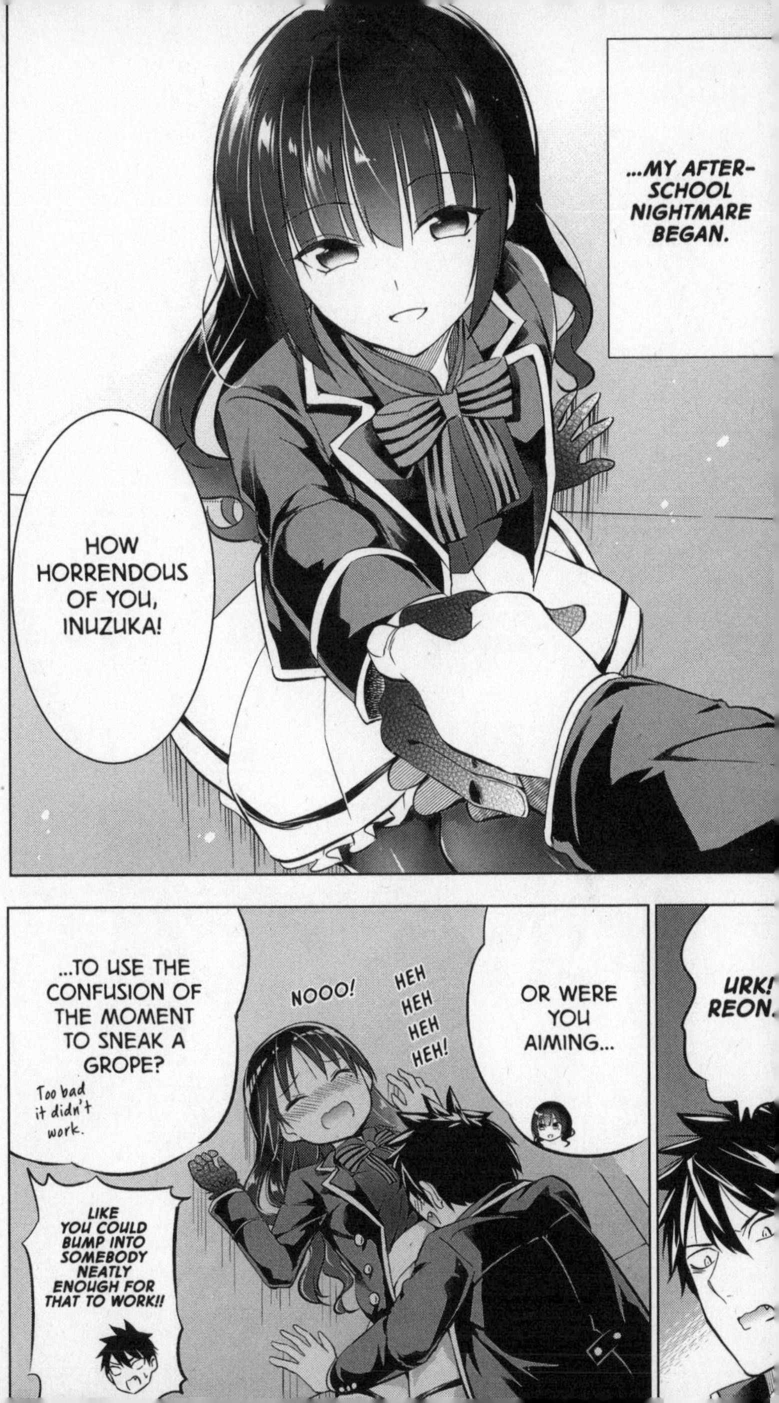
...MY AFTER-SCHOOL NIGHTMARE BEGAN.
HOW HORRENDOUS OF YOU, INUZUKA!
URK! REON.
OR WERE YOU AIMING...
HEH HEH HEH HEH!
NOOO!
...TO USE THE CONFUSION OF THE MOMENT TO SNEAK A GROPE?
Too bad it didn't work.
LIKE YOU COULD BUMP INTO SOMEBODY NEATLY ENOUGH FOR THAT TO WORK!!

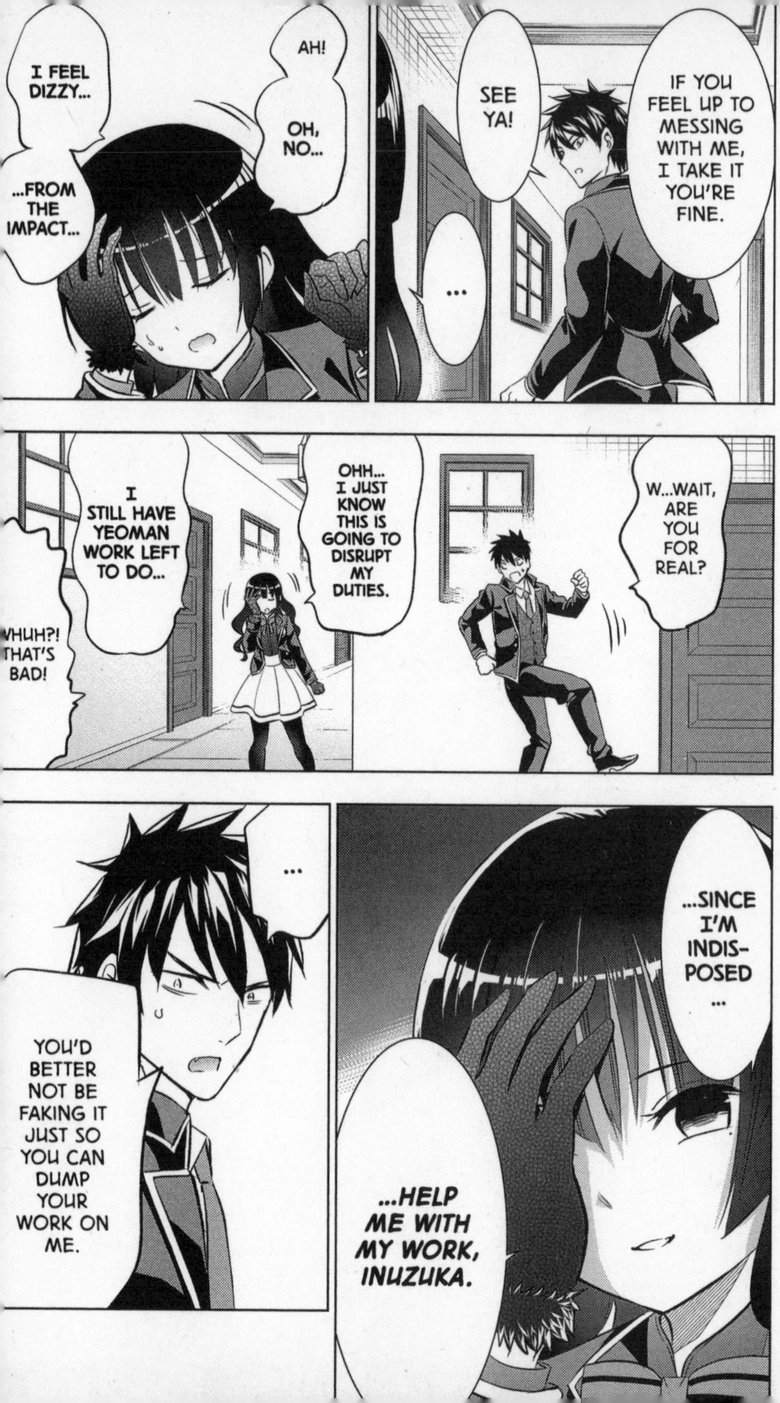
IF YOU FEEL UP TO MESSING WITH ME, I TAKE IT YOU'RE FINE.
SEE YA!
...
AH!
OH, NO...
I FEEL DIZZY...
...FROM THE IMPACT...
W...WAIT, ARE YOU FOR REAL?
OHH... I JUST KNOW THIS IS GOING TO DISRUPT MY DUTIES.
I STILL HAVE YEOMAN WORK LEFT TO DO...
WHUH?! THAT'S BAD!
...SINCE I'M INDIS-POSED ...
...HELP ME WITH MY WORK, INUZUKA.
...
YOU'D BETTER NOT BE FAKING IT JUST SO YOU CAN DUMP YOUR WORK ON ME.

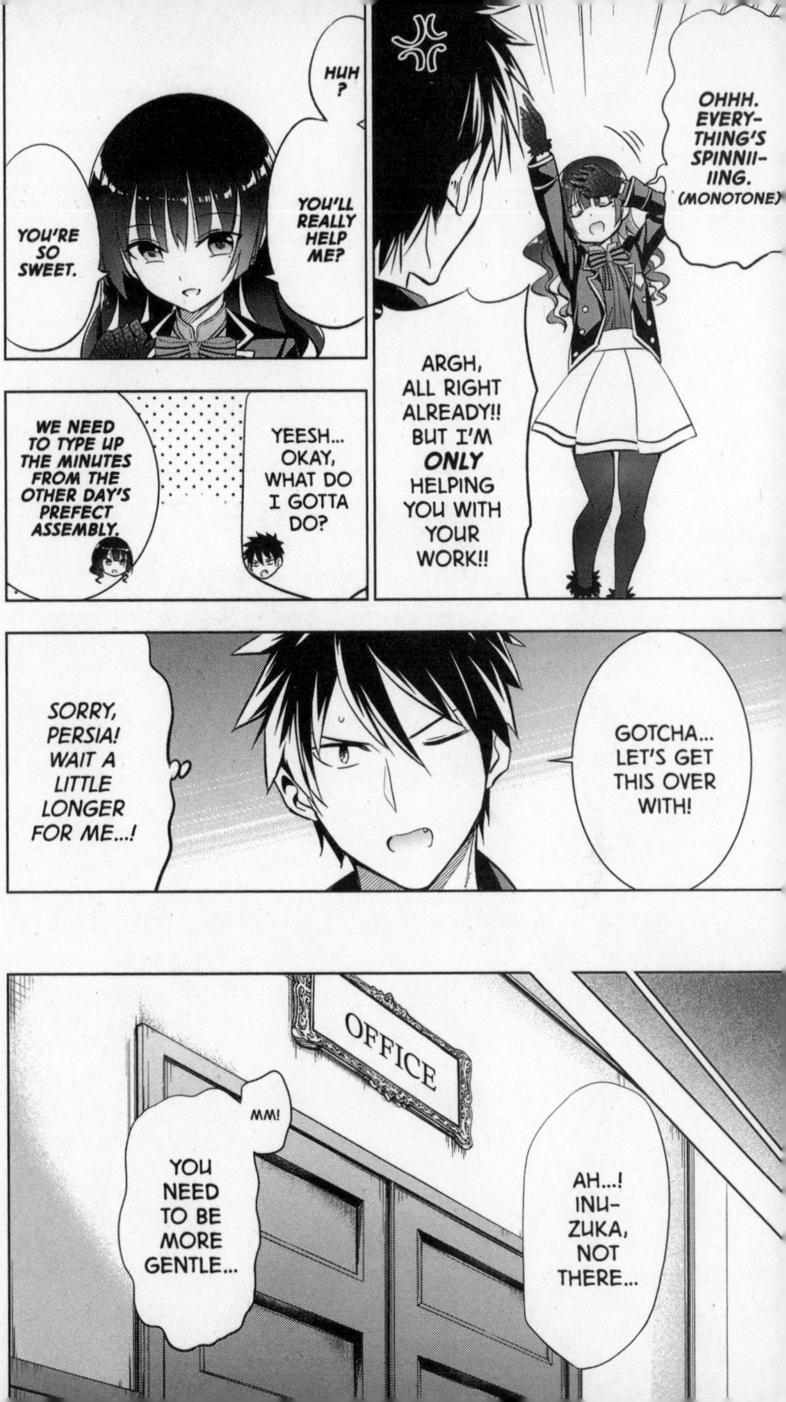
OHHH. EVERY-THING'S SPINNII-IING. (MONOTONE)
ARGH, ALL RIGHT ALREADY!! BUT I'M ONLY HELPING YOU WITH YOUR WORK!!
HUH?
YOU'LL REALLY HELP ME?
YOU'RE SO SWEET.
YEESH... OKAY, WHAT DO I GOTTA DO?
WE NEED TO TYPE UP THE MINUTES FROM THE OTHER DAY'S PREFECT ASSEMBLY.
GOTCHA... LET'S GET THIS OVER WITH!
SORRY, PERSIA! WAIT A LITTLE LONGER FOR ME...!
OFFICE
AH...! INU-ZUKA, NOT THERE...
MM!
YOU NEED TO BE MORE GENTLE...

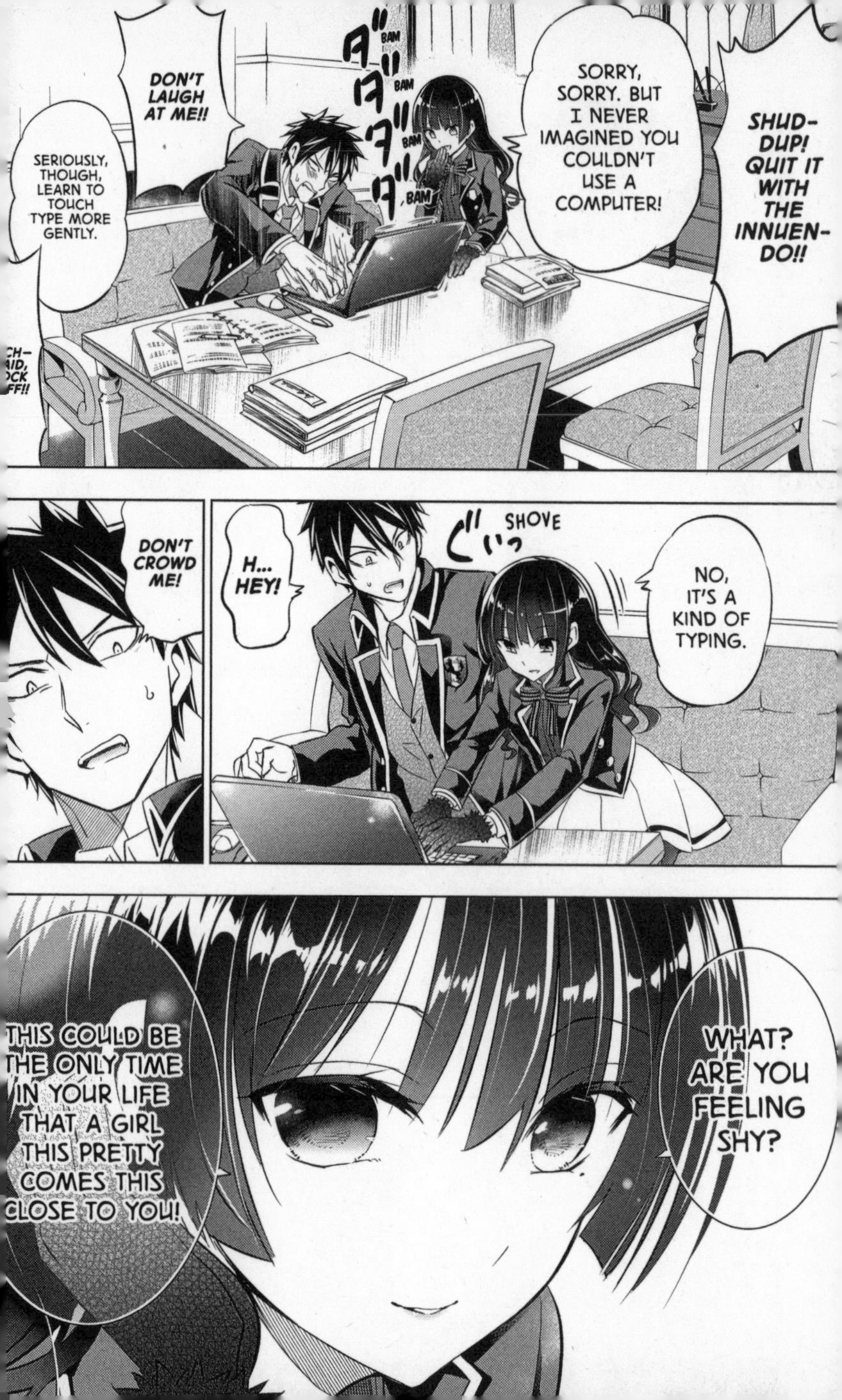
SHUD-DUP! QUIT IT WITH THE INNUEN-DO!!
SORRY, SORRY. BUT I NEVER IMAGINED YOU COULDN'T USE A COMPUTER!
BAM
BAM
BAM
BAM
DON'T LAUGH AT ME!!
SERIOUSLY, THOUGH, LEARN TO TOUCH TYPE MORE GENTLY.
SHOVE
NO, IT'S A KIND OF TYPING.
H... HEY!
DON'T CROWD ME!
WHAT? ARE YOU FEELING SHY?
THIS COULD BE THE ONLY TIME IN YOUR LIFE THAT A GIRL THIS PRETTY COMES THIS CLOSE TO YOU!

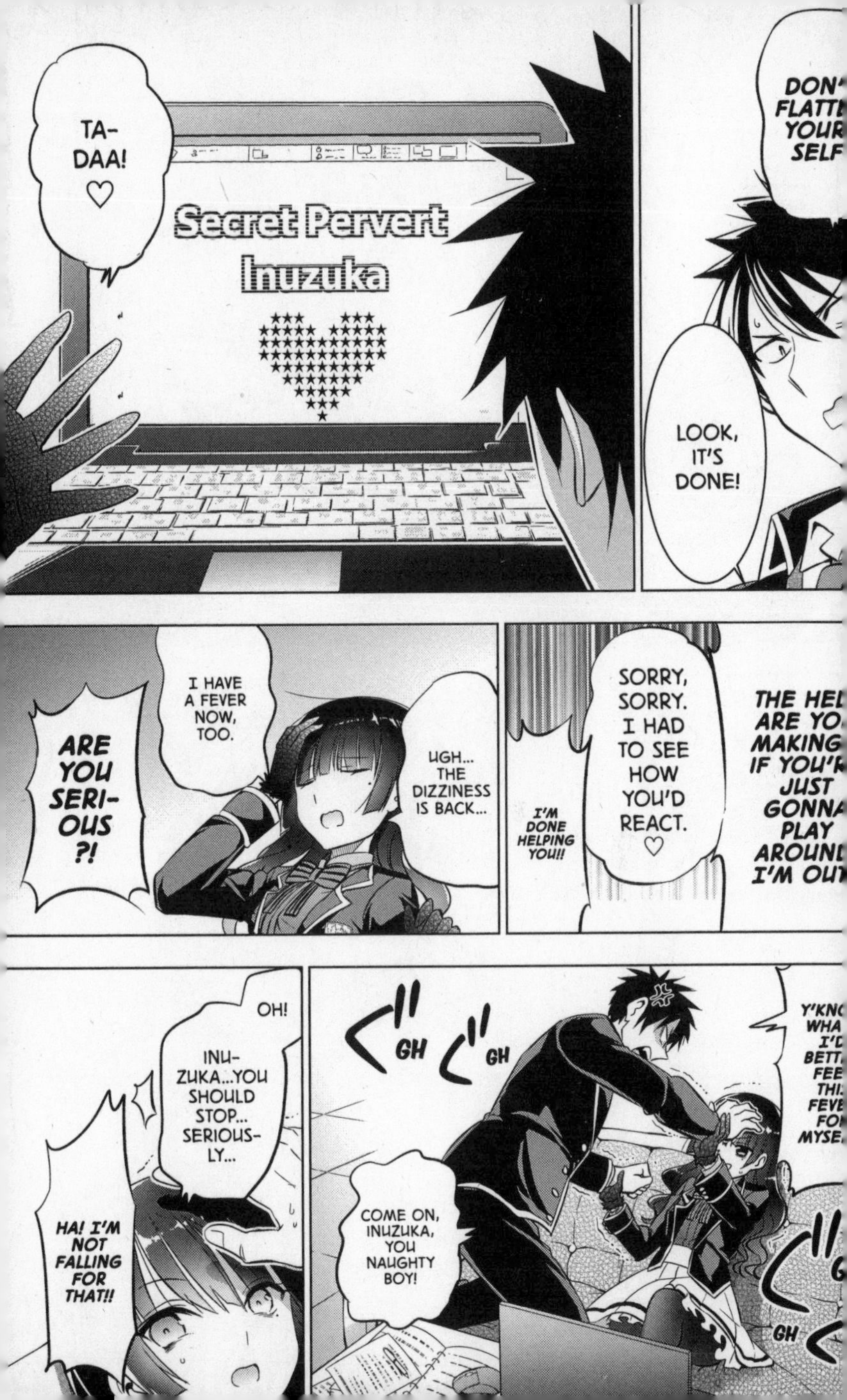
DON' FLATT YOUR SELF
LOOK, IT'S DONE!
TA-DAA! ♡
Secret Pervert Inuzuka
THE HEL ARE YO MAKING IF YOU'R JUST GONNA PLAY AROUNI I'M OU
SORRY, SORRY. I HAD TO SEE HOW YOU'D REACT. ♡
I'M DONE HELPING YOU!!
UGH... THE DIZZINESS IS BACK...
I HAVE A FEVER NOW, TOO.
ARE YOU SERI-OUS ?!
Y'KNO WHA I'D BETT FEE THI FEVE FOI MYSE
GH
GH
GH
GH
COME ON, INUZUKA, YOU NAUGHTY BOY!
OH!
INU-ZUKA...YOU SHOULD STOP... SERIOUS-LY...
HA! I'M NOT FALLING FOR THAT!!

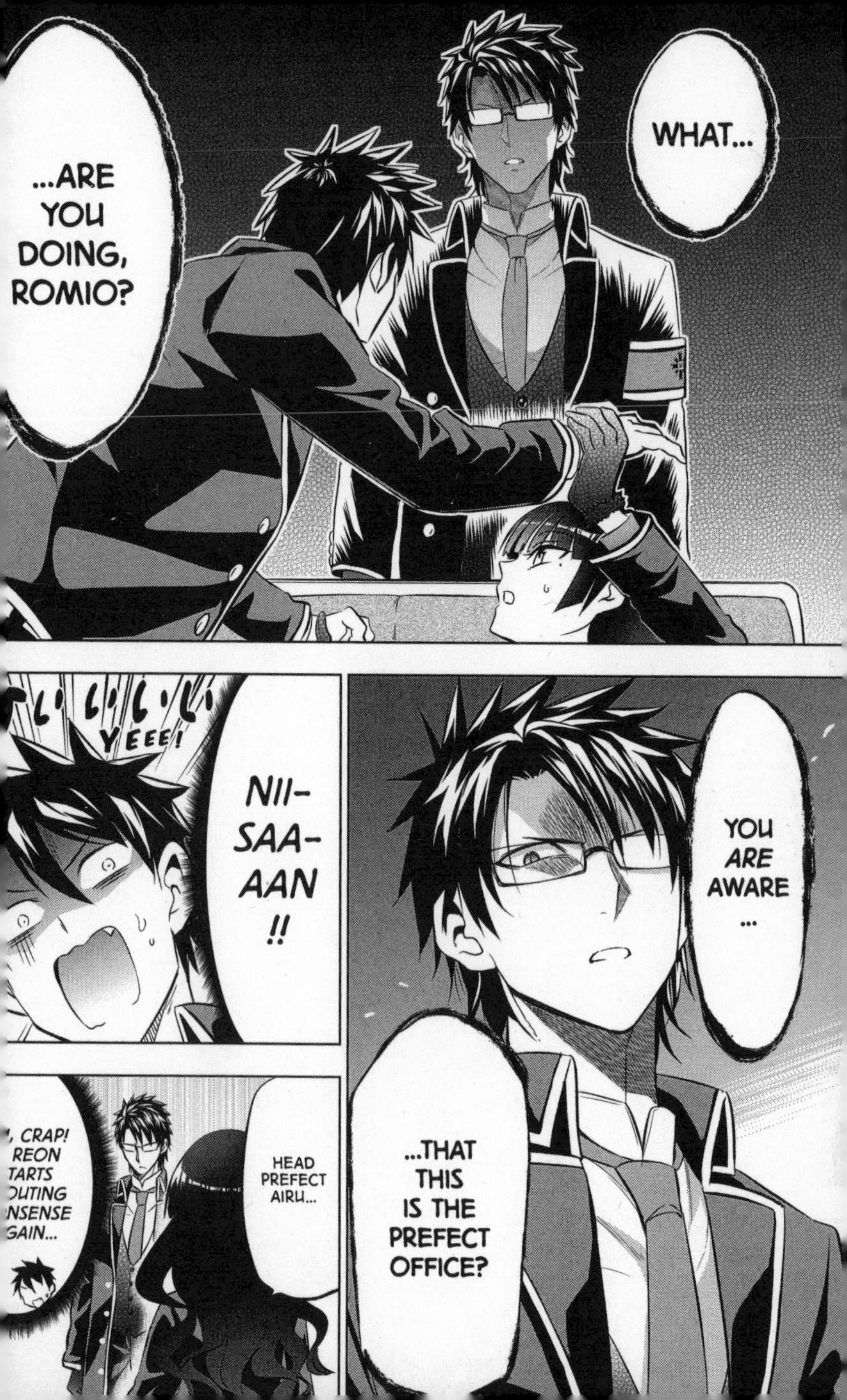
WHAT...
...ARE YOU DOING, ROMIO?
YOU ARE AWARE...
...THAT THIS IS THE PREFECT OFFICE?
NII-SAAA-AAN!!
YEEE!
HEAD PREFECT AIRU...
, CRAP! REON TARTS OUTING NSENSE GAIN...

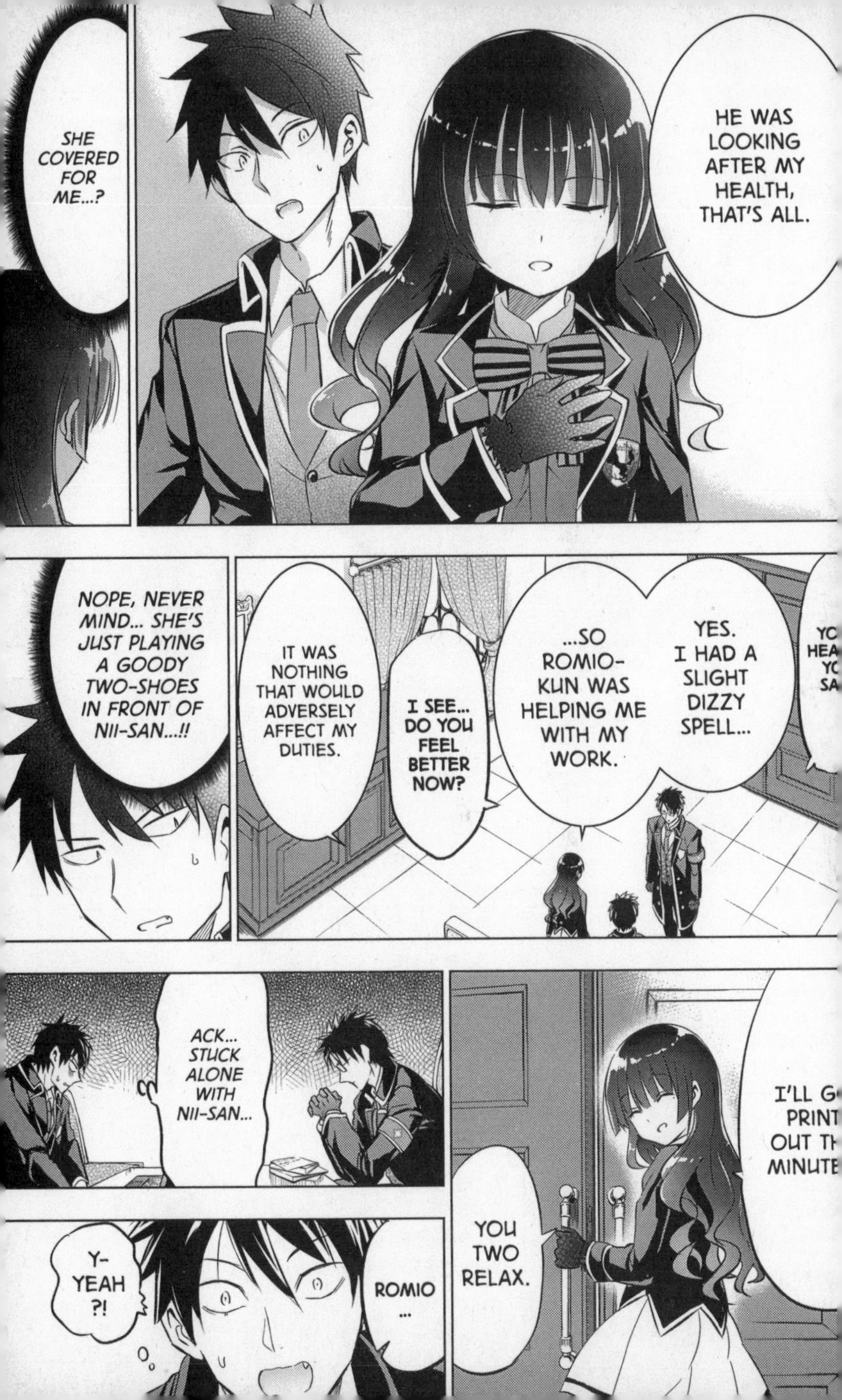
HE WAS LOOKING AFTER MY HEALTH, THAT'S ALL.
SHE COVERED FOR ME...?
YES. I HAD A SLIGHT DIZZY SPELL...
...SO ROMIO-KUN WAS HELPING ME WITH MY WORK.
I SEE... DO YOU FEEL BETTER NOW?
IT WAS NOTHING THAT WOULD ADVERSELY AFFECT MY DUTIES.
NOPE, NEVER MIND... SHE'S JUST PLAYING A GOODY TWO-SHOES IN FRONT OF NII-SAN...!!
I'LL G PRINT OUT TH MINUTE
YOU TWO RELAX.
ACK... STUCK ALONE WITH NII-SAN...
ROMIO...
Y-YEAH?!

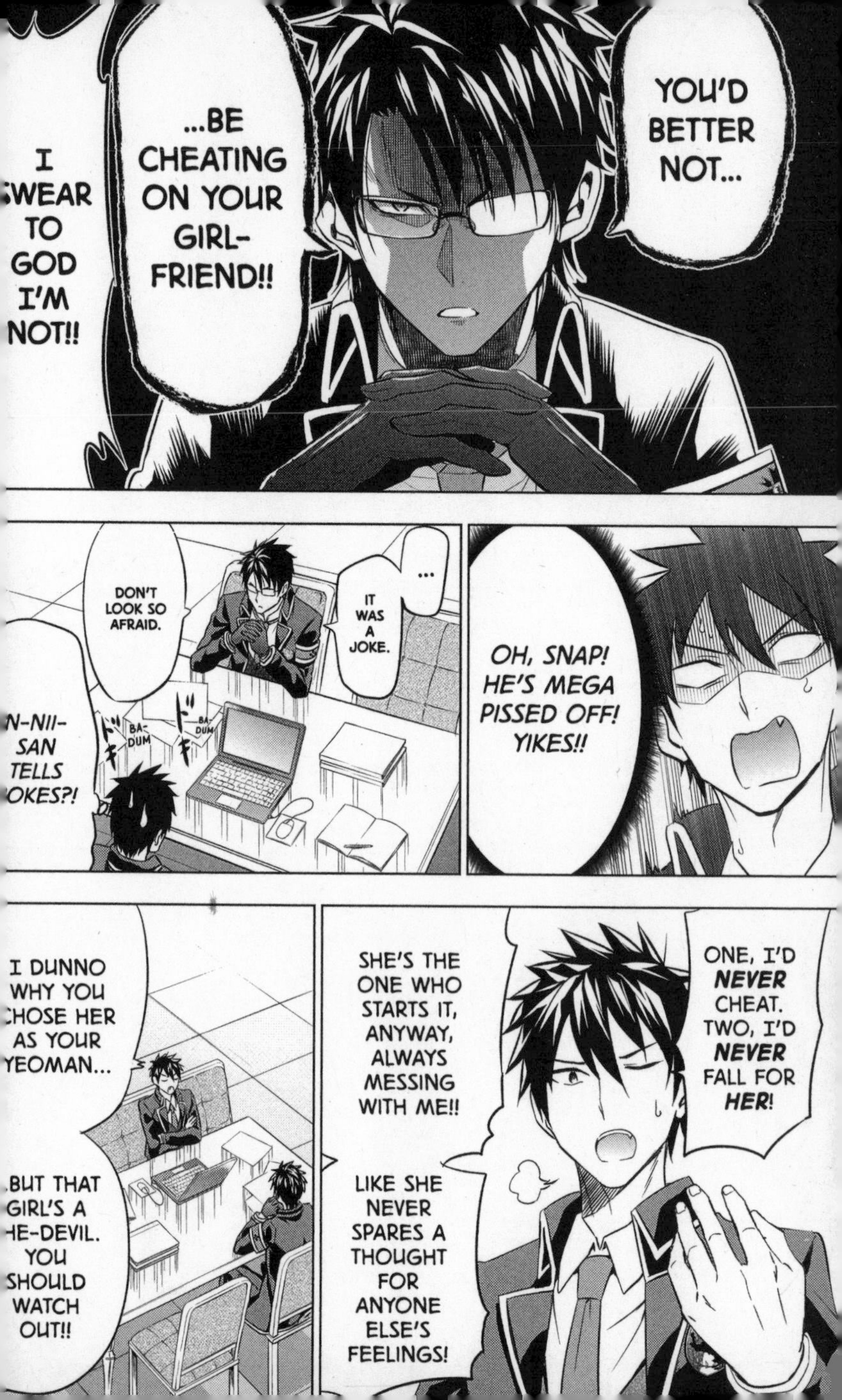
YOU'D BETTER NOT...
...BE CHEATING ON YOUR GIRL-FRIEND!!
I SWEAR TO GOD I'M NOT!!
OH, SNAP! HE'S MEGA PISSED OFF! YIKES!!
...
IT WAS A JOKE.
DON'T LOOK SO AFRAID.
BA-DUM
BA-DUM
N-NII-SAN TELLS JOKES?!
ONE, I'D **NEVER** CHEAT. TWO, I'D **NEVER** FALL FOR **HER**!
SHE'S THE ONE WHO STARTS IT, ANYWAY, ALWAYS MESSING WITH ME!!
LIKE SHE NEVER SPARES A THOUGHT FOR ANYONE ELSE'S FEELINGS!
I DUNNO WHY YOU CHOSE HER AS YOUR YEOMAN...
...BUT THAT GIRL'S A SHE-DEVIL. YOU SHOULD WATCH OUT!!

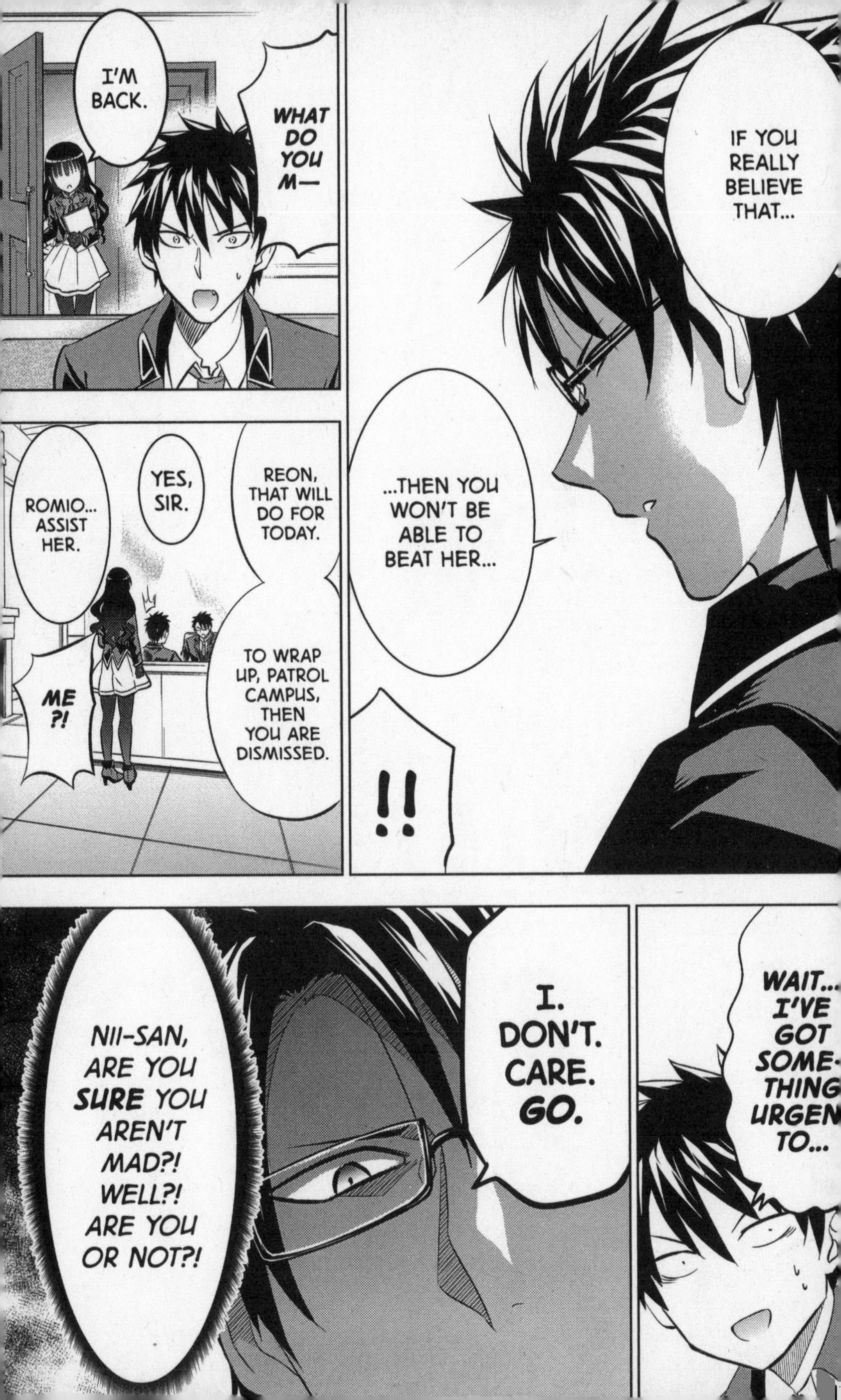
IF YOU REALLY BELIEVE THAT...
...THEN YOU WON'T BE ABLE TO BEAT HER...
!!
WHAT DO YOU M—
I'M BACK.
REON, THAT WILL DO FOR TODAY.
YES, SIR.
TO WRAP UP, PATROL CAMPUS, THEN YOU ARE DISMISSED.
ROMIO... ASSIST HER.
ME?!
WAIT... I'VE GOT SOME-THING URGEN TO...
I. DON'T. CARE. GO.
NII-SAN, ARE YOU SURE YOU AREN'T MAD?! WELL?! ARE YOU OR NOT?!

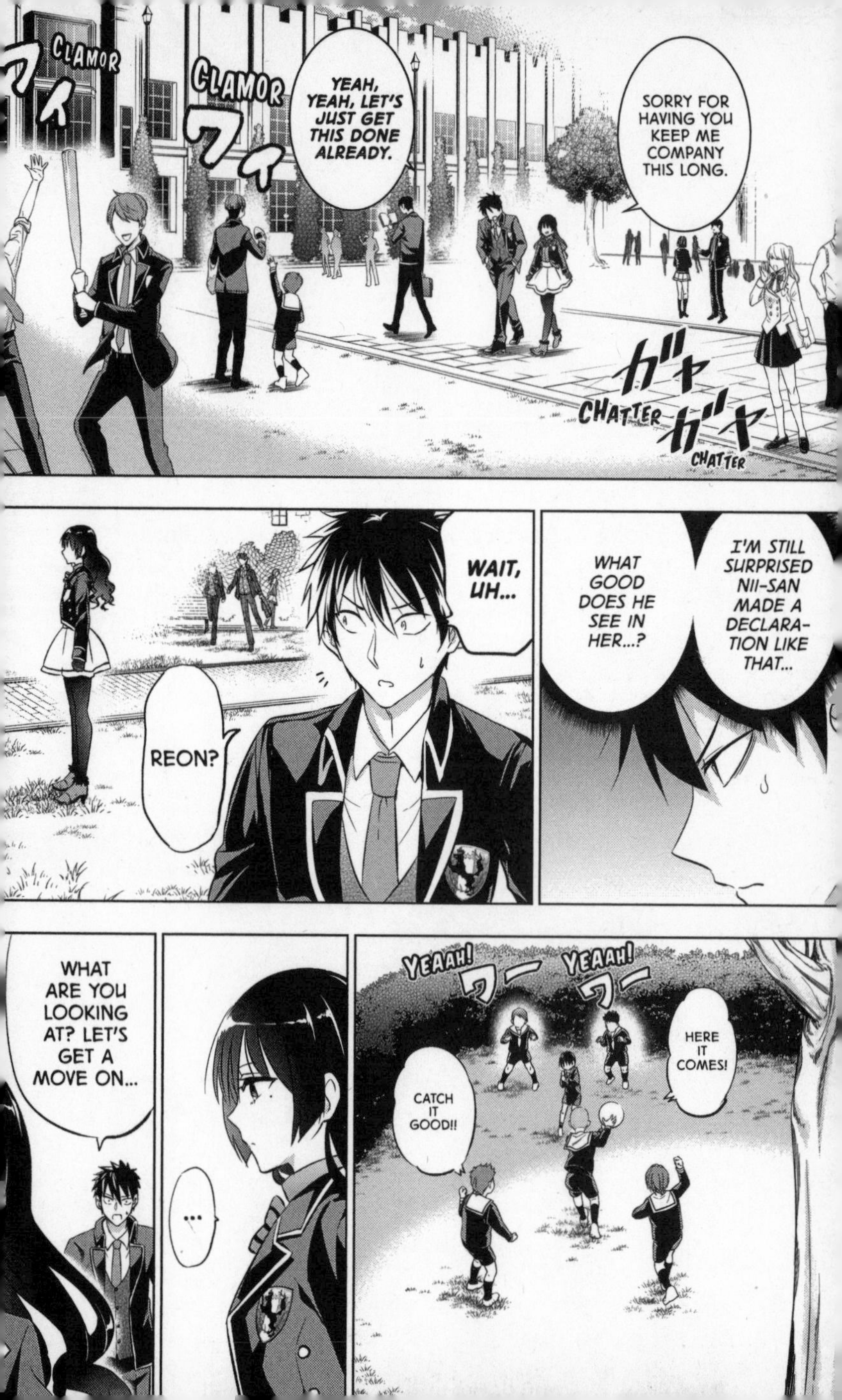
SORRY FOR HAVING YOU KEEP ME COMPANY THIS LONG.
YEAH, YEAH, LET'S JUST GET THIS DONE ALREADY.
CLAMOR
CLAMOR
CHATTER
CHATTER
I'M STILL SURPRISED NII-SAN MADE A DECLARATION LIKE THAT...
WHAT GOOD DOES HE SEE IN HER...?
WAIT, UH...
REON?
YEAAH!
YEAAH!
HERE IT COMES!
CATCH IT GOOD!!
...
WHAT ARE YOU LOOKING AT? LET'S GET A MOVE ON...

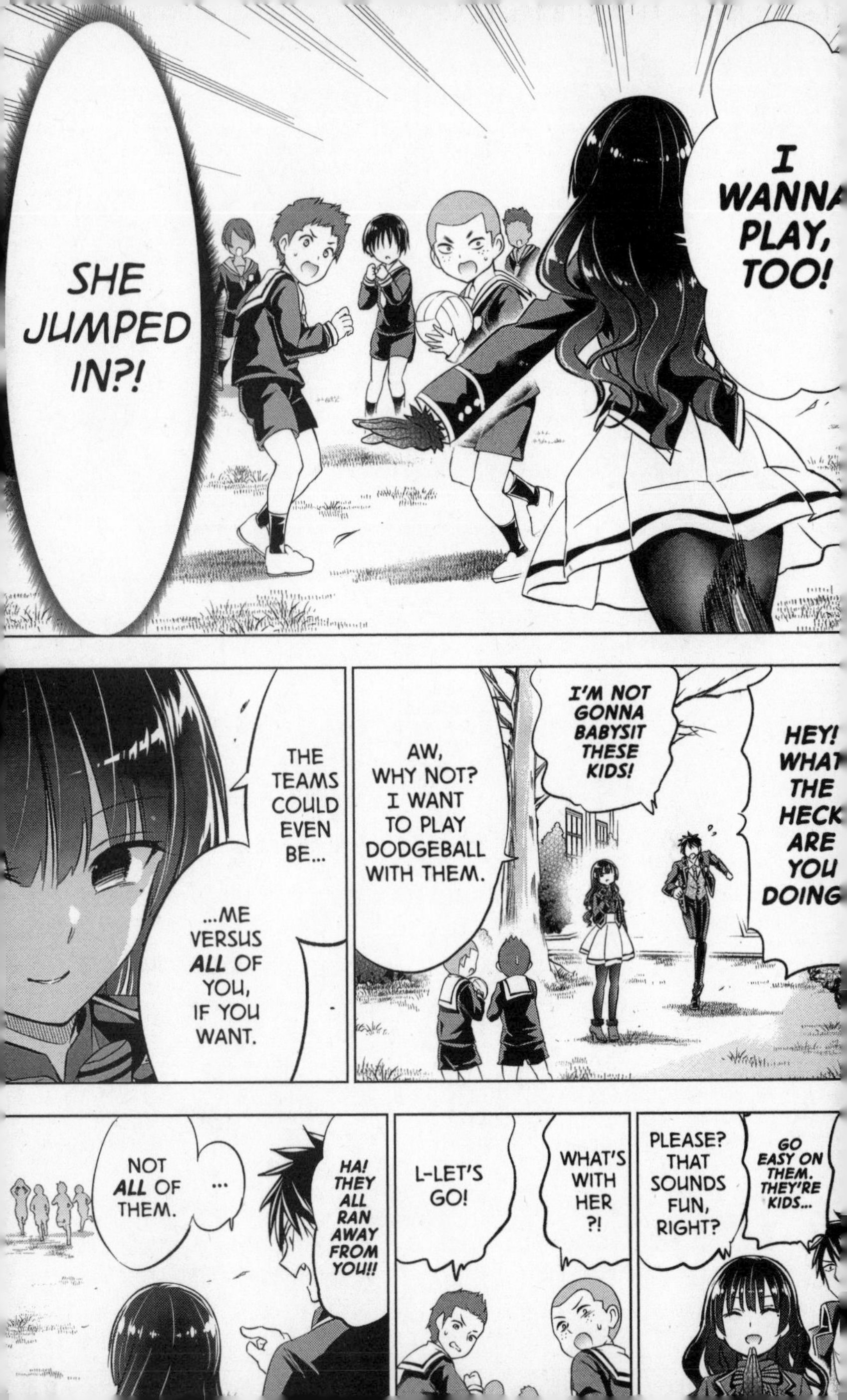
I WANNA PLAY, TOO!
SHE JUMPED IN?!
HEY! WHAT THE HECK ARE YOU DOING
I'M NOT GONNA BABYSIT THESE KIDS!
AW, WHY NOT? I WANT TO PLAY DODGEBALL WITH THEM.
THE TEAMS COULD EVEN BE...
...ME VERSUS ALL OF YOU, IF YOU WANT.
GO EASY ON THEM. THEY'RE KIDS...
PLEASE? THAT SOUNDS FUN, RIGHT?
WHAT'S WITH HER?!
L-LET'S GO!
HA! THEY ALL RAN AWAY FROM YOU!!
...
NOT ALL OF THEM.

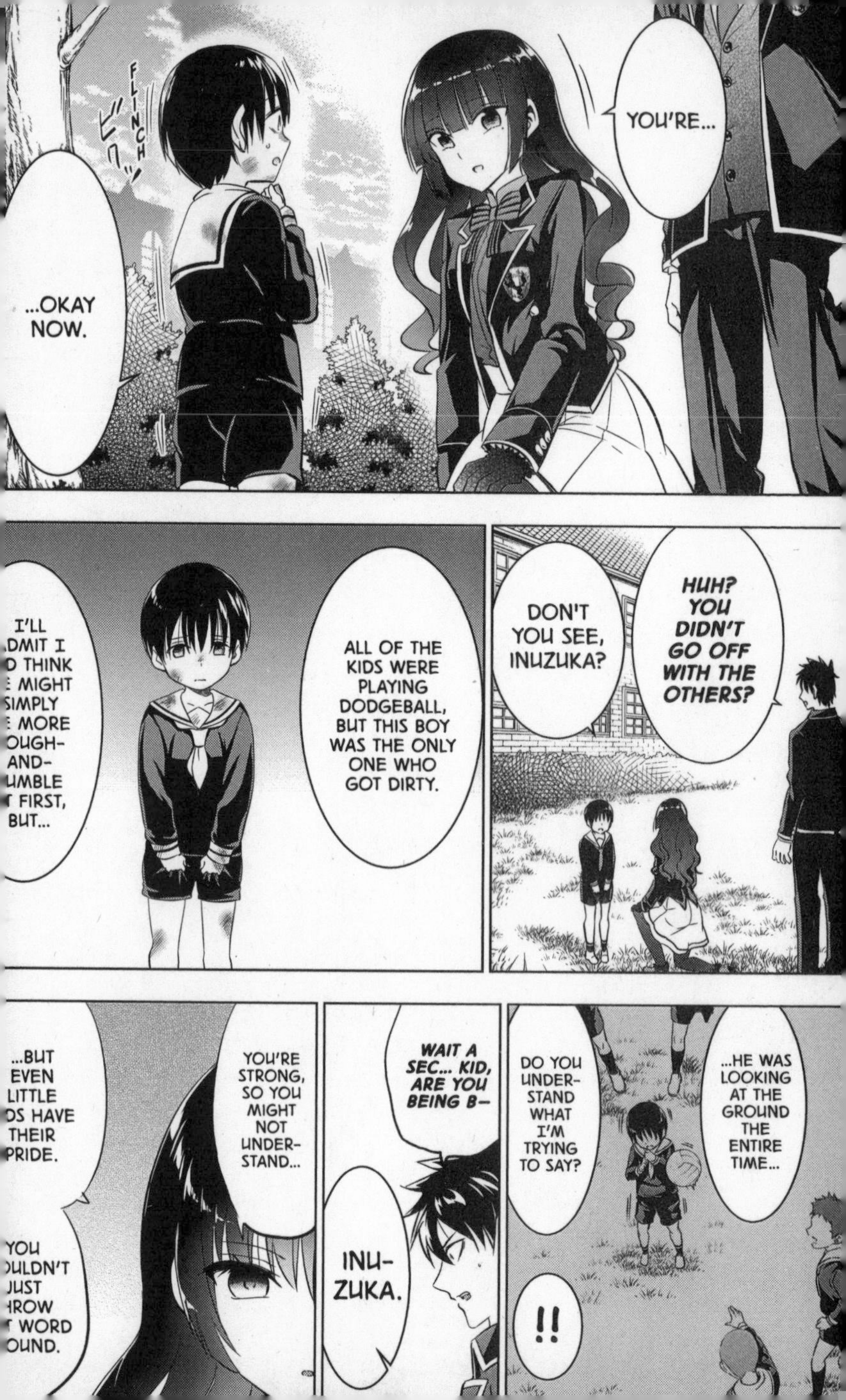
YOU'RE...
FLINCH
ビクッ
...OKAY NOW.
HUH? YOU DIDN'T GO OFF WITH THE OTHERS?
DON'T YOU SEE, INUZUKA?
ALL OF THE KIDS WERE PLAYING DODGEBALL, BUT THIS BOY WAS THE ONLY ONE WHO GOT DIRTY.
I'LL DMIT I D THINK E MIGHT SIMPLY E MORE OUGH-AND-UMBLE T FIRST, BUT...
...HE WAS LOOKING AT THE GROUND THE ENTIRE TIME...
DO YOU UNDER-STAND WHAT I'M TRYING TO SAY?
!!
WAIT A SEC... KID, ARE YOU BEING B—
INU-ZUKA.
YOU'RE STRONG, SO YOU MIGHT NOT UNDER-STAND...
...BUT EVEN LITTLE DS HAVE THEIR PRIDE.
YOU ULDN'T JUST HROW T WORD OUND.

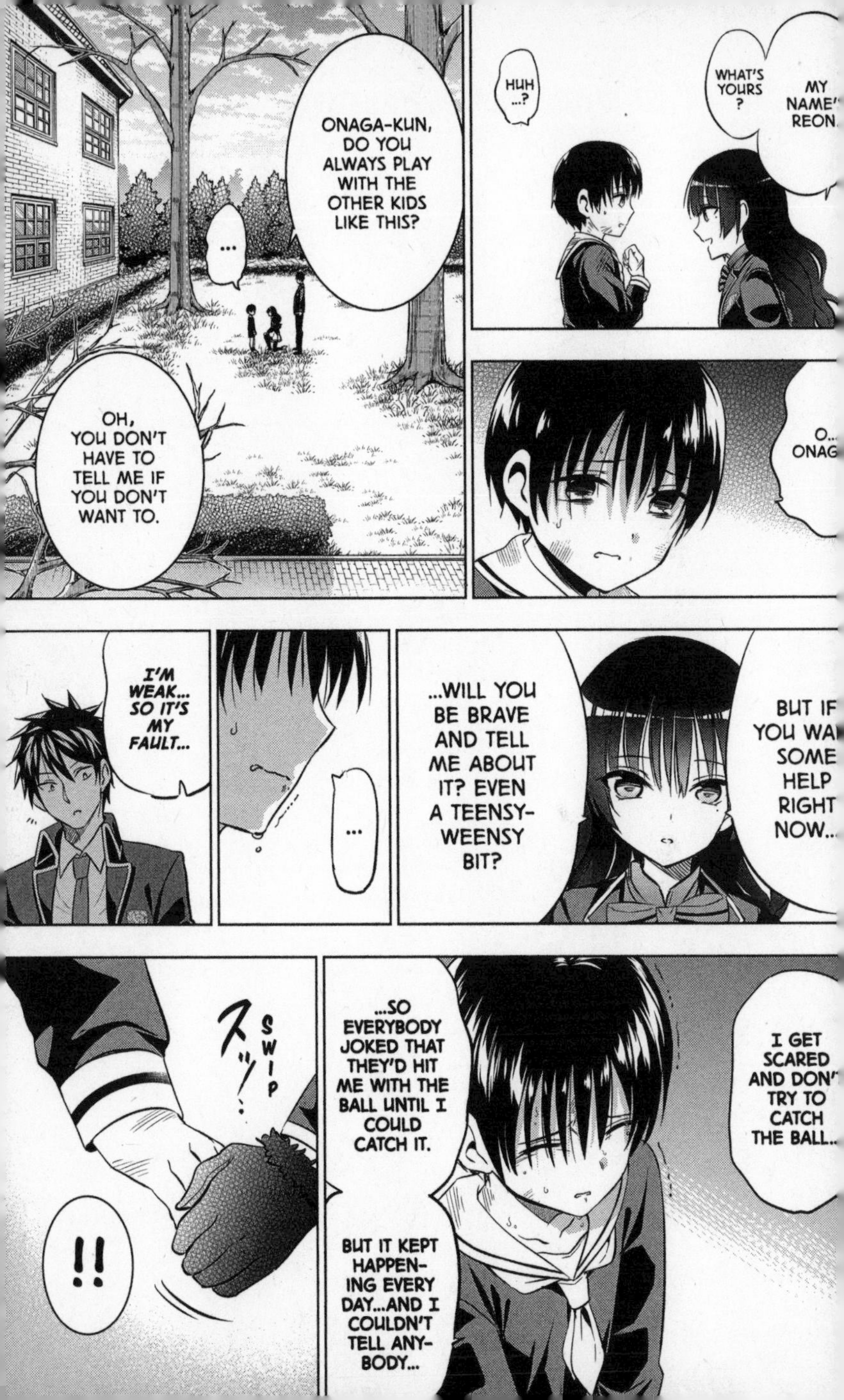
MY NAME'S REON.
WHAT'S YOURS?
HUH...?
O... ONAG
ONAGA-KUN, DO YOU ALWAYS PLAY WITH THE OTHER KIDS LIKE THIS?
...
OH, YOU DON'T HAVE TO TELL ME IF YOU DON'T WANT TO.
BUT IF YOU WA SOME HELP RIGHT NOW...
...WILL YOU BE BRAVE AND TELL ME ABOUT IT? EVEN A TEENSY-WEENSY BIT?
...
I'M WEAK... SO IT'S MY FAULT...
I GET SCARED AND DON' TRY TO CATCH THE BALL...
...SO EVERYBODY JOKED THAT THEY'D HIT ME WITH THE BALL UNTIL I COULD CATCH IT.
BUT IT KEPT HAPPENING EVERY DAY...AND I COULDN'T TELL ANYBODY...
SWIP
!!

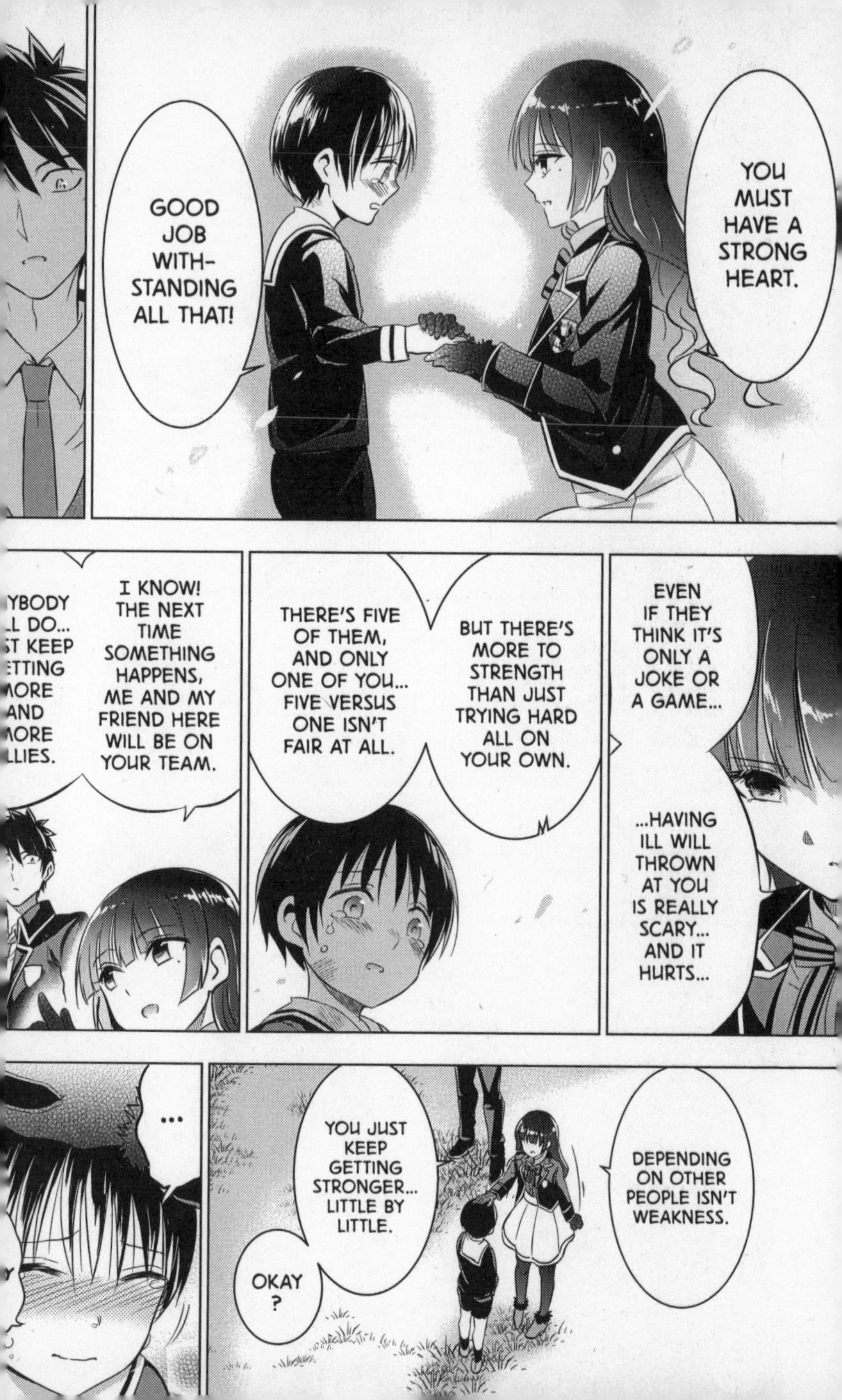
YOU MUST HAVE A STRONG HEART.
GOOD JOB WITH-STANDING ALL THAT!
EVEN IF THEY THINK IT'S ONLY A JOKE OR A GAME...
...HAVING ILL WILL THROWN AT YOU IS REALLY SCARY... AND IT HURTS...
BUT THERE'S MORE TO STRENGTH THAN JUST TRYING HARD ALL ON YOUR OWN.
THERE'S FIVE OF THEM, AND ONLY ONE OF YOU... FIVE VERSUS ONE ISN'T FAIR AT ALL.
I KNOW! THE NEXT TIME SOMETHING HAPPENS, ME AND MY FRIEND HERE WILL BE ON YOUR TEAM.
YBODY LL DO... ST KEEP ETTING MORE AND MORE LLIES.
DEPENDING ON OTHER PEOPLE ISN'T WEAKNESS.
YOU JUST KEEP GETTING STRONGER... LITTLE BY LITTLE.
OKAY?
...

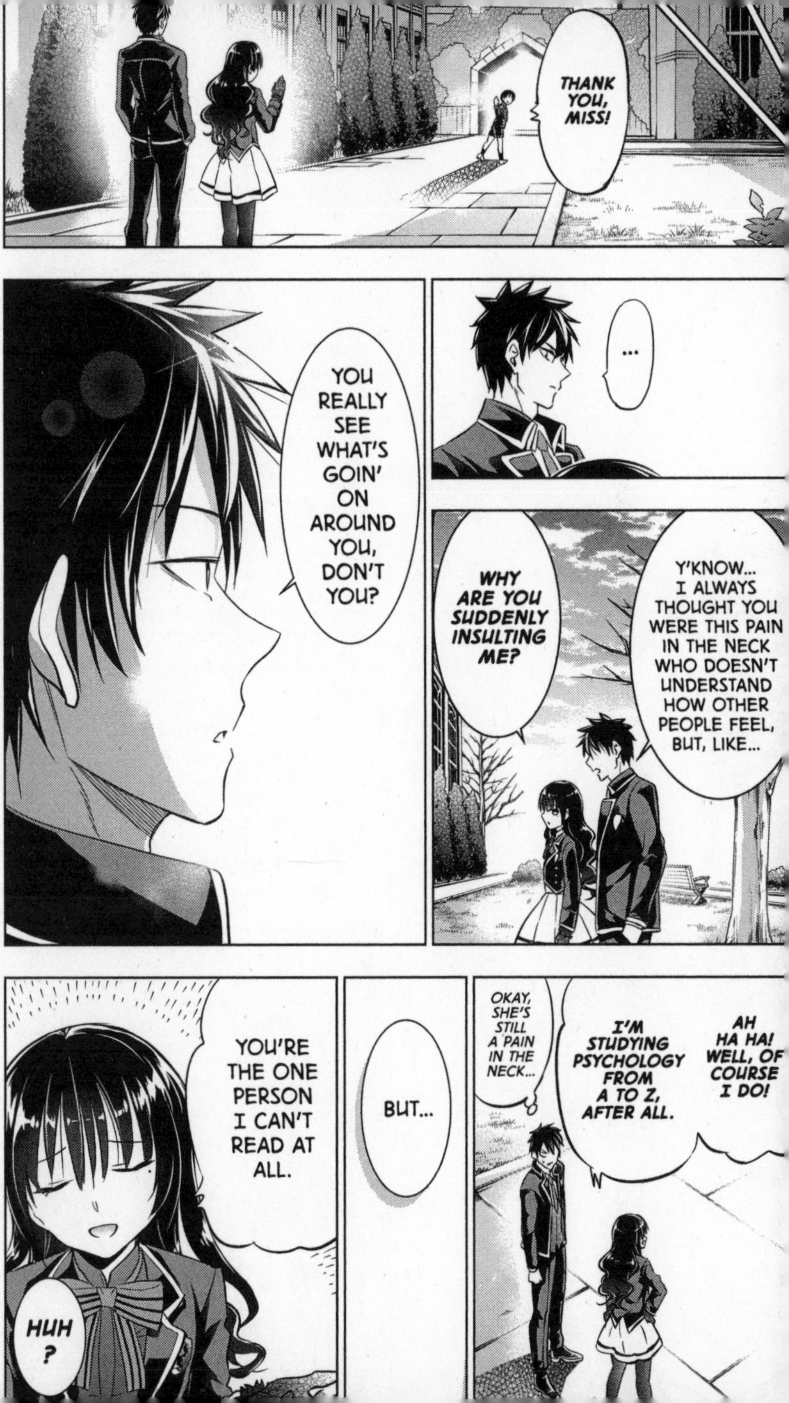
THANK YOU, MISS!
...
Y'KNOW... I ALWAYS THOUGHT YOU WERE THIS PAIN IN THE NECK WHO DOESN'T UNDERSTAND HOW OTHER PEOPLE FEEL, BUT, LIKE...
WHY ARE YOU SUDDENLY INSULTING ME?
YOU REALLY SEE WHAT'S GOIN' ON AROUND YOU, DON'T YOU?
AH HA HA! WELL, OF COURSE I DO!
I'M STUDYING PSYCHOLOGY FROM A TO Z, AFTER ALL.
OKAY, SHE'S STILL A PAIN IN THE NECK...
BUT...
YOU'RE THE ONE PERSON I CAN'T READ AT ALL.
HUH?

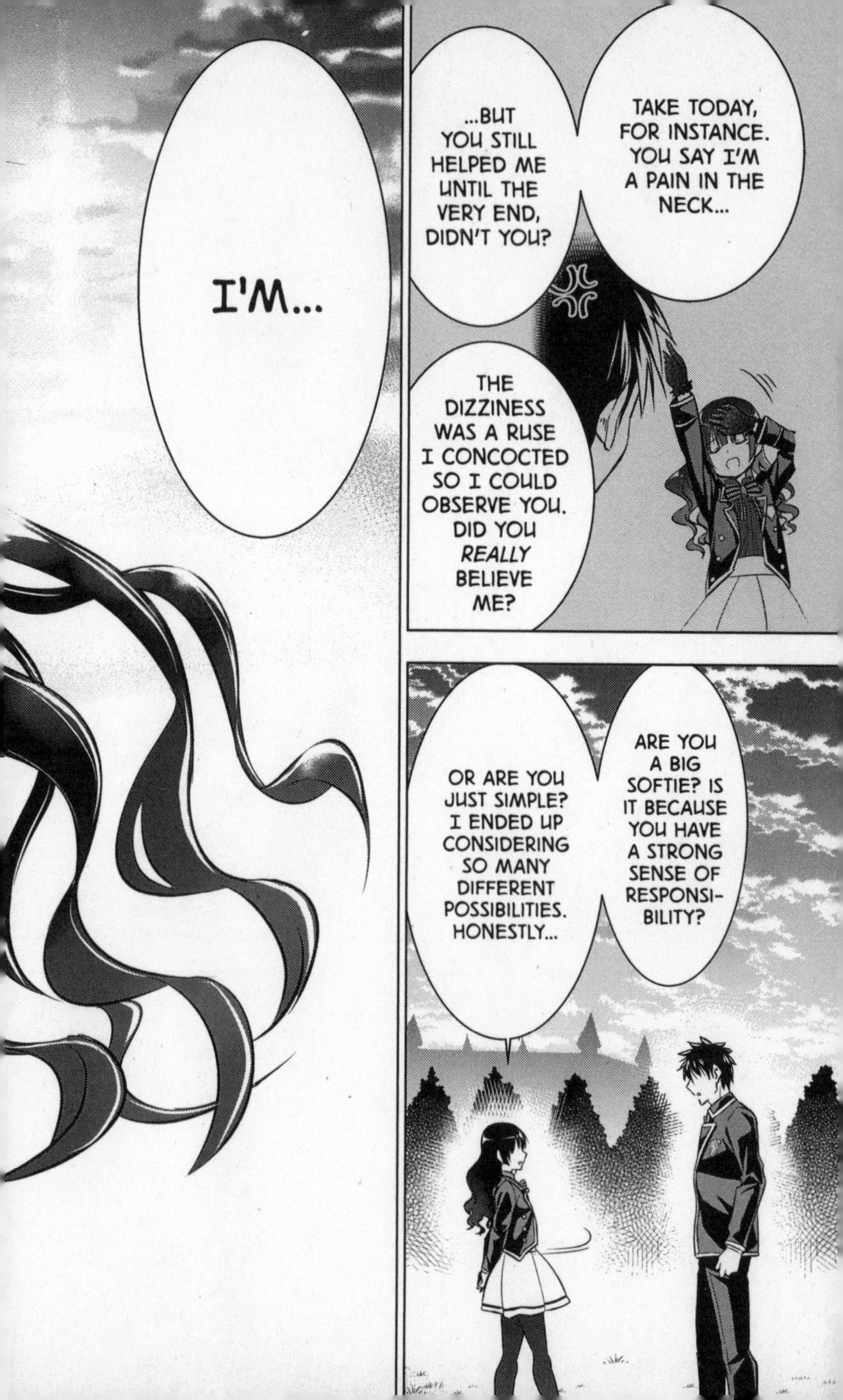
TAKE TODAY, FOR INSTANCE. YOU SAY I'M A PAIN IN THE NECK...
...BUT YOU STILL HELPED ME UNTIL THE VERY END, DIDN'T YOU?
THE DIZZINESS WAS A RUSE I CONCOCTED SO I COULD OBSERVE YOU. DID YOU *REALLY* BELIEVE ME?
ARE YOU A BIG SOFTIE? IS IT BECAUSE YOU HAVE A STRONG SENSE OF RESPONSI-BILITY?
OR ARE YOU JUST SIMPLE? I ENDED UP CONSIDERING SO MANY DIFFERENT POSSIBILITIES. HONESTLY...
I'M...

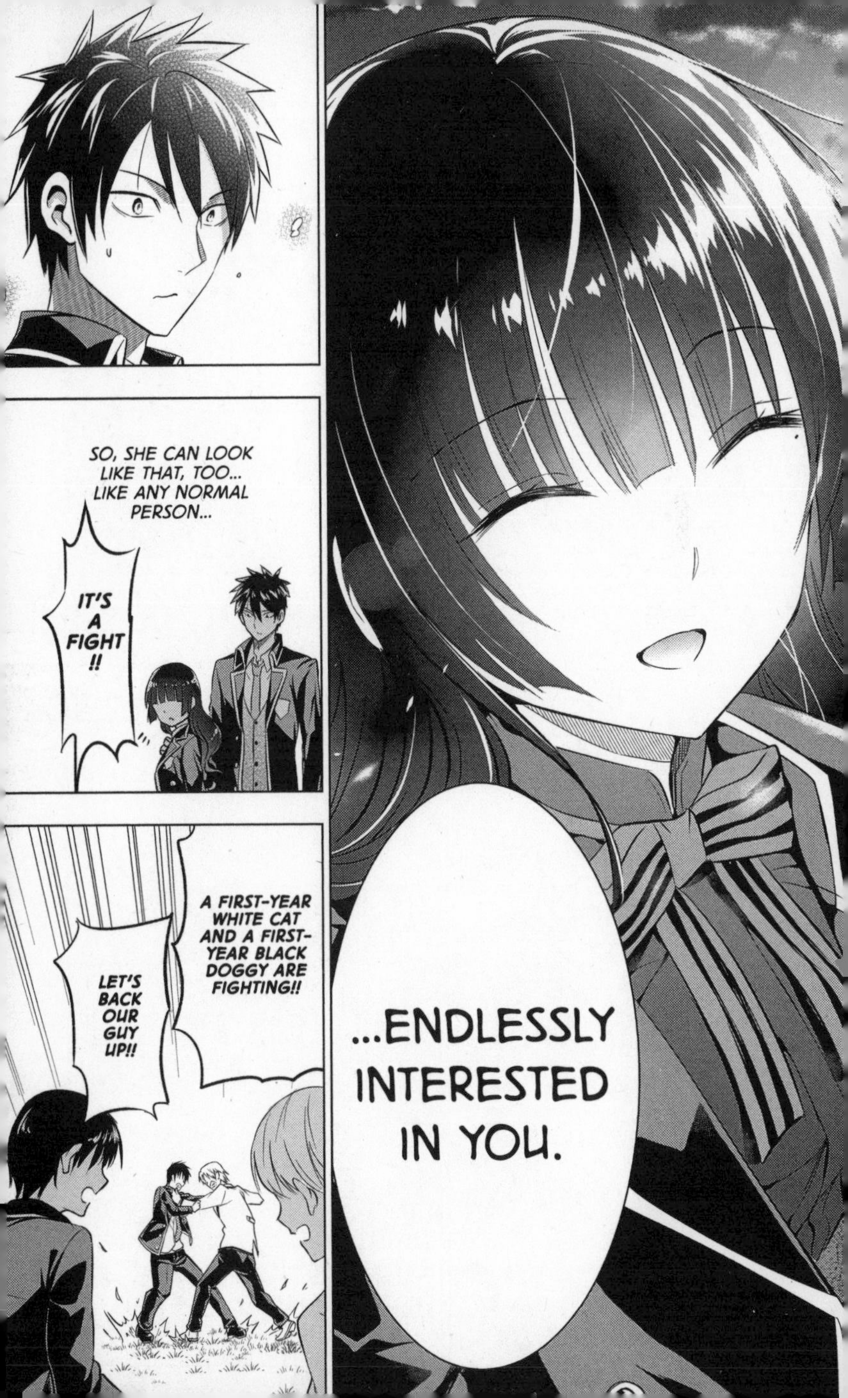
...ENDLESSLY INTERESTED IN YOU.
SO, SHE CAN LOOK LIKE THAT, TOO... LIKE ANY NORMAL PERSON...
IT'S A FIGHT!!
A FIRST-YEAR WHITE CAT AND A FIRST-YEAR BLACK DOGGY ARE FIGHTING!!
LET'S BACK OUR GUY UP!!

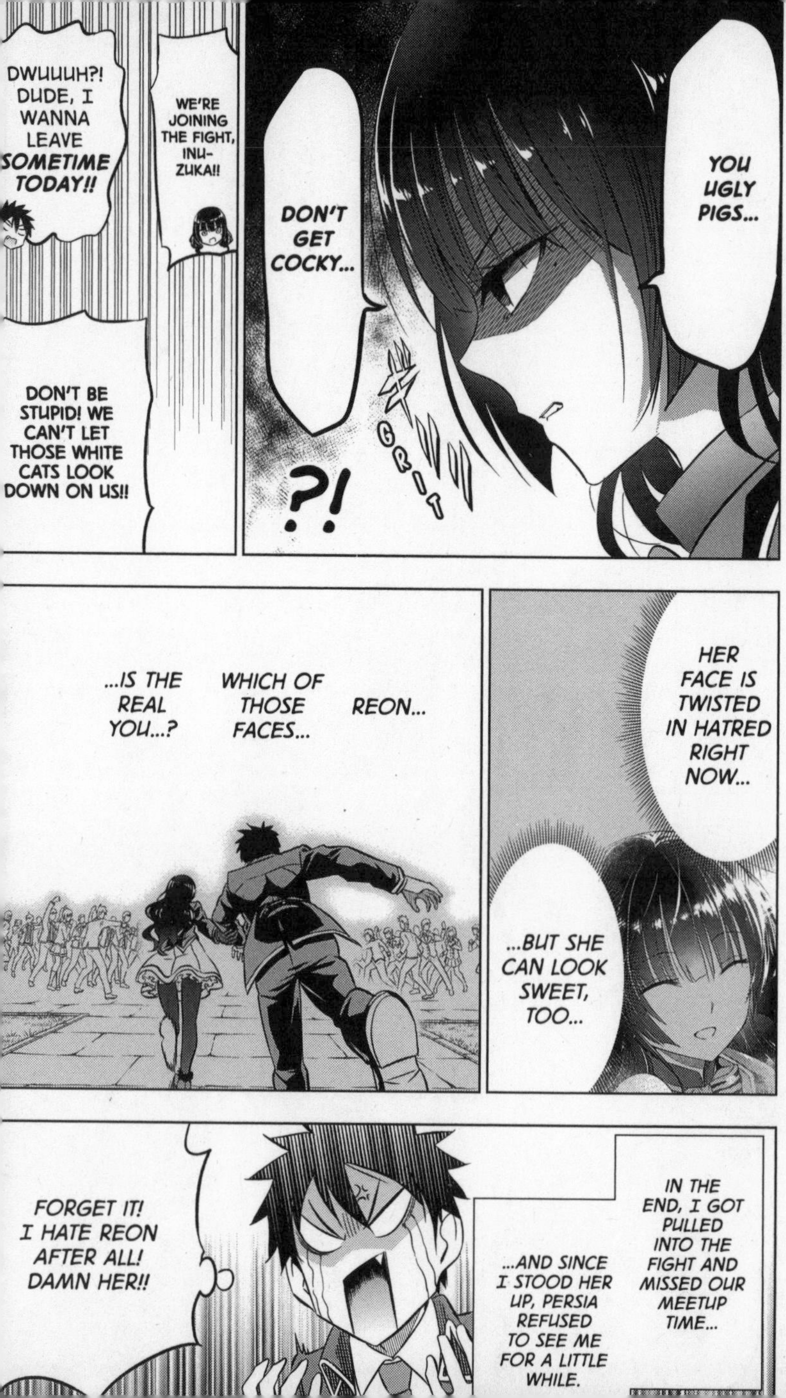
YOU UGLY PIGS...
DON'T GET COCKY...
GRIT
?!
WE'RE JOINING THE FIGHT, INU-ZUKA!!
DWUUUH?! DUDE, I WANNA LEAVE SOMETIME TODAY!!
DON'T BE STUPID! WE CAN'T LET THOSE WHITE CATS LOOK DOWN ON US!!
HER FACE IS TWISTED IN HATRED RIGHT NOW...
...BUT SHE CAN LOOK SWEET, TOO...
REON...
WHICH OF THOSE FACES...
...IS THE REAL YOU...?
IN THE END, I GOT PULLED INTO THE FIGHT AND MISSED OUR MEETUP TIME...
...AND SINCE I STOOD HER UP, PERSIA REFUSED TO SEE ME FOR A LITTLE WHILE.
FORGET IT! I HATE REON AFTER ALL! DAMN HER!!

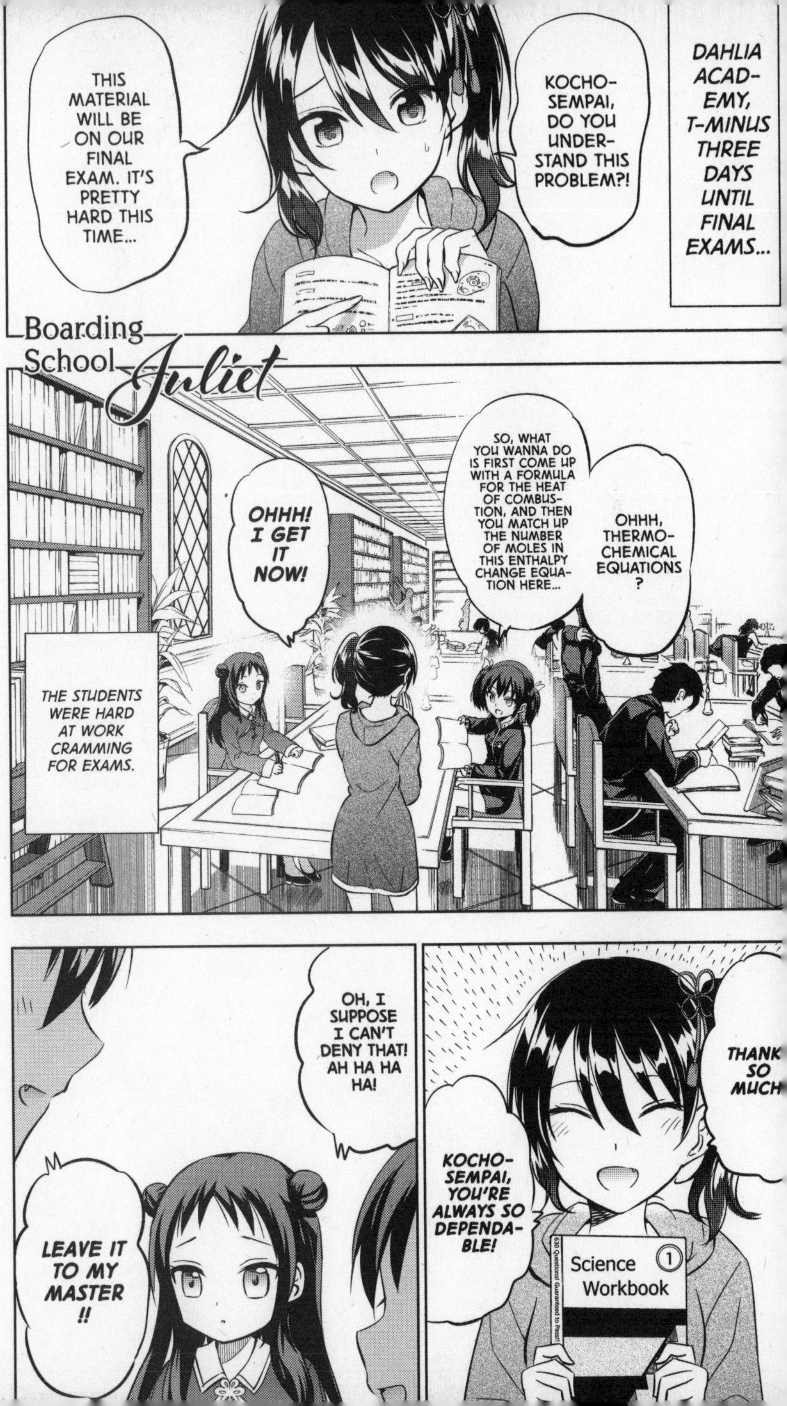
DAHLIA ACADEMY, T-MINUS THREE DAYS UNTIL FINAL EXAMS...
KOCHO-SEMPAI, DO YOU UNDERSTAND THIS PROBLEM?!
THIS MATERIAL WILL BE ON OUR FINAL EXAM. IT'S PRETTY HARD THIS TIME...
Boarding School Juliet
OHHH, THERMOCHEMICAL EQUATIONS?
SO, WHAT YOU WANNA DO IS FIRST COME UP WITH A FORMULA FOR THE HEAT OF COMBUSTION, AND THEN YOU MATCH UP THE NUMBER OF MOLES IN THIS ENTHALPY CHANGE EQUATION HERE...
OHHH! I GET IT NOW!
THE STUDENTS WERE HARD AT WORK CRAMMING FOR EXAMS.
THANK SO MUCH
KOCHO-SEMPAI, YOU'RE ALWAYS SO DEPENDABLE!
Science Workbook 1
630 Questions! Guaranteed to Pass!
OH, I SUPPOSE I CAN'T DENY THAT! AH HA HA HA!
LEAVE IT TO MY MASTER!!

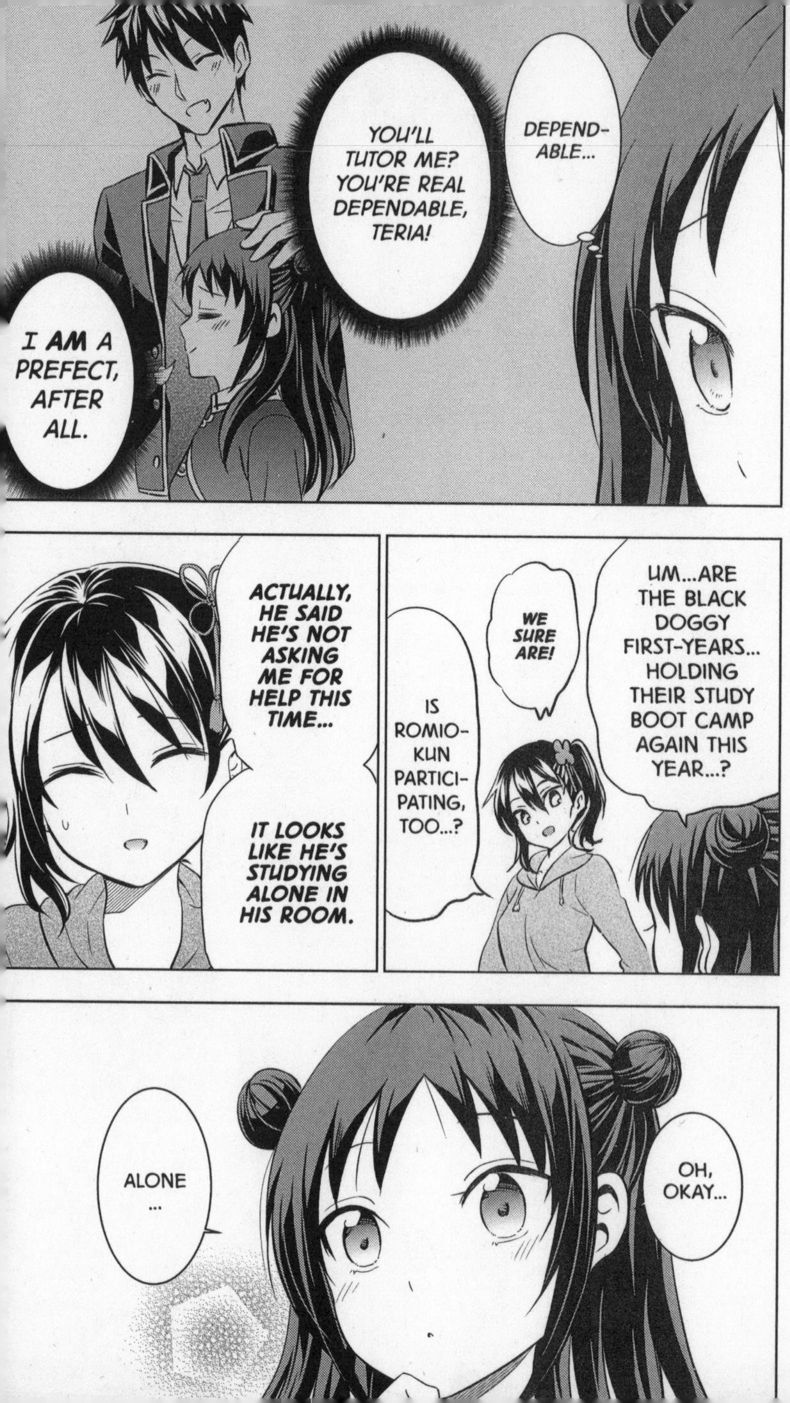
DEPEND-ABLE...
YOU'LL TUTOR ME? YOU'RE REAL DEPENDABLE, TERIA!
I AM A PREFECT, AFTER ALL.
UM...ARE THE BLACK DOGGY FIRST-YEARS... HOLDING THEIR STUDY BOOT CAMP AGAIN THIS YEAR...?
WE SURE ARE!
IS ROMIO-KUN PARTICIPATING, TOO...?
ACTUALLY, HE SAID HE'S NOT ASKING ME FOR HELP THIS TIME...
IT LOOKS LIKE HE'S STUDYING ALONE IN HIS ROOM.
OH, OKAY...
ALONE ...

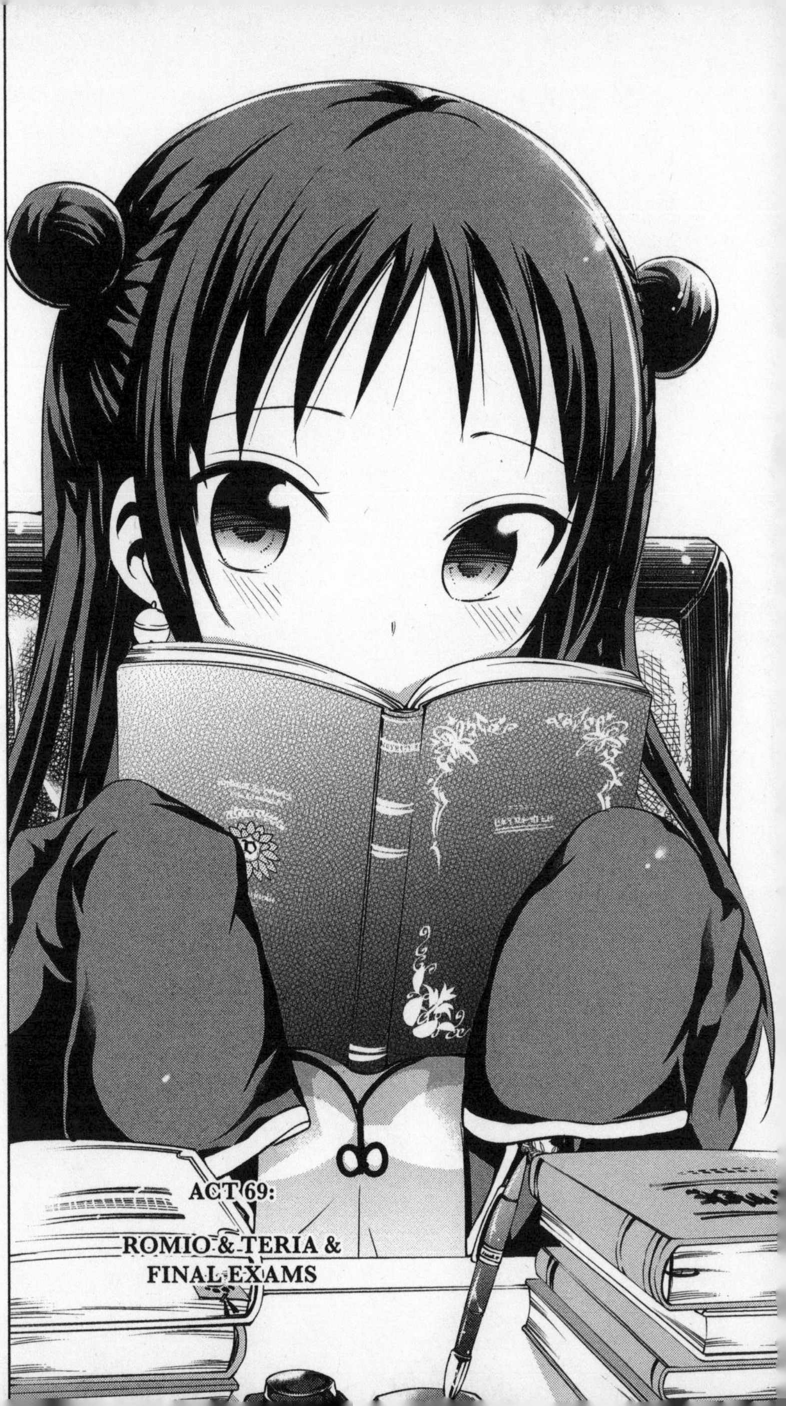
ACT 69:
ROMIO & TERIA &
FINAL EXAMS

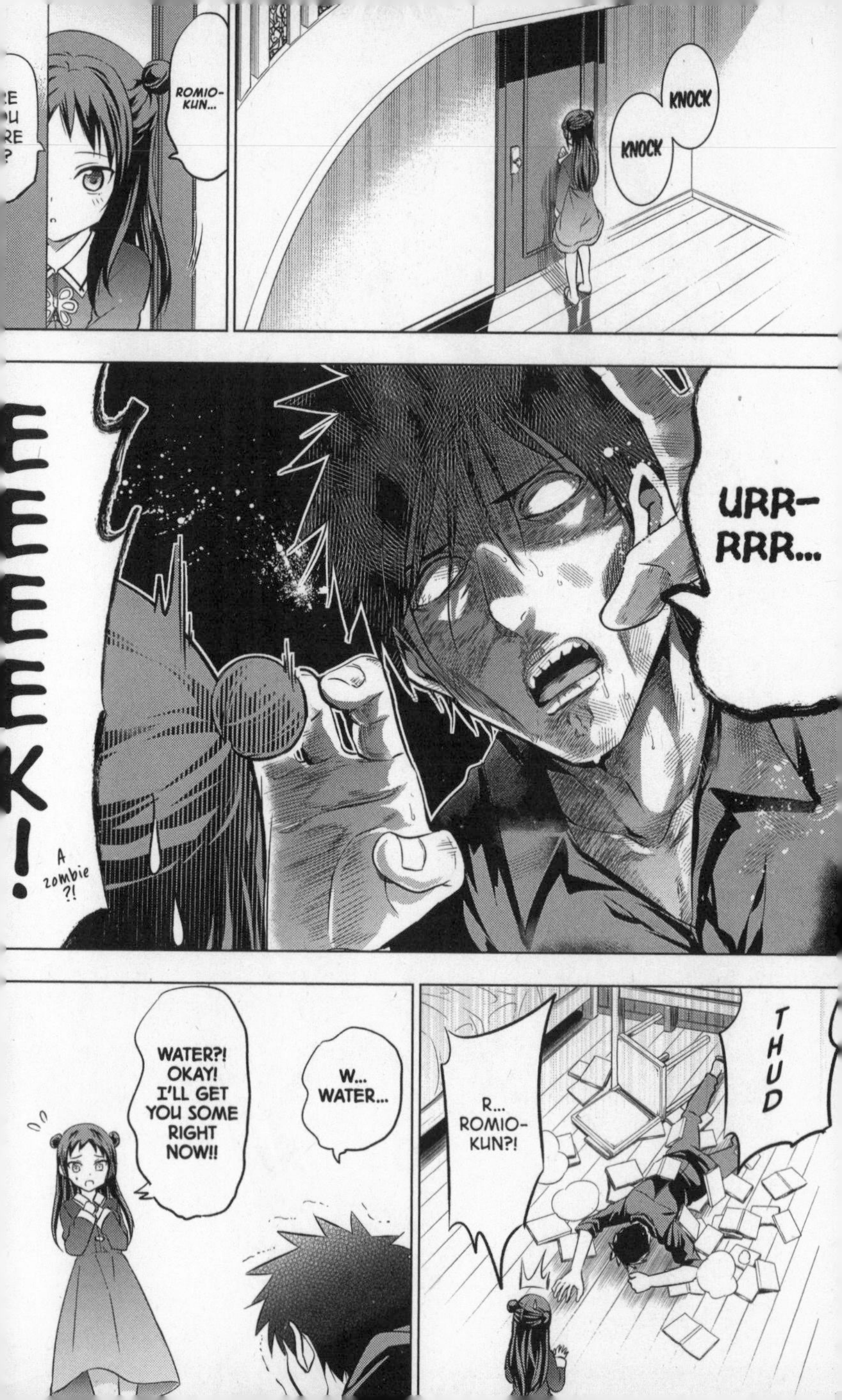
KNOCK
KNOCK
ROMIO-KUN...
URR-RRR...
EEEEK!
A zombie ?!
THUD
R... ROMIO-KUN?!
W... WATER...
WATER?! OKAY! I'LL GET YOU SOME RIGHT NOW!!

GULP

GULP

YOU'VE BEEN STUDYING THIS WHOLE TIME? WITHOUT SLEEP-ING...?

NOPE! HAVEN'T SLEPT SINCE EXAM BREAK BEGAN.

THAT WAS FOUR DAYS AGO, RIGHT...?!

PWAAAH! I'M ALIVE AGAIN!! THANKS!!

ROMIO-KUN, ARE YOU GETTING ENOUGH SLEEP...?

I GOTTA PUSH MYSELF AT LEAST THAT HARD THIS TIME!

YOU DON'T HAVE ENOUGH TIME? IT'S NOT GOOD TO PUSH YOURSELF TOO MUCH, THOUGH.

I GOT NO CHOICE BUT TO CUT INTO MY SLEEPING...

I'VE HAD A LOT GOING ON, SO I NEVER HAVE ENOUGH TIME.

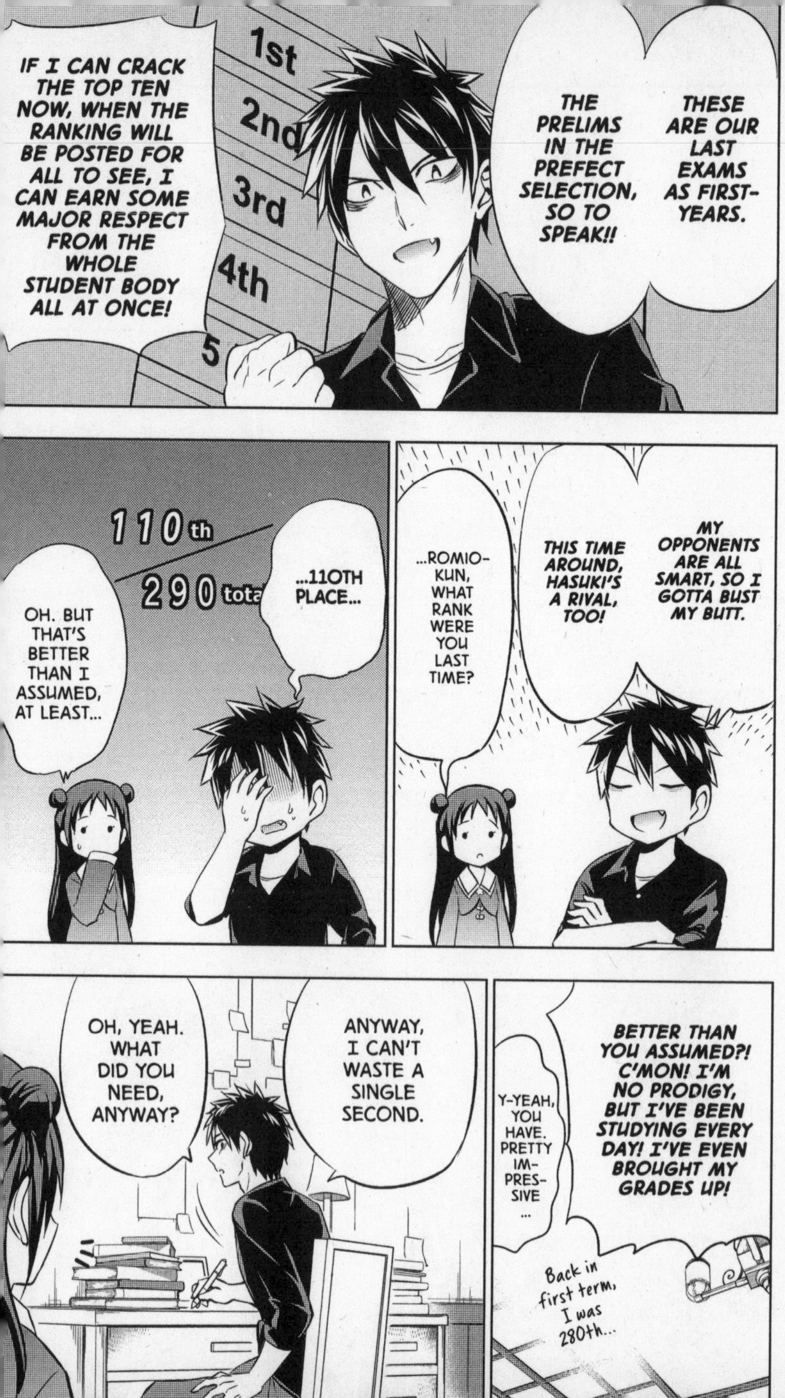
THESE ARE OUR LAST EXAMS AS FIRST-YEARS.
THE PRELIMS IN THE PREFECT SELECTION, SO TO SPEAK!!
1st
2nd
3rd
4th
5
IF I CAN CRACK THE TOP TEN NOW, WHEN THE RANKING WILL BE POSTED FOR ALL TO SEE, I CAN EARN SOME MAJOR RESPECT FROM THE WHOLE STUDENT BODY ALL AT ONCE!
MY OPPONENTS ARE ALL SMART, SO I GOTTA BUST MY BUTT.
THIS TIME AROUND, HASUKI'S A RIVAL, TOO!
...ROMIO-KUN, WHAT RANK WERE YOU LAST TIME?
110th
290 tota
...110TH PLACE...
OH. BUT THAT'S BETTER THAN I ASSUMED, AT LEAST...
BETTER THAN YOU ASSUMED?! C'MON! I'M NO PRODIGY, BUT I'VE BEEN STUDYING EVERY DAY! I'VE EVEN BROUGHT MY GRADES UP!
Y-YEAH, YOU HAVE. PRETTY IM-PRES-SIVE...
Back in first term, I was 280th...
ANYWAY, I CAN'T WASTE A SINGLE SECOND.
OH, YEAH. WHAT DID YOU NEED, ANYWAY?

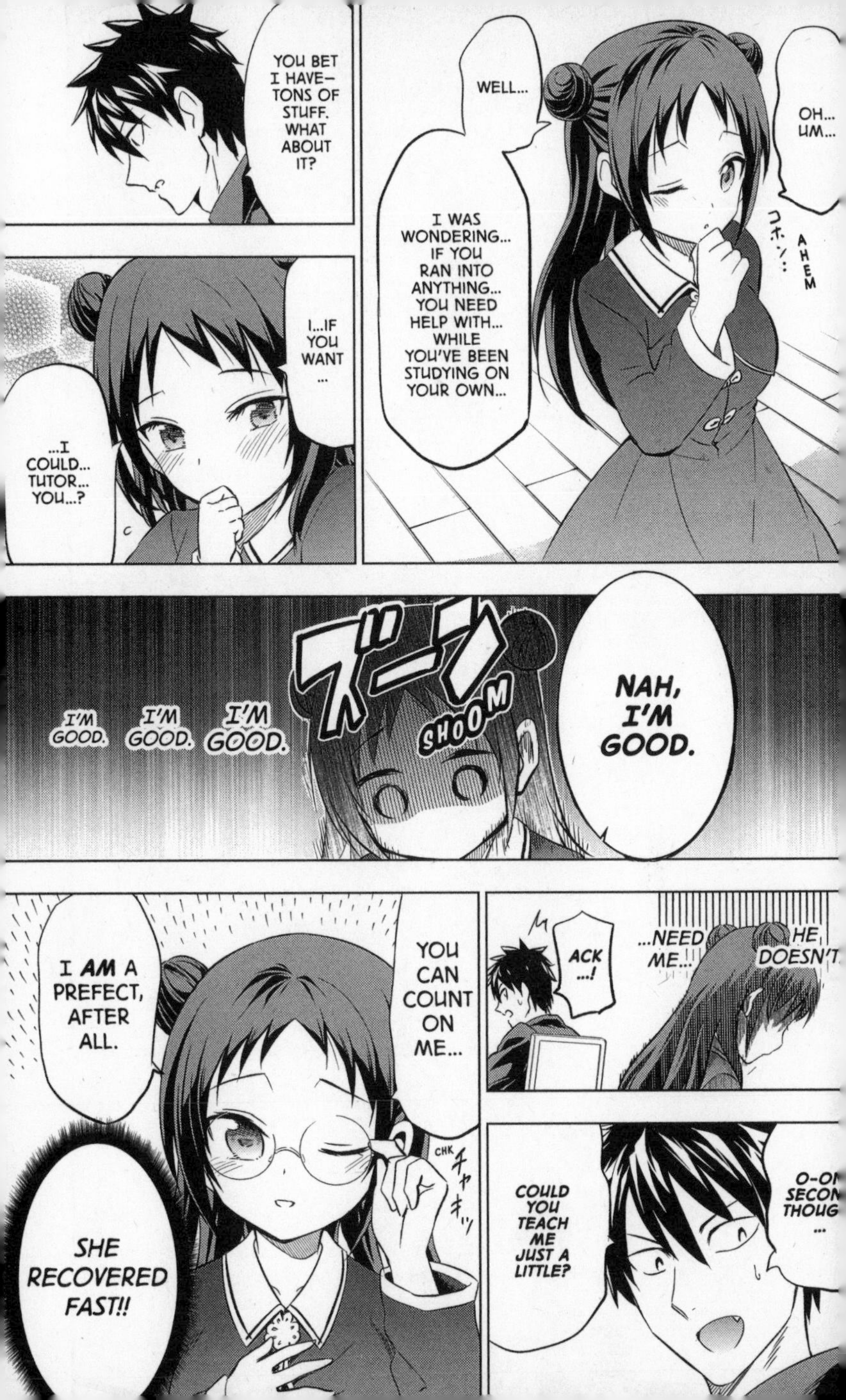
OH... UM...
コホン…
AHEM
WELL...
I WAS WONDERING... IF YOU RAN INTO ANYTHING... YOU NEED HELP WITH... WHILE YOU'VE BEEN STUDYING ON YOUR OWN...
YOU BET I HAVE— TONS OF STUFF. WHAT ABOUT IT?
I...IF YOU WANT ...
...I COULD... TUTOR... YOU...?
NAH, I'M GOOD.
ズーン
SHOOM
I'M GOOD. I'M GOOD. I'M GOOD.
HE DOESN'T
...NEED ME...
ACK ...!
O-ON SECON THOUG ...
COULD YOU TEACH ME JUST A LITTLE?
YOU CAN COUNT ON ME...
I **AM** A PREFECT, AFTER ALL.
CHK
チャキッ
SHE RECOVERED FAST!!

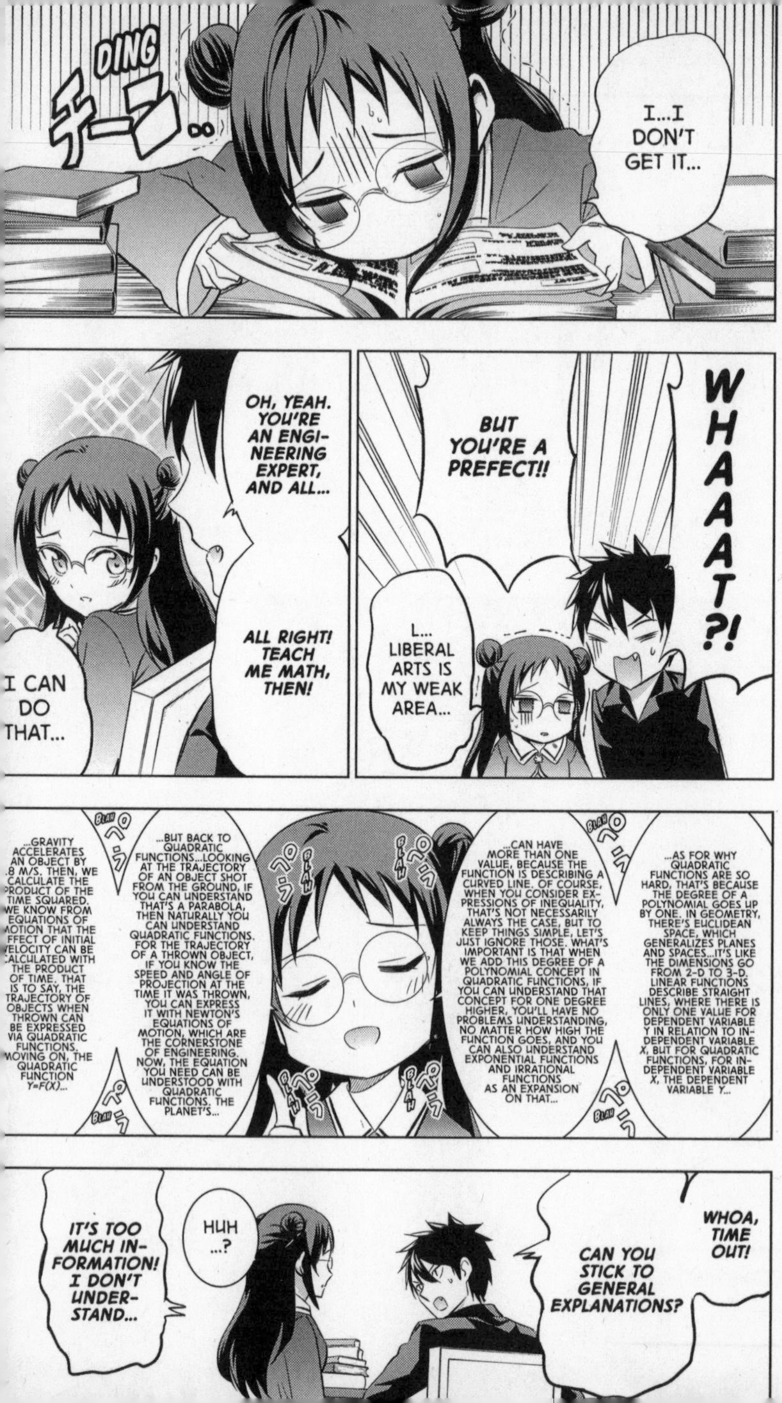
DING
チーン
I...I DON'T GET IT...
WHAAAT?!
BUT YOU'RE A PREFECT!!
L... LIBERAL ARTS IS MY WEAK AREA...
OH, YEAH. YOU'RE AN ENGI-NEERING EXPERT, AND ALL...
ALL RIGHT! TEACH ME MATH, THEN!
I CAN DO THAT...
BLAH
...AS FOR WHY QUADRATIC FUNCTIONS ARE SO HARD, THAT'S BECAUSE THE DEGREE OF A POLYNOMIAL GOES UP BY ONE. IN GEOMETRY, THERE'S EUCLIDEAN SPACE, WHICH GENERALIZES PLANES AND SPACES...IT'S LIKE THE DIMENSIONS GO FROM 2-D TO 3-D. LINEAR FUNCTIONS DESCRIBE STRAIGHT LINES, WHERE THERE IS ONLY ONE VALUE FOR DEPENDENT VARIABLE Y IN RELATION TO IN-DEPENDENT VARIABLE X, BUT FOR QUADRATIC FUNCTIONS, FOR IN-DEPENDENT VARIABLE X, THE DEPENDENT VARIABLE Y...
...CAN HAVE MORE THAN ONE VALUE, BECAUSE THE FUNCTION IS DESCRIBING A CURVED LINE. OF COURSE, WHEN YOU CONSIDER EX-PRESSIONS OF INEQUALITY, THAT'S NOT NECESSARILY ALWAYS THE CASE, BUT TO KEEP THINGS SIMPLE, LET'S JUST IGNORE THOSE. WHAT'S IMPORTANT IS THAT WHEN WE ADD THIS DEGREE OF A POLYNOMIAL CONCEPT IN QUADRATIC FUNCTIONS, IF YOU CAN UNDERSTAND THAT CONCEPT FOR ONE DEGREE HIGHER, YOU'LL HAVE NO PROBLEMS UNDERSTANDING, NO MATTER HOW HIGH THE FUNCTION GOES, AND YOU CAN ALSO UNDERSTAND EXPONENTIAL FUNCTIONS AND IRRATIONAL FUNCTIONS AS AN EXPANSION ON THAT...
...BUT BACK TO QUADRATIC FUNCTIONS...LOOKING AT THE TRAJECTORY OF AN OBJECT SHOT FROM THE GROUND, IF YOU CAN UNDERSTAND THAT'S A PARABOLA, THEN NATURALLY YOU CAN UNDERSTAND QUADRATIC FUNCTIONS. FOR THE TRAJECTORY OF A THROWN OBJECT, IF YOU KNOW THE SPEED AND ANGLE OF PROJECTION AT THE TIME IT WAS THROWN, YOU CAN EXPRESS IT WITH NEWTON'S EQUATIONS OF MOTION, WHICH ARE THE CORNERSTONE OF ENGINEERING. NOW, THE EQUATION YOU NEED CAN BE UNDERSTOOD WITH QUADRATIC FUNCTIONS. THE PLANET'S...
...GRAVITY ACCELERATES AN OBJECT BY .8 M/S. THEN, WE CALCULATE THE PRODUCT OF THE TIME SQUARED. WE KNOW FROM EQUATIONS OF MOTION THAT THE EFFECT OF INITIAL VELOCITY CAN BE CALCULATED WITH THE PRODUCT OF TIME. THAT IS TO SAY, THE TRAJECTORY OF OBJECTS WHEN THROWN CAN BE EXPRESSED VIA QUADRATIC FUNCTIONS. MOVING ON, THE QUADRATIC FUNCTION Y=F(X)...
WHOA, TIME OUT!
CAN YOU STICK TO GENERAL EXPLANATIONS?
HUH ...?
IT'S TOO MUCH IN-FORMATION! I DON'T UNDER-STAND...

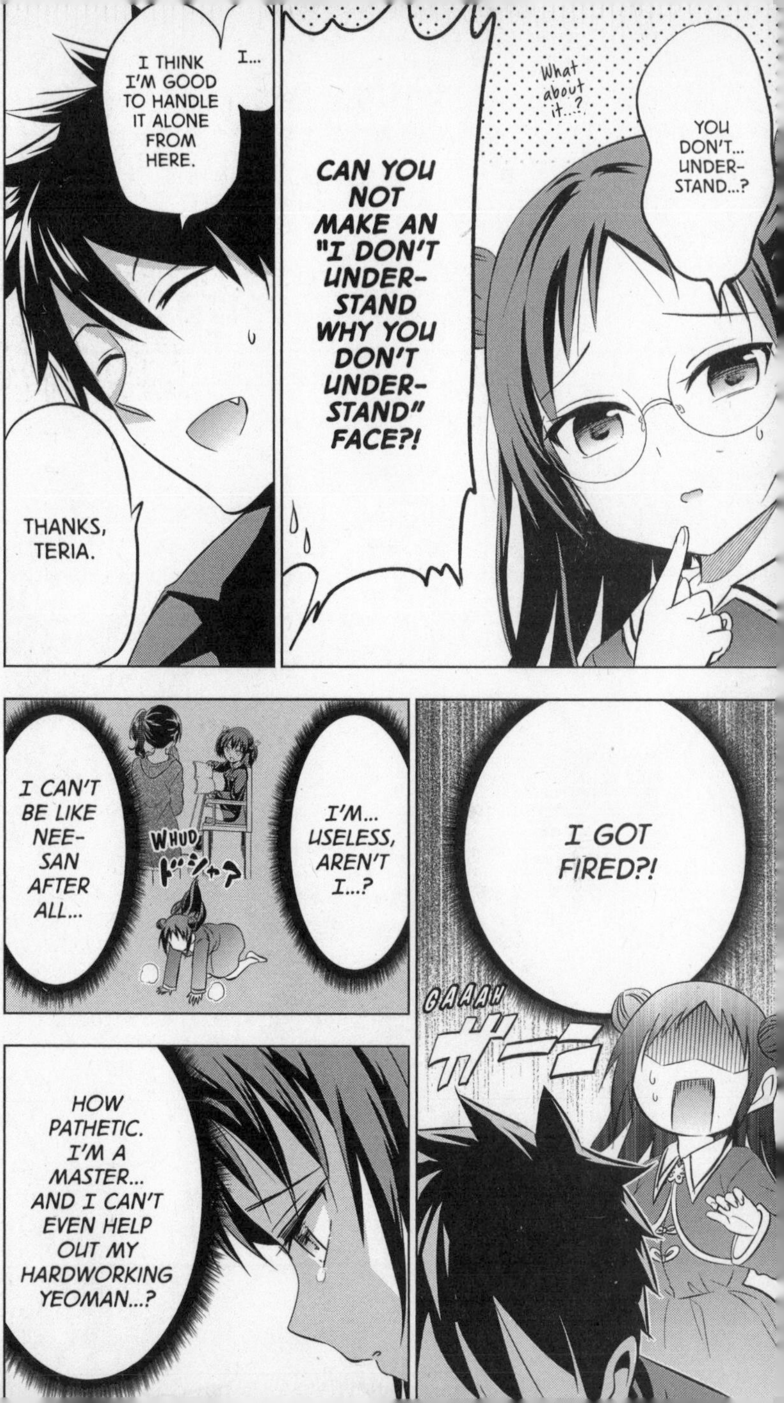

YOU DON'T... UNDER-STAND...?
What about it...?
CAN YOU NOT MAKE AN "I DON'T UNDER-STAND WHY YOU DON'T UNDER-STAND" FACE?!
I...
I THINK I'M GOOD TO HANDLE IT ALONE FROM HERE.
THANKS, TERIA.
I GOT FIRED?!
GAAAH
ザーン
I'M... USELESS, AREN'T I...?
WHUD
ドシャア
I CAN'T BE LIKE NEE-SAN AFTER ALL...
HOW PATHETIC. I'M A MASTER... AND I CAN'T EVEN HELP OUT MY HARDWORKING YEOMAN...?

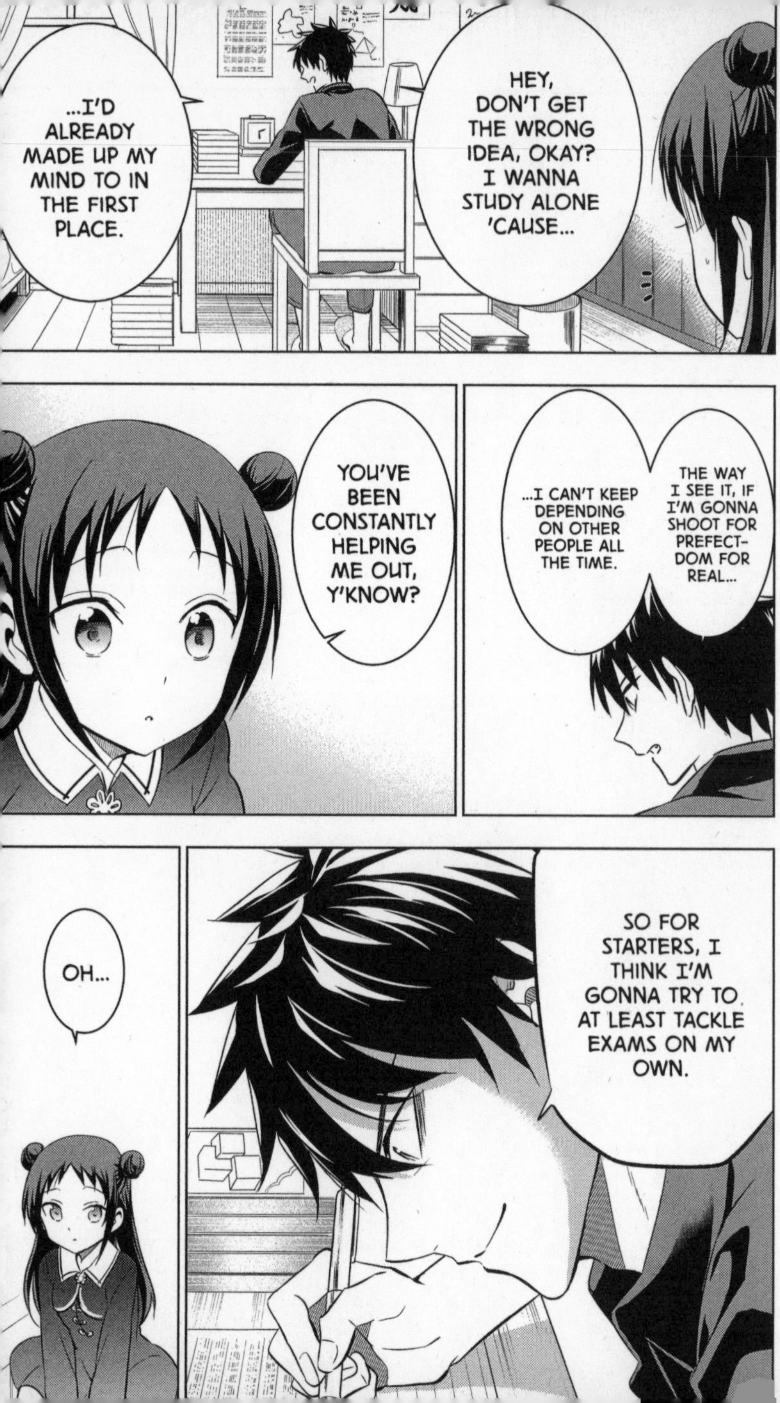
HEY, DON'T GET THE WRONG IDEA, OKAY? I WANNA STUDY ALONE 'CAUSE...
...I'D ALREADY MADE UP MY MIND TO IN THE FIRST PLACE.
THE WAY I SEE IT, IF I'M GONNA SHOOT FOR PREFECT-DOM FOR REAL...
...I CAN'T KEEP DEPENDING ON OTHER PEOPLE ALL THE TIME.
YOU'VE BEEN CONSTANTLY HELPING ME OUT, Y'KNOW?
SO FOR STARTERS, I THINK I'M GONNA TRY TO AT LEAST TACKLE EXAMS ON MY OWN.
OH...

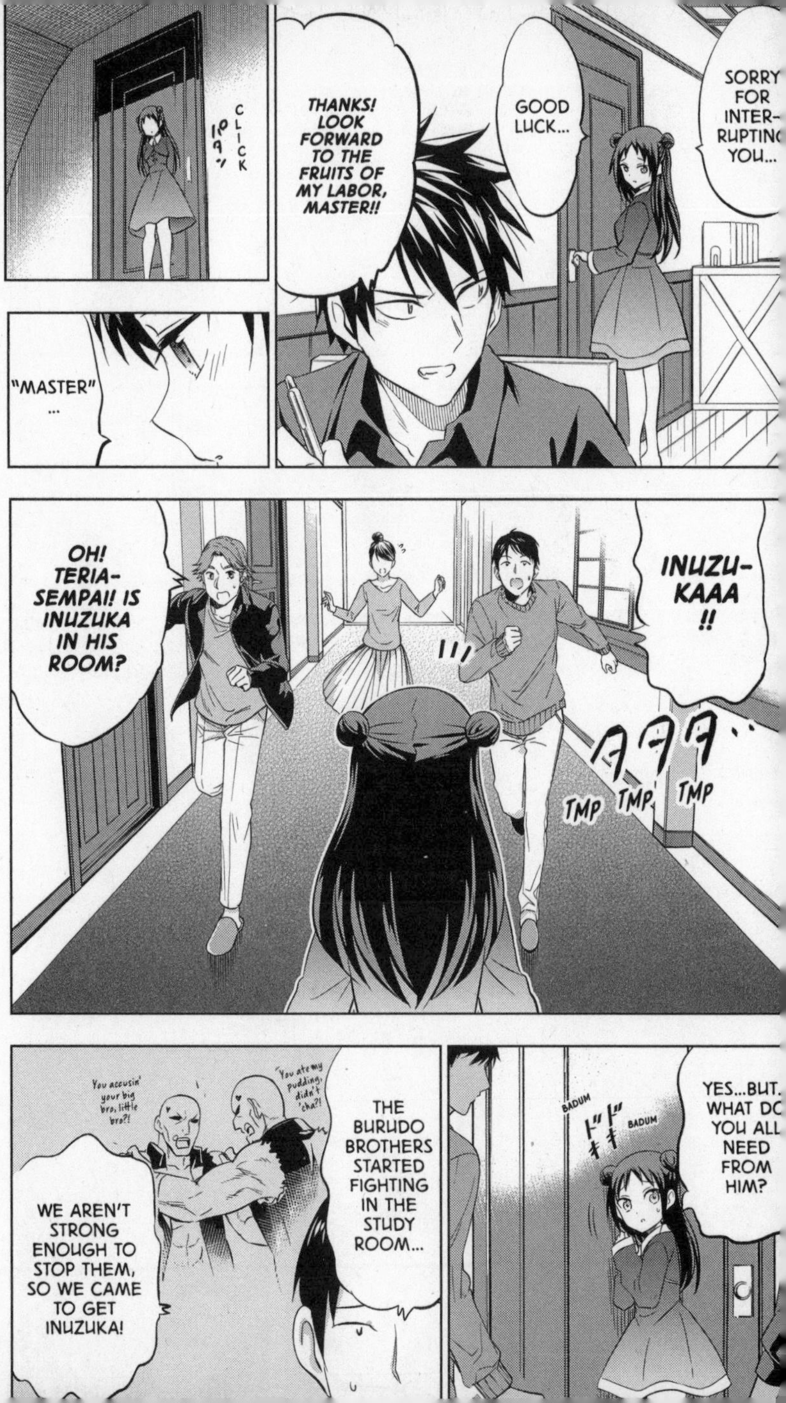
SORRY FOR INTERRUPTING YOU...
GOOD LUCK...
THANKS! LOOK FORWARD TO THE FRUITS OF MY LABOR, MASTER!!
CLICK
"MASTER" ...
INUZUKAAA!!
OH! TERIA-SEMPAI! IS INUZUKA IN HIS ROOM?
TMP TMP TMP
YES...BUT. WHAT DO YOU ALL NEED FROM HIM?
BADUM BADUM
THE BURUDO BROTHERS STARTED FIGHTING IN THE STUDY ROOM...
"You ate my pudding, didn't 'cha?!
You accusin' your big bro, little bro?!
WE AREN'T STRONG ENOUGH TO STOP THEM, SO WE CAME TO GET INUZUKA!

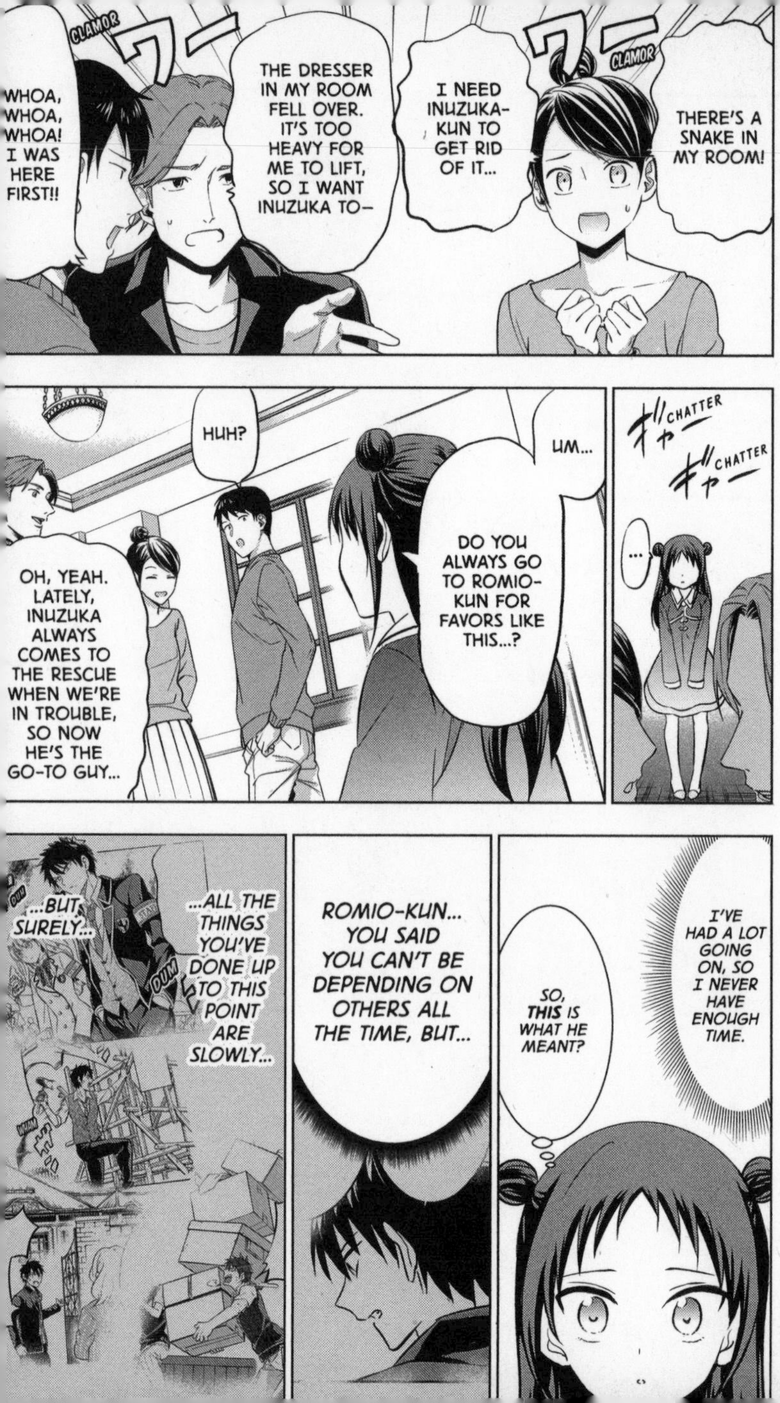
THERE'S A SNAKE IN MY ROOM!
CLAMOR
I NEED INUZUKA-KUN TO GET RID OF IT...
THE DRESSER IN MY ROOM FELL OVER. IT'S TOO HEAVY FOR ME TO LIFT, SO I WANT INUZUKA TO–
CLAMOR
WHOA, WHOA, WHOA! I WAS HERE FIRST!!
CHATTER
CHATTER
...
UM...
DO YOU ALWAYS GO TO ROMIO-KUN FOR FAVORS LIKE THIS...?
HUH?
OH, YEAH. LATELY, INUZUKA ALWAYS COMES TO THE RESCUE WHEN WE'RE IN TROUBLE, SO NOW HE'S THE GO-TO GUY...
I'VE HAD A LOT GOING ON, SO I NEVER HAVE ENOUGH TIME.
SO, THIS IS WHAT HE MEANT?
ROMIO-KUN... YOU SAID YOU CAN'T BE DEPENDING ON OTHERS ALL THE TIME, BUT...
...ALL THE THINGS YOU'VE DONE UP TO THIS POINT ARE SLOWLY...
DUM
...BUT, SURELY...

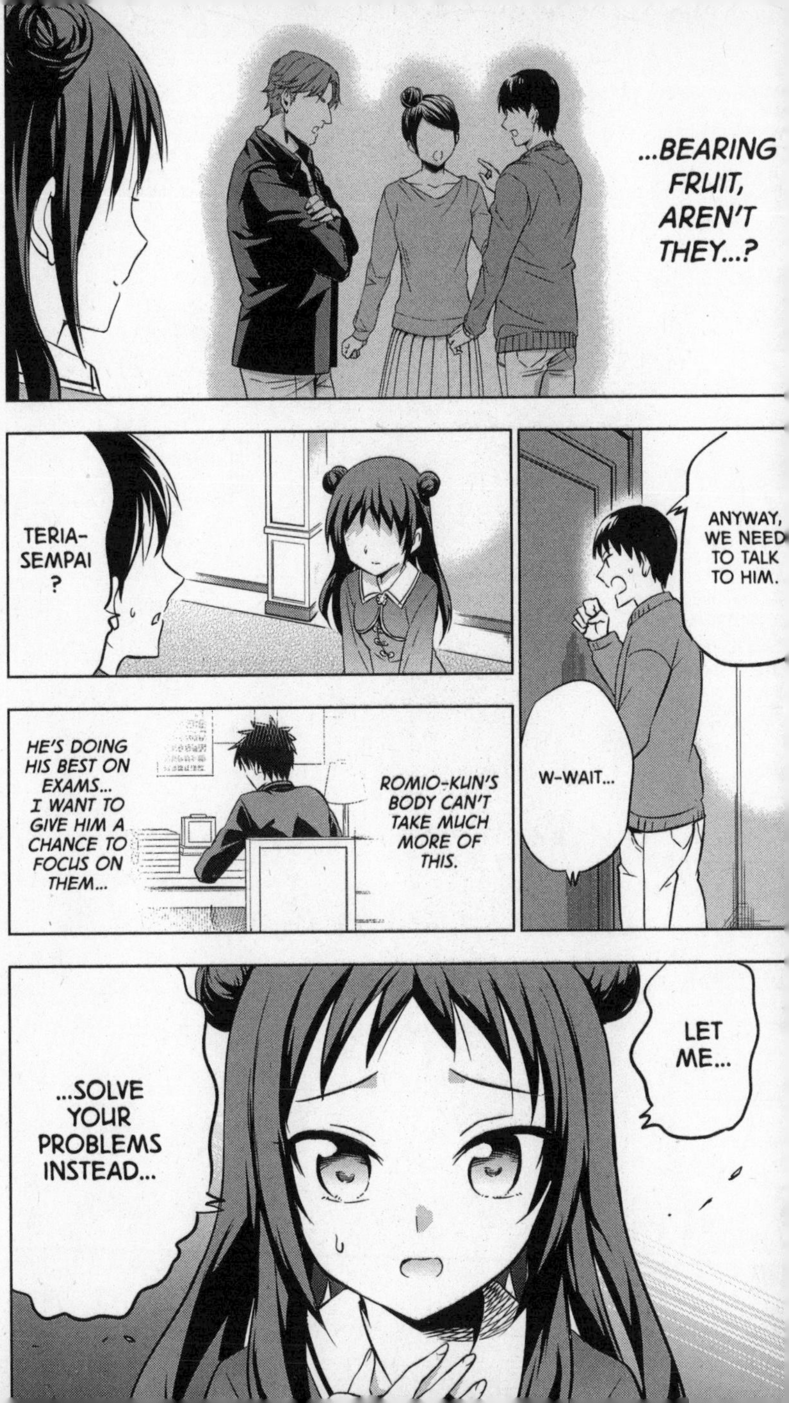

...BEARING FRUIT, AREN'T THEY...?
ANYWAY, WE NEED TO TALK TO HIM.
W-WAIT...
TERIA-SEMPAI?
ROMIO-KUN'S BODY CAN'T TAKE MUCH MORE OF THIS.
HE'S DOING HIS BEST ON EXAMS... I WANT TO GIVE HIM A CHANCE TO FOCUS ON THEM...
LET ME...
...SOLVE YOUR PROBLEMS INSTEAD...

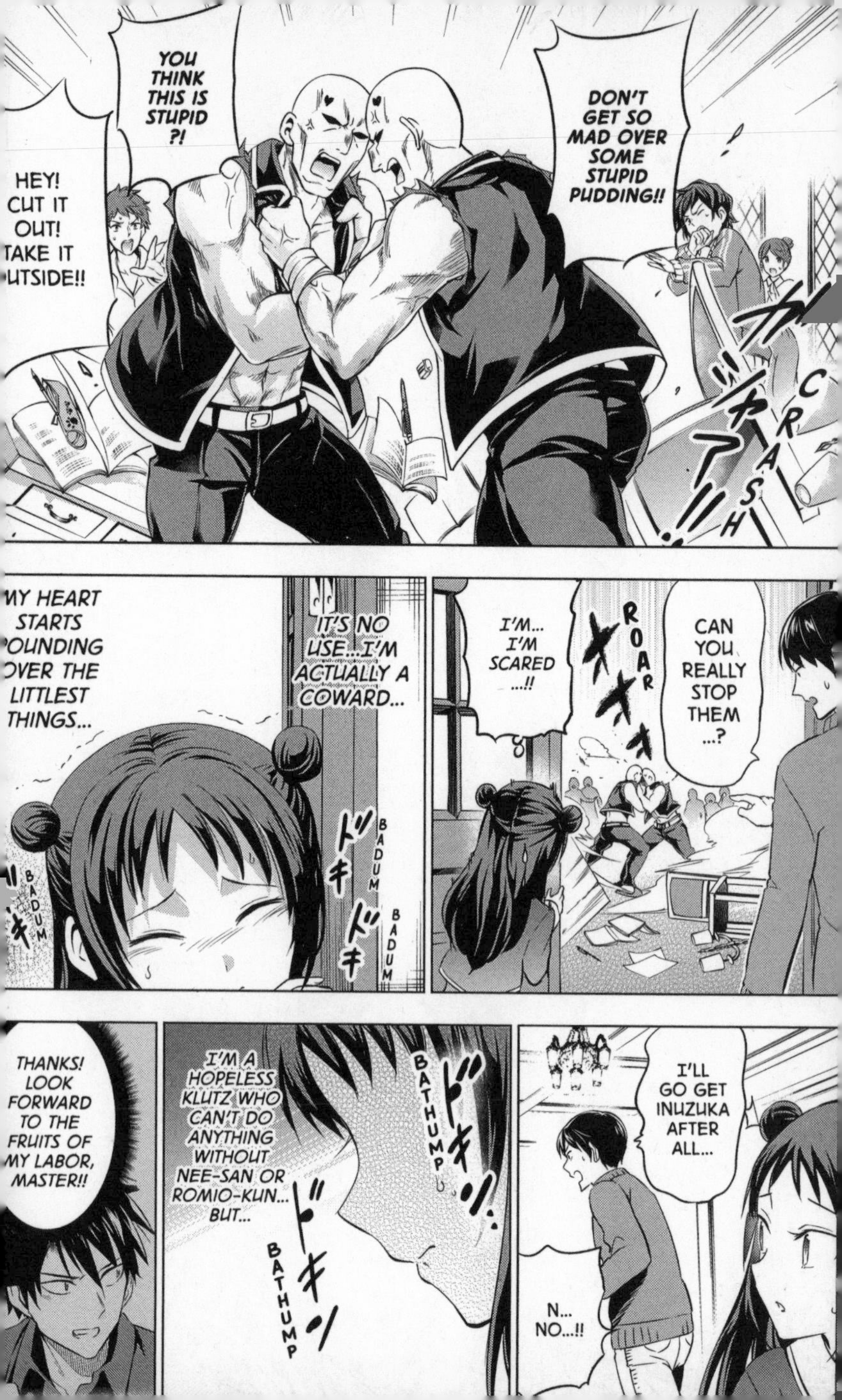
DON'T GET SO MAD OVER SOME STUPID PUDDING!!
YOU THINK THIS IS STUPID?!
HEY! CUT IT OUT! TAKE IT UTSIDE!!
CRASH
CAN YOU REALLY STOP THEM...?
ROAR
I'M... I'M SCARED...!!
IT'S NO USE...I'M ACTUALLY A COWARD...
BADUM
BADUM
MY HEART STARTS OUNDING VER THE LITTLEST THINGS...
BADUM
I'LL GO GET INUZUKA AFTER ALL...
N... NO...!!
BATHUMP
I'M A HOPELESS KLUTZ WHO CAN'T DO ANYTHING WITHOUT NEE-SAN OR ROMIO-KUN... BUT...
BATHUMP
THANKS! LOOK FORWARD TO THE FRUITS OF MY LABOR, MASTER!!

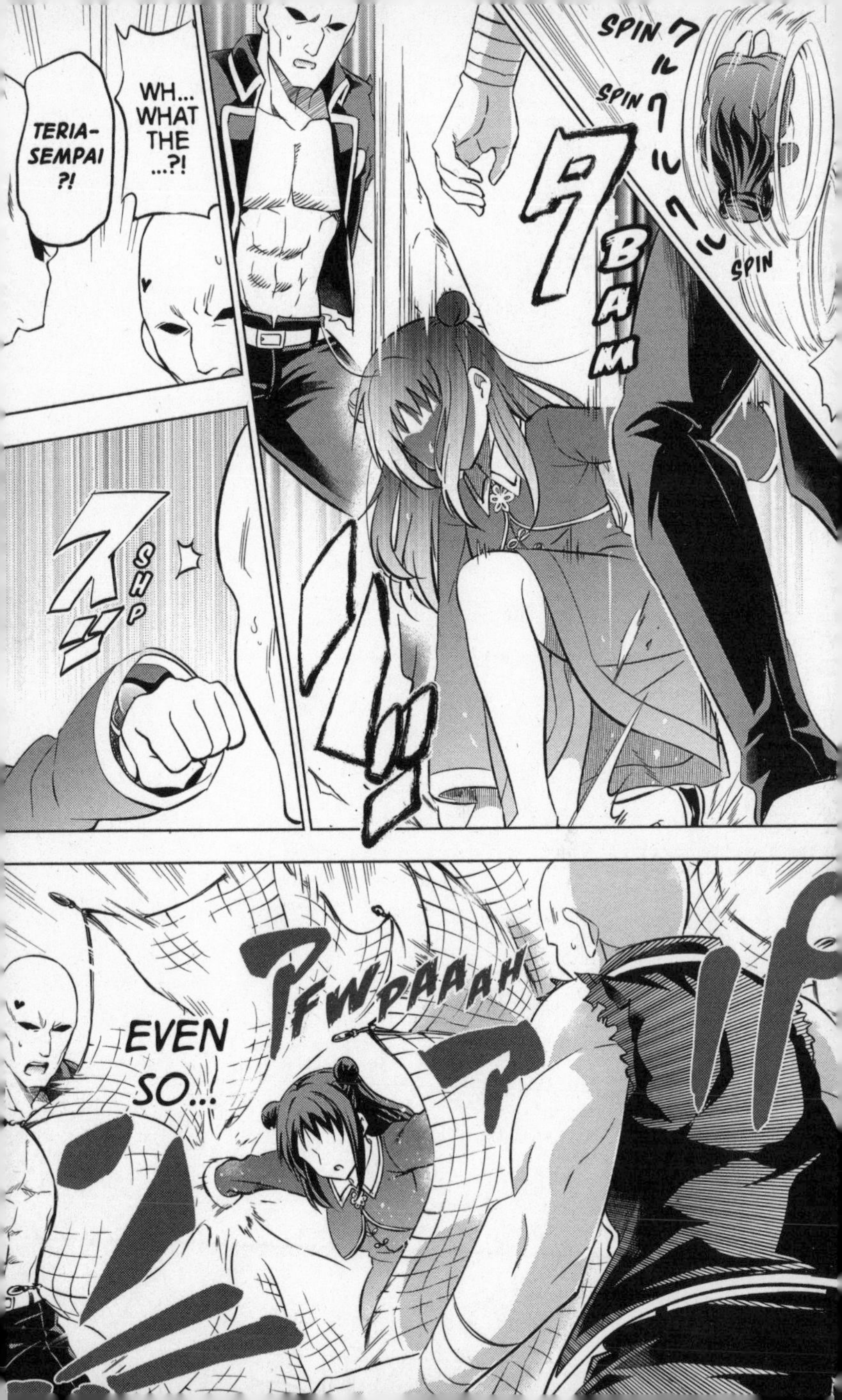
SPIN
SPIN
SPIN
BAM
WH... WHAT THE ...?!
TERIA-SEMPAI ?!
SHP
FWPAAAH
EVEN SO...!

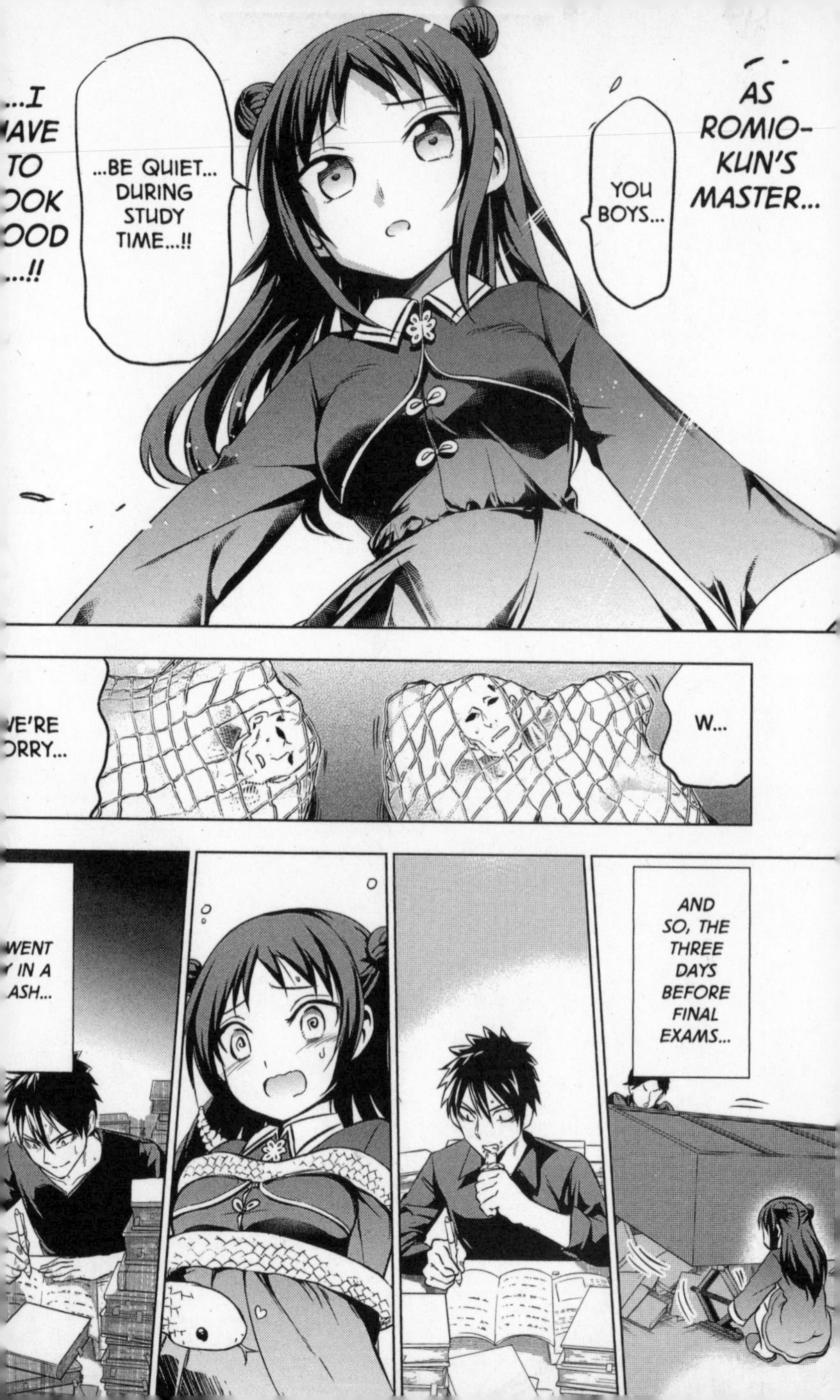
AS ROMIO-KUN'S MASTER...
YOU BOYS...
...BE QUIET... DURING STUDY TIME...!!
...I AVE TO OOK OOD ...!!
W...
VE'RE ORRY...
AND SO, THE THREE DAYS BEFORE FINAL EXAMS...
WENT IN A ASH...

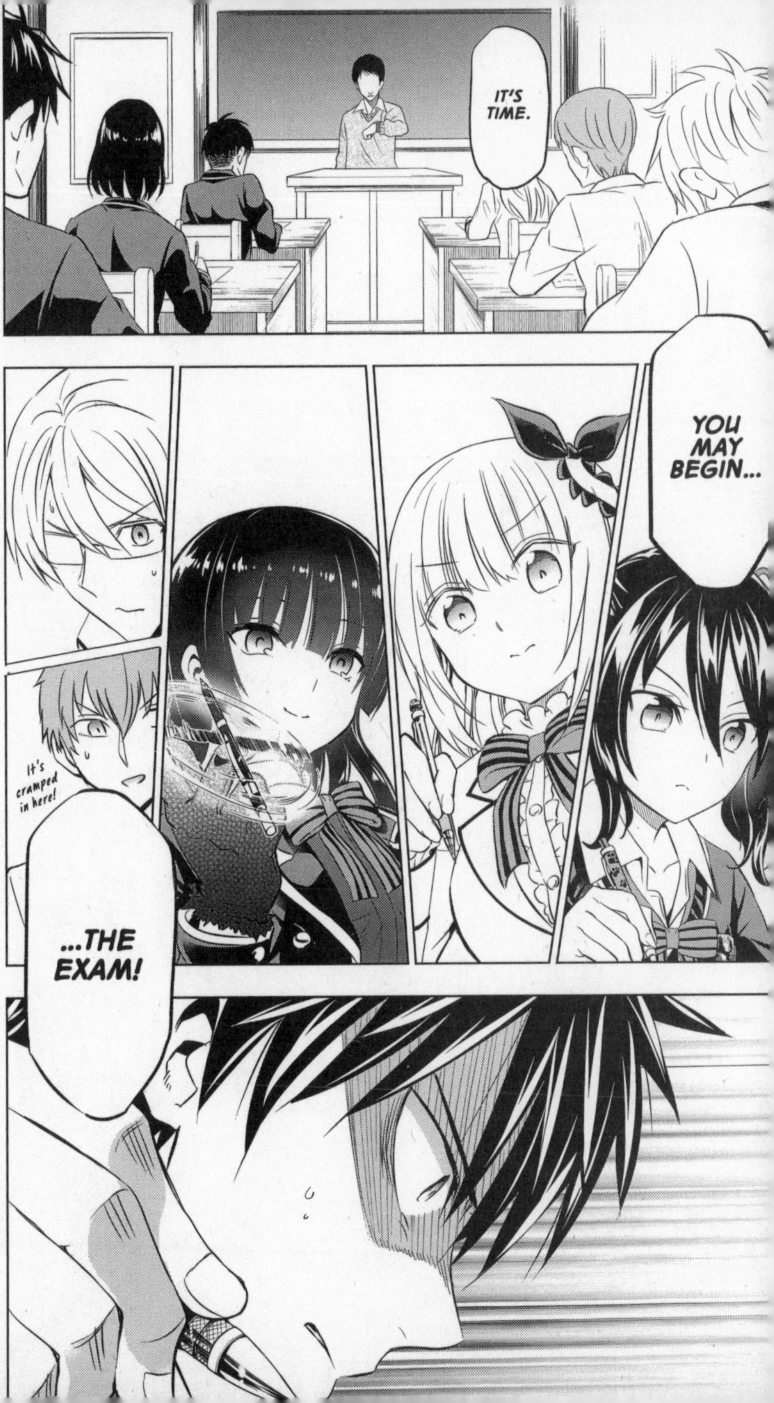
IT'S TIME.
YOU MAY BEGIN...
...THE EXAM!
It's cramped in here!

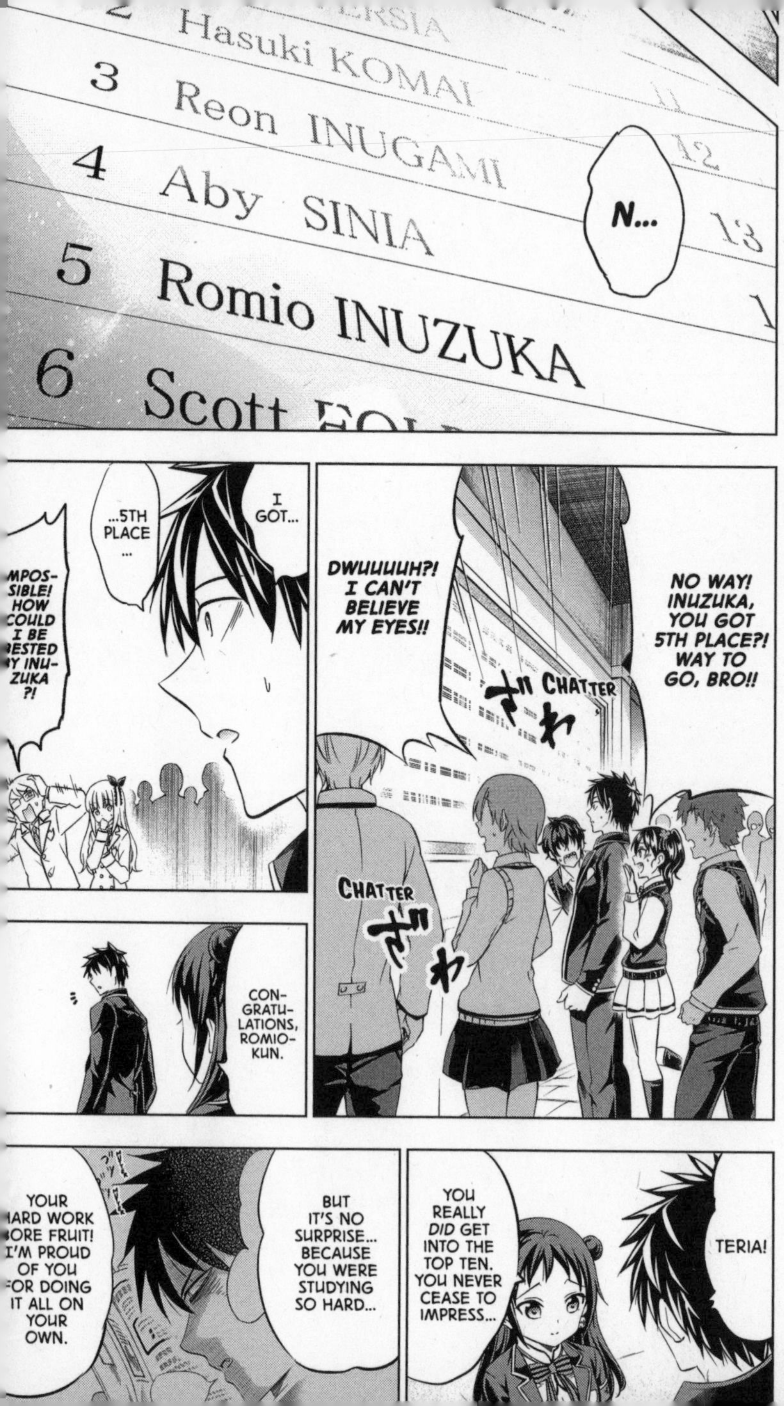
Hasuki KOMAI
3 Reon INUGAMI
4 Aby SINIA
5 Romio INUZUKA
6 Scott
N...
NO WAY! INUZUKA, YOU GOT 5TH PLACE?! WAY TO GO, BRO!!
DWUUUUH?! I CAN'T BELIEVE MY EYES!!
CHATTER
CHATTER
I GOT...
...5TH PLACE...
MPOSSIBLE! HOW COULD I BE BESTED BY INUZUKA?!
CONGRATULATIONS, ROMIO-KUN.
TERIA!
YOU REALLY DID GET INTO THE TOP TEN. YOU NEVER CEASE TO IMPRESS...
BUT IT'S NO SURPRISE... BECAUSE YOU WERE STUDYING SO HARD...
YOUR HARD WORK BORE FRUIT! I'M PROUD OF YOU FOR DOING IT ALL ON YOUR OWN.

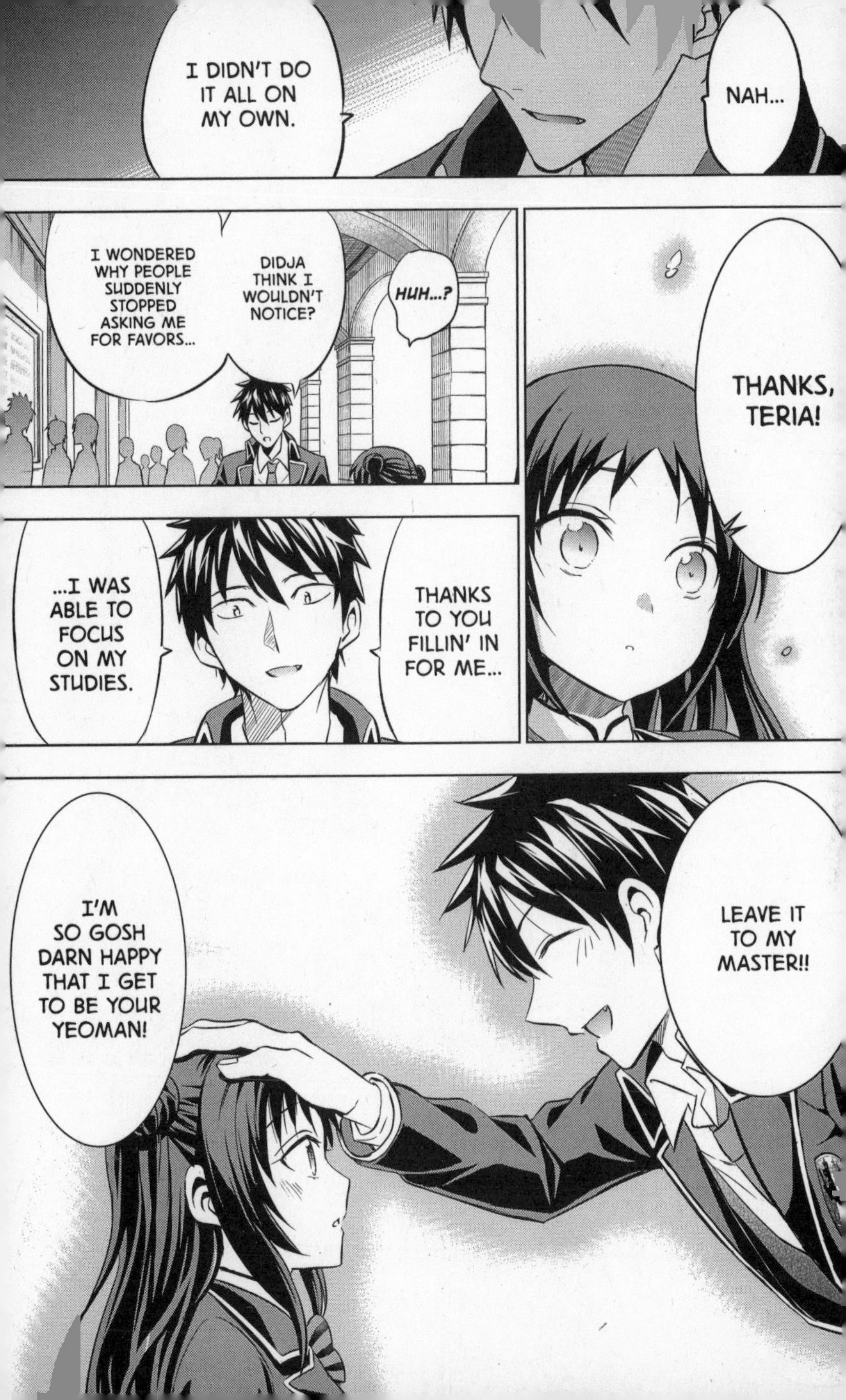
NAH...
I DIDN'T DO IT ALL ON MY OWN.
THANKS, TERIA!
HUH...?
DIDJA THINK I WOULDN'T NOTICE?
I WONDERED WHY PEOPLE SUDDENLY STOPPED ASKING ME FOR FAVORS...
THANKS TO YOU FILLIN' IN FOR ME...
...I WAS ABLE TO FOCUS ON MY STUDIES.
LEAVE IT TO MY MASTER!!
I'M SO GOSH DARN HAPPY THAT I GET TO BE YOUR YEOMAN!

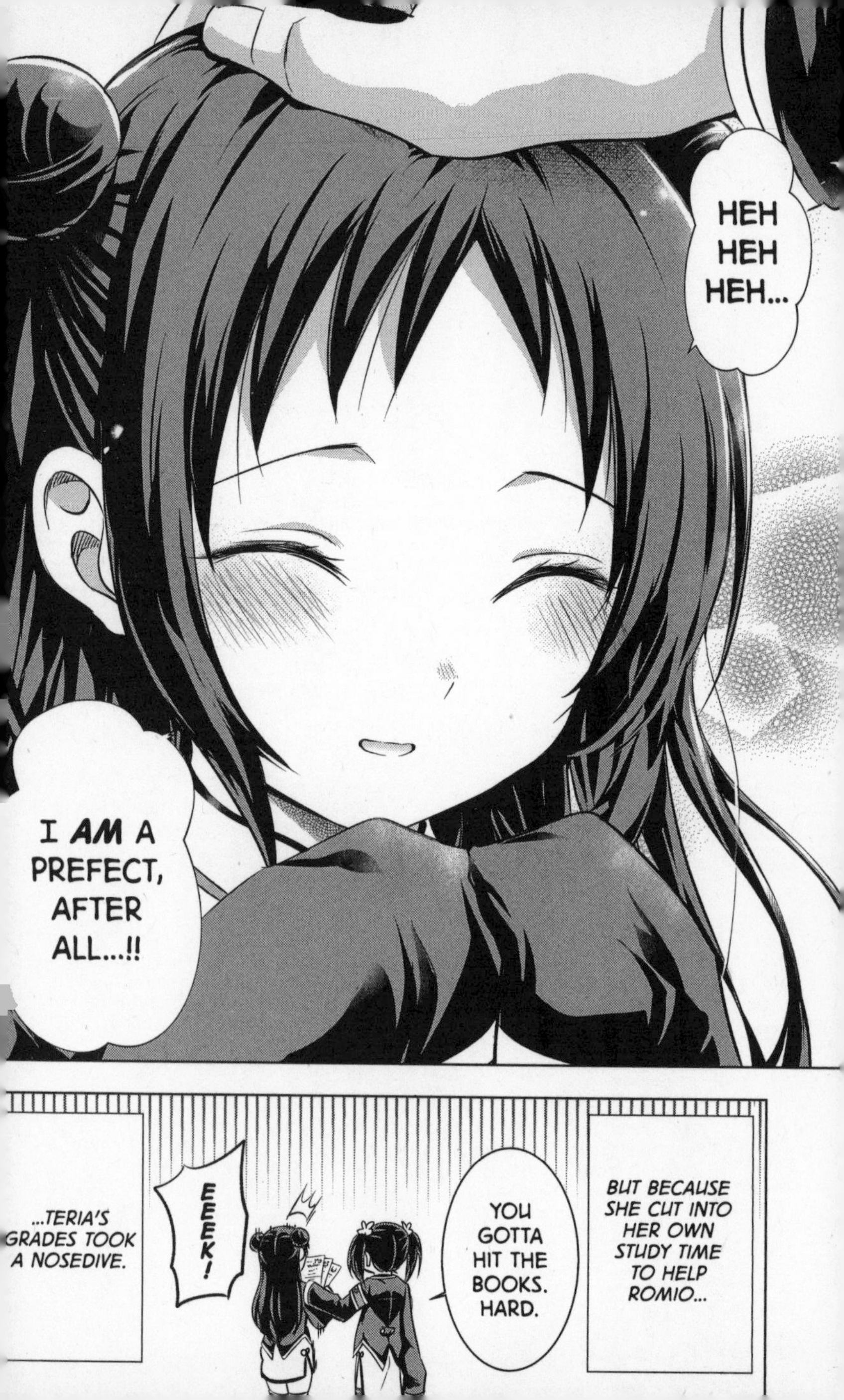
HEH HEH HEH...
I *AM* A PREFECT, AFTER ALL...!!
BUT BECAUSE SHE CUT INTO HER OWN STUDY TIME TO HELP ROMIO...
YOU GOTTA HIT THE BOOKS. HARD.
EEEK!
...TERIA'S GRADES TOOK A NOSEDIVE.

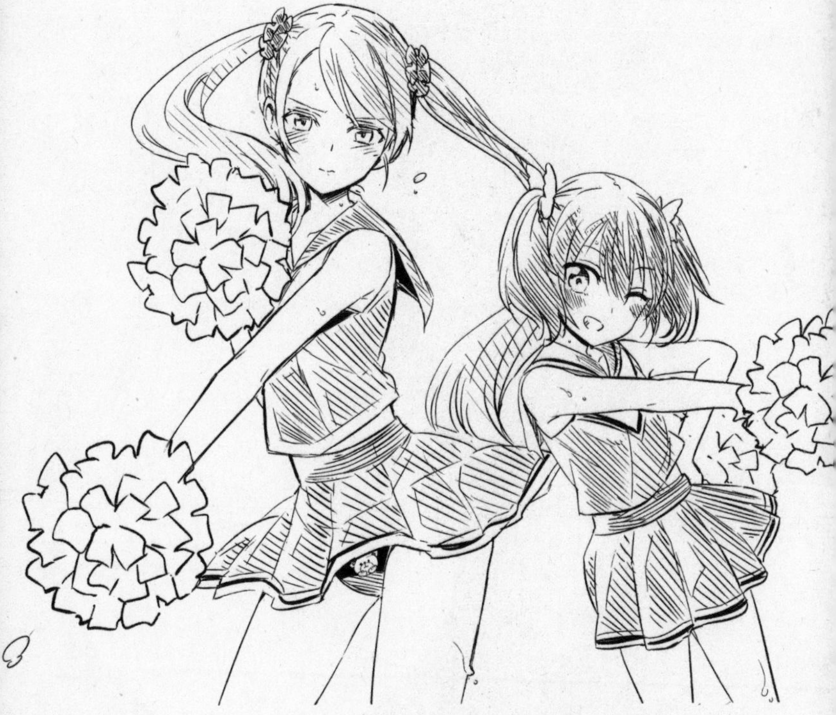

To LOVE, or not to LOVE

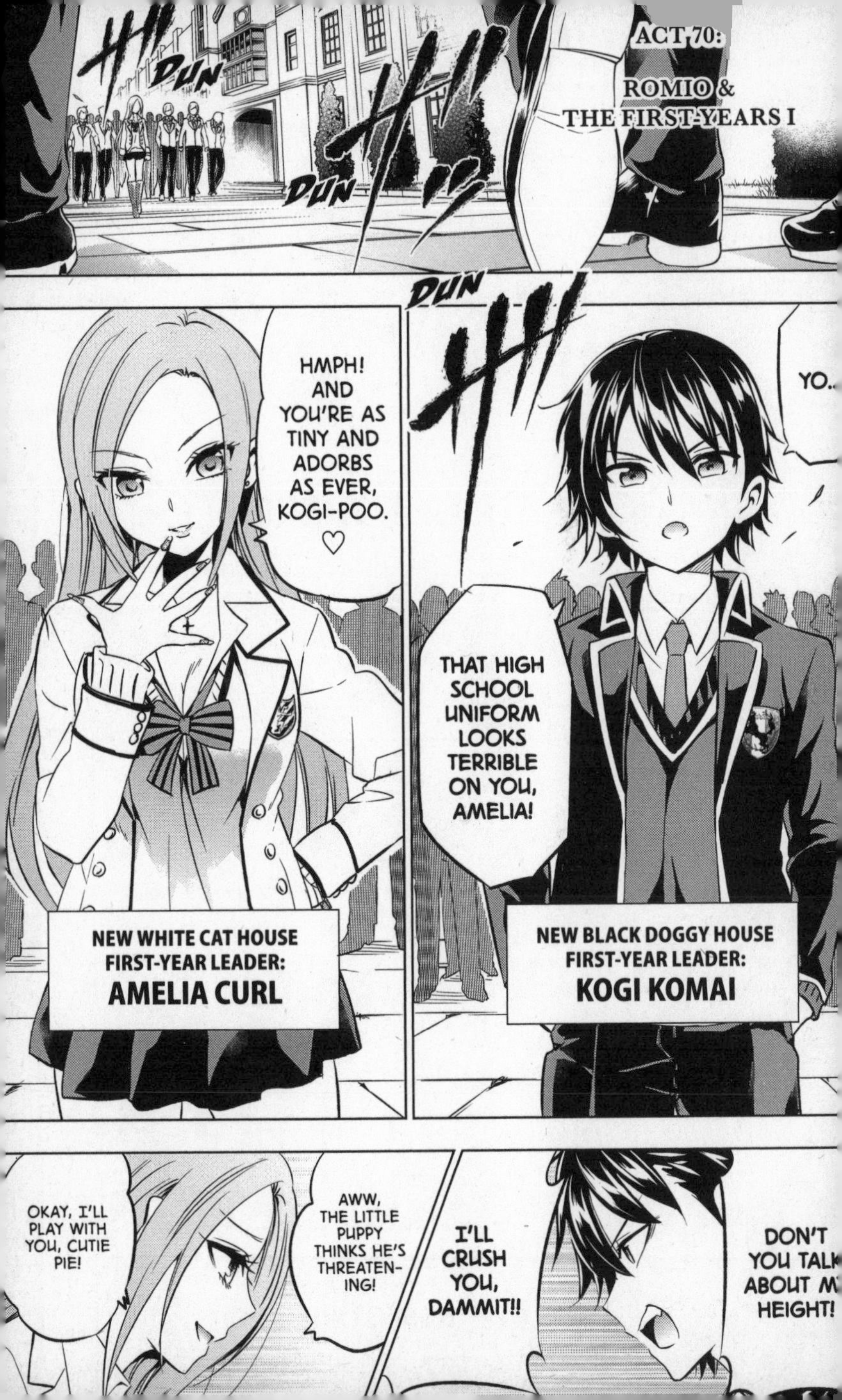
ACT 70:
ROMIO & THE FIRST-YEARS I
DUN
DUN
DUN
YO..
DUN
THAT HIGH SCHOOL UNIFORM LOOKS TERRIBLE ON YOU, AMELIA!
NEW BLACK DOGGY HOUSE FIRST-YEAR LEADER: KOGI KOMAI
HMPH! AND YOU'RE AS TINY AND ADORBS AS EVER, KOGI-POO. ♡
NEW WHITE CAT HOUSE FIRST-YEAR LEADER: AMELIA CURL
DON'T YOU TALK ABOUT M HEIGHT!
I'LL CRUSH YOU, DAMMIT!!
AWW, THE LITTLE PUPPY THINKS HE'S THREATEN-ING!
OKAY, I'LL PLAY WITH YOU, CUTIE PIE!

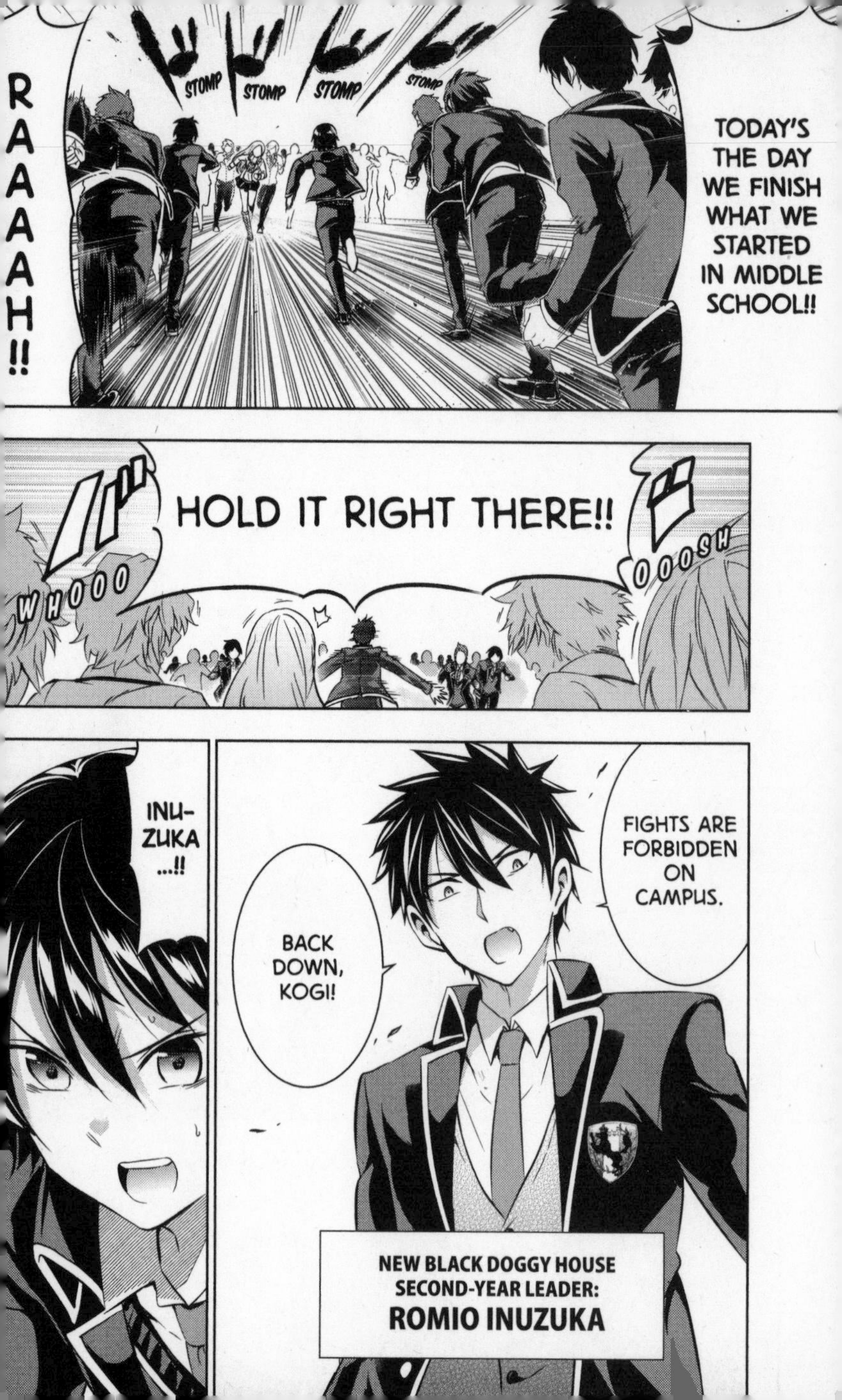
TODAY'S THE DAY WE FINISH WHAT WE STARTED IN MIDDLE SCHOOL!!
STOMP
STOMP
STOMP
STOMP
RAAAAAH!!
HOLD IT RIGHT THERE!!
WHOOO OOOSH
FIGHTS ARE FORBIDDEN ON CAMPUS.
BACK DOWN, KOGI!
NEW BLACK DOGGY HOUSE SECOND-YEAR LEADER: ROMIO INUZUKA
INU-ZUKA ...!!

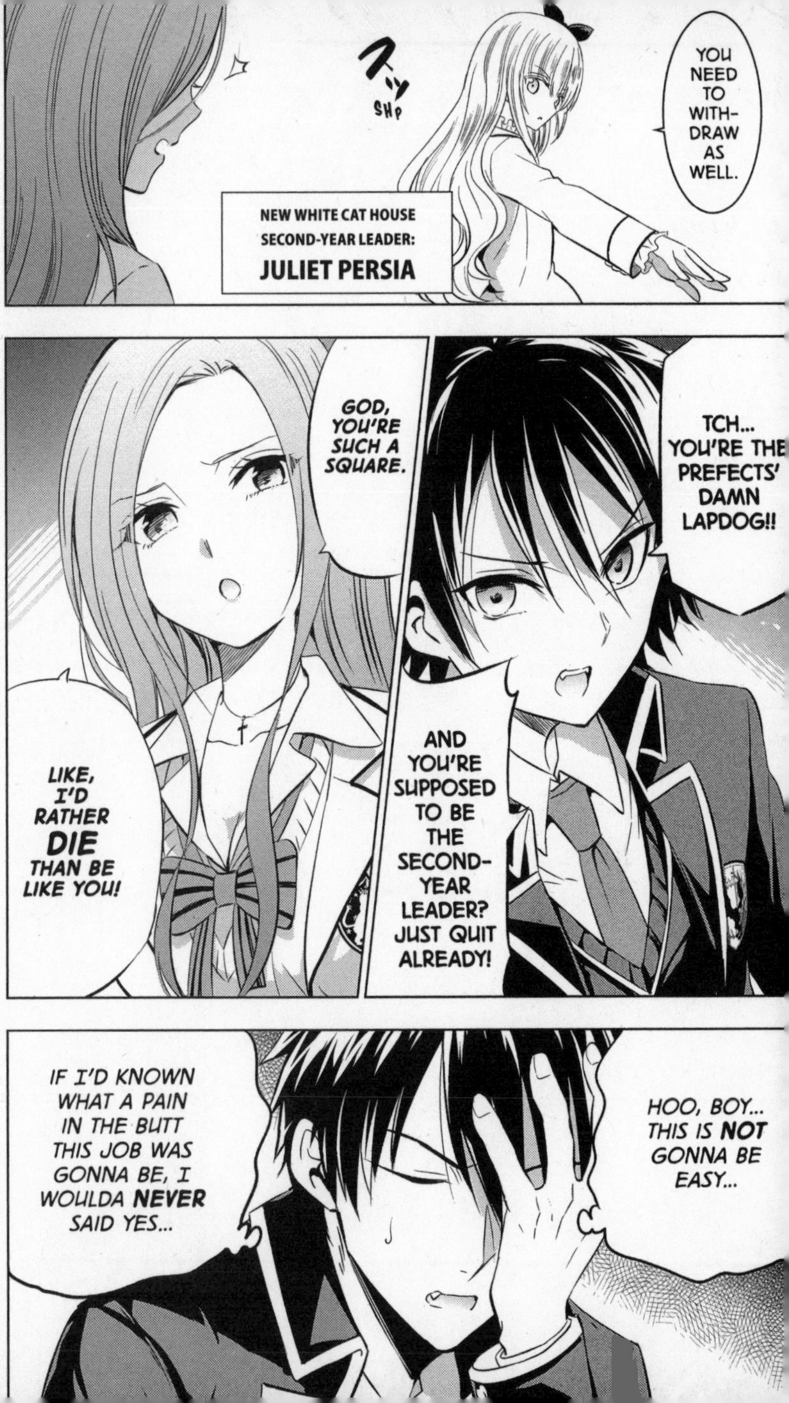
YOU NEED TO WITH-DRAW AS WELL.
SHP
NEW WHITE CAT HOUSE SECOND-YEAR LEADER: JULIET PERSIA
TCH... YOU'RE THE PREFECTS' DAMN LAPDOG!!
AND YOU'RE SUPPOSED TO BE THE SECOND-YEAR LEADER? JUST QUIT ALREADY!
GOD, YOU'RE SUCH A SQUARE.
LIKE, I'D RATHER DIE THAN BE LIKE YOU!
HOO, BOY... THIS IS NOT GONNA BE EASY...
IF I'D KNOWN WHAT A PAIN IN THE BUTT THIS JOB WAS GONNA BE, I WOULDA NEVER SAID YES...

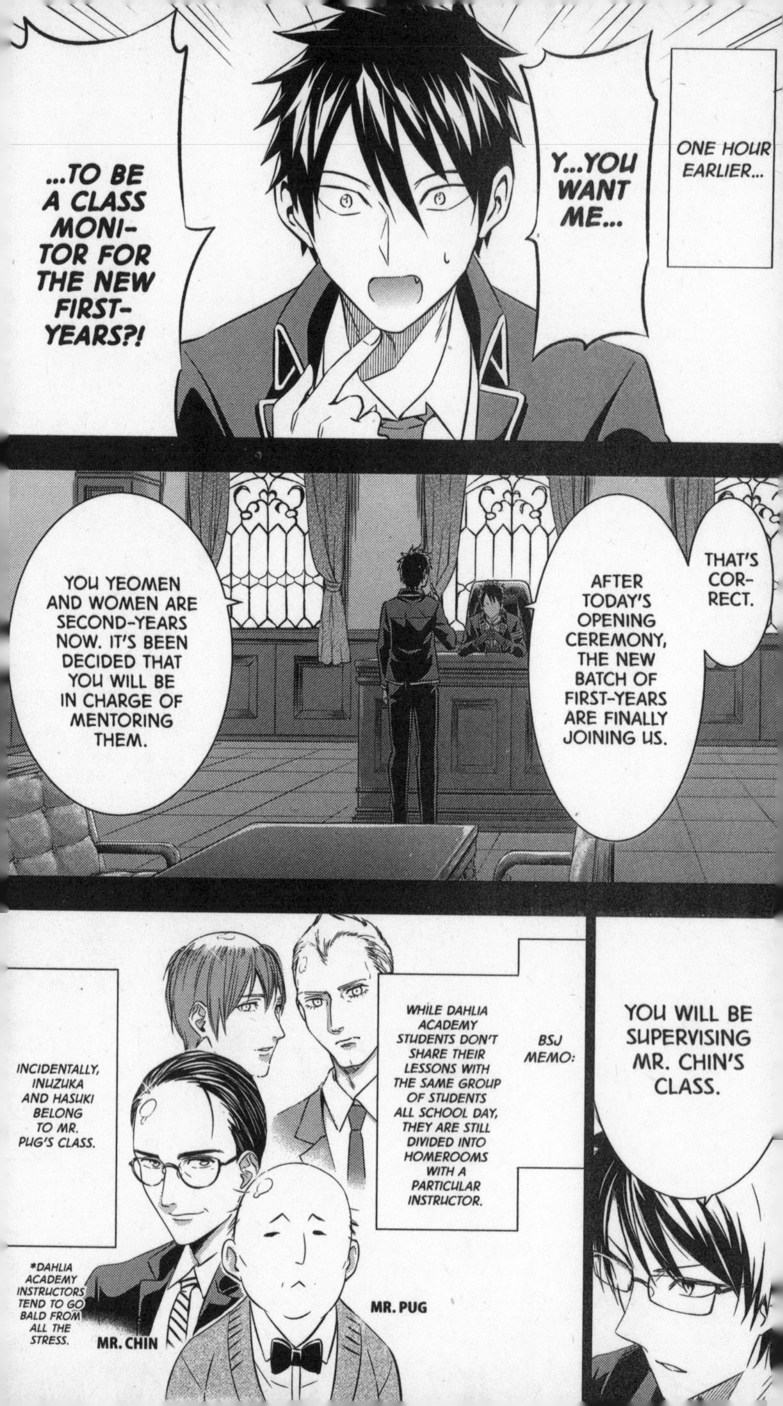
ONE HOUR EARLIER...
Y...YOU WANT ME...
...TO BE A CLASS MONI-TOR FOR THE NEW FIRST-YEARS?!
THAT'S COR-RECT.
AFTER TODAY'S OPENING CEREMONY, THE NEW BATCH OF FIRST-YEARS ARE FINALLY JOINING US.
YOU YEOMEN AND WOMEN ARE SECOND-YEARS NOW. IT'S BEEN DECIDED THAT YOU WILL BE IN CHARGE OF MENTORING THEM.
YOU WILL BE SUPERVISING MR. CHIN'S CLASS.
BSJ MEMO:
WHILE DAHLIA ACADEMY STUDENTS DON'T SHARE THEIR LESSONS WITH THE SAME GROUP OF STUDENTS ALL SCHOOL DAY, THEY ARE STILL DIVIDED INTO HOMEROOMS WITH A PARTICULAR INSTRUCTOR.
INCIDENTALLY, INUZUKA AND HASUKI BELONG TO MR. PUG'S CLASS.
MR. PUG
*DAHLIA ACADEMY INSTRUCTORS TEND TO GO BALD FROM ALL THE STRESS.
MR. CHIN

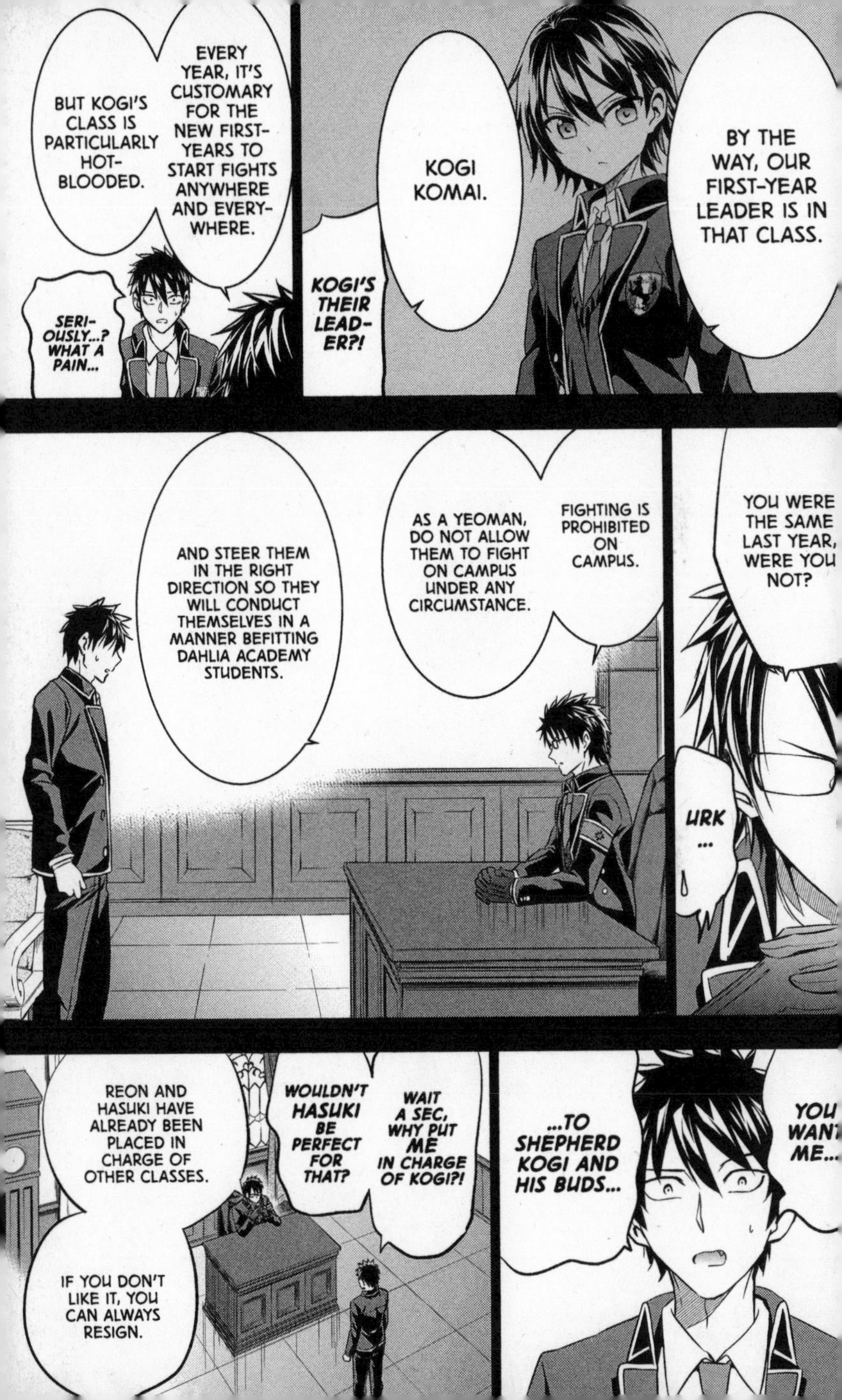
BY THE WAY, OUR FIRST-YEAR LEADER IS IN THAT CLASS.
KOGI KOMAI.
KOGI'S THEIR LEADER?!
EVERY YEAR, IT'S CUSTOMARY FOR THE NEW FIRST-YEARS TO START FIGHTS ANYWHERE AND EVERYWHERE.
BUT KOGI'S CLASS IS PARTICULARLY HOT-BLOODED.
SERIOUSLY...? WHAT A PAIN...
YOU WERE THE SAME LAST YEAR, WERE YOU NOT?
URK...
FIGHTING IS PROHIBITED ON CAMPUS.
AS A YEOMAN, DO NOT ALLOW THEM TO FIGHT ON CAMPUS UNDER ANY CIRCUMSTANCE.
AND STEER THEM IN THE RIGHT DIRECTION SO THEY WILL CONDUCT THEMSELVES IN A MANNER BEFITTING DAHLIA ACADEMY STUDENTS.
YOU WANT ME...
...TO SHEPHERD KOGI AND HIS BUDS...
WAIT A SEC, WHY PUT ME IN CHARGE OF KOGI?!
WOULDN'T HASUKI BE PERFECT FOR THAT?
REON AND HASUKI HAVE ALREADY BEEN PLACED IN CHARGE OF OTHER CLASSES.
IF YOU DON'T LIKE IT, YOU CAN ALWAYS RESIGN.

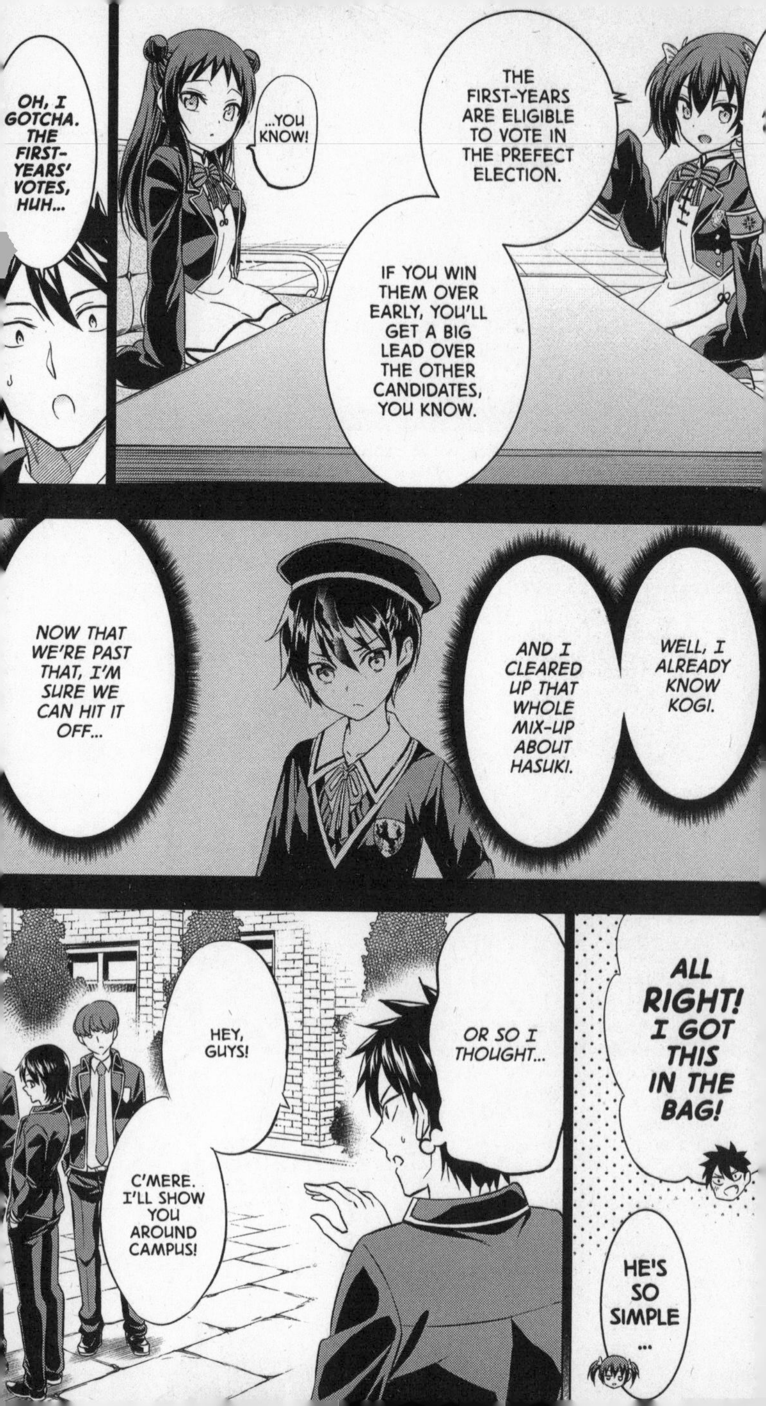
THE FIRST-YEARS ARE ELIGIBLE TO VOTE IN THE PREFECT ELECTION.
IF YOU WIN THEM OVER EARLY, YOU'LL GET A BIG LEAD OVER THE OTHER CANDIDATES, YOU KNOW.
...YOU KNOW!
OH, I GOTCHA. THE FIRST-YEARS' VOTES, HUH...
WELL, I ALREADY KNOW KOGI.
AND I CLEARED UP THAT WHOLE MIX-UP ABOUT HASUKI.
NOW THAT WE'RE PAST THAT, I'M SURE WE CAN HIT IT OFF...
ALL RIGHT! I GOT THIS IN THE BAG!
HE'S SO SIMPLE ...
OR SO I THOUGHT...
HEY, GUYS!
C'MERE. I'LL SHOW YOU AROUND CAMPUS!

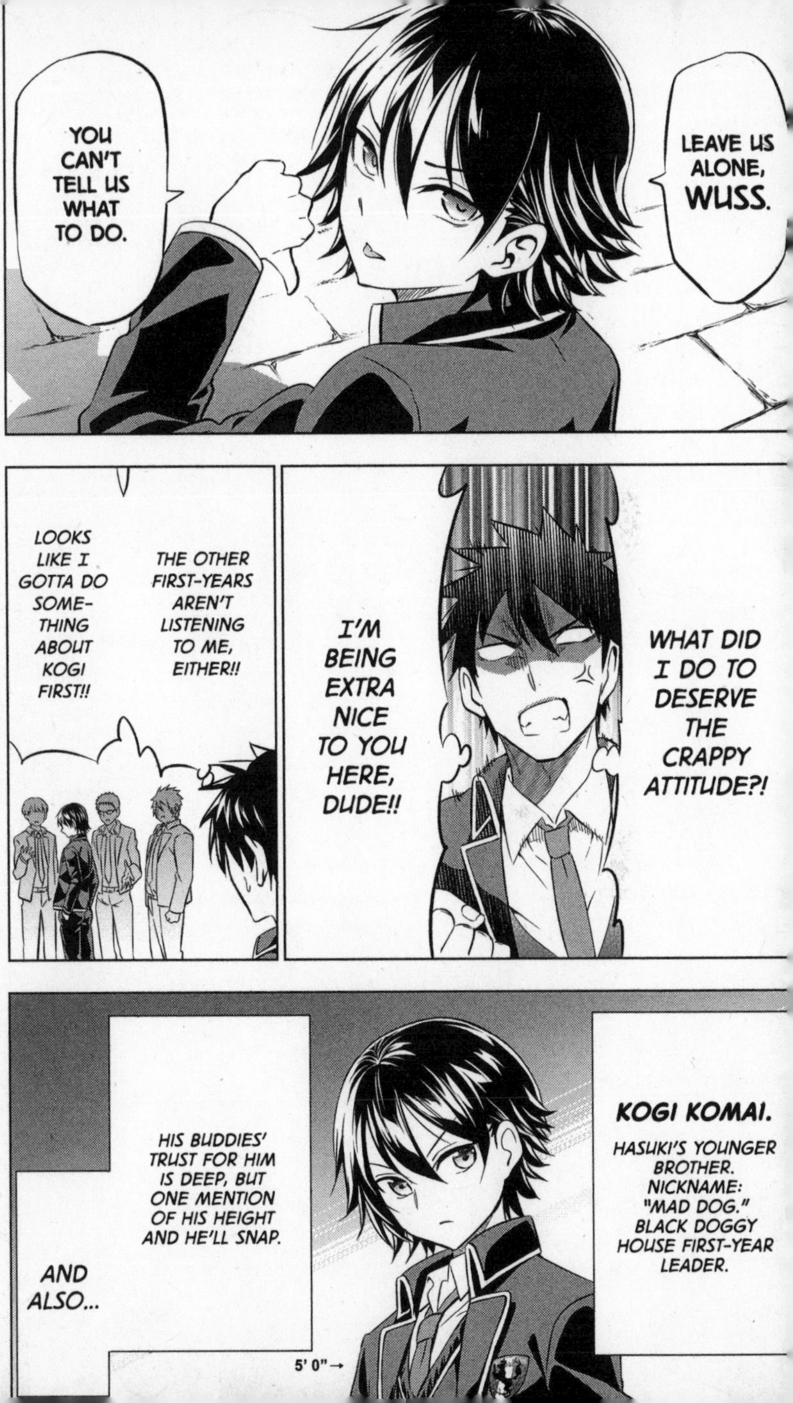
LEAVE US ALONE, WUSS.
YOU CAN'T TELL US WHAT TO DO.
WHAT DID I DO TO DESERVE THE CRAPPY ATTITUDE?!
I'M BEING EXTRA NICE TO YOU HERE, DUDE!!
THE OTHER FIRST-YEARS AREN'T LISTENING TO ME, EITHER!!
LOOKS LIKE I GOTTA DO SOME-THING ABOUT KOGI FIRST!!
KOGI KOMAI.
HASUKI'S YOUNGER BROTHER. NICKNAME: "MAD DOG." BLACK DOGGY HOUSE FIRST-YEAR LEADER.
HIS BUDDIES' TRUST FOR HIM IS DEEP, BUT ONE MENTION OF HIS HEIGHT AND HE'LL SNAP.
AND ALSO...
5' 0"→

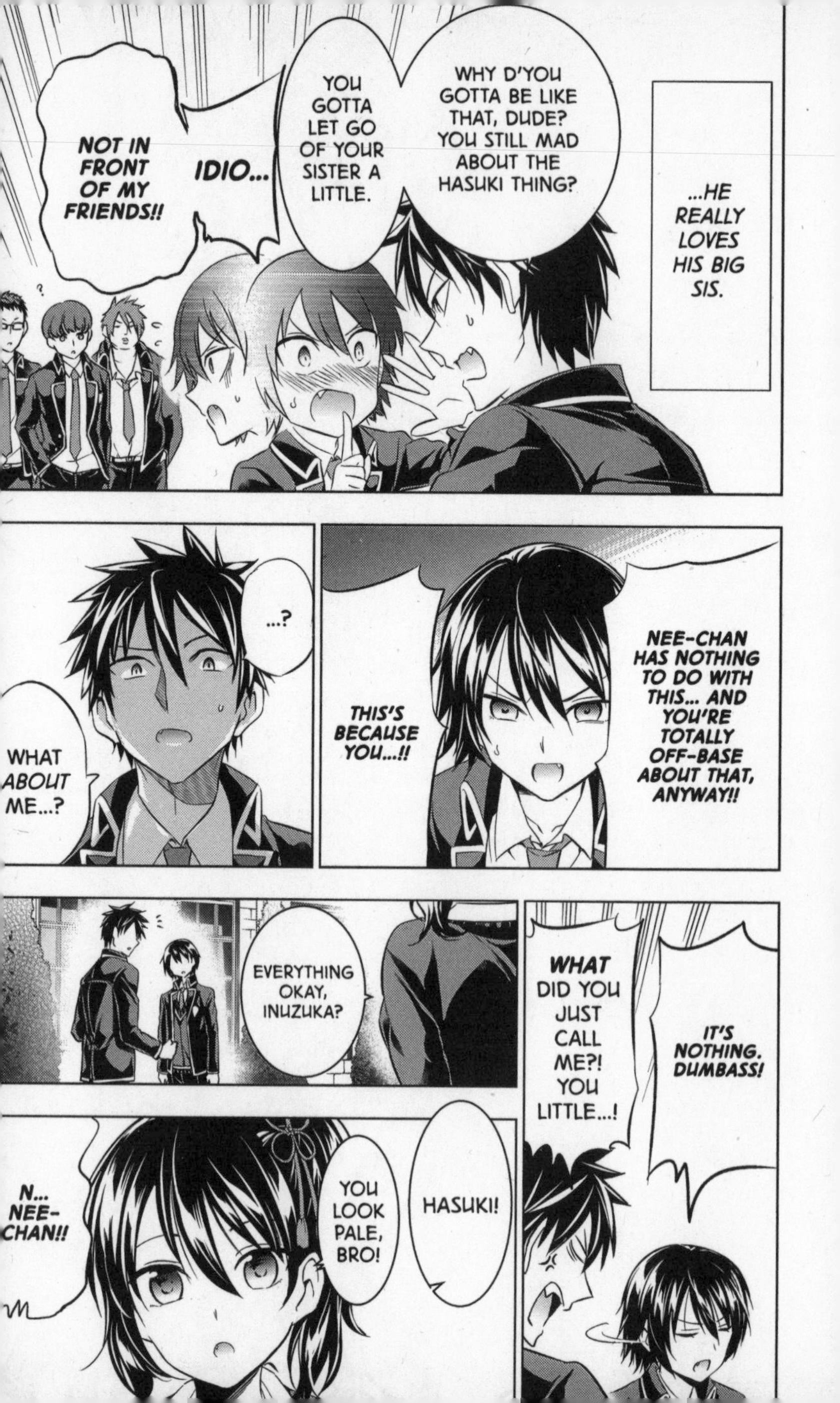
...HE REALLY LOVES HIS BIG SIS.
WHY D'YOU GOTTA BE LIKE THAT, DUDE? YOU STILL MAD ABOUT THE HASUKI THING?
YOU GOTTA LET GO OF YOUR SISTER A LITTLE.
IDIO...
NOT IN FRONT OF MY FRIENDS!!
NEE-CHAN HAS NOTHING TO DO WITH THIS... AND YOU'RE TOTALLY OFF-BASE ABOUT THAT, ANYWAY!!
THIS'S BECAUSE YOU...!!
...?
WHAT ABOUT ME...?
IT'S NOTHING. DUMBASS!
WHAT DID YOU JUST CALL ME?! YOU LITTLE...!
EVERYTHING OKAY, INUZUKA?
HASUKI!
YOU LOOK PALE, BRO!
N... NEE-CHAN!!

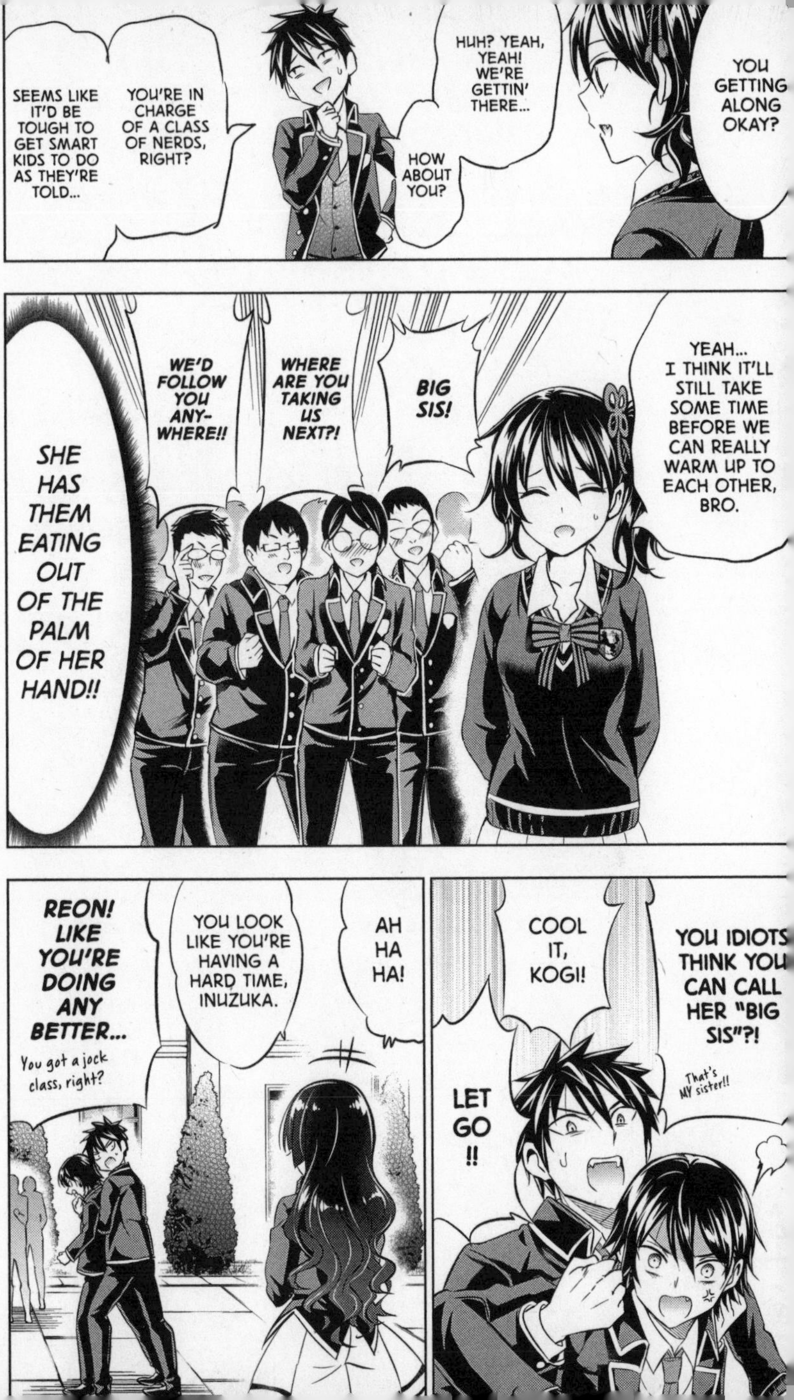
YOU GETTING ALONG OKAY?
HUH? YEAH, YEAH! WE'RE GETTIN' THERE...
HOW ABOUT YOU?
YOU'RE IN CHARGE OF A CLASS OF NERDS, RIGHT?
SEEMS LIKE IT'D BE TOUGH TO GET SMART KIDS TO DO AS THEY'RE TOLD...
YEAH... I THINK IT'LL STILL TAKE SOME TIME BEFORE WE CAN REALLY WARM UP TO EACH OTHER, BRO.
BIG SIS!
WHERE ARE YOU TAKING US NEXT?!
WE'D FOLLOW YOU ANY-WHERE!!
SHE HAS THEM EATING OUT OF THE PALM OF HER HAND!!
YOU IDIOTS THINK YOU CAN CALL HER "BIG SIS"?!
That's MY sister!!
COOL IT, KOGI!
LET GO !!
AH HA HA!
YOU LOOK LIKE YOU'RE HAVING A HARD TIME, INUZUKA.
REON! LIKE YOU'RE DOING ANY BETTER...
You got a jock class, right?

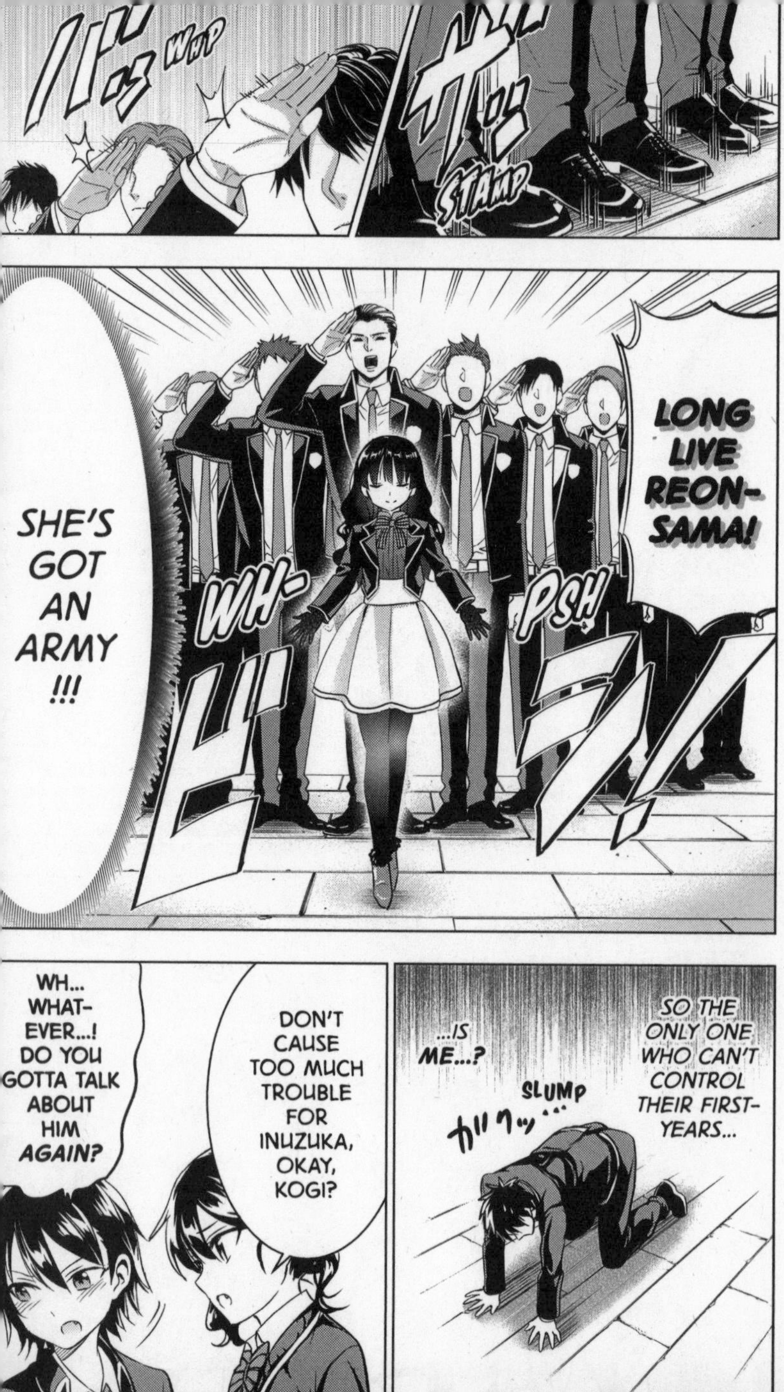
STAMP
WHIP
LONG LIVE REON-SAMA!
PSH
WH-
SHE'S GOT AN ARMY!!!
SO THE ONLY ONE WHO CAN'T CONTROL THEIR FIRST-YEARS...
...IS ME...?
SLUMP
DON'T CAUSE TOO MUCH TROUBLE FOR INUZUKA, OKAY, KOGI?
WH... WHATEVER...! DO YOU GOTTA TALK ABOUT HIM AGAIN?

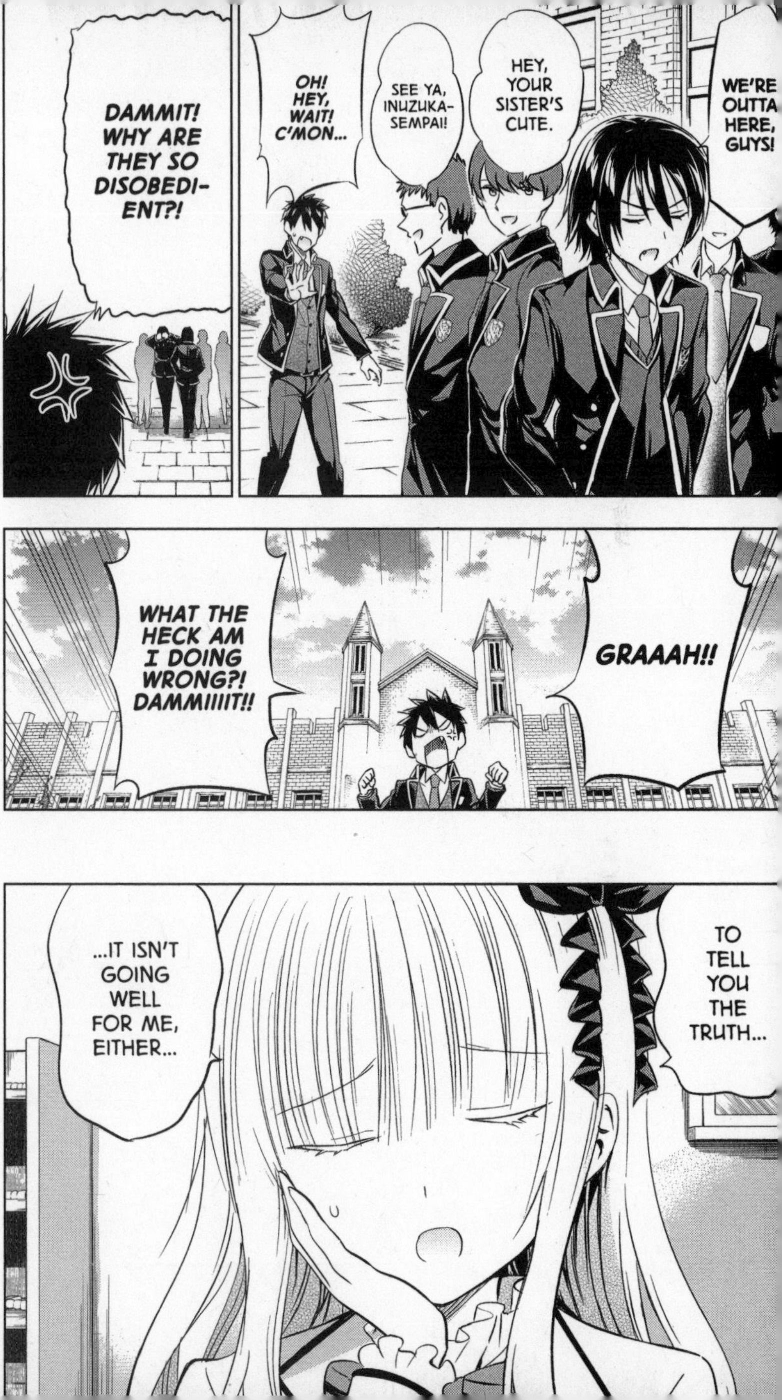
WE'RE OUTTA HERE, GUYS!
HEY, YOUR SISTER'S CUTE.
SEE YA, INUZUKA-SEMPAI!
OH! HEY, WAIT! C'MON...
DAMMIT! WHY ARE THEY SO DISOBEDIENT?!
GRAAAH!!
WHAT THE HECK AM I DOING WRONG?! DAMMIIIIT!!
TO TELL YOU THE TRUTH...
...IT ISN'T GOING WELL FOR ME, EITHER...

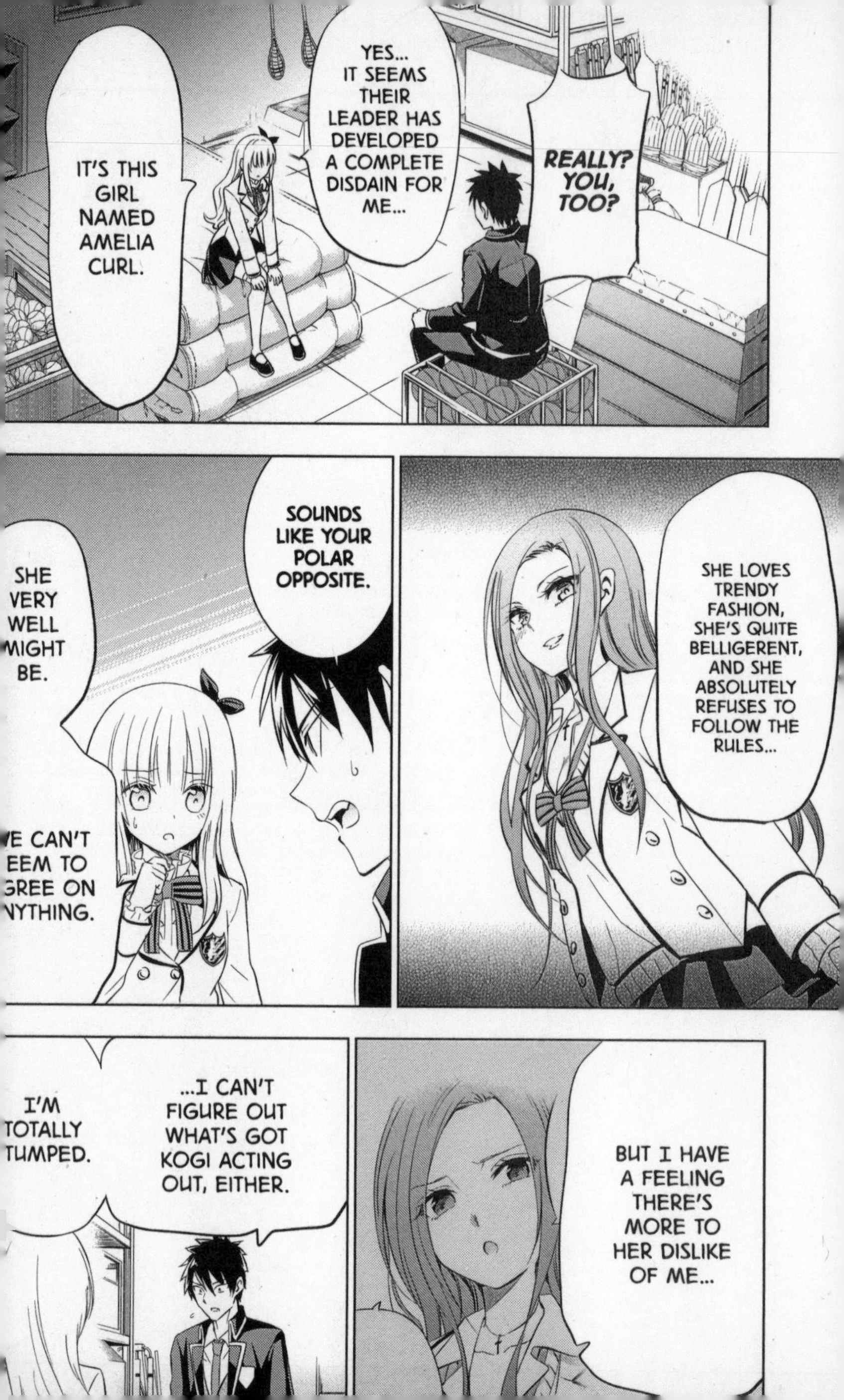
REALLY? YOU, TOO?
YES... IT SEEMS THEIR LEADER HAS DEVELOPED A COMPLETE DISDAIN FOR ME...
IT'S THIS GIRL NAMED AMELIA CURL.
SHE LOVES TRENDY FASHION, SHE'S QUITE BELLIGERENT, AND SHE ABSOLUTELY REFUSES TO FOLLOW THE RULES...
SOUNDS LIKE YOUR POLAR OPPOSITE.
SHE VERY WELL MIGHT BE.
E CAN'T EEM TO GREE ON NYTHING.
BUT I HAVE A FEELING THERE'S MORE TO HER DISLIKE OF ME...
...I CAN'T FIGURE OUT WHAT'S GOT KOGI ACTING OUT, EITHER.
I'M TOTALLY TUMPED.

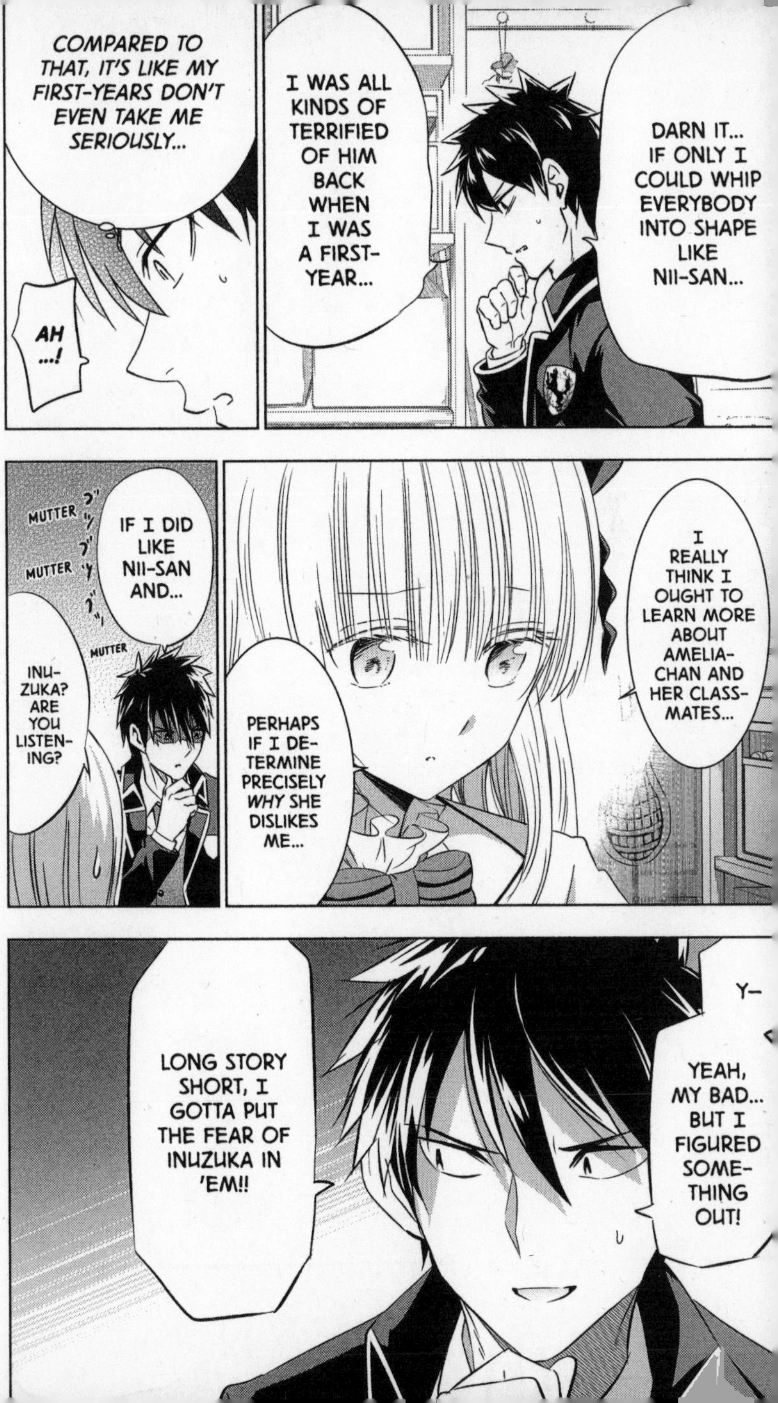
DARN IT... IF ONLY I COULD WHIP EVERYBODY INTO SHAPE LIKE NII-SAN...
I WAS ALL KINDS OF TERRIFIED OF HIM BACK WHEN I WAS A FIRST-YEAR...
COMPARED TO THAT, IT'S LIKE MY FIRST-YEARS DON'T EVEN TAKE ME SERIOUSLY...
AH ...!
I REALLY THINK I OUGHT TO LEARN MORE ABOUT AMELIA-CHAN AND HER CLASSMATES...
PERHAPS IF I DETERMINE PRECISELY *WHY* SHE DISLIKES ME...
MUTTER
MUTTER
IF I DID LIKE NII-SAN AND...
MUTTER
INUZUKA? ARE YOU LISTENING?
Y—
YEAH, MY BAD... BUT I FIGURED SOMETHING OUT!
LONG STORY SHORT, I GOTTA PUT THE FEAR OF INUZUKA IN 'EM!!

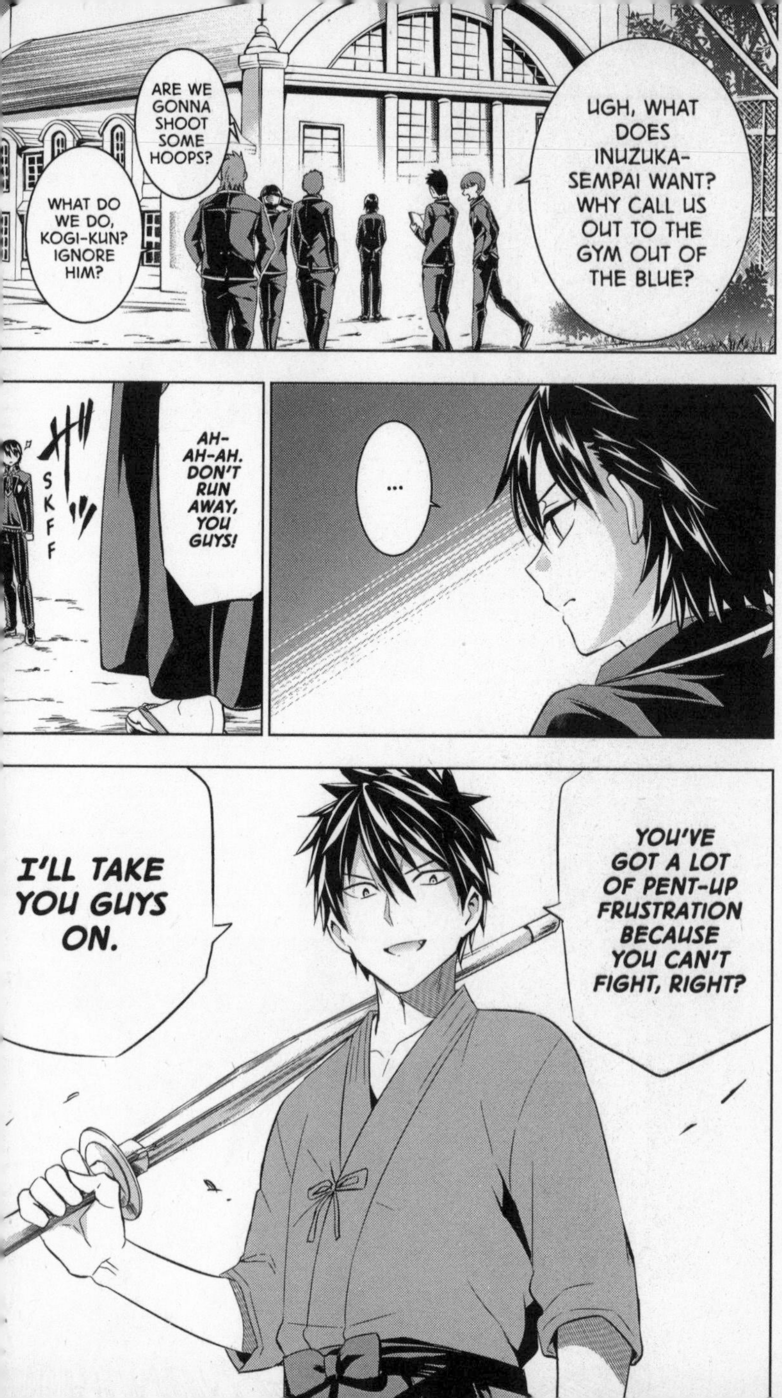
UGH, WHAT DOES INUZUKA-SEMPAI WANT? WHY CALL US OUT TO THE GYM OUT OF THE BLUE?
ARE WE GONNA SHOOT SOME HOOPS?
WHAT DO WE DO, KOGI-KUN? IGNORE HIM?
...
AH-AH-AH. DON'T RUN AWAY, YOU GUYS!
SKFF
YOU'VE GOT A LOT OF PENT-UP FRUSTRATION BECAUSE YOU CAN'T FIGHT, RIGHT?
I'LL TAKE YOU GUYS ON.

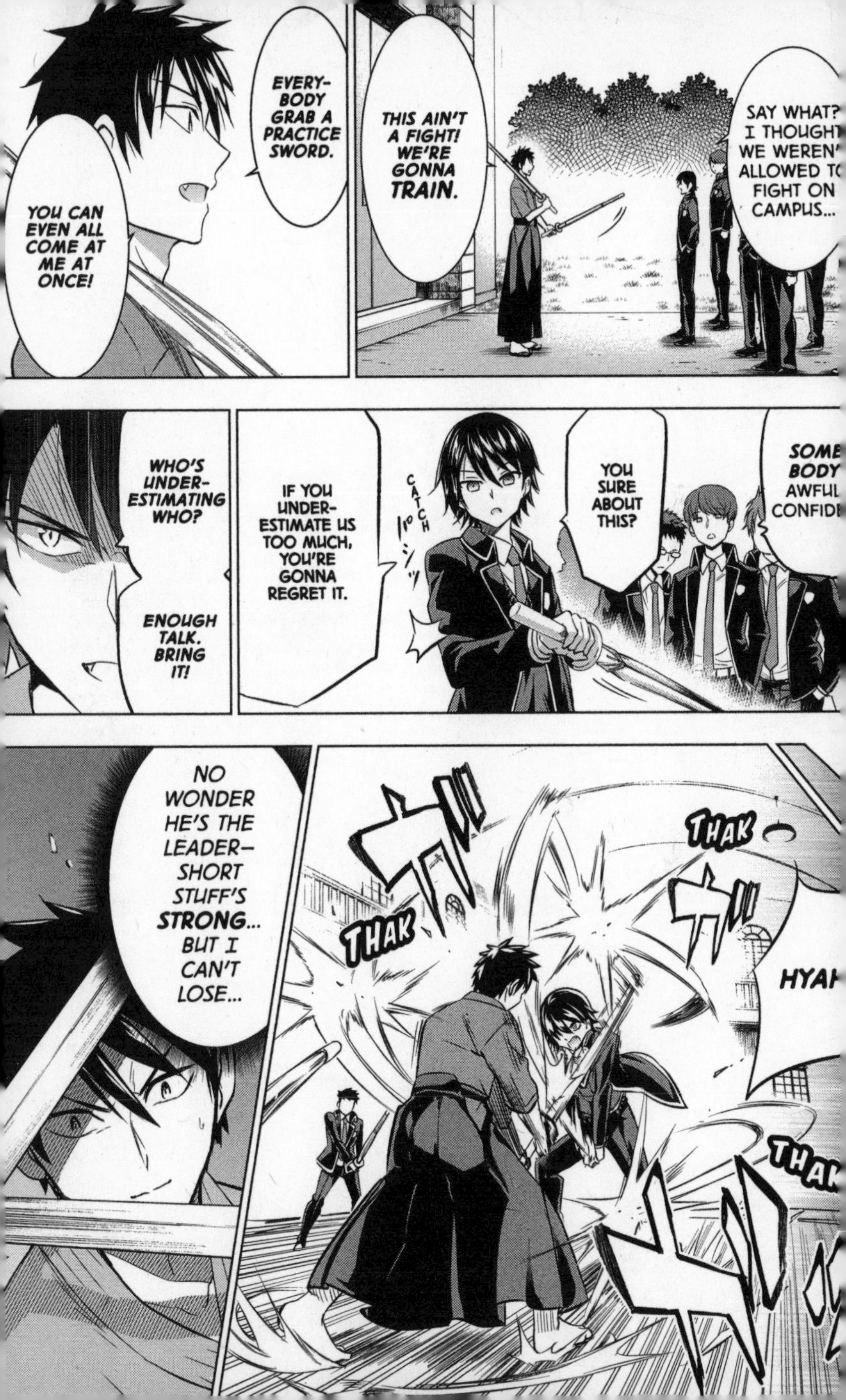
SAY WHAT? I THOUGHT WE WEREN' ALLOWED TO FIGHT ON CAMPUS...
THIS AIN'T A FIGHT! WE'RE GONNA TRAIN.
EVERY-BODY GRAB A PRACTICE SWORD.
YOU CAN EVEN ALL COME AT ME AT ONCE!
SOME BODY AWFUL CONFID
YOU SURE ABOUT THIS?
CATCH
IF YOU UNDER-ESTIMATE US TOO MUCH, YOU'RE GONNA REGRET IT.
WHO'S UNDER-ESTIMATING WHO?
ENOUGH TALK. BRING IT!
THAK
HYA
THAK
THAK
NO WONDER HE'S THE LEADER—SHORT STUFF'S STRONG... BUT I CAN'T LOSE...

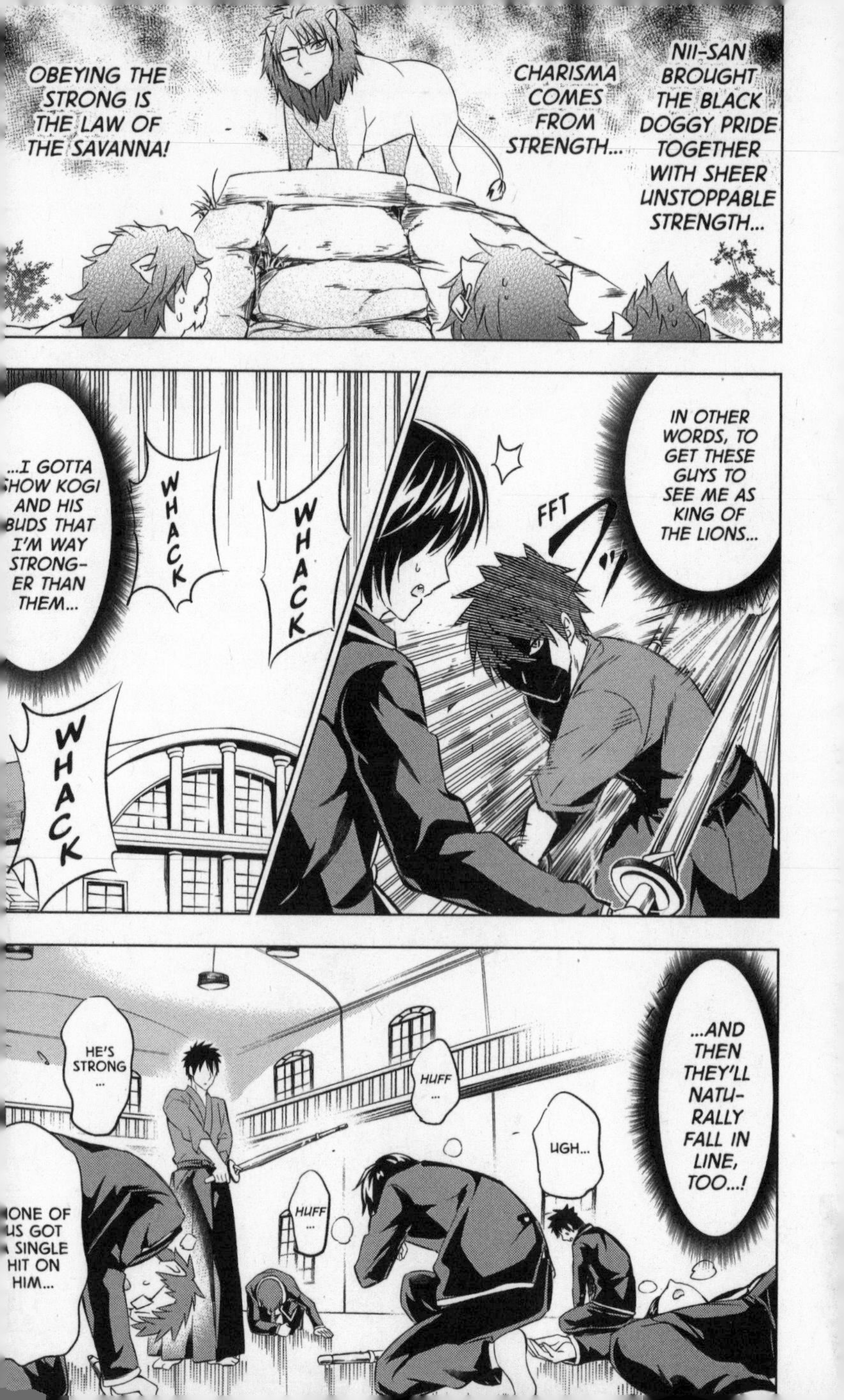
NII-SAN BROUGHT THE BLACK DOGGY PRIDE TOGETHER WITH SHEER UNSTOPPABLE STRENGTH...
CHARISMA COMES FROM STRENGTH...
OBEYING THE STRONG IS THE LAW OF THE SAVANNA!
IN OTHER WORDS, TO GET THESE GUYS TO SEE ME AS KING OF THE LIONS...
FFT
...I GOTTA SHOW KOGI AND HIS BUDS THAT I'M WAY STRONGER THAN THEM...
WHACK
WHACK
WHACK
...AND THEN THEY'LL NATURALLY FALL IN LINE, TOO...!
UGH...
HUFF...
HUFF...
HE'S STRONG...
ONE OF US GOT SINGLE HIT ON HIM...

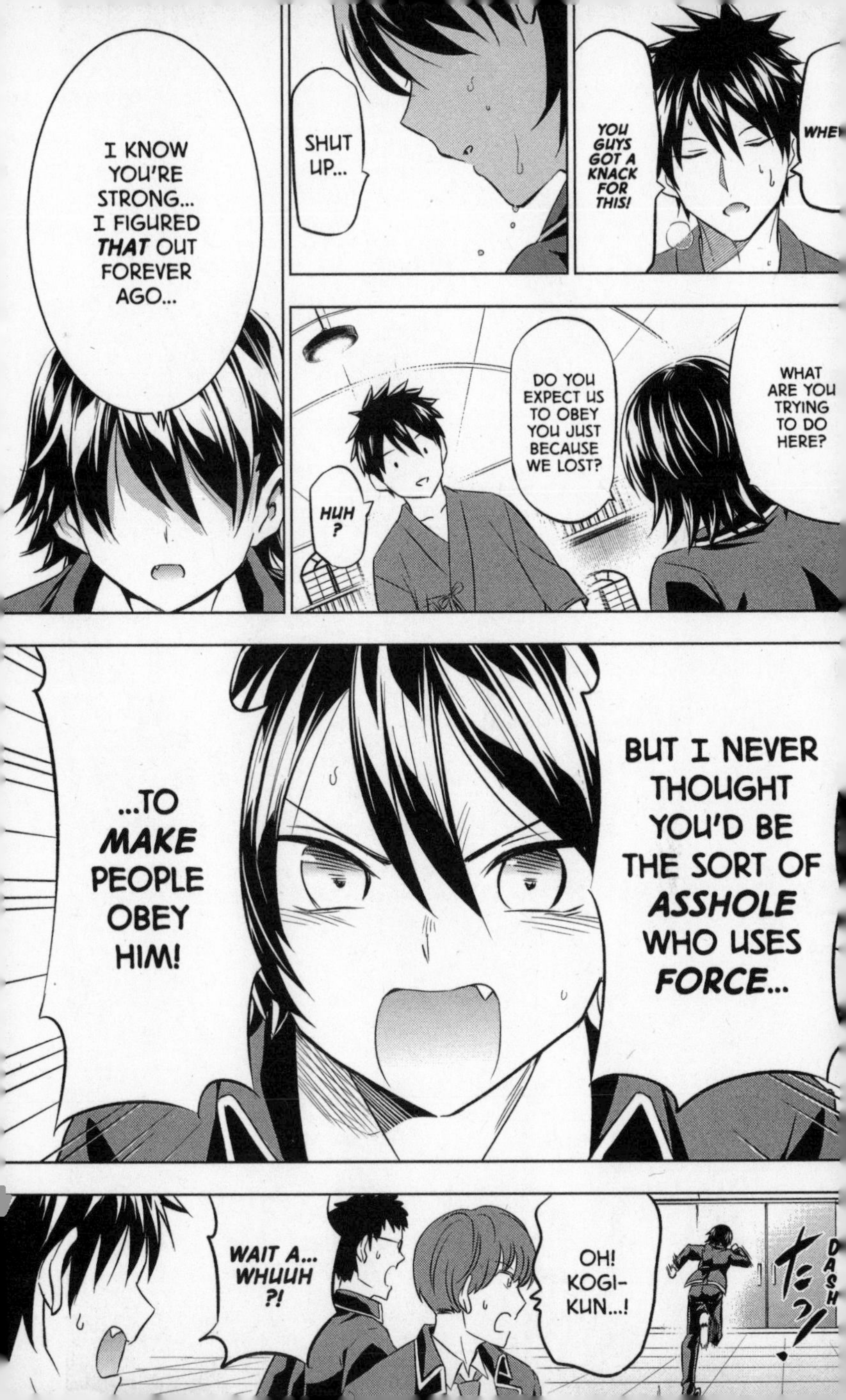
WHE
YOU GUYS GOT A KNACK FOR THIS!
SHUT UP...
WHAT ARE YOU TRYING TO DO HERE?
DO YOU EXPECT US TO OBEY YOU JUST BECAUSE WE LOST?
HUH?
I KNOW YOU'RE STRONG... I FIGURED THAT OUT FOREVER AGO...
BUT I NEVER THOUGHT YOU'D BE THE SORT OF ASSHOLE WHO USES FORCE...
...TO MAKE PEOPLE OBEY HIM!
DASH
OH! KOGI-KUN...!
WAIT A... WHUUH?!

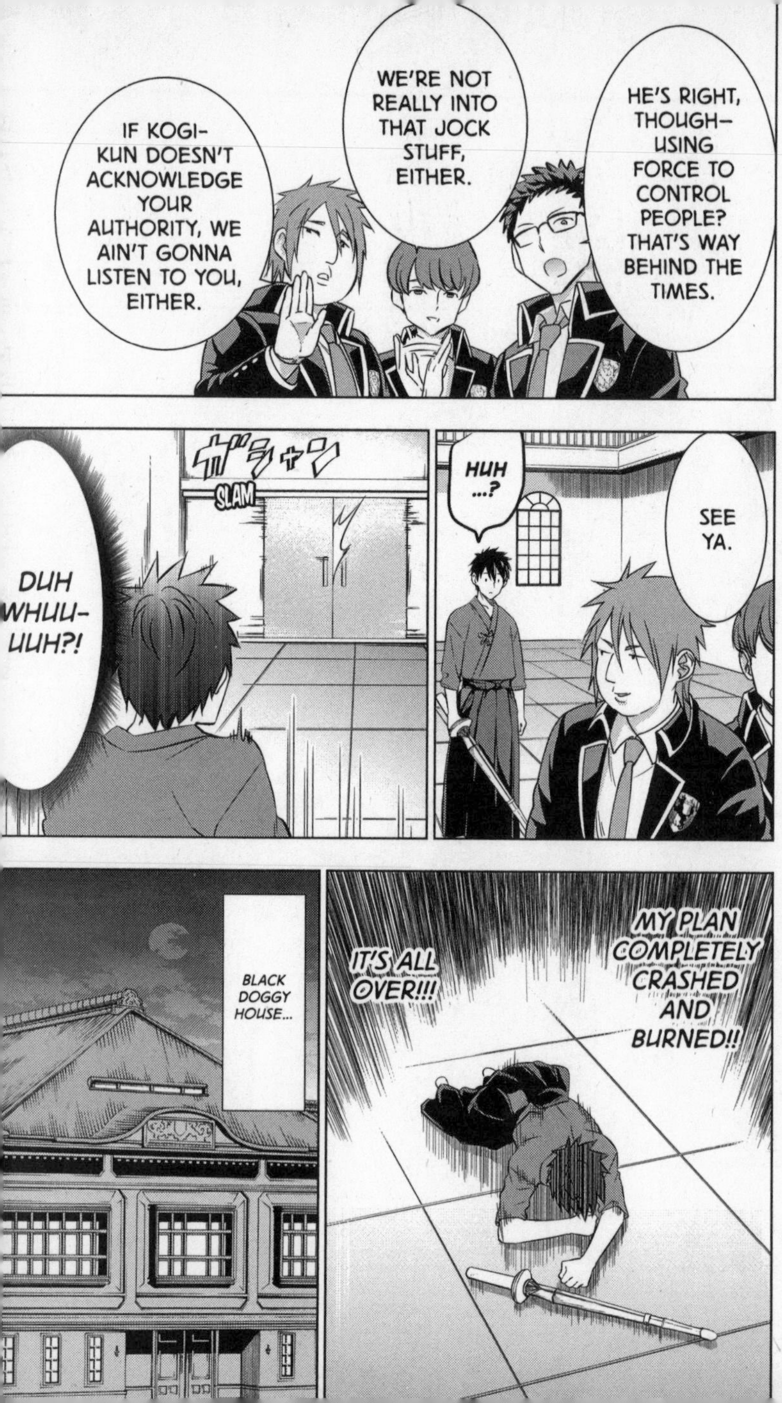
HE'S RIGHT, THOUGH— USING FORCE TO CONTROL PEOPLE? THAT'S WAY BEHIND THE TIMES.
WE'RE NOT REALLY INTO THAT JOCK STUFF, EITHER.
IF KOGI-KUN DOESN'T ACKNOWLEDGE YOUR AUTHORITY, WE AIN'T GONNA LISTEN TO YOU, EITHER.
SEE YA.
HUH ...?
ガシャン
SLAM
DUH WHUU-UUH?!
MY PLAN COMPLETELY CRASHED AND BURNED!!
IT'S ALL OVER!!!
BLACK DOGGY HOUSE...

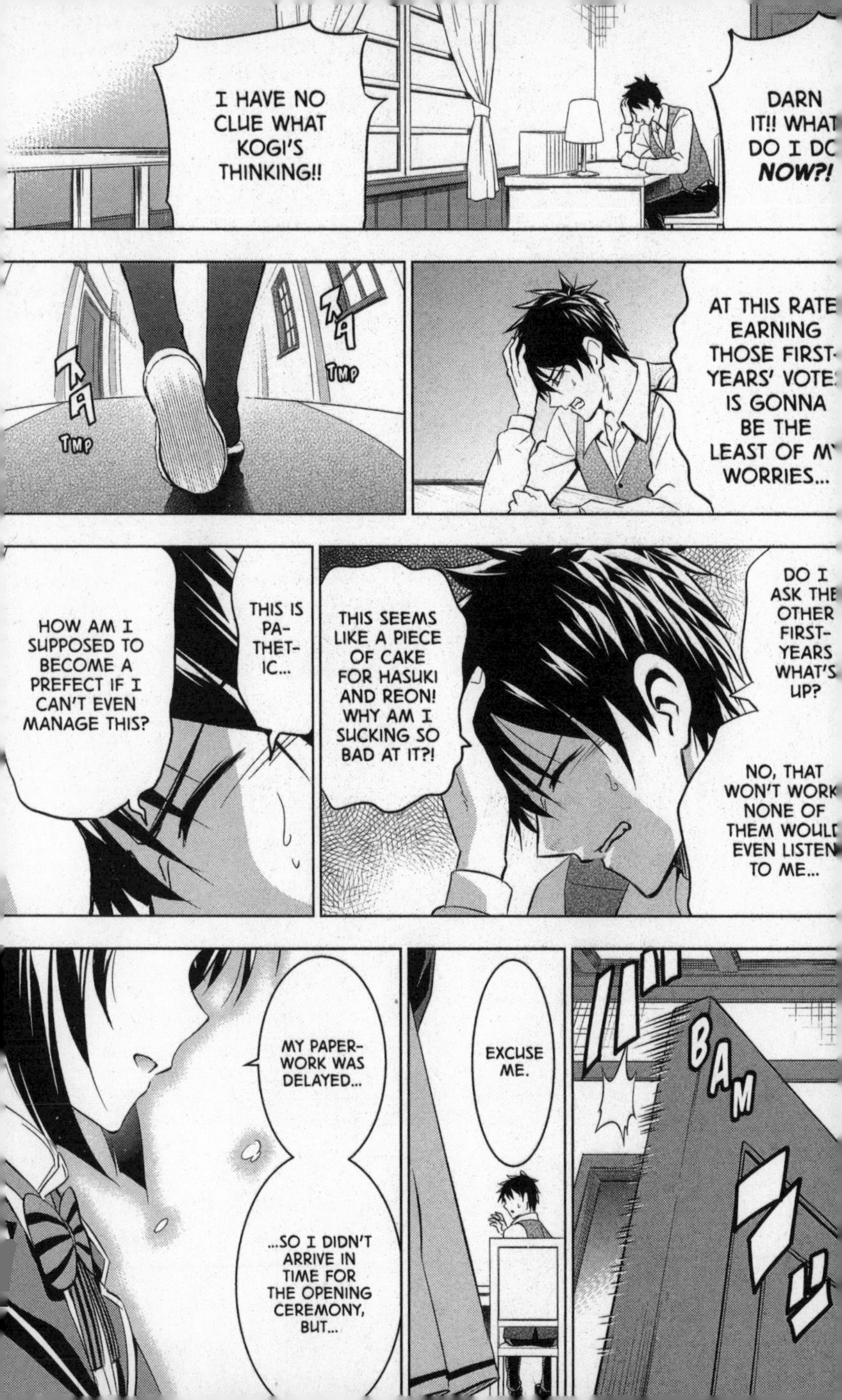
DARN IT!! WHAT DO I DO NOW?!
I HAVE NO CLUE WHAT KOGI'S THINKING!!
AT THIS RATE EARNING THOSE FIRST-YEARS' VOTES IS GONNA BE THE LEAST OF MY WORRIES...
TMP
TMP
DO I ASK THE OTHER FIRST-YEARS WHAT'S UP?
NO, THAT WON'T WORK NONE OF THEM WOULD EVEN LISTEN TO ME...
THIS SEEMS LIKE A PIECE OF CAKE FOR HASUKI AND REON! WHY AM I SUCKING SO BAD AT IT?!
THIS IS PATHETIC...
HOW AM I SUPPOSED TO BECOME A PREFECT IF I CAN'T EVEN MANAGE THIS?
BAM
EXCUSE ME.
MY PAPERWORK WAS DELAYED...
...SO I DIDN'T ARRIVE IN TIME FOR THE OPENING CEREMONY, BUT...

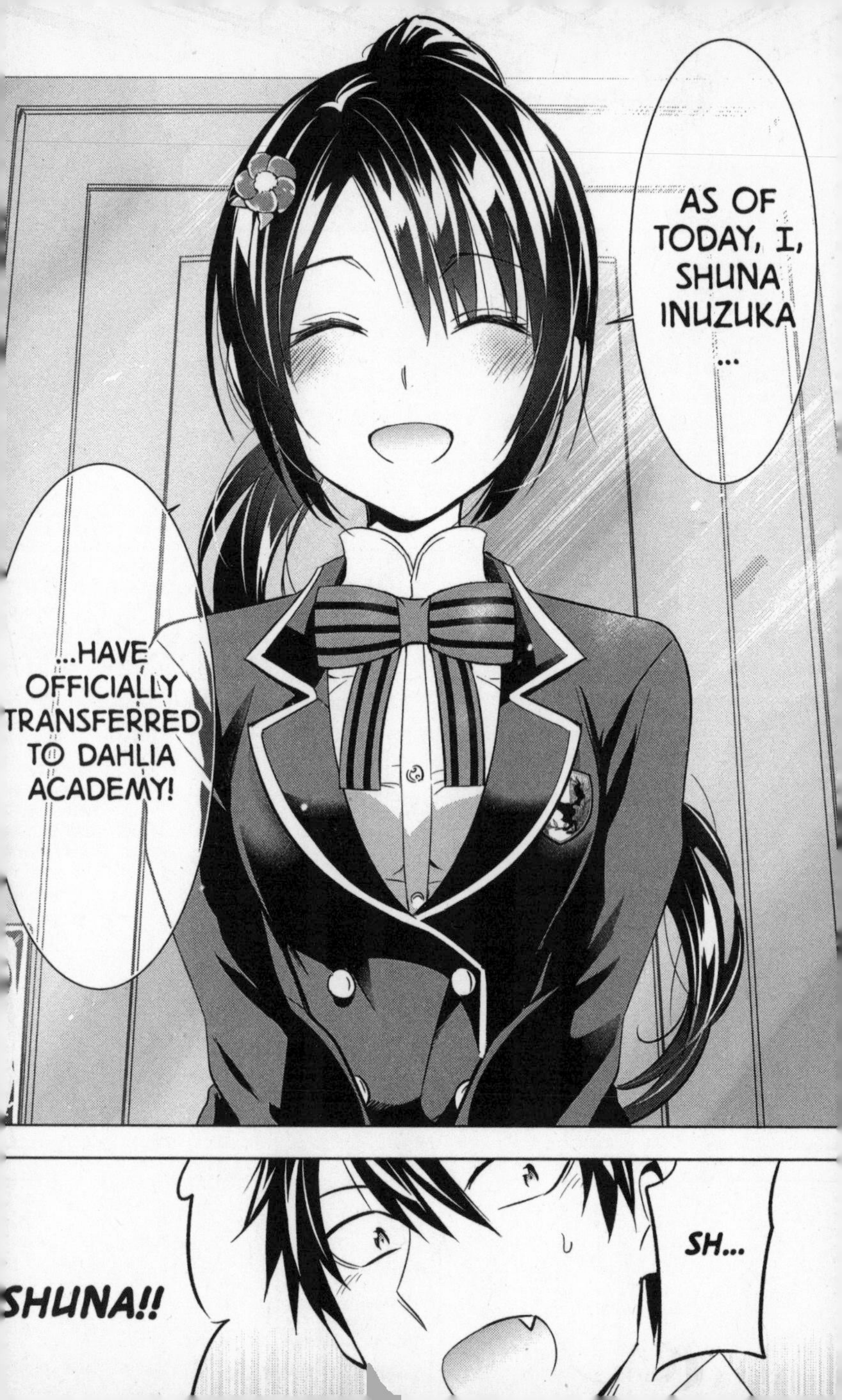
AS OF TODAY, I, SHUNA INUZUKA ...
...HAVE OFFICIALLY TRANSFERRED TO DAHLIA ACADEMY!
SH...
SHUNA!!

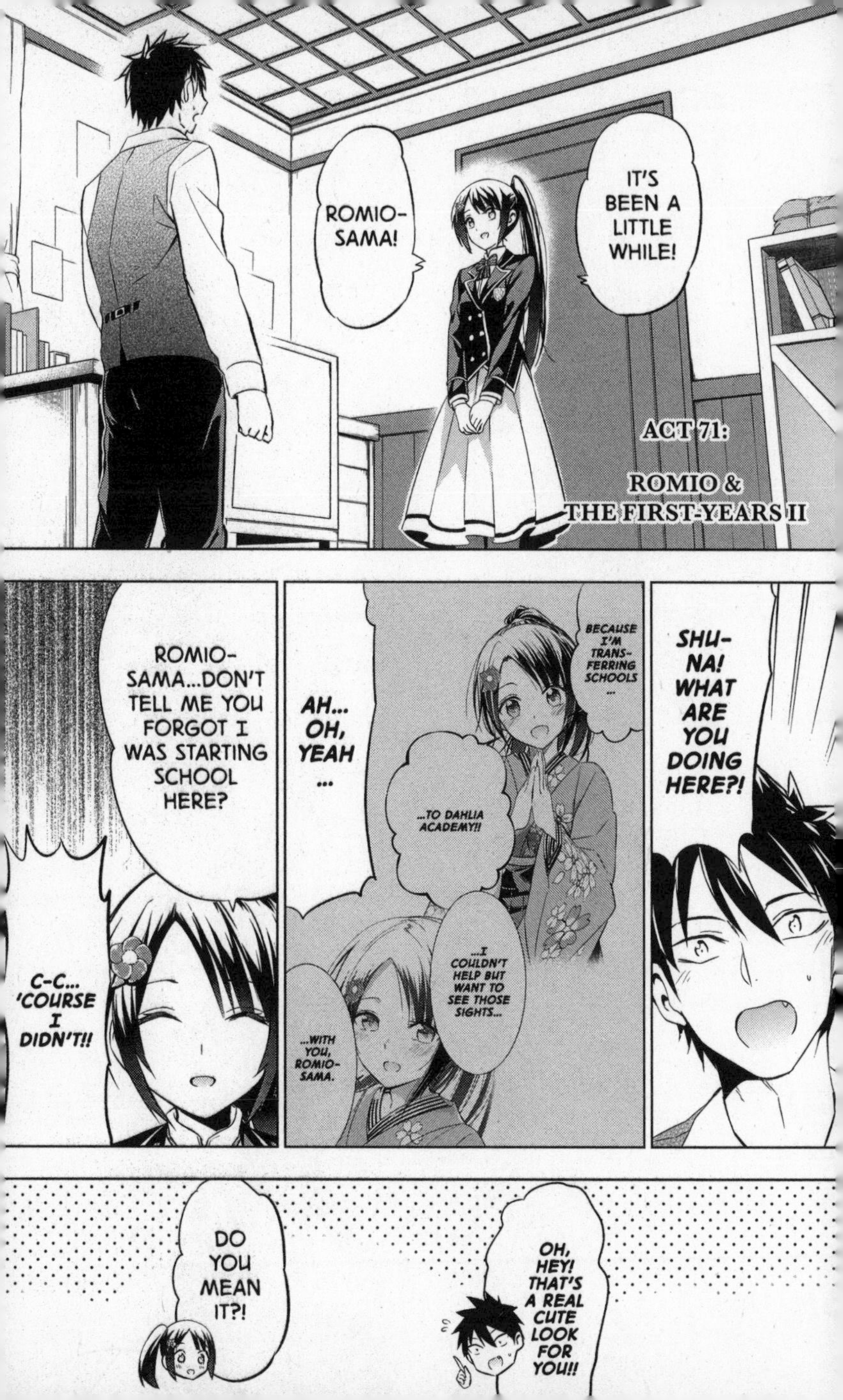
IT'S BEEN A LITTLE WHILE!
ROMIO-SAMA!
ACT 71:
ROMIO & THE FIRST-YEARS II
SHU-NA! WHAT ARE YOU DOING HERE?!
BECAUSE I'M TRANSFERRING SCHOOLS...
...TO DAHLIA ACADEMY!!
...I COULDN'T HELP BUT WANT TO SEE THOSE SIGHTS...
...WITH YOU, ROMIO-SAMA.
AH... OH, YEAH...
ROMIO-SAMA...DON'T TELL ME YOU FORGOT I WAS STARTING SCHOOL HERE?
C-C... 'COURSE I DIDN'T!!
OH, HEY! THAT'S A REAL CUTE LOOK FOR YOU!!
DO YOU MEAN IT?!

IT'S SOOTH-ING.

...IS OW ABY IRST-ARS GHTA ME!

YEAH, YEAH, THAT'S IT... THIS INNOCENCE!

IT'S THE FIRST TIME I'VE WORN A SCHOOL UNIFORM...

I FEEL A BIT SHY.

TWIRL

I'LL BEGIN WITH MAKING YOUR BED.

WELL, ROMIO-SAMA...

HUH ?

OME ON, U DON'T AFTA DO THAT!!

YOUR SHEETS NEED TO BE WASHED. I'LL GO FETCH FRESH ONES FROM THE LINEN ROOM.

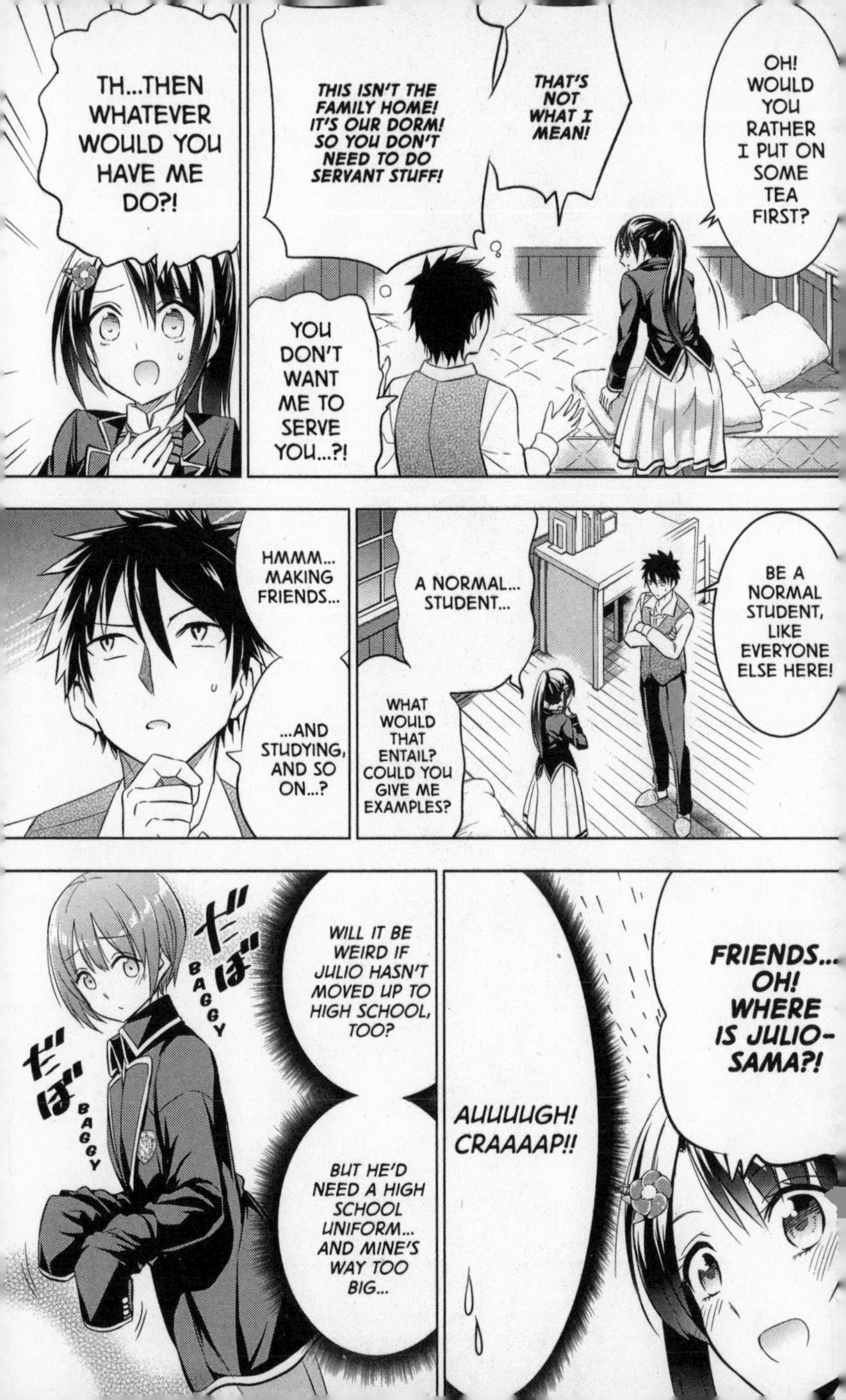
OH! WOULD YOU RATHER I PUT ON SOME TEA FIRST?
THAT'S NOT WHAT I MEAN!
THIS ISN'T THE FAMILY HOME! IT'S OUR DORM! SO YOU DON'T NEED TO DO SERVANT STUFF!
YOU DON'T WANT ME TO SERVE YOU...?!
TH...THEN WHATEVER WOULD YOU HAVE ME DO?!
BE A NORMAL STUDENT, LIKE EVERYONE ELSE HERE!
A NORMAL... STUDENT...
WHAT WOULD THAT ENTAIL? COULD YOU GIVE ME EXAMPLES?
HMMM... MAKING FRIENDS...
...AND STUDYING, AND SO ON...?
FRIENDS... OH! WHERE IS JULIO-SAMA?!
AUUUUGH! CRAAAAP!!
WILL IT BE WEIRD IF JULIO HASN'T MOVED UP TO HIGH SCHOOL, TOO?
BUT HE'D NEED A HIGH SCHOOL UNIFORM... AND MINE'S WAY TOO BIG...
だぼ BAGGY
だぼ BAGGY

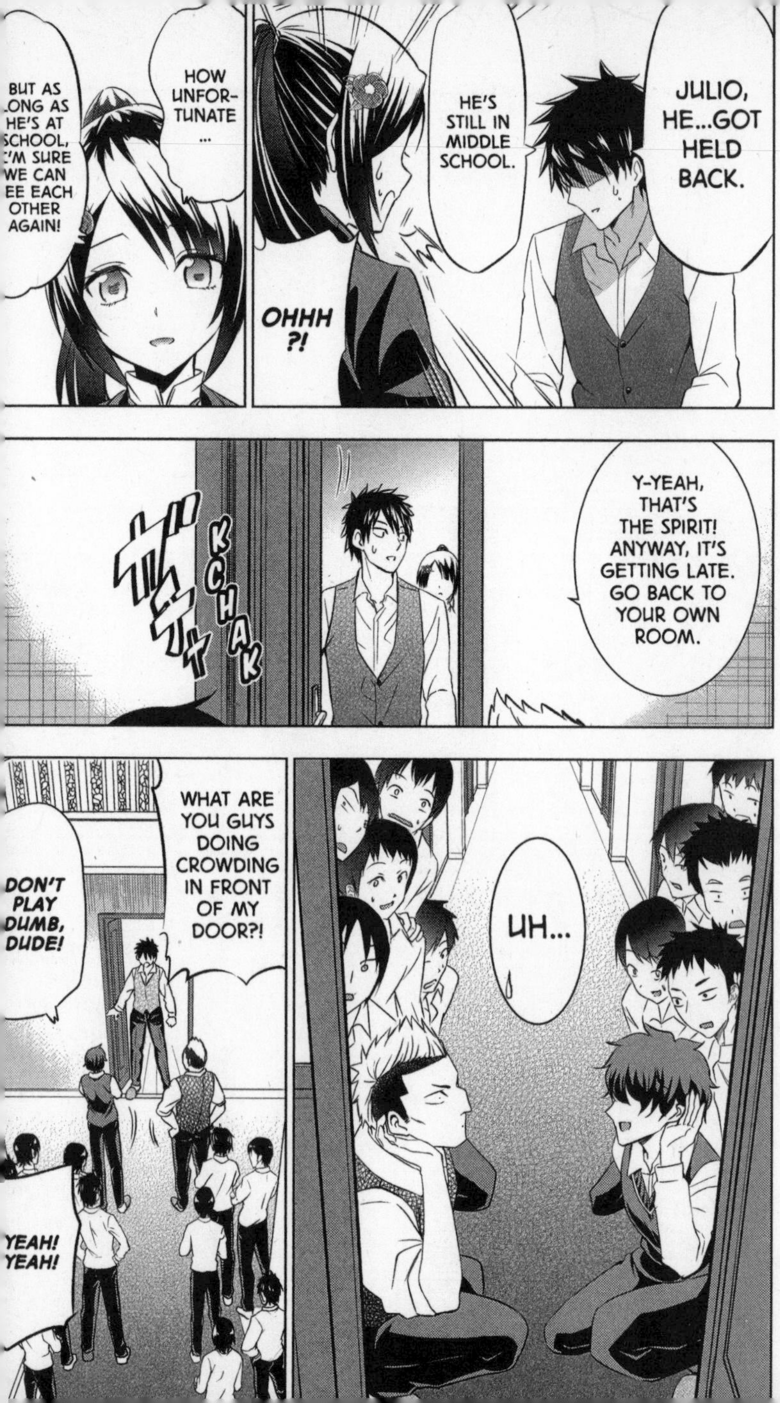
JULIO, HE...GOT HELD BACK.
HE'S STILL IN MIDDLE SCHOOL.
OHHH?!
HOW UNFORTUNATE...
BUT AS LONG AS HE'S AT SCHOOL, I'M SURE WE CAN SEE EACH OTHER AGAIN!
Y-YEAH, THAT'S THE SPIRIT! ANYWAY, IT'S GETTING LATE. GO BACK TO YOUR OWN ROOM.
KCHAK
UH...
WHAT ARE YOU GUYS DOING CROWDING IN FRONT OF MY DOOR?!
DON'T PLAY DUMB, DUDE!
YEAH! YEAH!

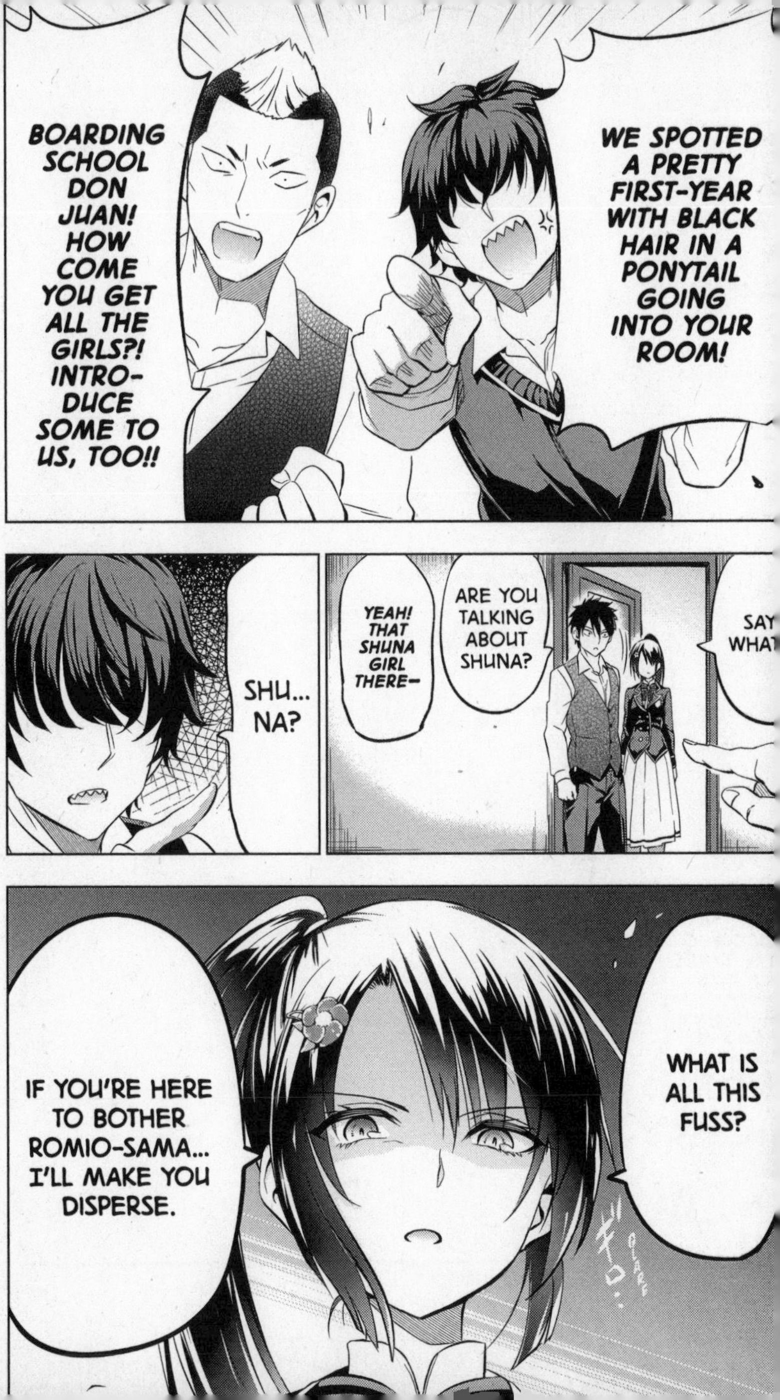
WE SPOTTED A PRETTY FIRST-YEAR WITH BLACK HAIR IN A PONYTAIL GOING INTO YOUR ROOM!
BOARDING SCHOOL DON JUAN! HOW COME YOU GET ALL THE GIRLS?! INTRO-DUCE SOME TO US, TOO!!
SAY WHAT
ARE YOU TALKING ABOUT SHUNA?
YEAH! THAT SHUNA GIRL THERE—
SHU... NA?
WHAT IS ALL THIS FUSS?
IF YOU'RE HERE TO BOTHER ROMIO-SAMA... I'LL MAKE YOU DISPERSE.
GLARE

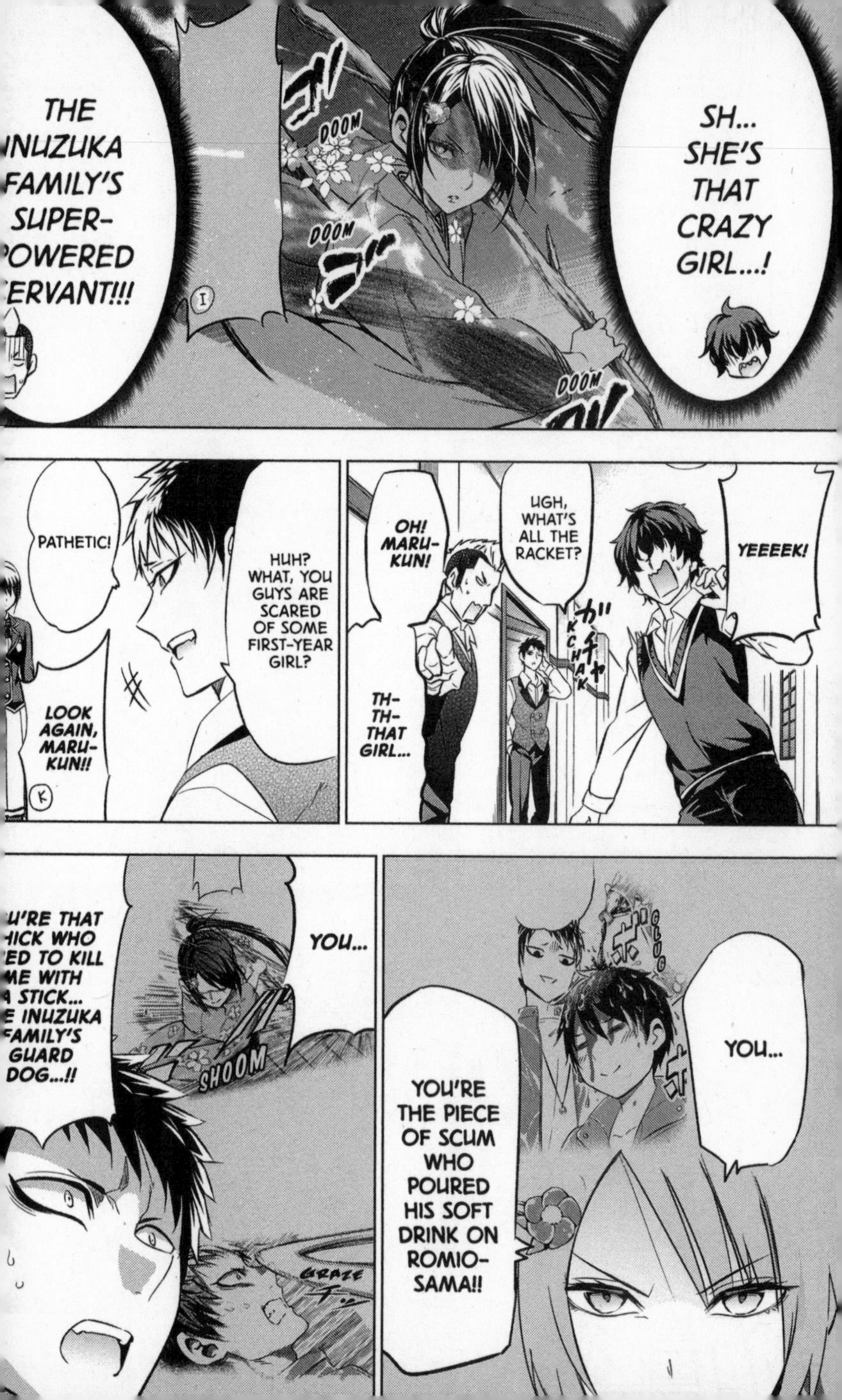
SH... SHE'S THAT CRAZY GIRL...!
DOOM
DOOM
DOOM
THE NUZUKA FAMILY'S SUPER- OWERED ERVANT!!!
YEEEEK!
UGH, WHAT'S ALL THE RACKET?
KCHAK
OH! MARU-KUN!
TH- TH- THAT GIRL...
HUH? WHAT, YOU GUYS ARE SCARED OF SOME FIRST-YEAR GIRL?
PATHETIC!
LOOK AGAIN, MARU-KUN!!
YOU...
GLUG
YOU'RE THE PIECE OF SCUM WHO POURED HIS SOFT DRINK ON ROMIO-SAMA!!
YOU...
U'RE THAT HICK WHO ED TO KILL ME WITH A STICK... E INUZUKA FAMILY'S GUARD DOG...!!
SHOOM
GRAZE

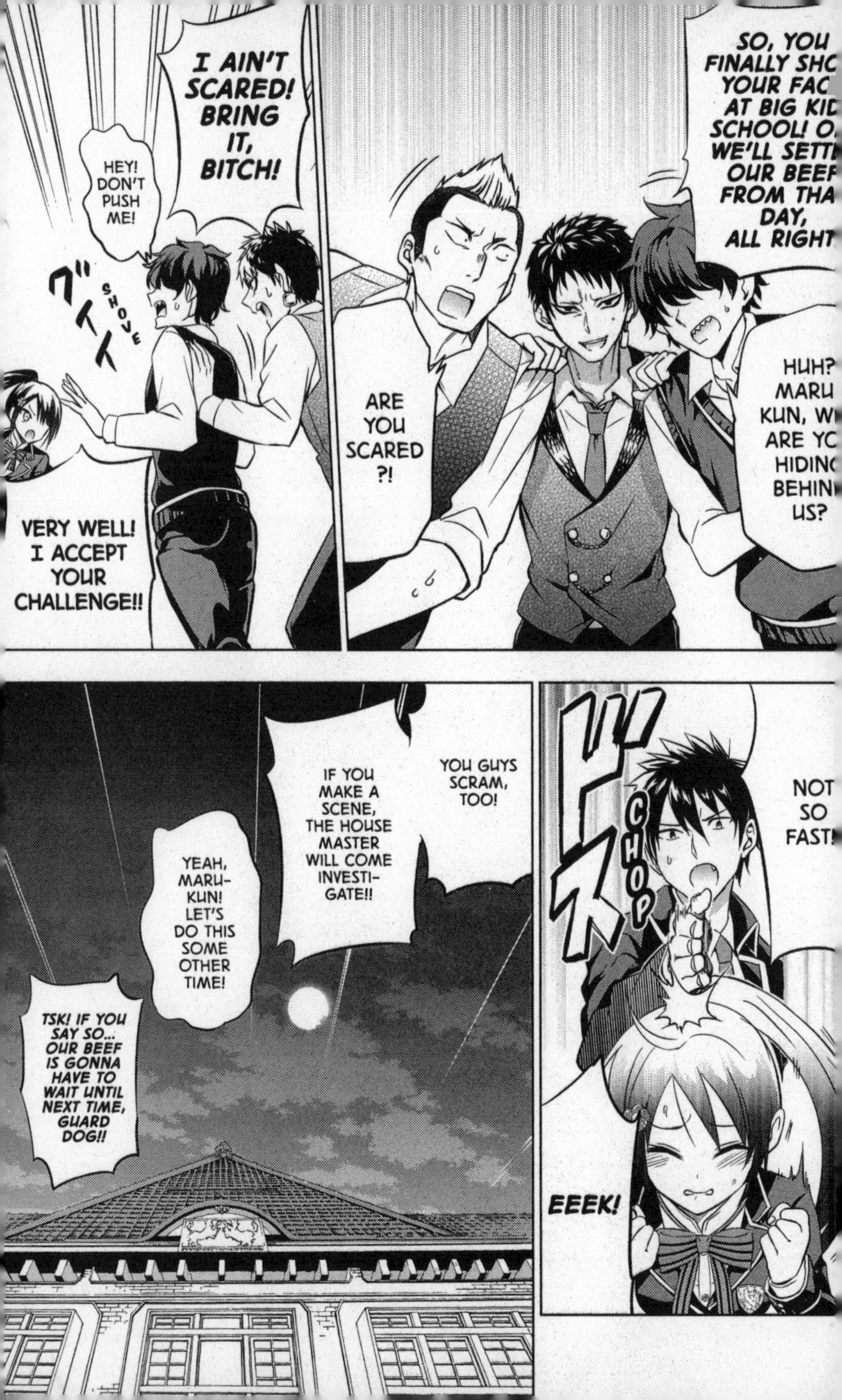
SO, YOU FINALLY SHO YOUR FAC AT BIG KID SCHOOL! O WE'LL SETT OUR BEEF FROM THA DAY, ALL RIGHT
HUH? MARU KUN, W ARE YO HIDIN BEHIN US?
ARE YOU SCARED ?!
I AIN'T SCARED! BRING IT, BITCH!
HEY! DON'T PUSH ME!
グイイ
SHOVE
VERY WELL! I ACCEPT YOUR CHALLENGE!!
NOT SO FAST!
ドス
CHOP
EEEK!
YOU GUYS SCRAM, TOO!
IF YOU MAKE A SCENE, THE HOUSE MASTER WILL COME INVESTIGATE!!
YEAH, MARU-KUN! LET'S DO THIS SOME OTHER TIME!
TSK! IF YOU SAY SO... OUR BEEF IS GONNA HAVE TO WAIT UNTIL NEXT TIME, GUARD DOG!!

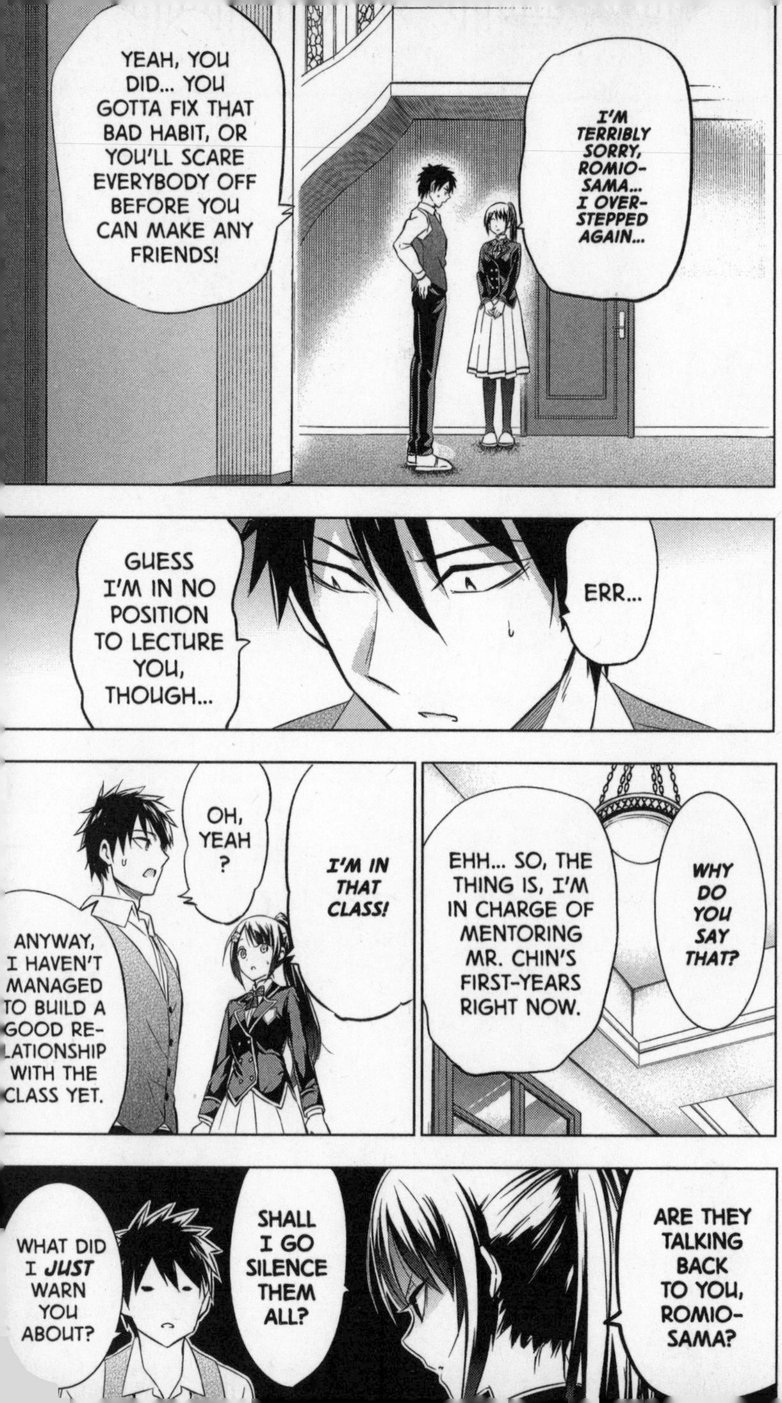
I'M TERRIBLY SORRY, ROMIO-SAMA... I OVER-STEPPED AGAIN...
YEAH, YOU DID... YOU GOTTA FIX THAT BAD HABIT, OR YOU'LL SCARE EVERYBODY OFF BEFORE YOU CAN MAKE ANY FRIENDS!
ERR...
GUESS I'M IN NO POSITION TO LECTURE YOU, THOUGH...
WHY DO YOU SAY THAT?
EHH... SO, THE THING IS, I'M IN CHARGE OF MENTORING MR. CHIN'S FIRST-YEARS RIGHT NOW.
ANYWAY, I HAVEN'T MANAGED TO BUILD A GOOD RE-LATIONSHIP WITH THE CLASS YET.
I'M IN THAT CLASS!
OH, YEAH?
ARE THEY TALKING BACK TO YOU, ROMIO-SAMA?
SHALL I GO SILENCE THEM ALL?
WHAT DID I JUST WARN YOU ABOUT?

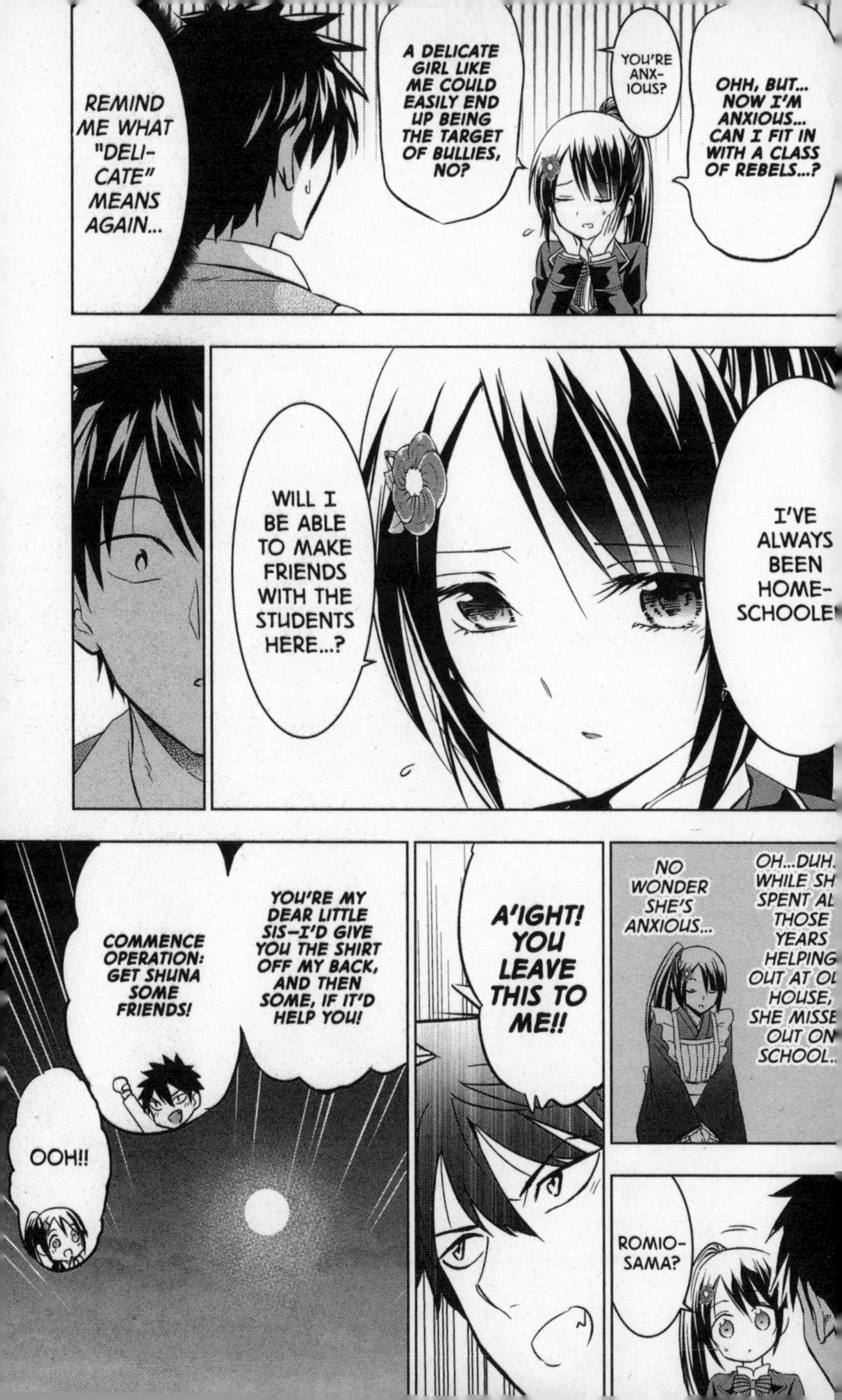
OHH, BUT... NOW I'M ANXIOUS... CAN I FIT IN WITH A CLASS OF REBELS...?
YOU'RE ANX-IOUS?
A DELICATE GIRL LIKE ME COULD EASILY END UP BEING THE TARGET OF BULLIES, NO?
REMIND ME WHAT "DELI-CATE" MEANS AGAIN...
I'VE ALWAYS BEEN HOME-SCHOOLE
WILL I BE ABLE TO MAKE FRIENDS WITH THE STUDENTS HERE...?
OH...DUH. WHILE SH SPENT AL THOSE YEARS HELPING OUT AT OU HOUSE, SHE MISSE OUT ON SCHOOL..
NO WONDER SHE'S ANXIOUS...
ROMIO-SAMA?
A'IGHT! YOU LEAVE THIS TO ME!!
YOU'RE MY DEAR LITTLE SIS—I'D GIVE YOU THE SHIRT OFF MY BACK, AND THEN SOME, IF IT'D HELP YOU!
COMMENCE OPERATION: GET SHUNA SOME FRIENDS!
OOH!!

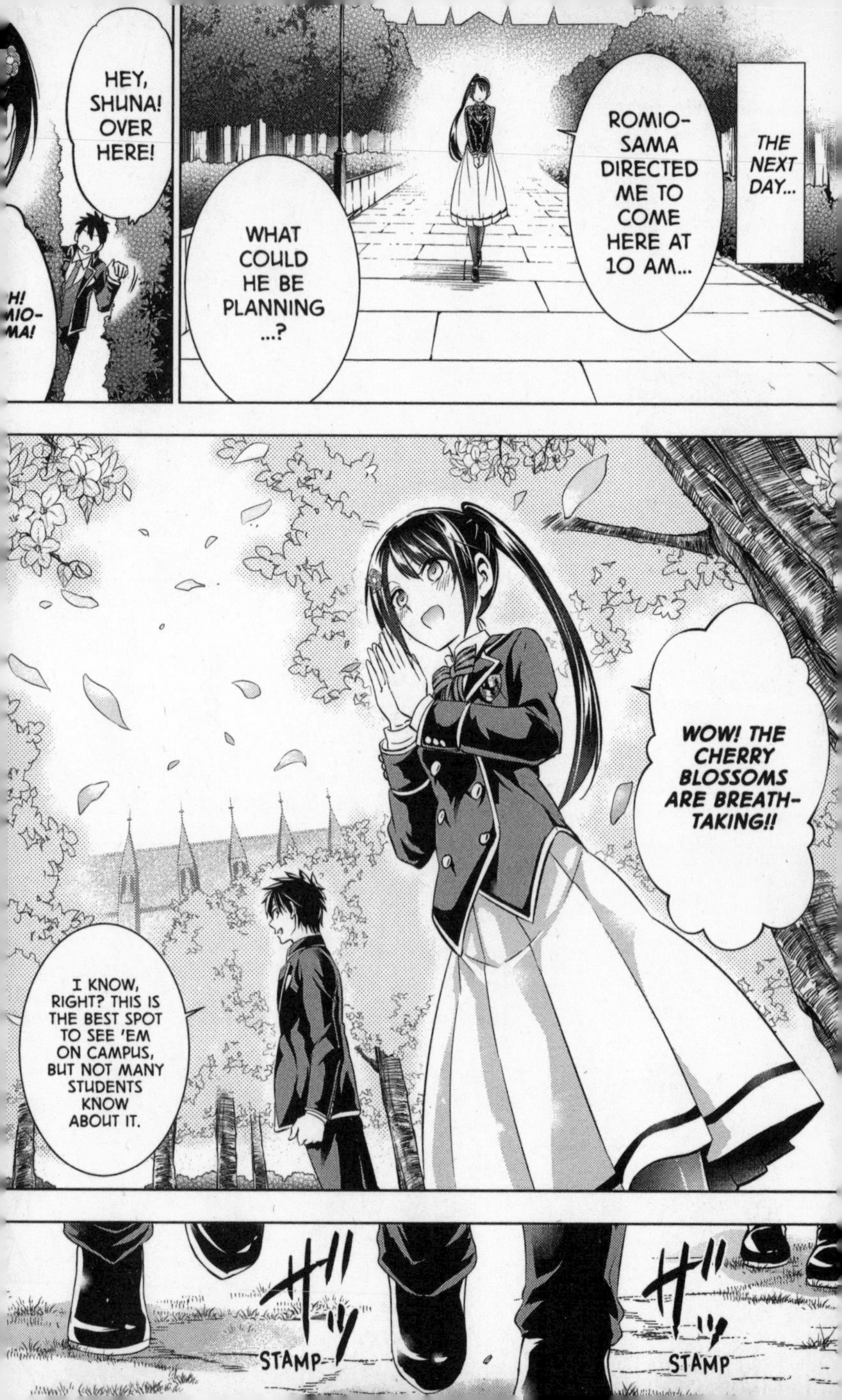
THE NEXT DAY...
ROMIO-SAMA DIRECTED ME TO COME HERE AT 10 AM...
WHAT COULD HE BE PLANNING ...?
HEY, SHUNA! OVER HERE!
WOW! THE CHERRY BLOSSOMS ARE BREATH-TAKING!!
I KNOW, RIGHT? THIS IS THE BEST SPOT TO SEE 'EM ON CAMPUS, BUT NOT MANY STUDENTS KNOW ABOUT IT.
ザッ
STAMP
ザッ
STAMP

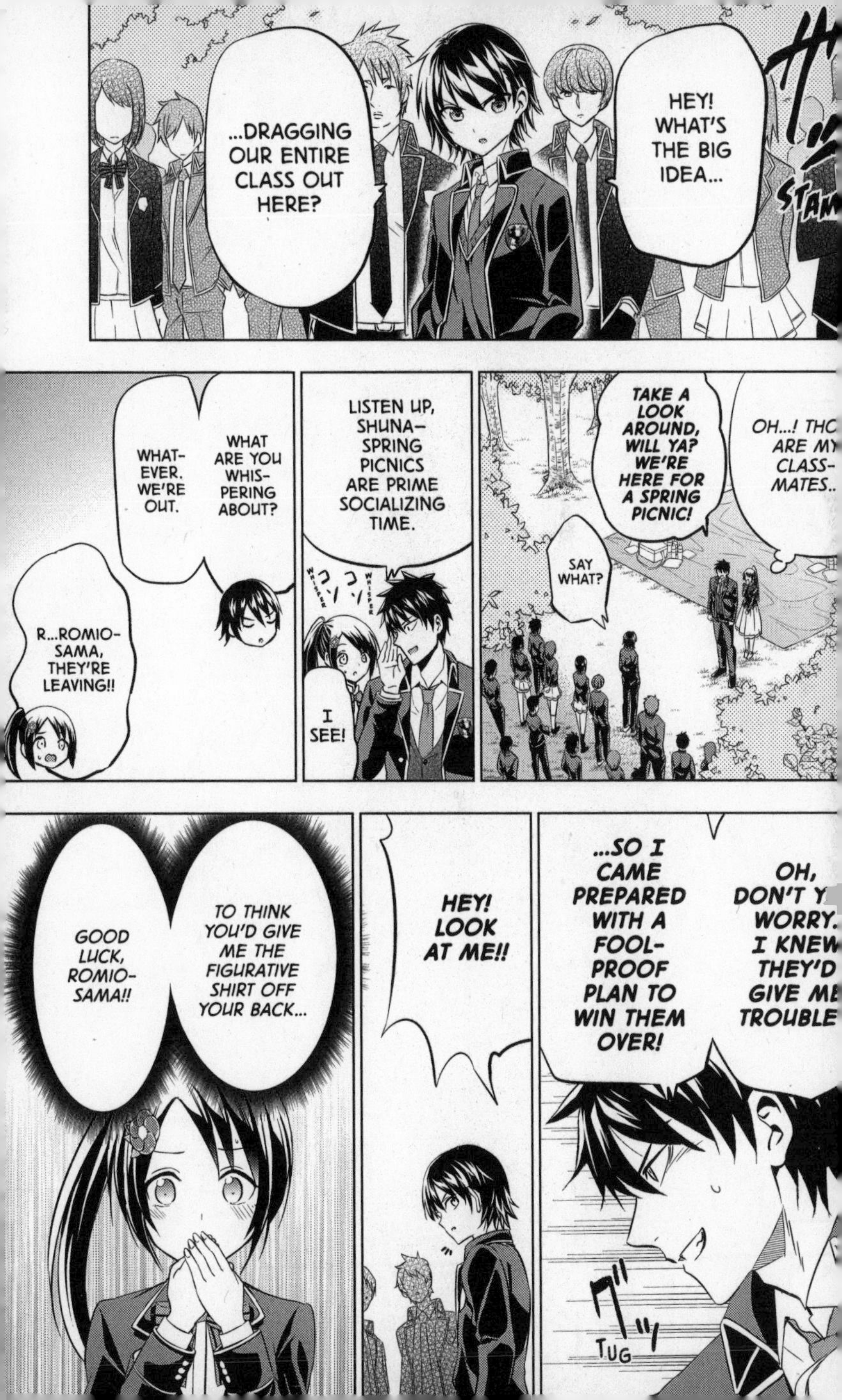
HEY! WHAT'S THE BIG IDEA...
...DRAGGING OUR ENTIRE CLASS OUT HERE?
OH...! THO ARE MY CLASS-MATES..
TAKE A LOOK AROUND, WILL YA? WE'RE HERE FOR A SPRING PICNIC!
SAY WHAT?
LISTEN UP, SHUNA— SPRING PICNICS ARE PRIME SOCIALIZING TIME.
WHISPER
WHISPER
I SEE!
WHAT ARE YOU WHIS-PERING ABOUT?
WHAT-EVER. WE'RE OUT.
R...ROMIO-SAMA, THEY'RE LEAVING!!
OH, DON'T Y WORRY. I KNEW THEY'D GIVE ME TROUBLE
...SO I CAME PREPARED WITH A FOOL-PROOF PLAN TO WIN THEM OVER!
TUG
HEY! LOOK AT ME!!
TO THINK YOU'D GIVE ME THE FIGURATIVE SHIRT OFF YOUR BACK...
GOOD LUCK, ROMIO-SAMA!!

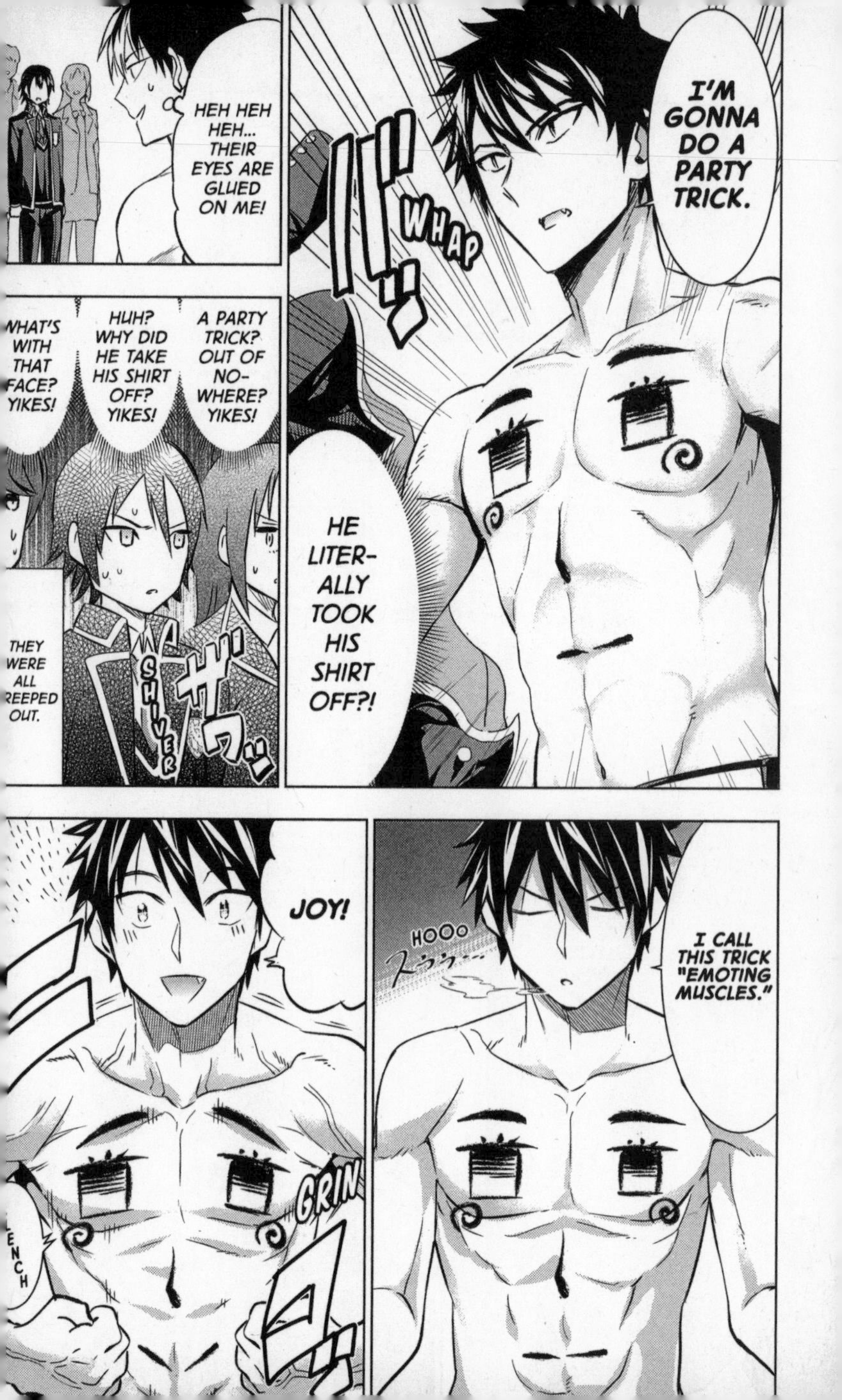
I'M GONNA DO A PARTY TRICK.
WHAP
HE LITERALLY TOOK HIS SHIRT OFF?!
HEH HEH HEH... THEIR EYES ARE GLUED ON ME!
A PARTY TRICK? OUT OF NOWHERE? YIKES!
HUH? WHY DID HE TAKE HIS SHIRT OFF? YIKES!
WHAT'S WITH THAT FACE? YIKES!
THEY WERE ALL REEPED OUT.
SHIVER
I CALL THIS TRICK "EMOTING MUSCLES."
HOOO
JOY!
GRIN

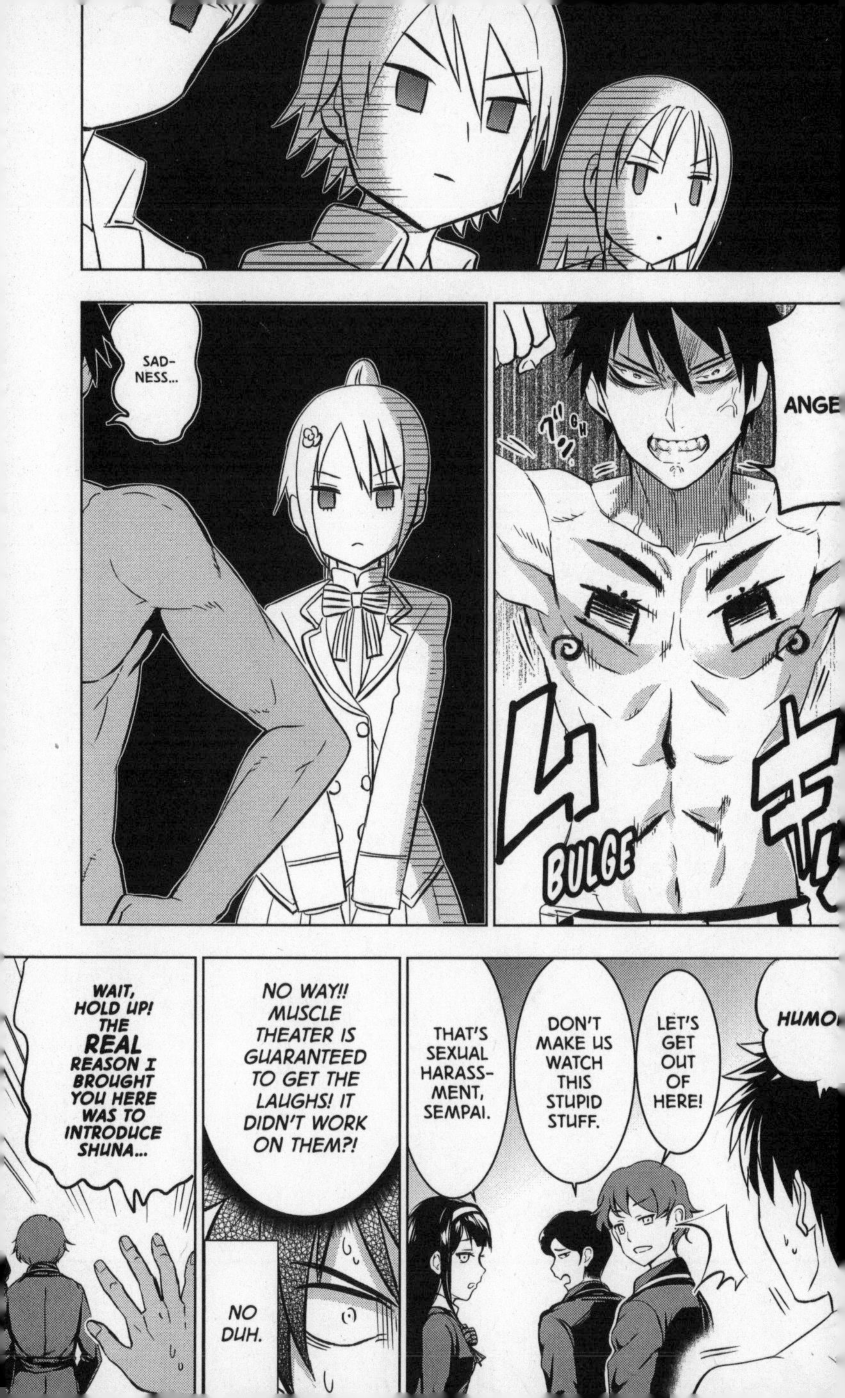
ANGE
BULGE
SAD-NESS...
HUMO
LET'S GET OUT OF HERE!
DON'T MAKE US WATCH THIS STUPID STUFF.
THAT'S SEXUAL HARASS-MENT, SEMPAI.
NO WAY!! MUSCLE THEATER IS GUARANTEED TO GET THE LAUGHS! IT DIDN'T WORK ON THEM?!
NO DUH.
WAIT, HOLD UP! THE REAL REASON I BROUGHT YOU HERE WAS TO INTRODUCE SHUNA...

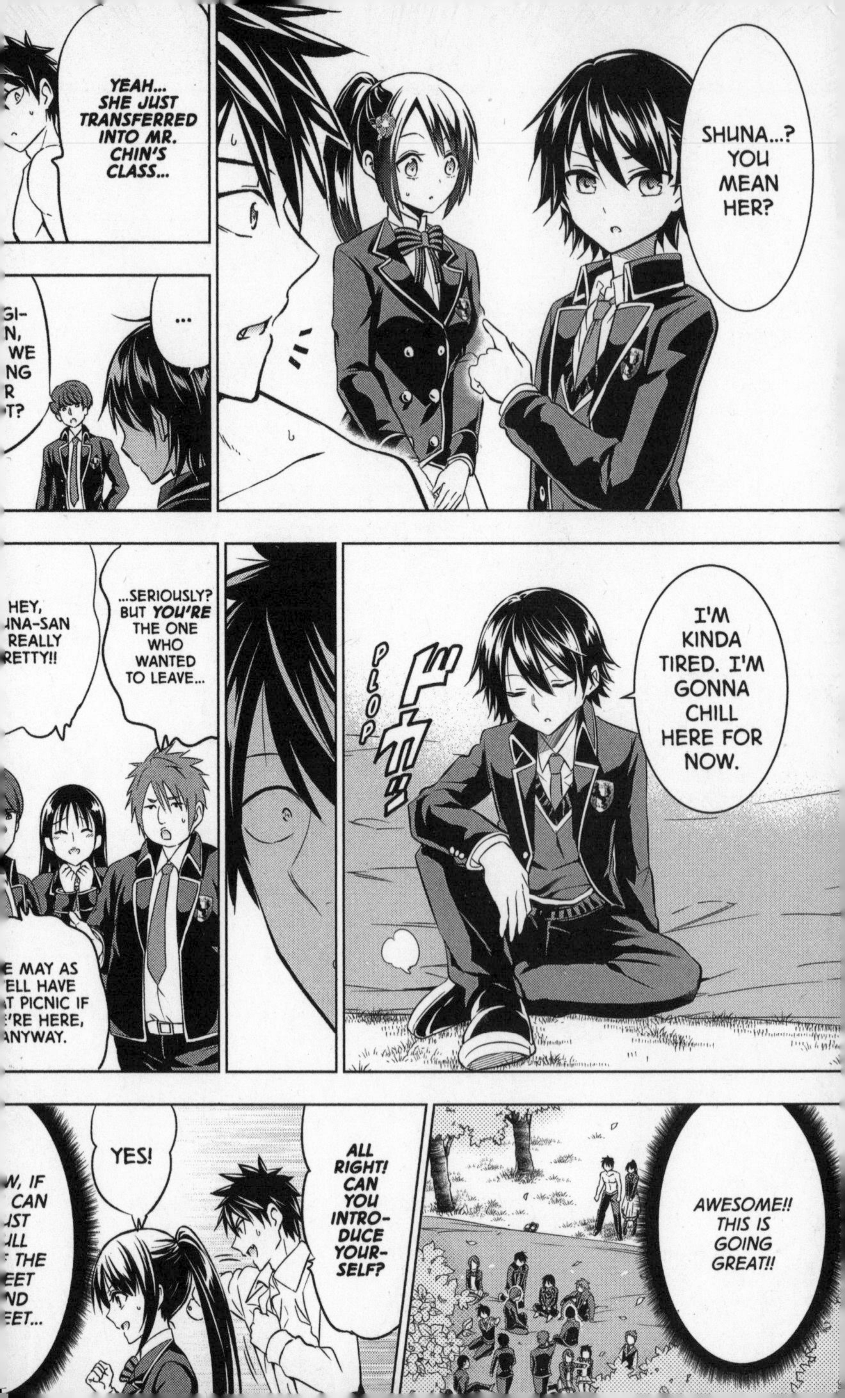
SHUNA...? YOU MEAN HER?
YEAH... SHE JUST TRANSFERRED INTO MR. CHIN'S CLASS...
...
GI- N, WE NG R T?
I'M KINDA TIRED. I'M GONNA CHILL HERE FOR NOW.
PLOP
...SERIOUSLY? BUT YOU'RE THE ONE WHO WANTED TO LEAVE...
HEY, INA-SAN REALLY RETTY!!
E MAY AS ELL HAVE T PICNIC IF 'RE HERE, ANYWAY.
AWESOME!! THIS IS GOING GREAT!!
ALL RIGHT! CAN YOU INTRODUCE YOURSELF?
YES!
W, IF CAN JST ULL THE EET ND EET...

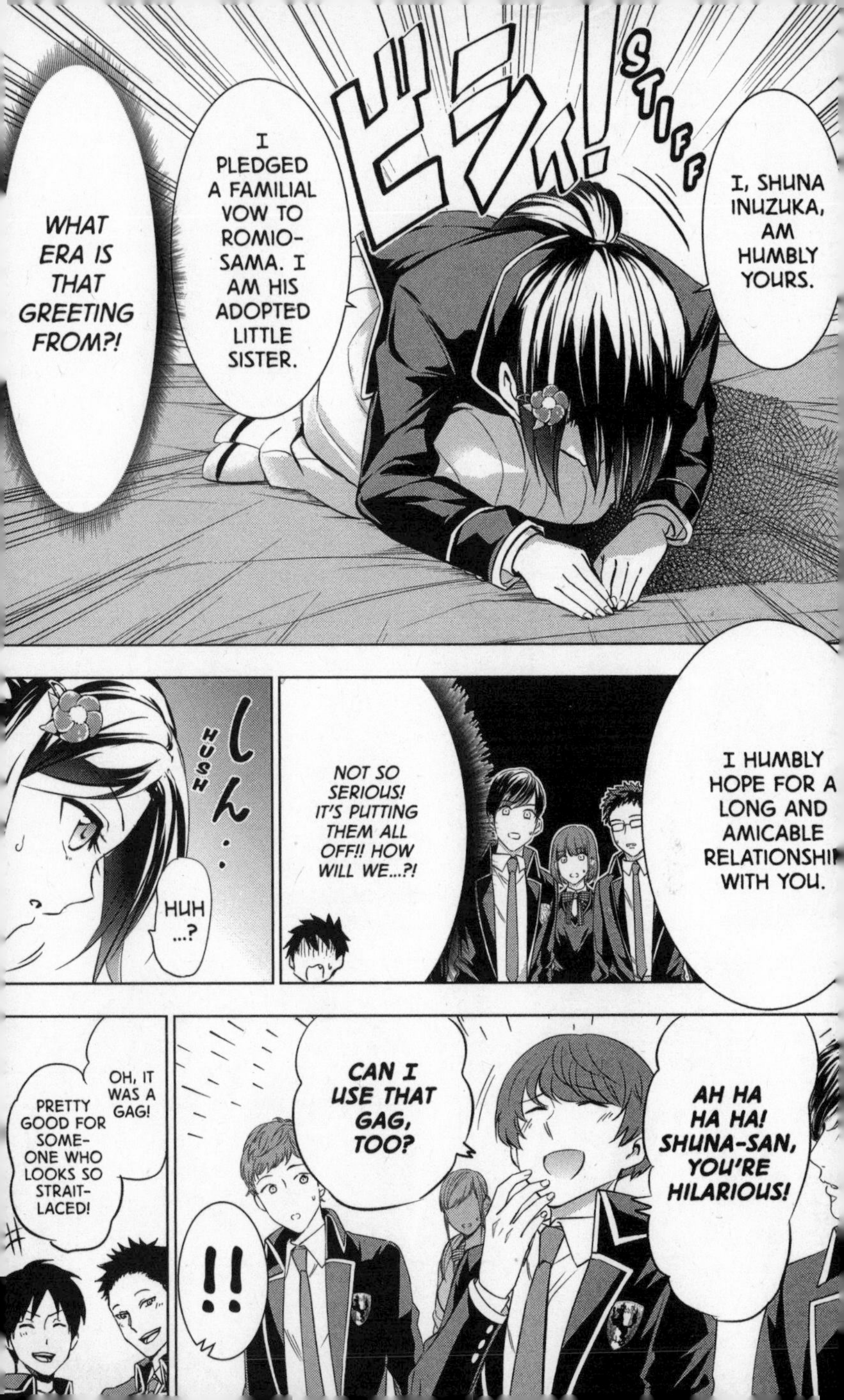
STIFF
I, SHUNA INUZUKA, AM HUMBLY YOURS.
I PLEDGED A FAMILIAL VOW TO ROMIO-SAMA. I AM HIS ADOPTED LITTLE SISTER.
WHAT ERA IS THAT GREETING FROM?!
I HUMBLY HOPE FOR A LONG AND AMICABLE RELATIONSHI WITH YOU.
NOT SO SERIOUS! IT'S PUTTING THEM ALL OFF!! HOW WILL WE...?!
HUSH
HUH ...?
AH HA HA HA! SHUNA-SAN, YOU'RE HILARIOUS!
CAN I USE THAT GAG, TOO?
!!
OH, IT WAS A GAG!
PRETTY GOOD FOR SOME-ONE WHO LOOKS SO STRAIT-LACED!

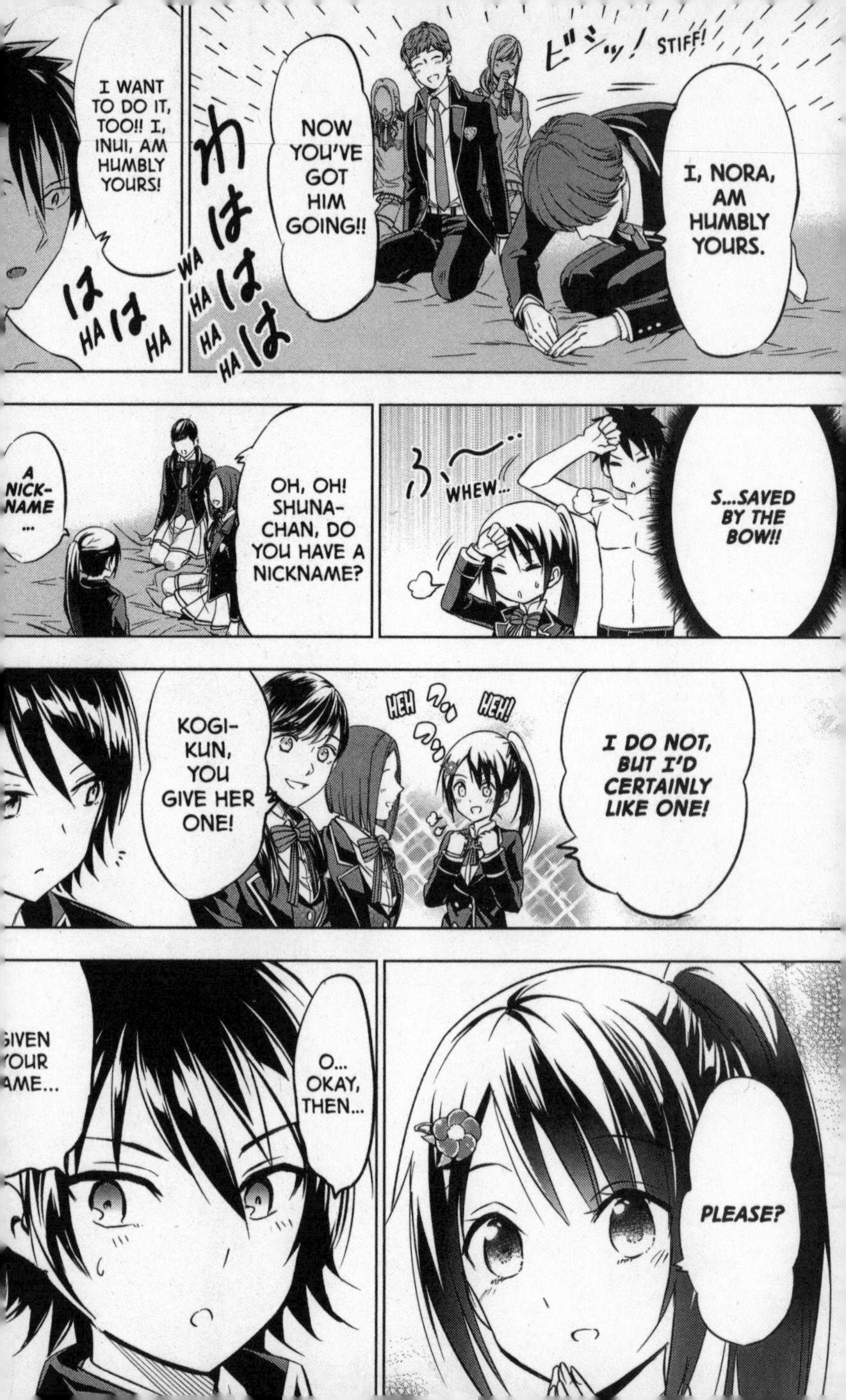
ビシッ! STIFF!
I, NORA, AM HUMBLY YOURS.
NOW YOU'VE GOT HIM GOING!!
わははは WA HA HA HA HA
I WANT TO DO IT, TOO!! I, INUI, AM HUMBLY YOURS!
はは HA HA
S...SAVED BY THE BOW!!
ふ〜・・ WHEW...
OH, OH! SHUNA-CHAN, DO YOU HAVE A NICKNAME?
A NICK-NAME ...
I DO NOT, BUT I'D CERTAINLY LIKE ONE!
HEH HEH!
KOGI-KUN, YOU GIVE HER ONE!
PLEASE?
O... OKAY, THEN...
GIVEN YOUR AME...

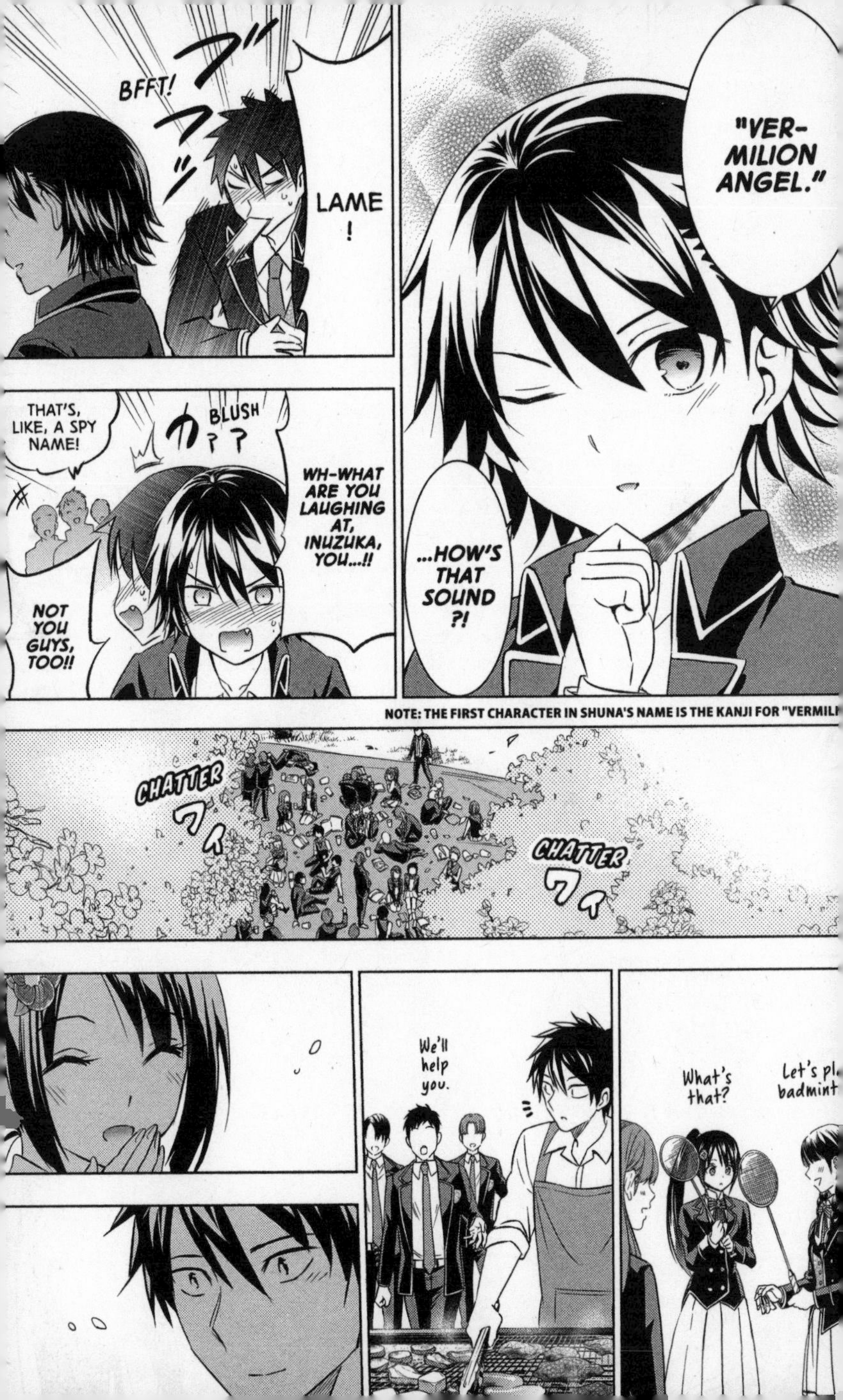
"VERMILION ANGEL."
...HOW'S THAT SOUND?!
BFFT!
LAME!
THAT'S, LIKE, A SPY NAME!
BLUSH
WH-WHAT ARE YOU LAUGHING AT, INUZUKA, YOU...!!
NOT YOU GUYS, TOO!!
NOTE: THE FIRST CHARACTER IN SHUNA'S NAME IS THE KANJI FOR "VERMIL
CHATTER
CHATTER
Let's pl badmint
What's that?
We'll help you.

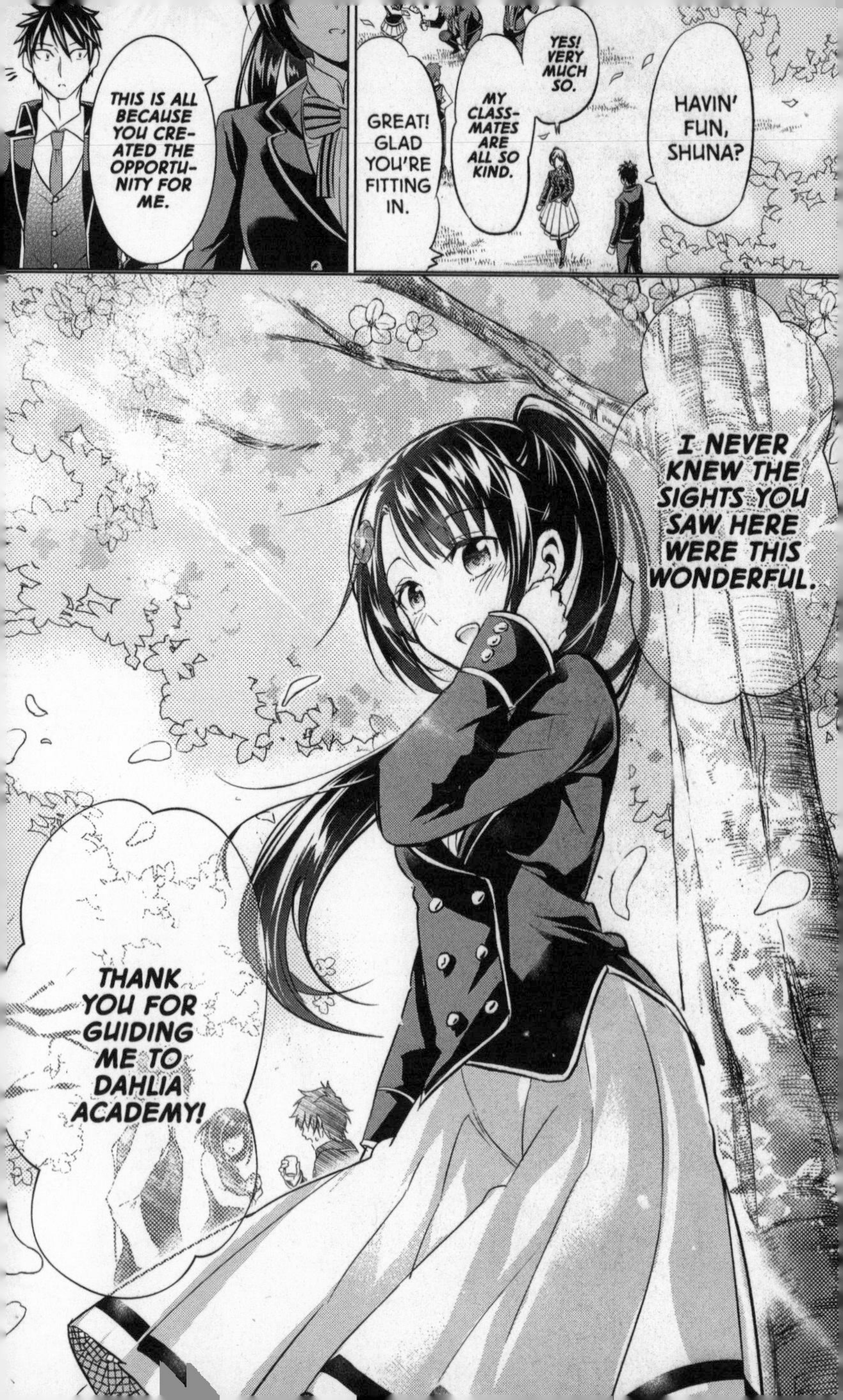
HAVIN' FUN, SHUNA?
YES! VERY MUCH SO.
MY CLASS-MATES ARE ALL SO KIND.
GREAT! GLAD YOU'RE FITTING IN.
THIS IS ALL BECAUSE YOU CRE-ATED THE OPPORTU-NITY FOR ME.
I NEVER KNEW THE SIGHTS YOU SAW HERE WERE THIS WONDERFUL.
THANK YOU FOR GUIDING ME TO DAHLIA ACADEMY!

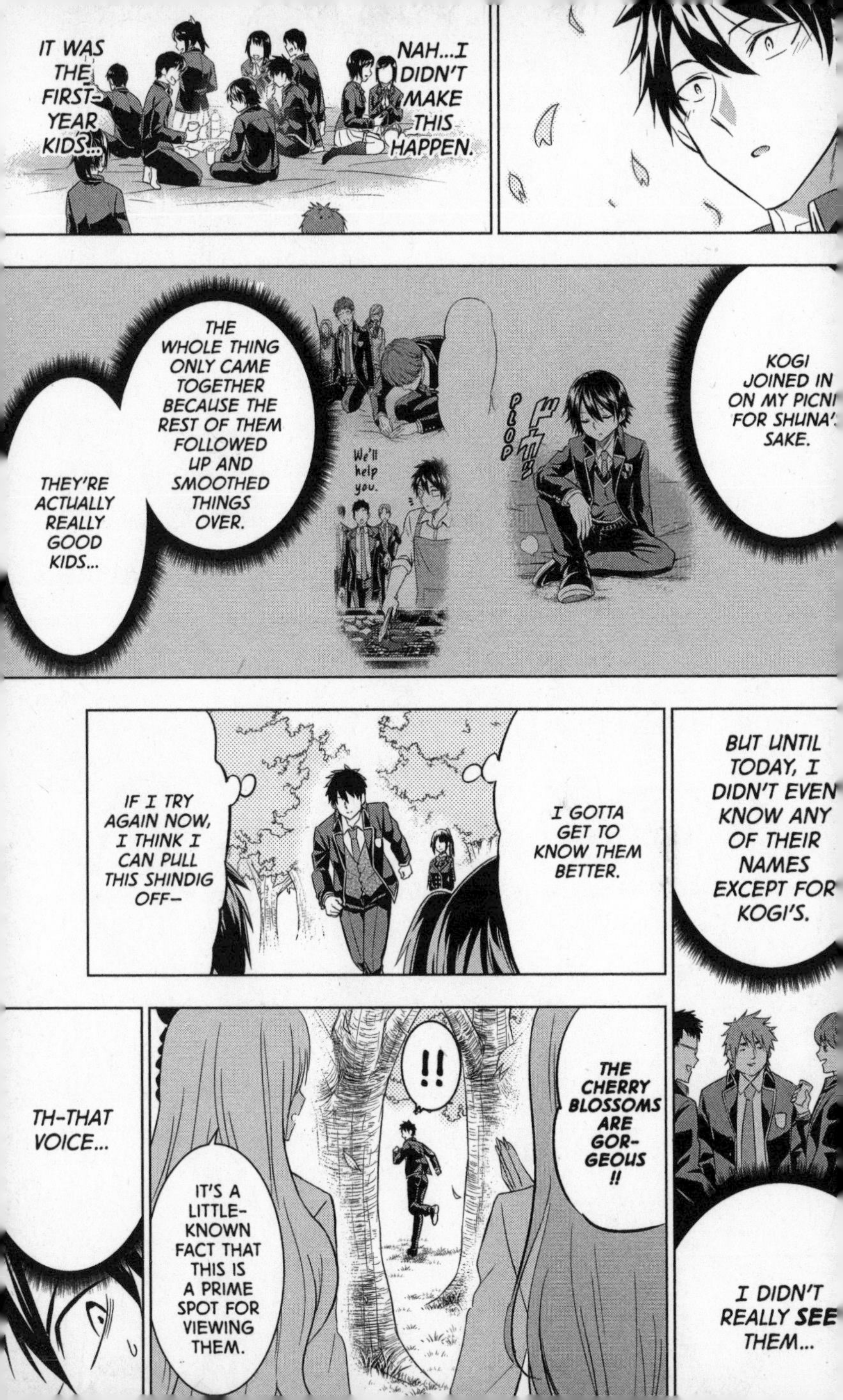
NAH...I DIDN'T MAKE THIS HAPPEN.
IT WAS THE FIRST-YEAR KIDS...
KOGI JOINED IN ON MY PICNI FOR SHUNA'S SAKE.
PLOP
We'll help you.
THE WHOLE THING ONLY CAME TOGETHER BECAUSE THE REST OF THEM FOLLOWED UP AND SMOOTHED THINGS OVER.
THEY'RE ACTUALLY REALLY GOOD KIDS...
BUT UNTIL TODAY, I DIDN'T EVEN KNOW ANY OF THEIR NAMES EXCEPT FOR KOGI'S.
I GOTTA GET TO KNOW THEM BETTER.
IF I TRY AGAIN NOW, I THINK I CAN PULL THIS SHINDIG OFF–
I DIDN'T REALLY SEE THEM...
THE CHERRY BLOSSOMS ARE GORGEOUS!!
!!
IT'S A LITTLE-KNOWN FACT THAT THIS IS A PRIME SPOT FOR VIEWING THEM.
TH-THAT VOICE...

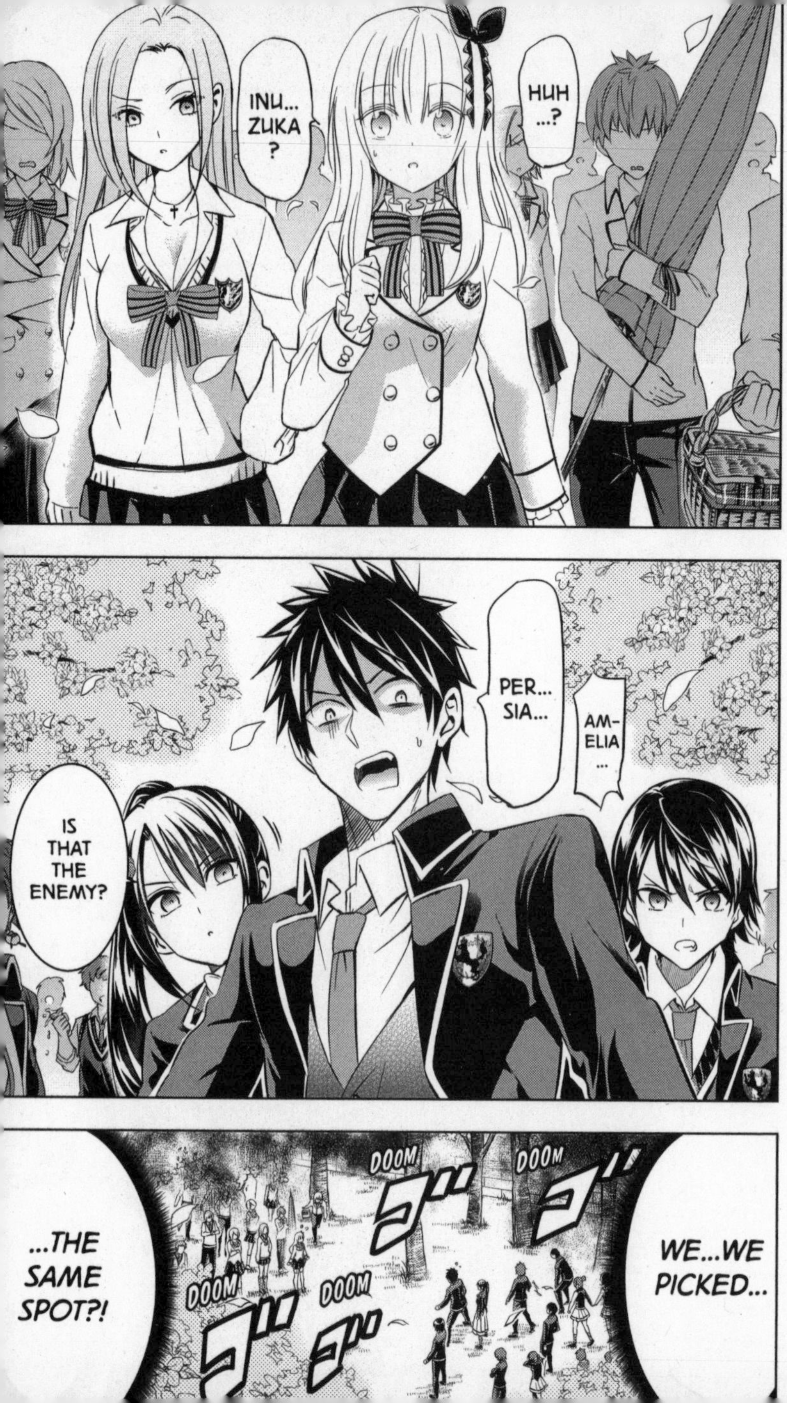
HUH ...?
INU... ZUKA ?
AM-ELIA ...
PER... SIA...
IS THAT THE ENEMY?
WE...WE PICKED...
DOOM
DOOM
DOOM
DOOM
...THE SAME SPOT?!

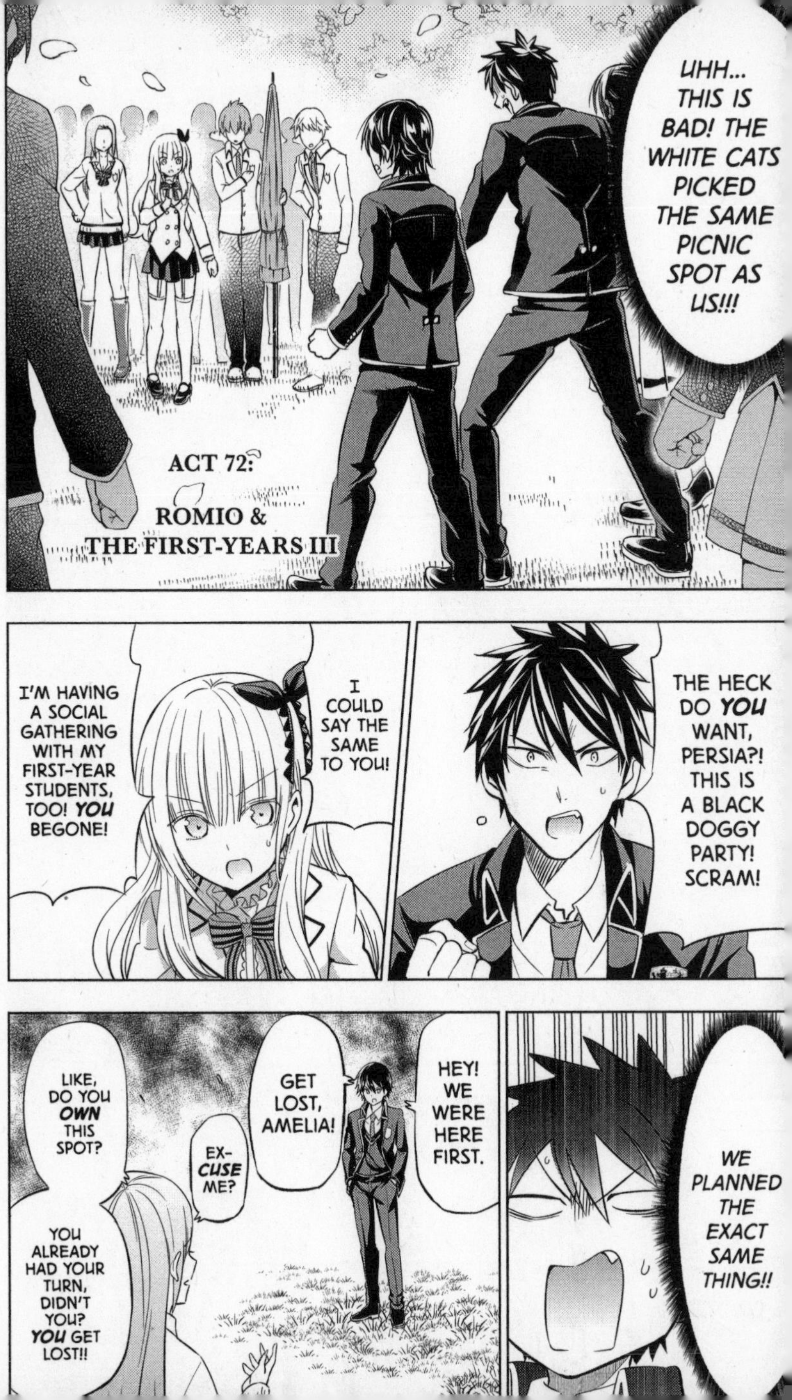
UHH... THIS IS BAD! THE WHITE CATS PICKED THE SAME PICNIC SPOT AS US!!!
ACT 72:
ROMIO & THE FIRST-YEARS III
THE HECK DO YOU WANT, PERSIA?! THIS IS A BLACK DOGGY PARTY! SCRAM!
I COULD SAY THE SAME TO YOU!
I'M HAVING A SOCIAL GATHERING WITH MY FIRST-YEAR STUDENTS, TOO! YOU BEGONE!
WE PLANNED THE EXACT SAME THING!!
HEY! WE WERE HERE FIRST.
GET LOST, AMELIA!
EX-CUSE ME?
LIKE, DO YOU OWN THIS SPOT?
YOU ALREADY HAD YOUR TURN, DIDN'T YOU? YOU GET LOST!!

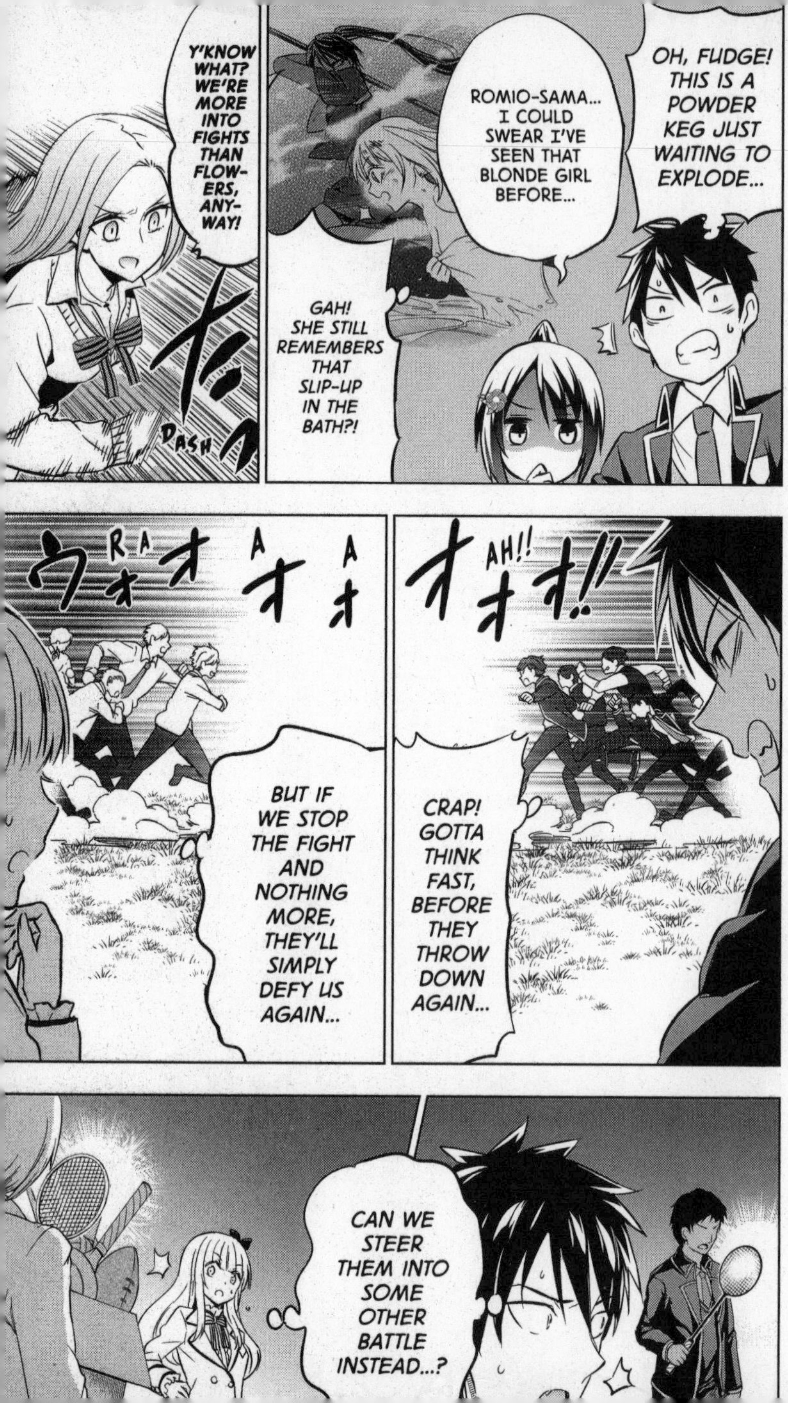
OH, FUDGE! THIS IS A POWDER KEG JUST WAITING TO EXPLODE...
ROMIO-SAMA... I COULD SWEAR I'VE SEEN THAT BLONDE GIRL BEFORE...
GAH! SHE STILL REMEMBERS THAT SLIP-UP IN THE BATH?!
Y'KNOW WHAT? WE'RE MORE INTO FIGHTS THAN FLOW-ERS, ANY-WAY!
DASH
RA A A AH!!
CRAP! GOTTA THINK FAST, BEFORE THEY THROW DOWN AGAIN...
BUT IF WE STOP THE FIGHT AND NOTHING MORE, THEY'LL SIMPLY DEFY US AGAIN...
CAN WE STEER THEM INTO SOME OTHER BATTLE INSTEAD...?

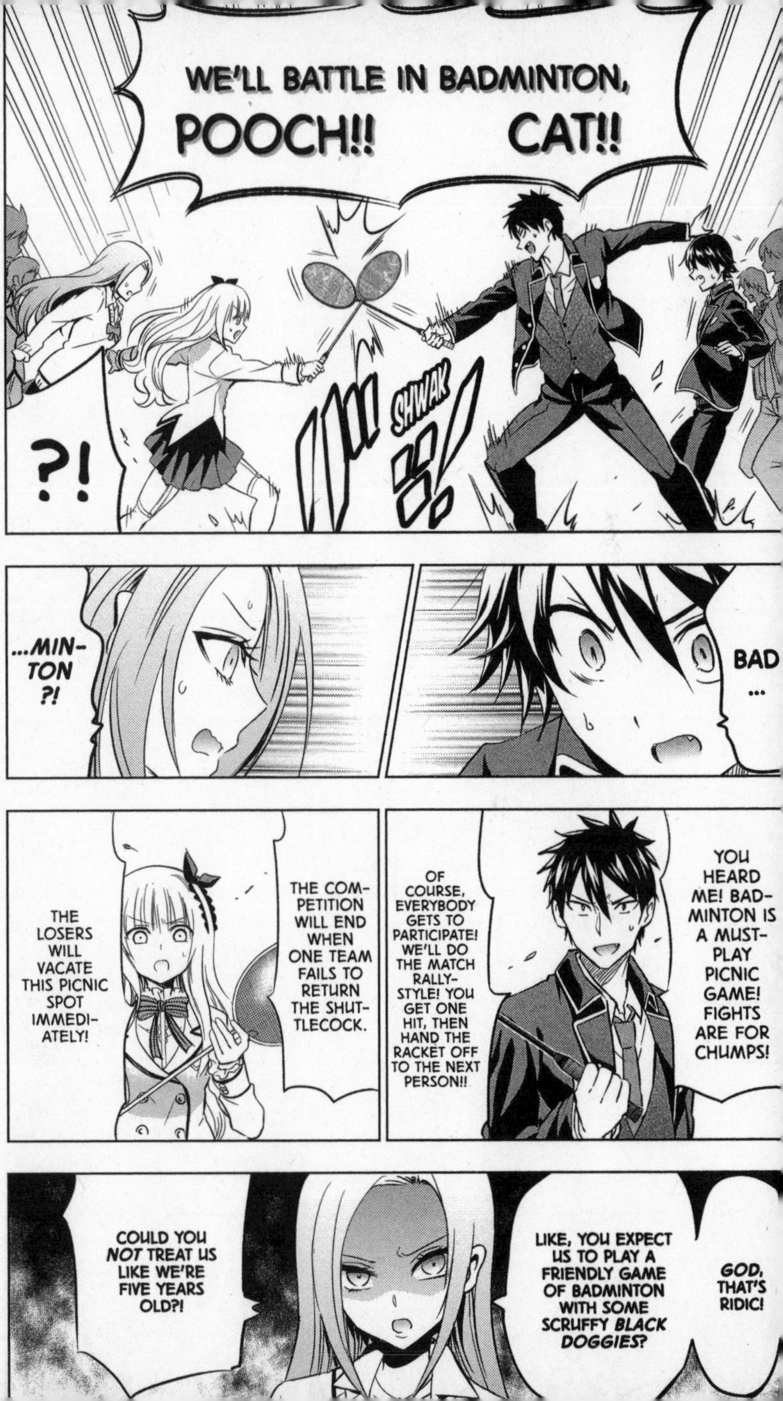
WE'LL BATTLE IN BADMINTON,
POOCH!! CAT!!
SHWAK
?!
BAD ...
...MIN-TON ?!
YOU HEARD ME! BADMINTON IS A MUST-PLAY PICNIC GAME! FIGHTS ARE FOR CHUMPS!
OF COURSE, EVERYBODY GETS TO PARTICIPATE! WE'LL DO THE MATCH RALLY-STYLE! YOU GET ONE HIT, THEN HAND THE RACKET OFF TO THE NEXT PERSON!!
THE COMPETITION WILL END WHEN ONE TEAM FAILS TO RETURN THE SHUTTLECOCK.
THE LOSERS WILL VACATE THIS PICNIC SPOT IMMEDIATELY!
GOD, THAT'S RIDIC!
LIKE, YOU EXPECT US TO PLAY A FRIENDLY GAME OF BADMINTON WITH SOME SCRUFFY *BLACK DOGGIES*?
COULD YOU *NOT* TREAT US LIKE WE'RE FIVE YEARS OLD?!

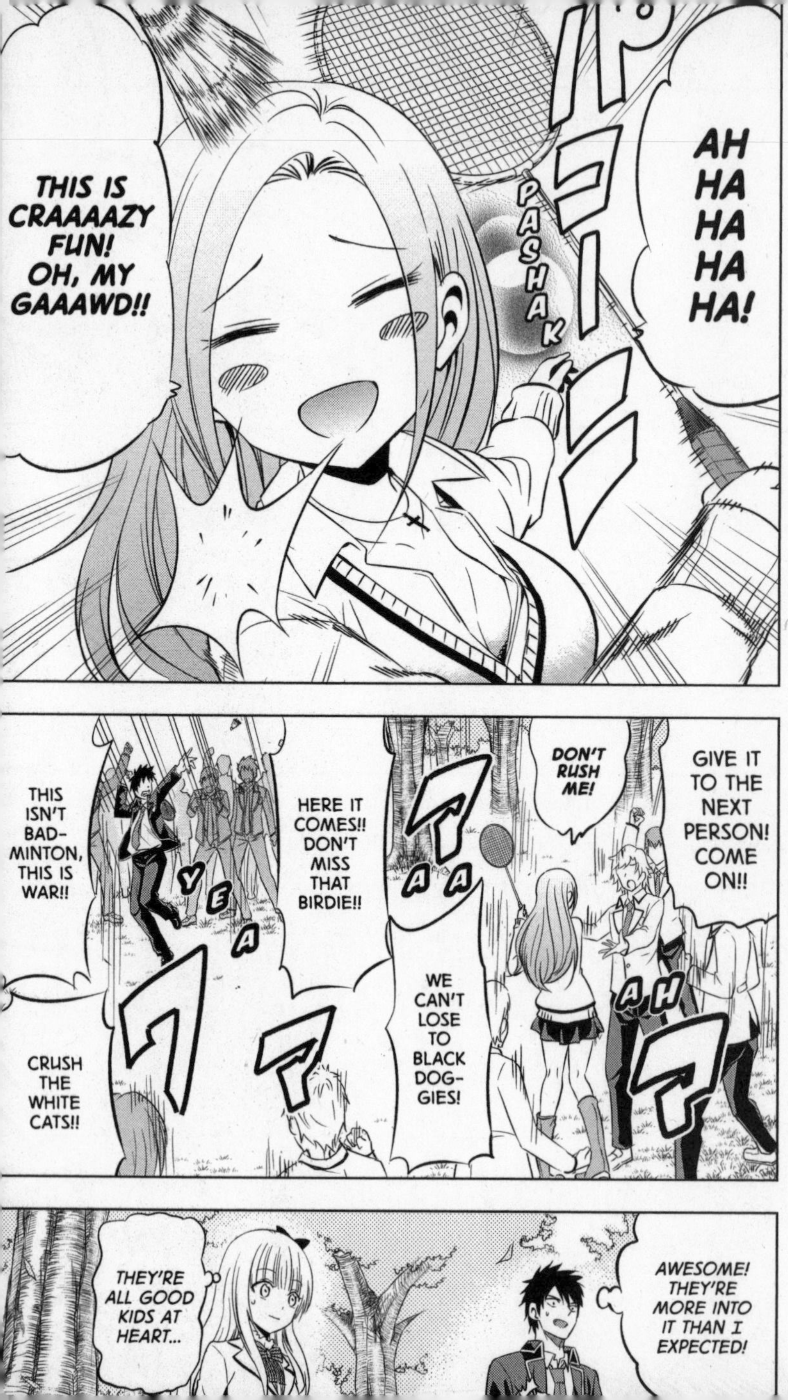
AH HA HA HA HA HA!
PASHAK
THIS IS CRAAAAZY FUN! OH, MY GAAAWD!!
GIVE IT TO THE NEXT PERSON! COME ON!!
DON'T RUSH ME!
AH
AA
HERE IT COMES!! DON'T MISS THAT BIRDIE!!
WE CAN'T LOSE TO BLACK DOG-GIES!
YEA
THIS ISN'T BAD-MINTON, THIS IS WAR!!
CRUSH THE WHITE CATS!!
AWESOME! THEY'RE MORE INTO IT THAN I EXPECTED!
THEY'RE ALL GOOD KIDS AT HEART...

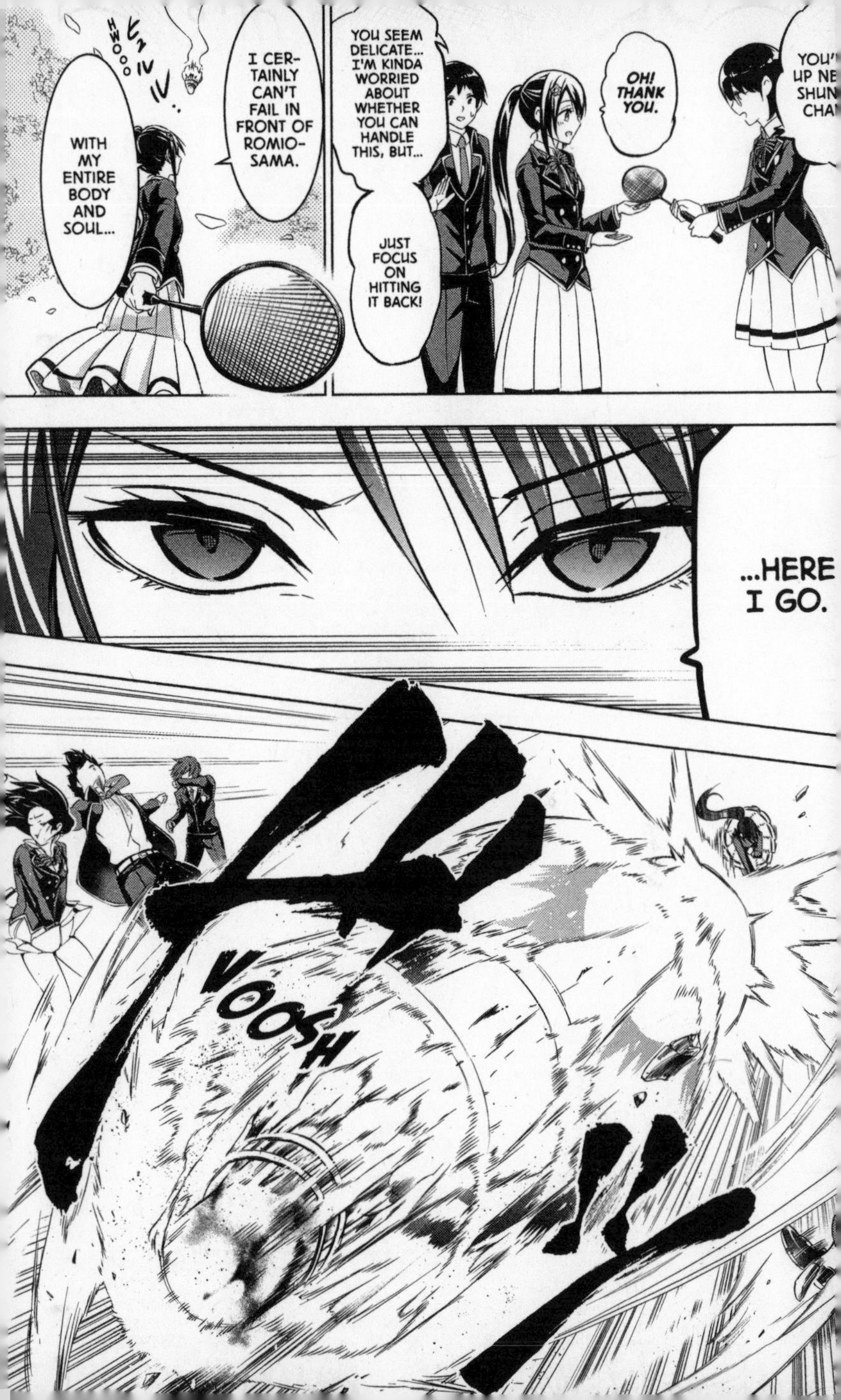
YOU' UP NE SHUN CHA
OH! THANK YOU.
YOU SEEM DELICATE... I'M KINDA WORRIED ABOUT WHETHER YOU CAN HANDLE THIS, BUT...
JUST FOCUS ON HITTING IT BACK!
I CERTAINLY CAN'T FAIL IN FRONT OF ROMIO-SAMA.
HWOOO
WITH MY ENTIRE BODY AND SOUL...
...HERE I GO.
VOOSH

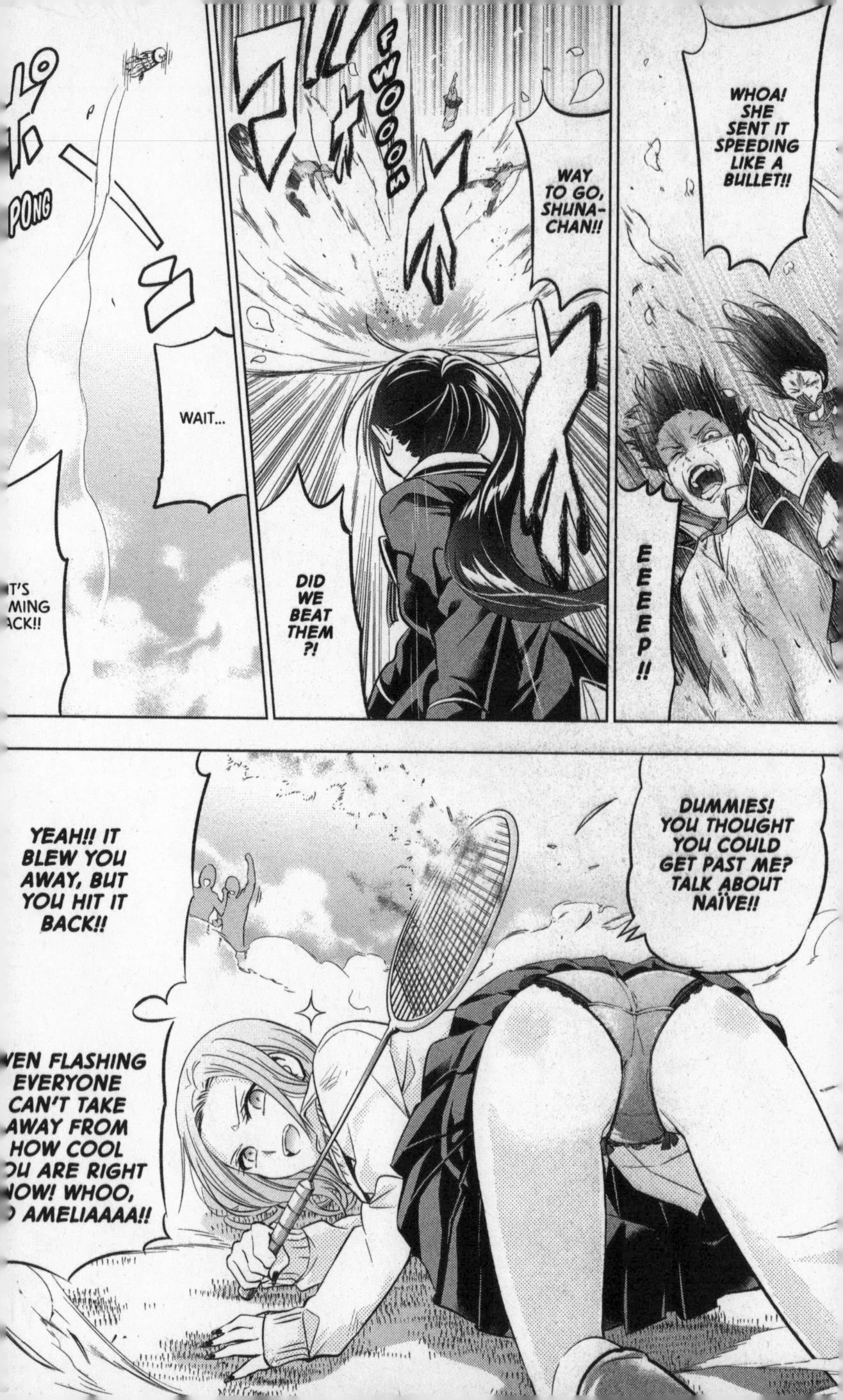
WHOA! SHE SENT IT SPEEDING LIKE A BULLET!!
EEEEEP!!
FWOOOOM
WAY TO GO, SHUNA-CHAN!!
DID WE BEAT THEM?!
PONG
WAIT...
T'S MING ACK!!
DUMMIES! YOU THOUGHT YOU COULD GET PAST ME? TALK ABOUT NAÏVE!!
YEAH!! IT BLEW YOU AWAY, BUT YOU HIT IT BACK!!
VEN FLASHING EVERYONE CAN'T TAKE AWAY FROM HOW COOL OU ARE RIGHT OW! WHOO, AMELIAAAA!!

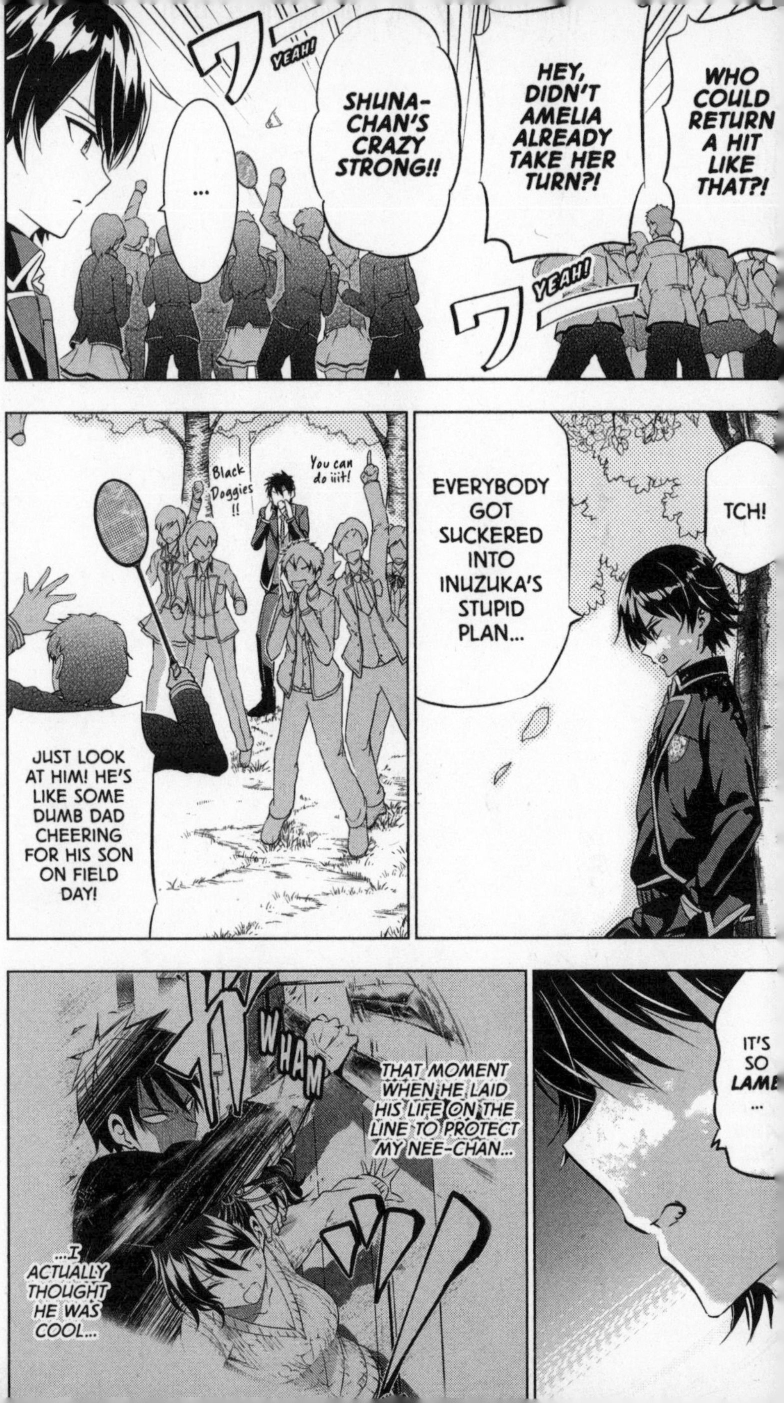
WHO COULD RETURN A HIT LIKE THAT?!
YEAH!
HEY, DIDN'T AMELIA ALREADY TAKE HER TURN?!
SHUNA-CHAN'S CRAZY STRONG!!
YEAH!
...
TCH!
EVERYBODY GOT SUCKERED INTO INUZUKA'S STUPID PLAN...
You can do iiit!
Black Doggies !!
JUST LOOK AT HIM! HE'S LIKE SOME DUMB DAD CHEERING FOR HIS SON ON FIELD DAY!
IT'S SO LAME ...
WHAM
THAT MOMENT WHEN HE LAID HIS LIFE ON THE LINE TO PROTECT MY NEE-CHAN...
...I ACTUALLY THOUGHT HE WAS COOL...

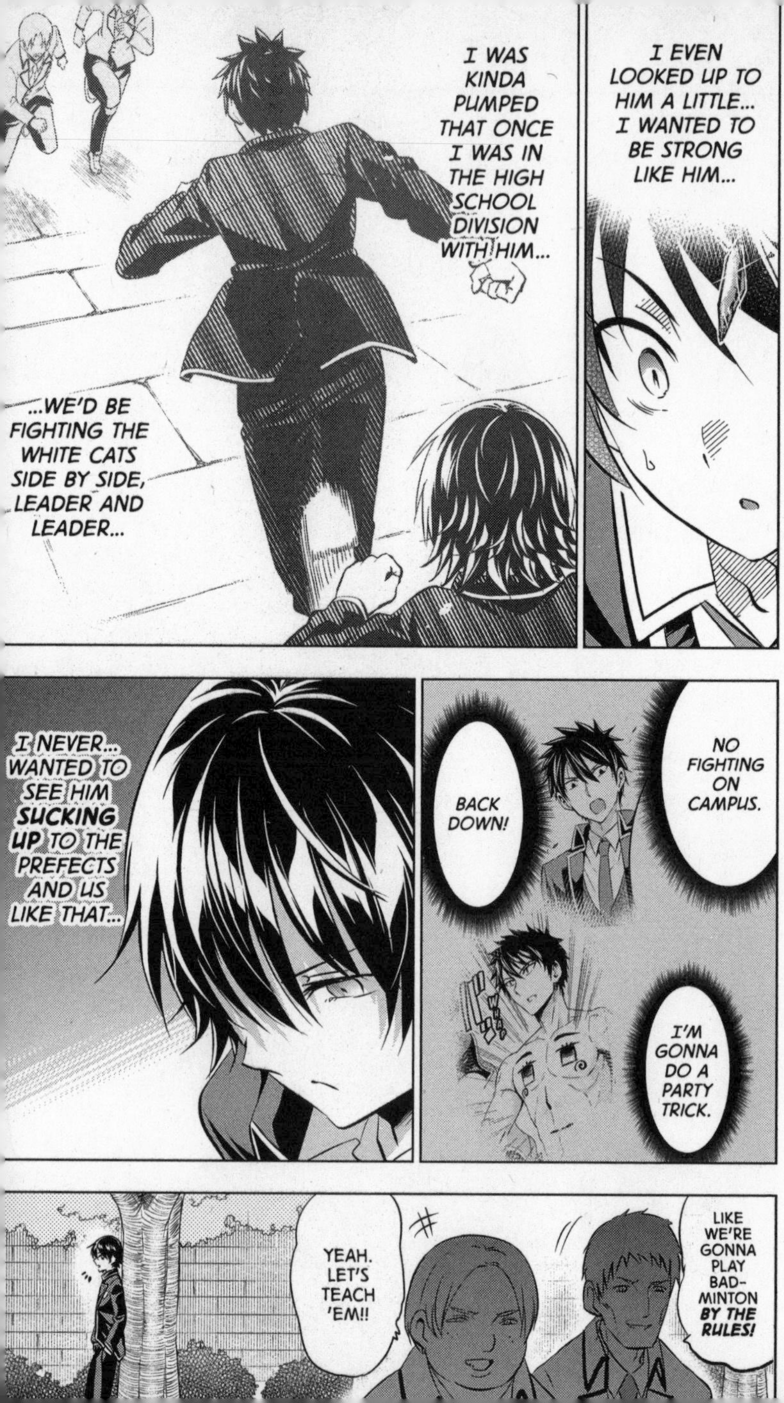
I EVEN LOOKED UP TO HIM A LITTLE... I WANTED TO BE STRONG LIKE HIM...
I WAS KINDA PUMPED THAT ONCE I WAS IN THE HIGH SCHOOL DIVISION WITH HIM...
...WE'D BE FIGHTING THE WHITE CATS SIDE BY SIDE, LEADER AND LEADER...
NO FIGHTING ON CAMPUS.
BACK DOWN!
I'M GONNA DO A PARTY TRICK.
I NEVER... WANTED TO SEE HIM **SUCKING UP** TO THE PREFECTS AND US LIKE THAT...
LIKE WE'RE GONNA PLAY BADMINTON ***BY THE RULES!***
YEAH. LET'S TEACH 'EM!!

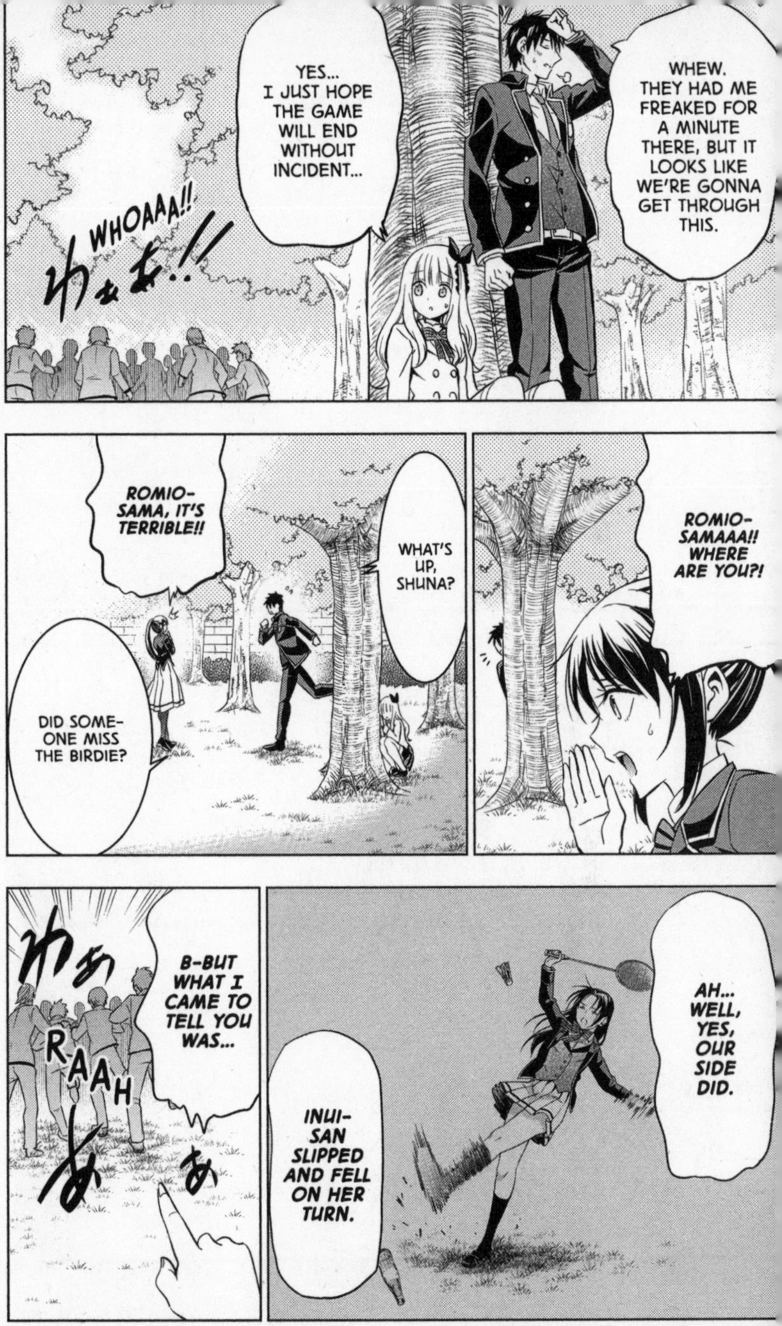
WHEW. THEY HAD ME FREAKED FOR A MINUTE THERE, BUT IT LOOKS LIKE WE'RE GONNA GET THROUGH THIS.
YES... I JUST HOPE THE GAME WILL END WITHOUT INCIDENT...
WHOAAA!!
ROMIO-SAMAAA!! WHERE ARE YOU?!
WHAT'S UP, SHUNA?
ROMIO-SAMA, IT'S TERRIBLE!!
DID SOME-ONE MISS THE BIRDIE?
AH... WELL, YES, OUR SIDE DID.
INUI-SAN SLIPPED AND FELL ON HER TURN.
B-BUT WHAT I CAME TO TELL YOU WAS...
RAAH

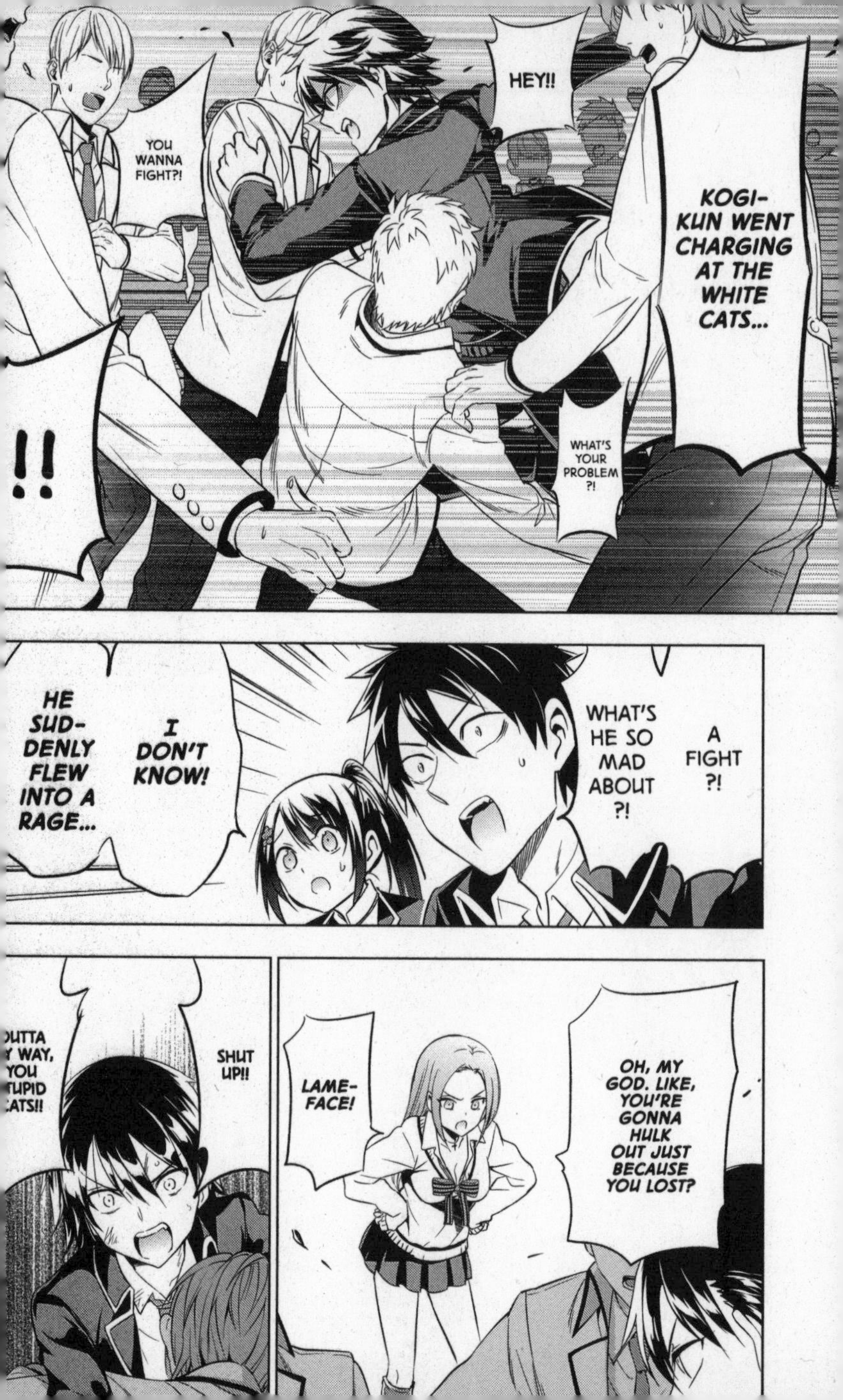
KOGI-KUN WENT CHARGING AT THE WHITE CATS...
HEY!!
WHAT'S YOUR PROBLEM?!
YOU WANNA FIGHT?!
!!
A FIGHT?!
WHAT'S HE SO MAD ABOUT?!
I DON'T KNOW!
HE SUDDENLY FLEW INTO A RAGE...
OH, MY GOD. LIKE, YOU'RE GONNA HULK OUT JUST BECAUSE YOU LOST?
LAME-FACE!
SHUT UP!!
UTTA Y WAY, YOU TUPID ATS!!

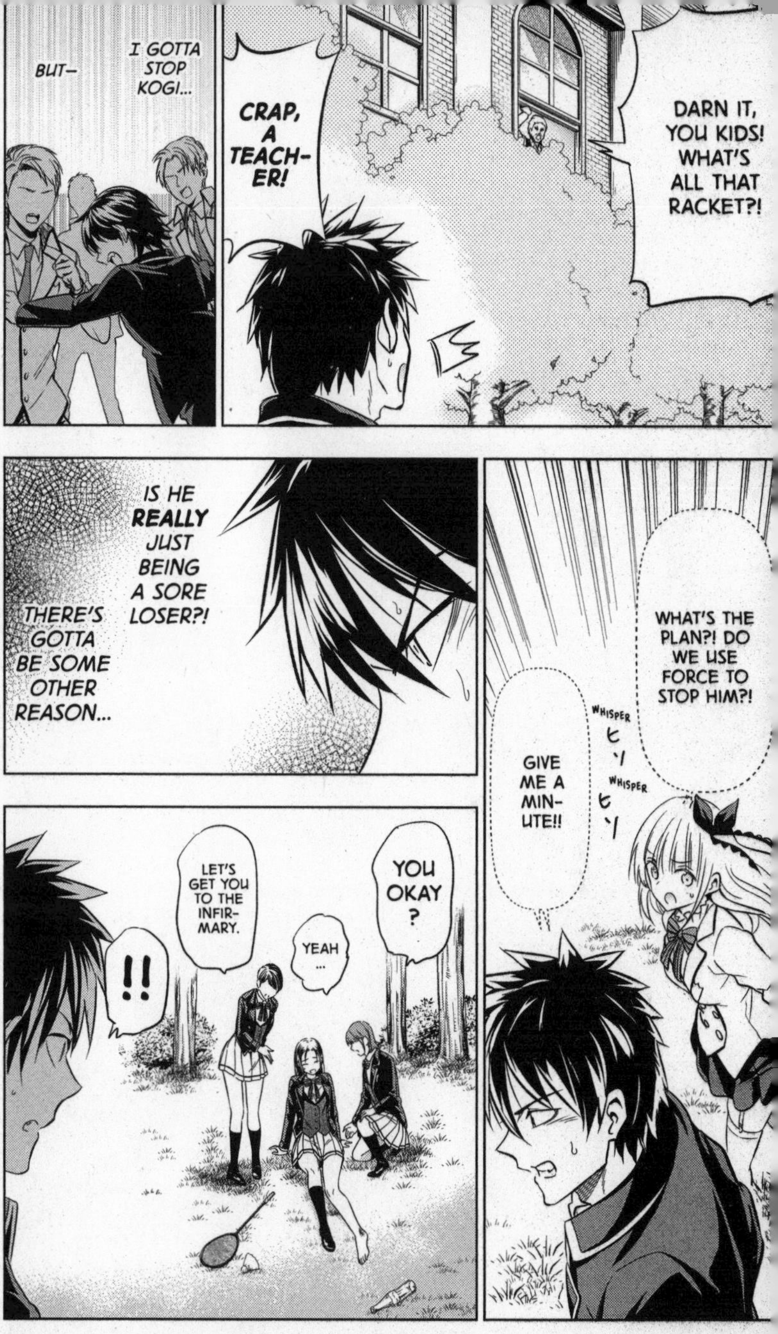
DARN IT, YOU KIDS! WHAT'S ALL THAT RACKET?!
CRAP, A TEACHER-ER!
I GOTTA STOP KOGI...
BUT—
WHAT'S THE PLAN?! DO WE USE FORCE TO STOP HIM?!
WHISPER
ヒソ
WHISPER
ヒソ
GIVE ME A MIN-UTE!!
IS HE REALLY JUST BEING A SORE LOSER?!
THERE'S GOTTA BE SOME OTHER REASON...
YOU OKAY?
YEAH...
LET'S GET YOU TO THE INFIR-MARY.
!!

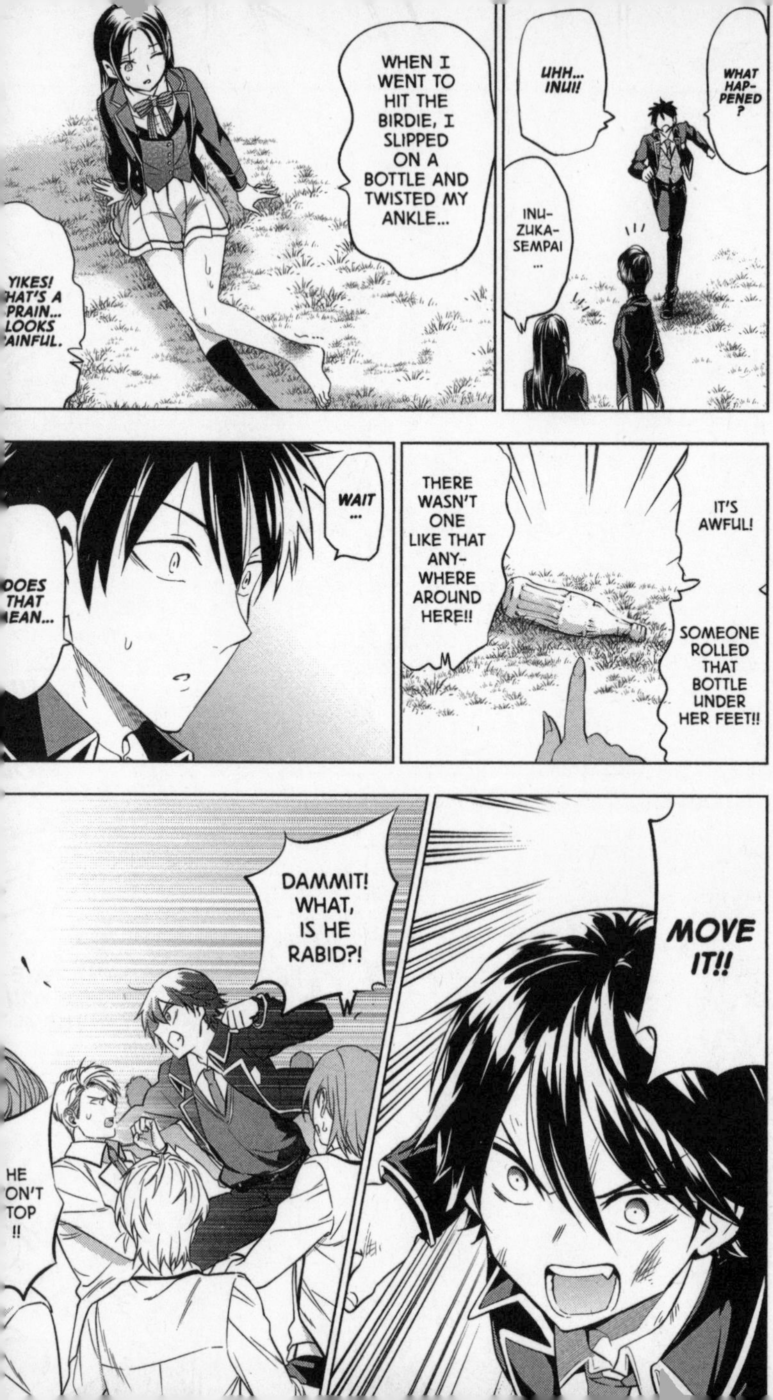
WHAT HAP-PENED ?
UHH... INUI!
INU-ZUKA-SEMPAI ...
WHEN I WENT TO HIT THE BIRDIE, I SLIPPED ON A BOTTLE AND TWISTED MY ANKLE...
YIKES! HAT'S A PRAIN... LOOKS AINFUL.
IT'S AWFUL!
THERE WASN'T ONE LIKE THAT ANY-WHERE AROUND HERE!!
SOMEONE ROLLED THAT BOTTLE UNDER HER FEET!!
WAIT ...
DOES THAT EAN...
MOVE IT!!
DAMMIT! WHAT, IS HE RABID?!
HE ON'T TOP !!

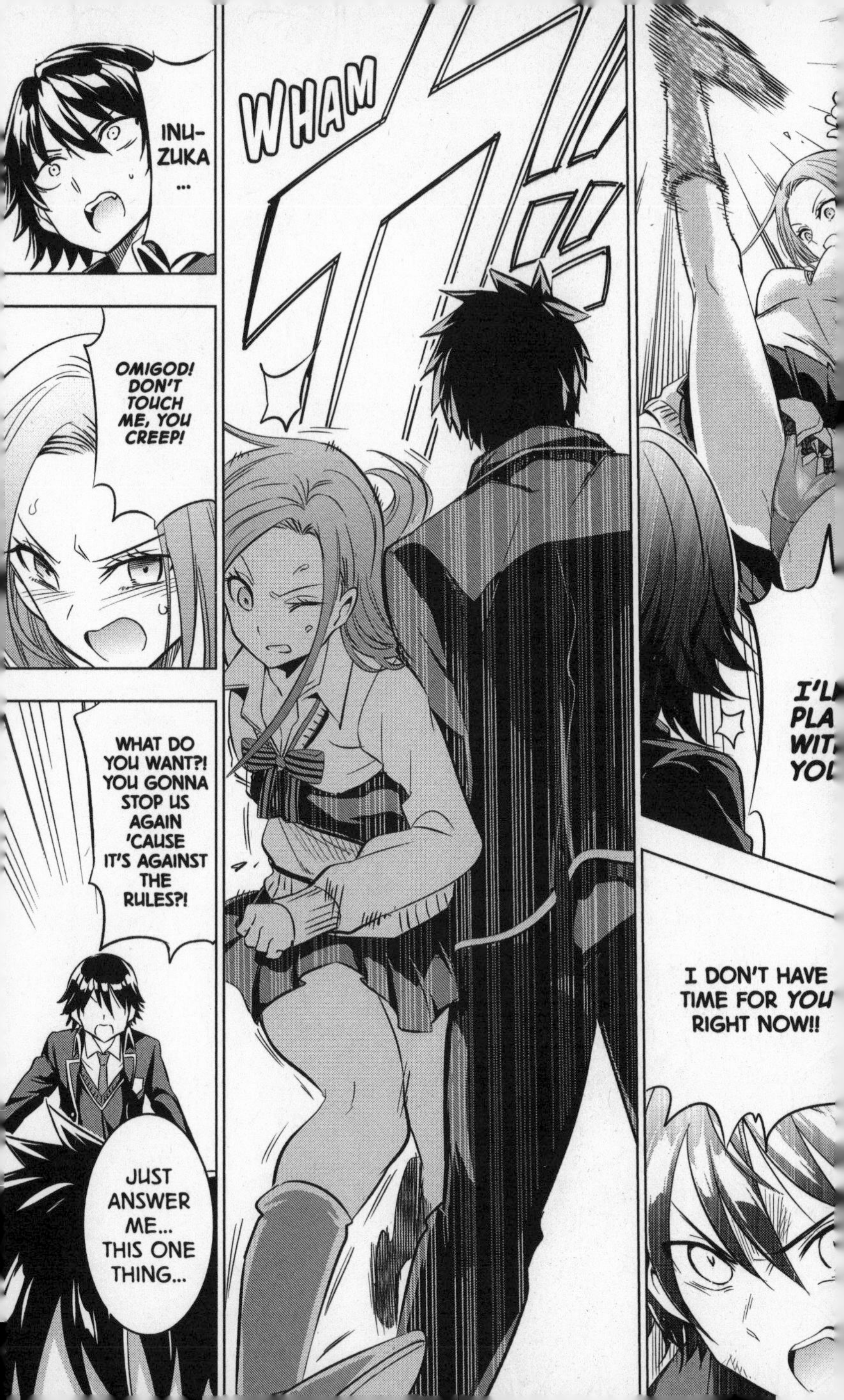
I DON'T HAVE TIME FOR YOU RIGHT NOW!!
WHAM
INU-ZUKA...
OMIGOD! DON'T TOUCH ME, YOU CREEP!
WHAT DO YOU WANT?! YOU GONNA STOP US AGAIN 'CAUSE IT'S AGAINST THE RULES?!
JUST ANSWER ME... THIS ONE THING...

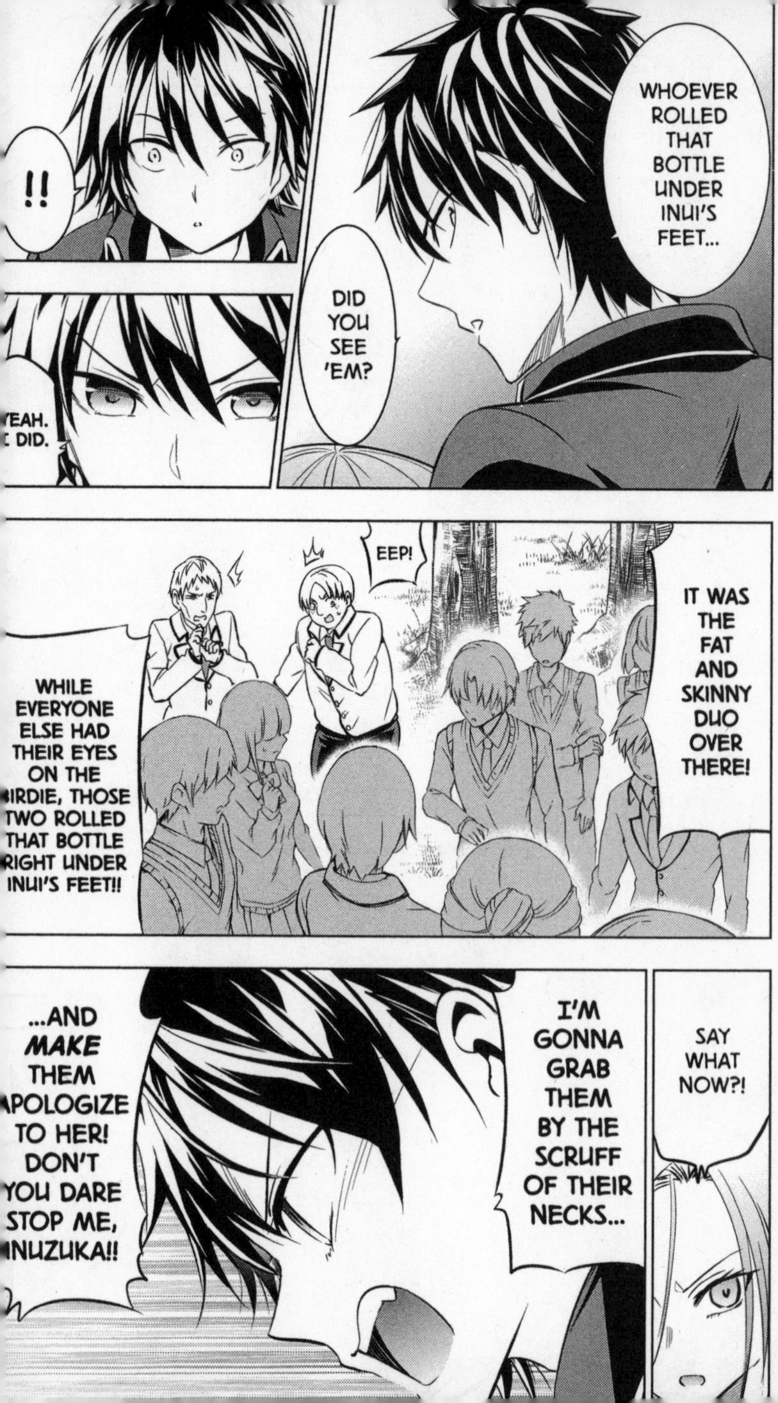
WHOEVER ROLLED THAT BOTTLE UNDER INUI'S FEET...
DID YOU SEE 'EM?
!!
YEAH. I DID.
IT WAS THE FAT AND SKINNY DUO OVER THERE!
EEP!
WHILE EVERYONE ELSE HAD THEIR EYES ON THE BIRDIE, THOSE TWO ROLLED THAT BOTTLE RIGHT UNDER INUI'S FEET!!
SAY WHAT NOW?!
I'M GONNA GRAB THEM BY THE SCRUFF OF THEIR NECKS...
...AND *MAKE* THEM APOLOGIZE TO HER! DON'T YOU DARE STOP ME, INUZUKA!!

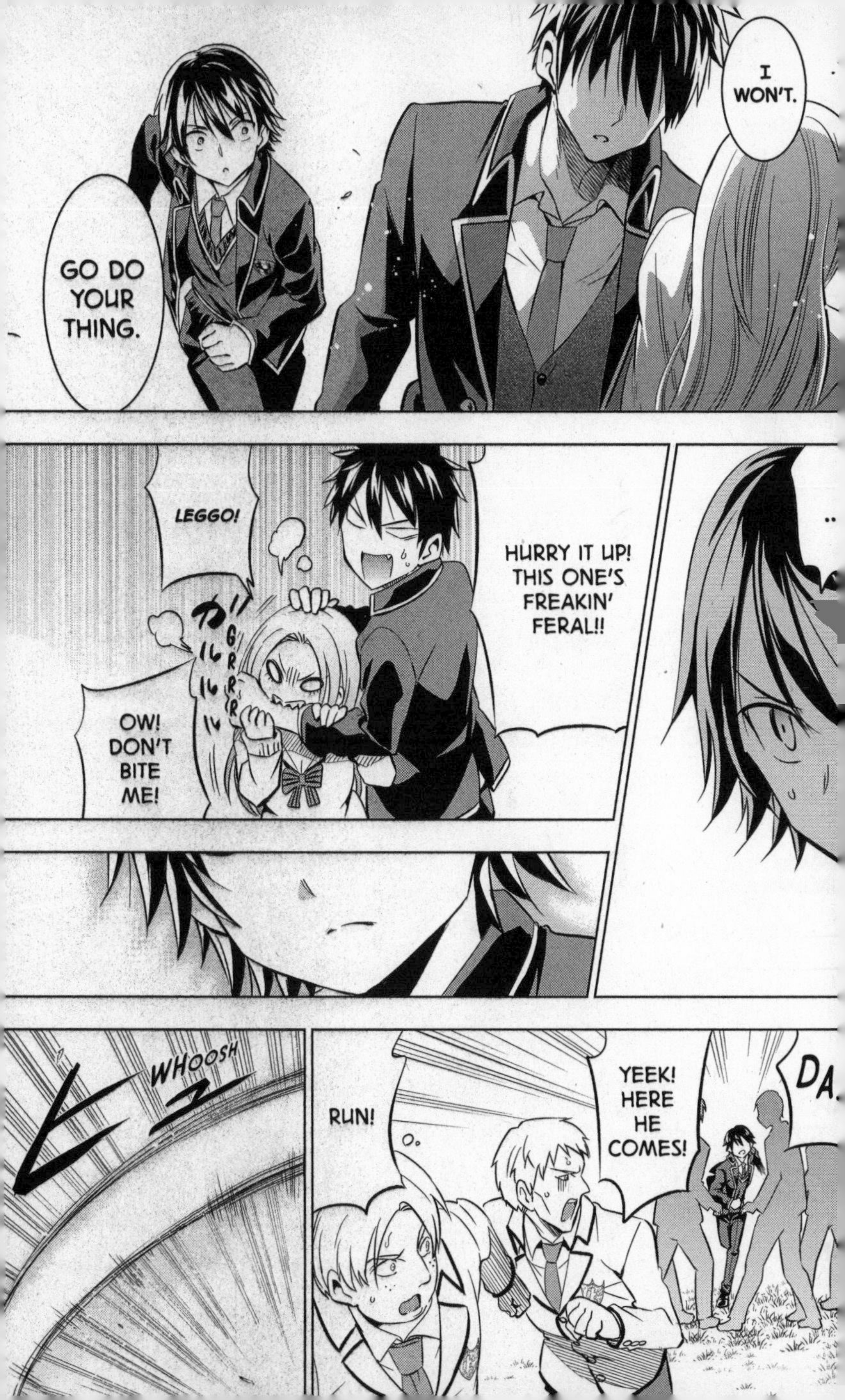
I WON'T.
GO DO YOUR THING.
..
HURRY IT UP! THIS ONE'S FREAKIN' FERAL!!
LEGGO!
GRRRR
OW! DON'T BITE ME!
DA...
YEEK! HERE HE COMES!
RUN!
WHOOSH

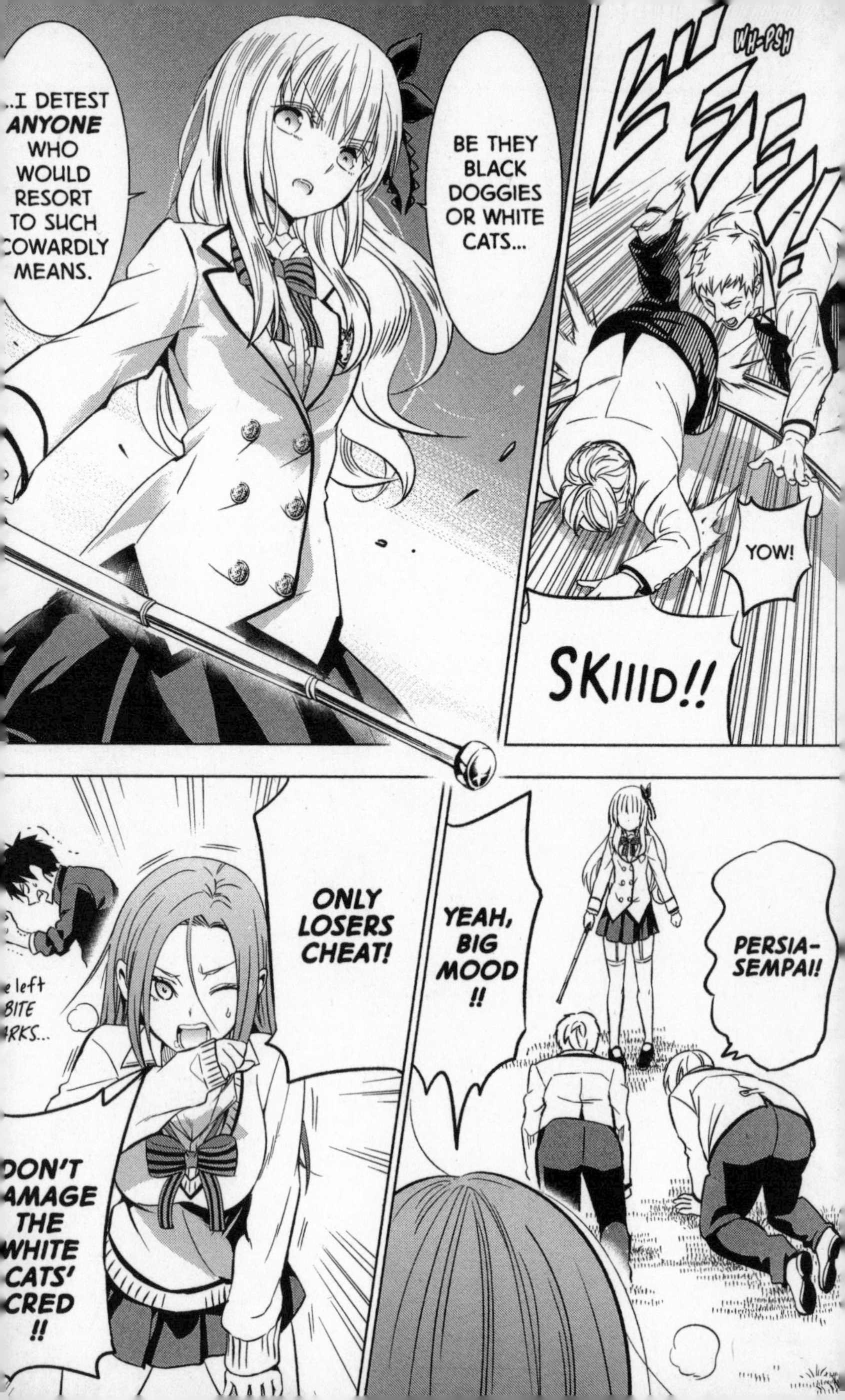
WH-PSH
YOW!
SKIIID!!
BE THEY BLACK DOGGIES OR WHITE CATS...
..I DETEST ANYONE WHO WOULD RESORT TO SUCH COWARDLY MEANS.
PERSIA-SEMPAI!
YEAH, BIG MOOD!!
ONLY LOSERS CHEAT!
e left BITE RKS...
ON'T AMAGE THE WHITE CATS' CRED!!

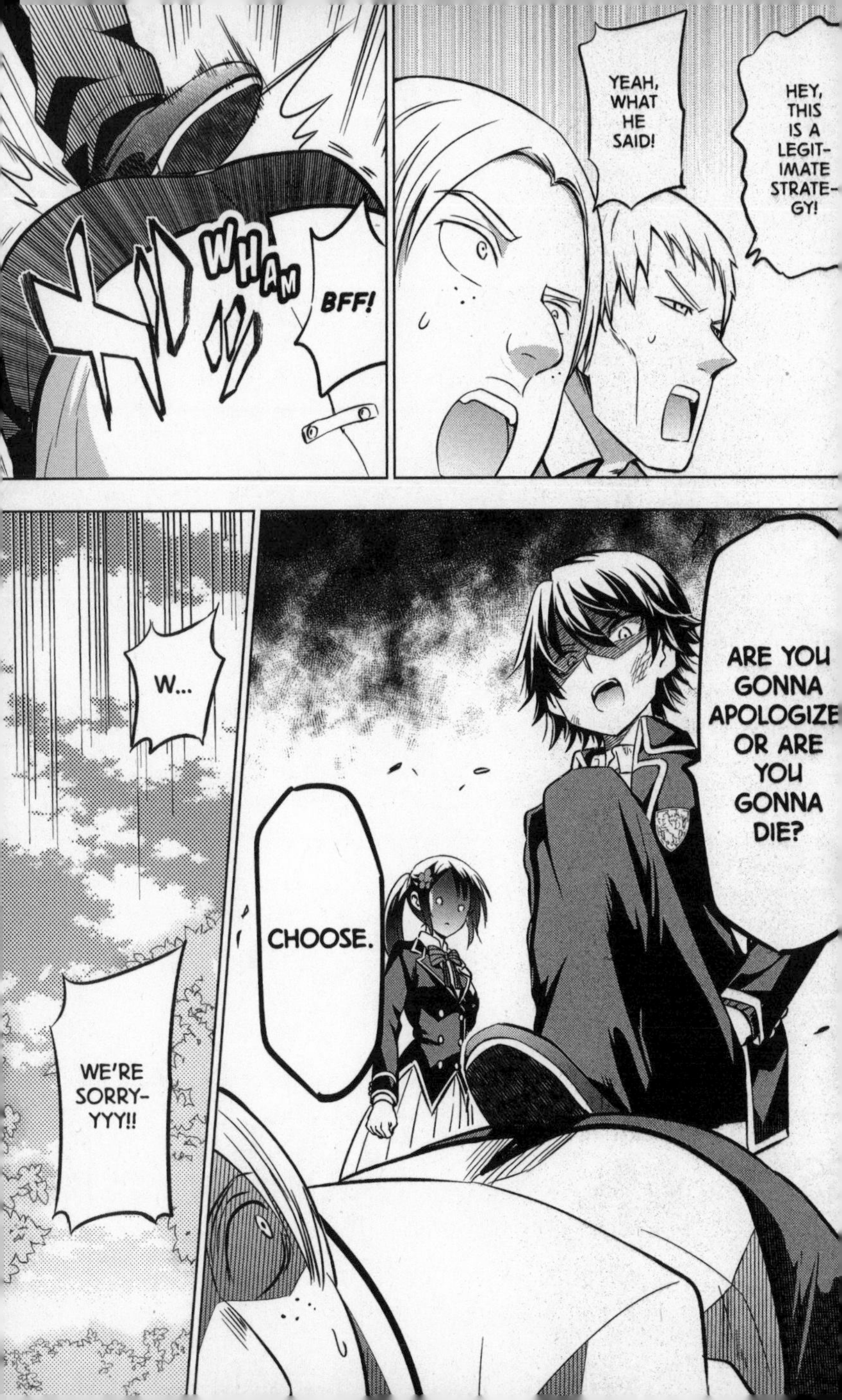
HEY, THIS IS A LEGIT-IMATE STRATE-GY!
YEAH, WHAT HE SAID!
WHAM
BFF!
ARE YOU GONNA APOLOGIZE OR ARE YOU GONNA DIE?
CHOOSE.
W...
WE'RE SORRY-YYY!!

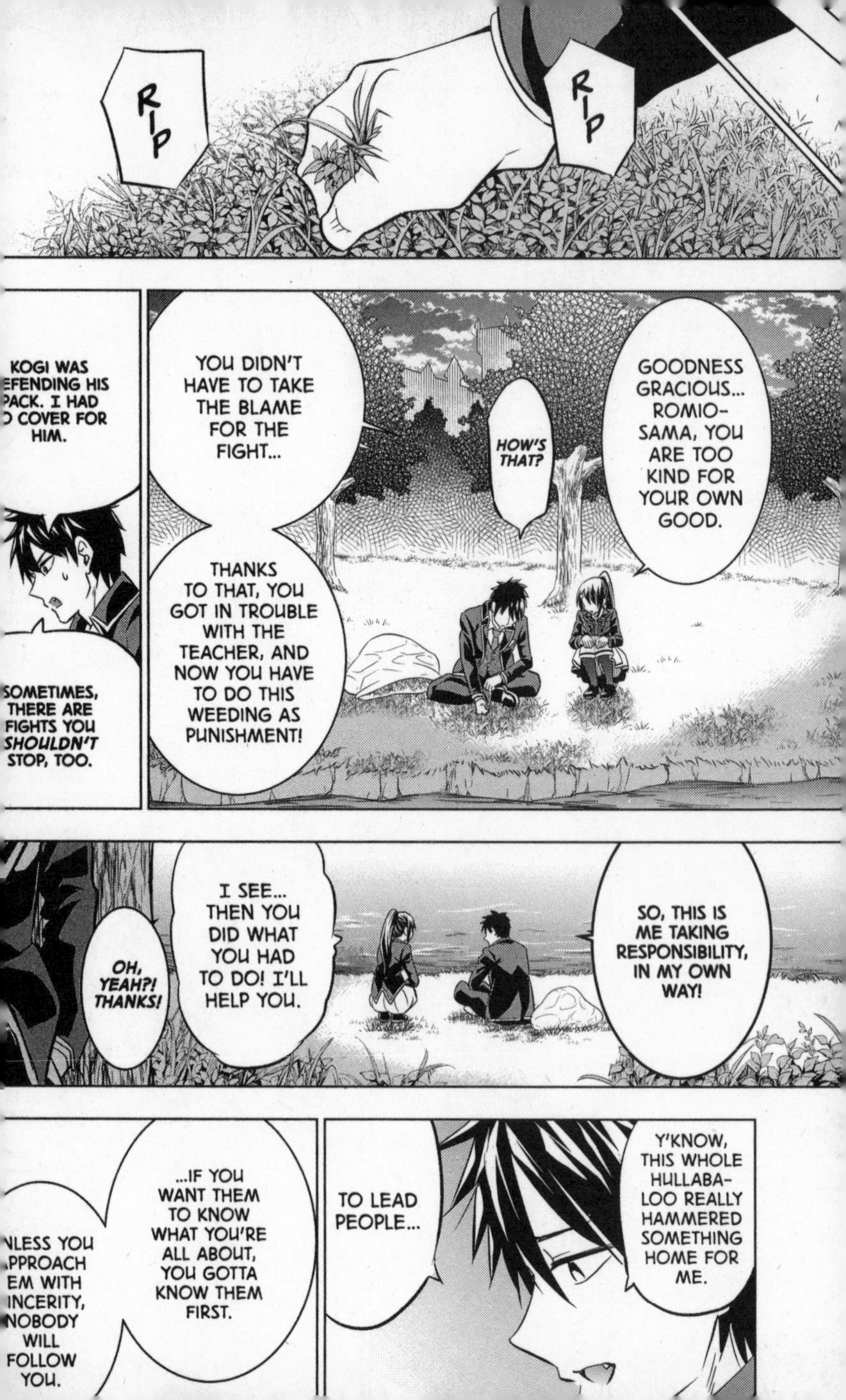
RIP
RIP
GOODNESS GRACIOUS... ROMIO-SAMA, YOU ARE TOO KIND FOR YOUR OWN GOOD.
HOW'S THAT?
YOU DIDN'T HAVE TO TAKE THE BLAME FOR THE FIGHT...
THANKS TO THAT, YOU GOT IN TROUBLE WITH THE TEACHER, AND NOW YOU HAVE TO DO THIS WEEDING AS PUNISHMENT!
KOGI WAS EFENDING HIS PACK. I HAD O COVER FOR HIM.
SOMETIMES, THERE ARE FIGHTS YOU SHOULDN'T STOP, TOO.
SO, THIS IS ME TAKING RESPONSIBILITY, IN MY OWN WAY!
I SEE... THEN YOU DID WHAT YOU HAD TO DO! I'LL HELP YOU.
OH, YEAH?! THANKS!
Y'KNOW, THIS WHOLE HULLABALOO REALLY HAMMERED SOMETHING HOME FOR ME.
TO LEAD PEOPLE...
...IF YOU WANT THEM TO KNOW WHAT YOU'RE ALL ABOUT, YOU GOTTA KNOW THEM FIRST.
NLESS YOU PPROACH EM WITH INCERITY, NOBODY WILL FOLLOW YOU.

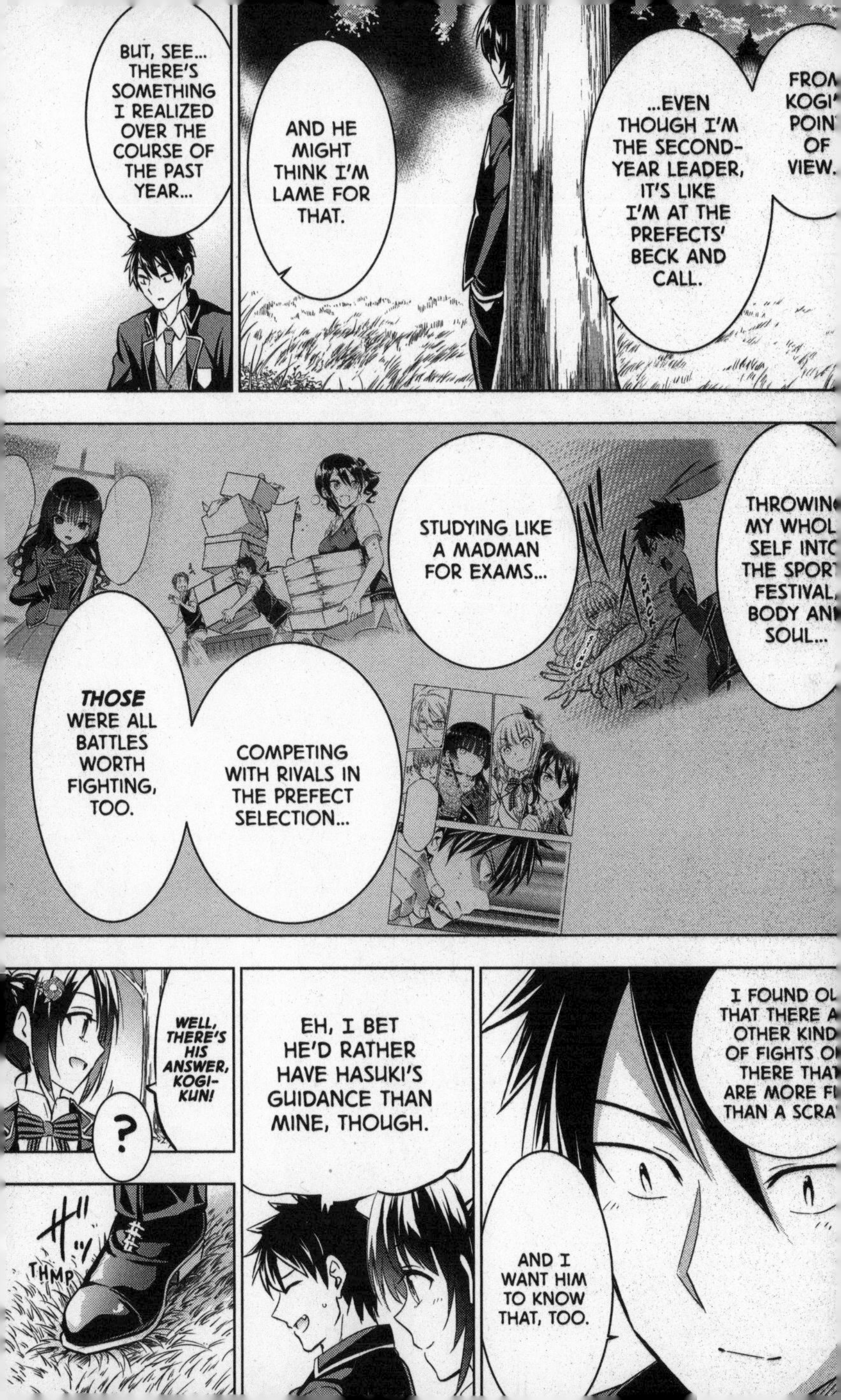
FROM KOGI' POINT OF VIEW.
...EVEN THOUGH I'M THE SECOND-YEAR LEADER, IT'S LIKE I'M AT THE PREFECTS' BECK AND CALL.
AND HE MIGHT THINK I'M LAME FOR THAT.
BUT, SEE... THERE'S SOMETHING I REALIZED OVER THE COURSE OF THE PAST YEAR...
THROWIN MY WHOL SELF INTO THE SPORT FESTIVAL, BODY AN SOUL...
STUDYING LIKE A MADMAN FOR EXAMS...
COMPETING WITH RIVALS IN THE PREFECT SELECTION...
THOSE WERE ALL BATTLES WORTH FIGHTING, TOO.
I FOUND OU THAT THERE A OTHER KIND OF FIGHTS O THERE THAT ARE MORE F THAN A SCRA
AND I WANT HIM TO KNOW THAT, TOO.
EH, I BET HE'D RATHER HAVE HASUKI'S GUIDANCE THAN MINE, THOUGH.
WELL, THERE'S HIS ANSWER, KOGI-KUN!
?
THMP

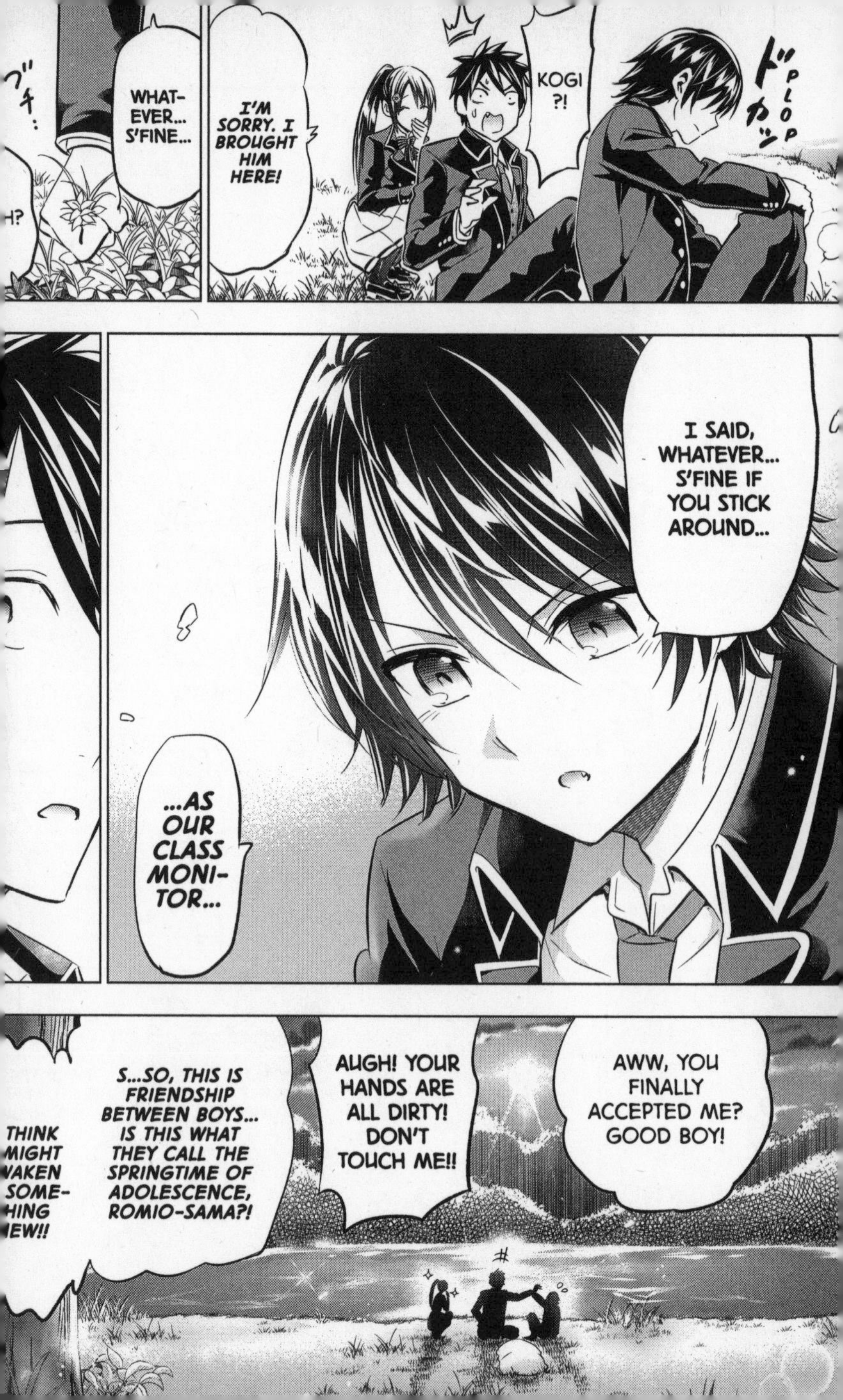
ドカッ
PLOP
KOGI ?!
I'M SORRY. I BROUGHT HIM HERE!
WHAT-EVER... S'FINE...
ブチ…
H?
I SAID, WHATEVER... S'FINE IF YOU STICK AROUND...
...AS OUR CLASS MONI-TOR...
AWW, YOU FINALLY ACCEPTED ME? GOOD BOY!
AUGH! YOUR HANDS ARE ALL DIRTY! DON'T TOUCH ME!!
S...SO, THIS IS FRIENDSHIP BETWEEN BOYS... IS THIS WHAT THEY CALL THE SPRINGTIME OF ADOLESCENCE, ROMIO-SAMA?!
THINK MIGHT VAKEN SOME-HING EW!!

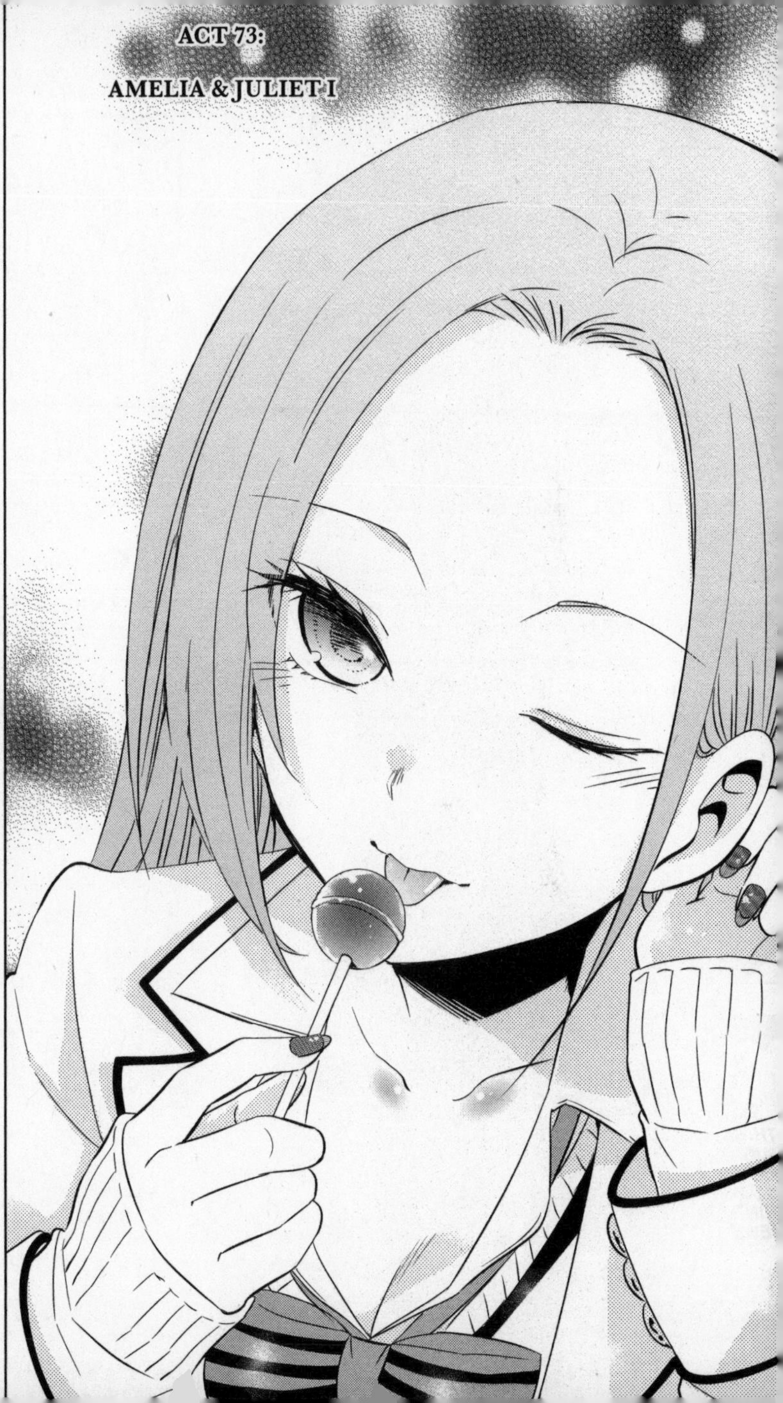
ACT 73:
AMELIA & JULIET I

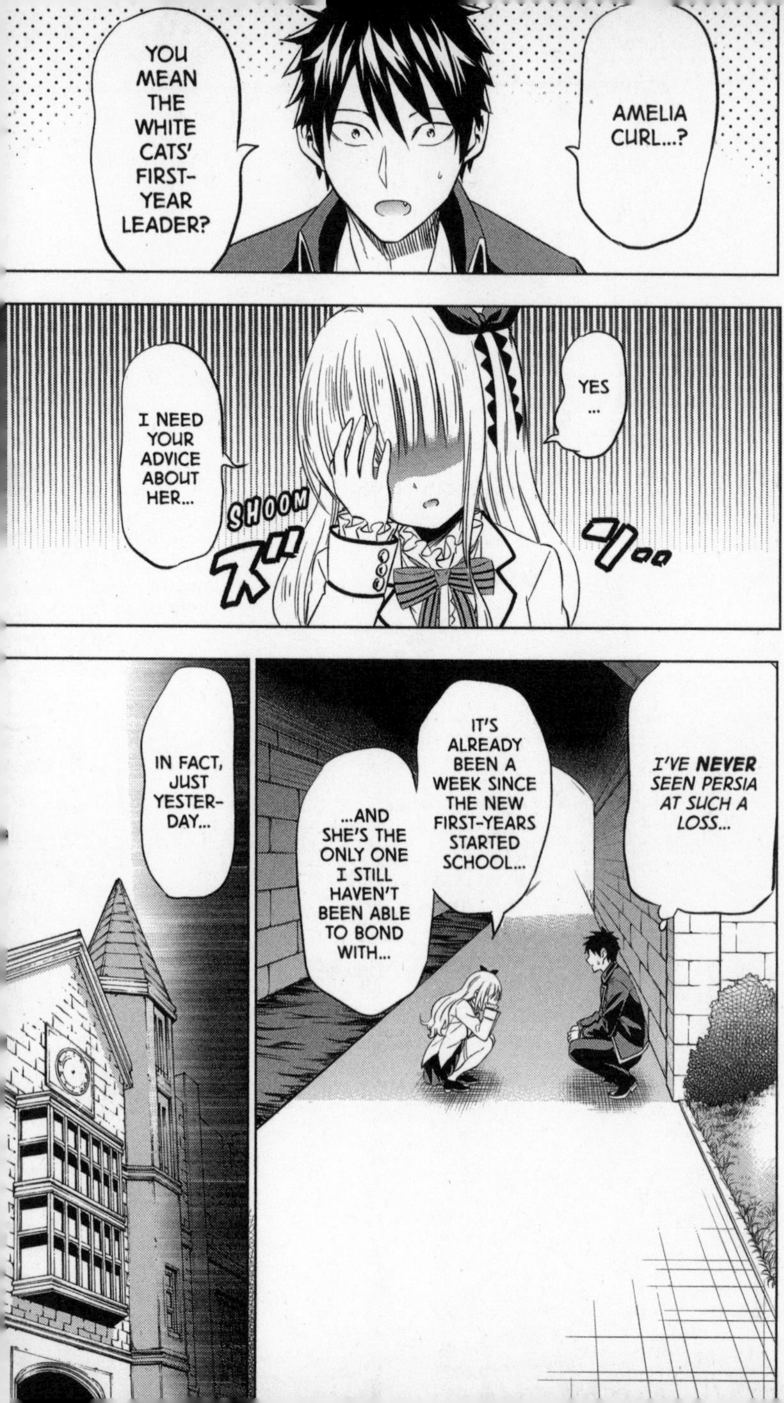

AMELIA CURL...?
YOU MEAN THE WHITE CATS' FIRST-YEAR LEADER?
YES ...
I NEED YOUR ADVICE ABOUT HER...
SHOOM
I'VE NEVER SEEN PERSIA AT SUCH A LOSS...
IT'S ALREADY BEEN A WEEK SINCE THE NEW FIRST-YEARS STARTED SCHOOL...
...AND SHE'S THE ONLY ONE I STILL HAVEN'T BEEN ABLE TO BOND WITH...
IN FACT, JUST YESTER-DAY...

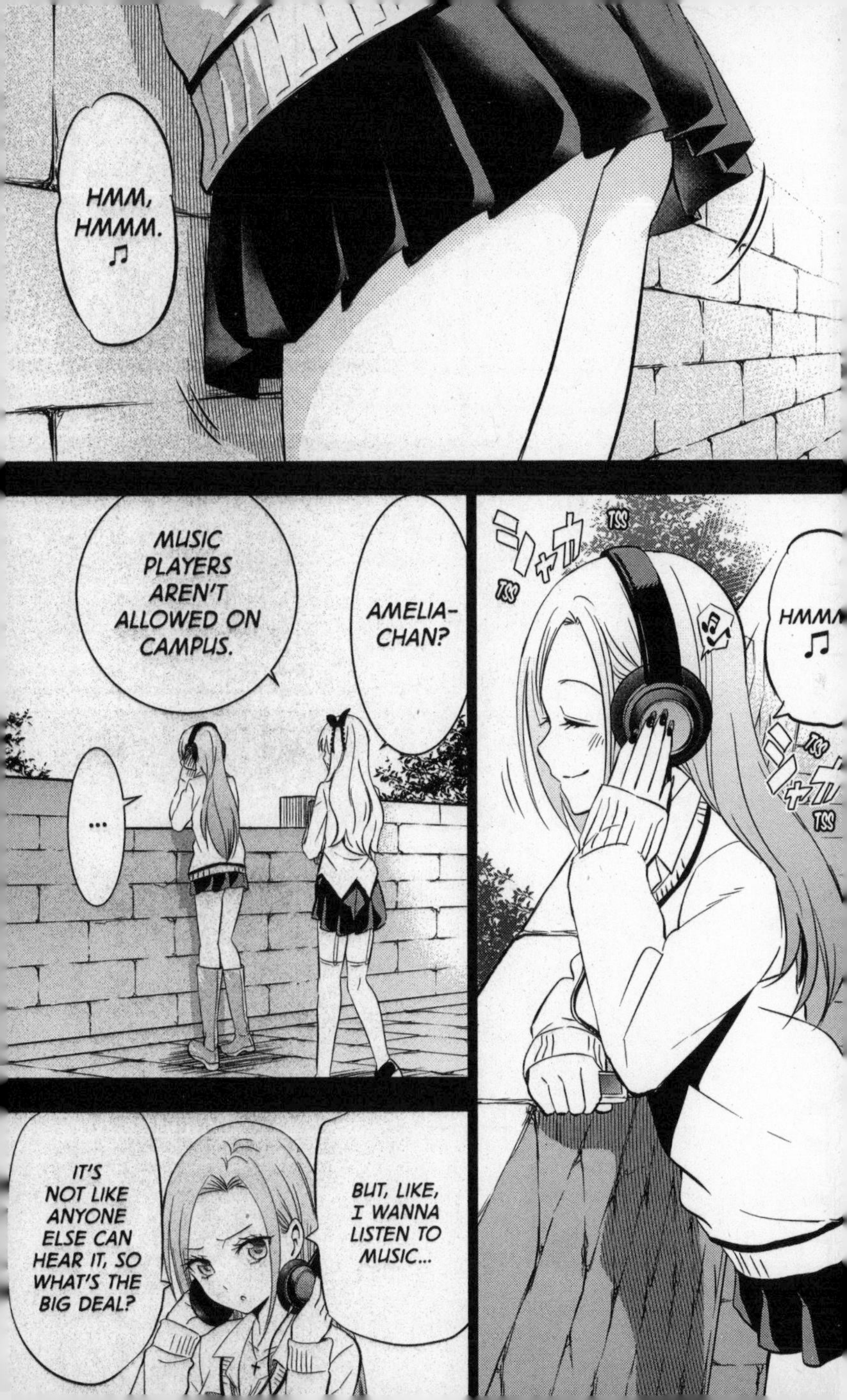
HMM, HMMM. ♫
TSS
TSS
HMMM ♫
TSS
TSS
AMELIA-CHAN?
MUSIC PLAYERS AREN'T ALLOWED ON CAMPUS.
...
BUT, LIKE, I WANNA LISTEN TO MUSIC...
IT'S NOT LIKE ANYONE ELSE CAN HEAR IT, SO WHAT'S THE BIG DEAL?

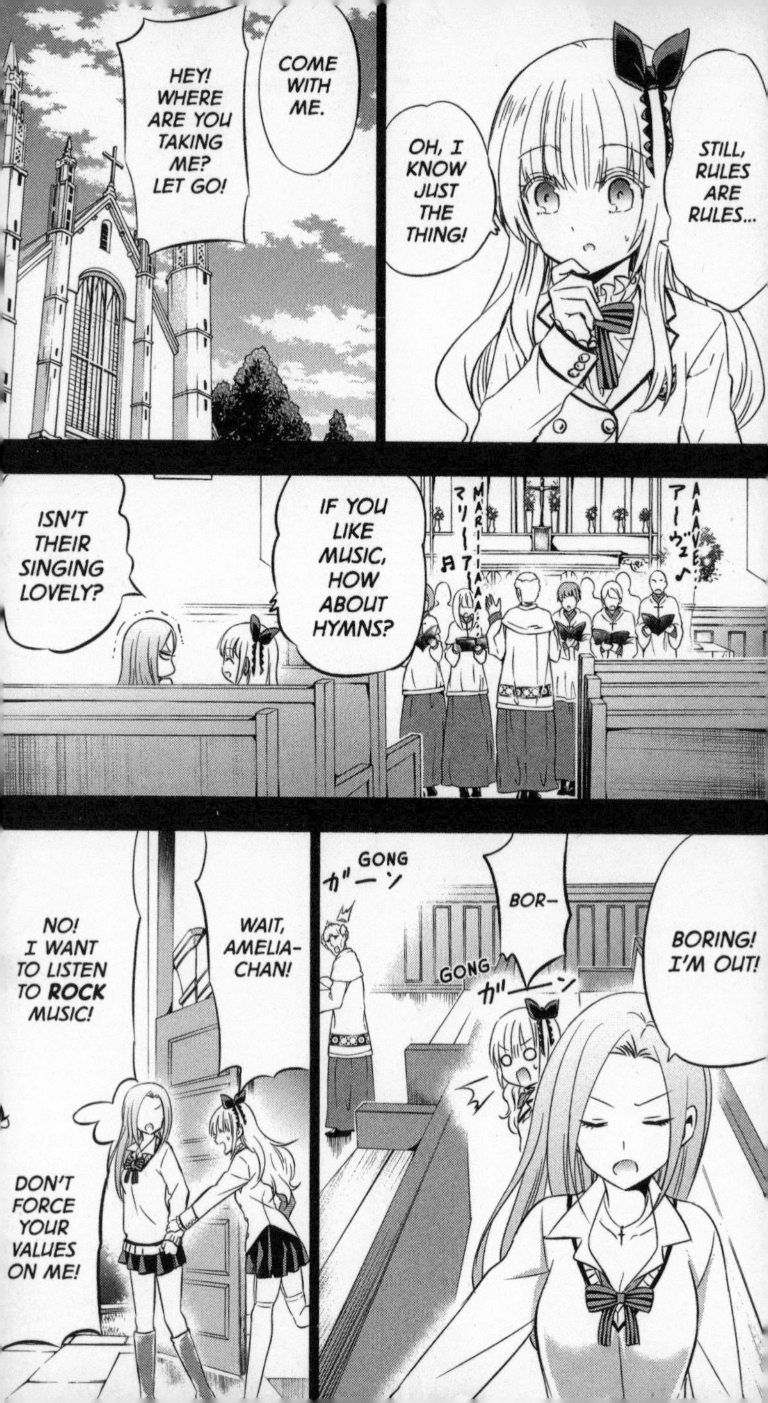
STILL, RULES ARE RULES...
OH, I KNOW JUST THE THING!
COME WITH ME.
HEY! WHERE ARE YOU TAKING ME? LET GO!
AAAVE...
アーヴェ
MARI-AAA...
マリーア
IF YOU LIKE MUSIC, HOW ABOUT HYMNS?
ISN'T THEIR SINGING LOVELY?
BOR-
BORING! I'M OUT!
GONG
ガーン
GONG
ガーン
WAIT, AMELIA-CHAN!
NO! I WANT TO LISTEN TO **ROCK** MUSIC!
DON'T FORCE YOUR VALUES ON ME!

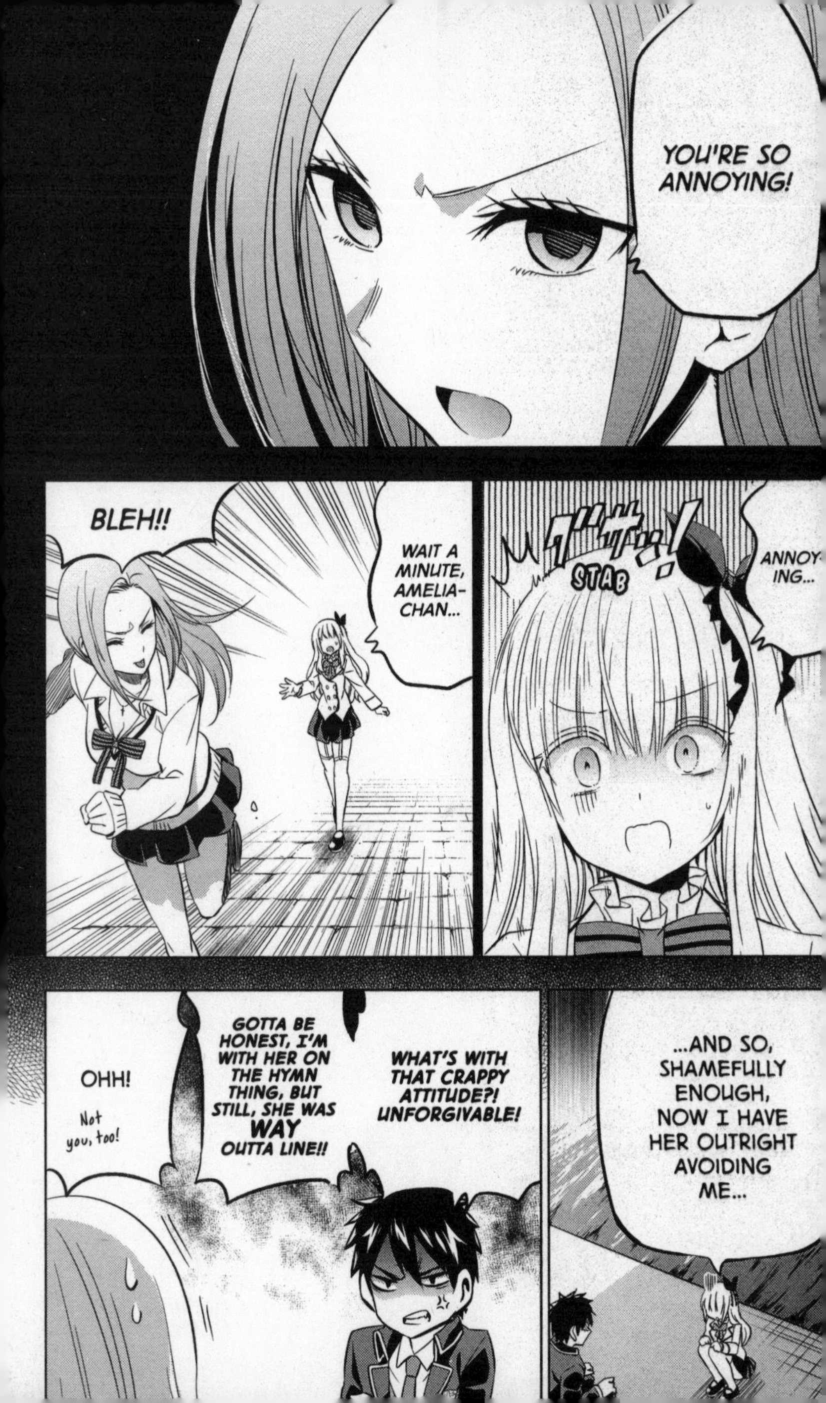
YOU'RE SO ANNOYING!
STAB
ANNOY-ING...
WAIT A MINUTE, AMELIA-CHAN...
BLEH!!
...AND SO, SHAMEFULLY ENOUGH, NOW I HAVE HER OUTRIGHT AVOIDING ME...
WHAT'S WITH THAT CRAPPY ATTITUDE?! UNFORGIVABLE!
GOTTA BE HONEST, I'M WITH HER ON THE HYMN THING, BUT STILL, SHE WAS WAY OUTTA LINE!!
OHH!
Not you, too!

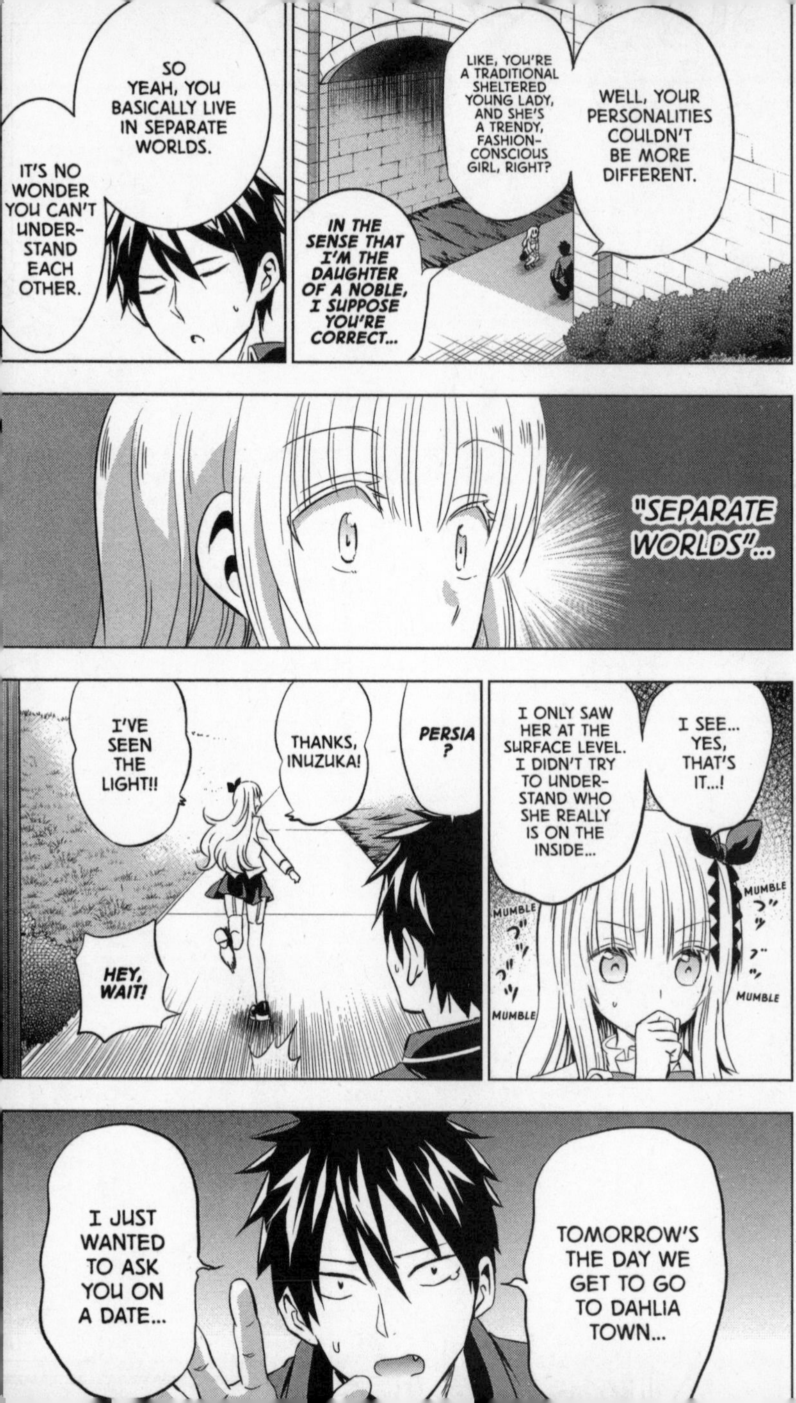
WELL, YOUR PERSONALITIES COULDN'T BE MORE DIFFERENT.
LIKE, YOU'RE A TRADITIONAL SHELTERED YOUNG LADY, AND SHE'S A TRENDY, FASHION-CONSCIOUS GIRL, RIGHT?
IN THE SENSE THAT I'M THE DAUGHTER OF A NOBLE, I SUPPOSE YOU'RE CORRECT...
SO YEAH, YOU BASICALLY LIVE IN SEPARATE WORLDS.
IT'S NO WONDER YOU CAN'T UNDER-STAND EACH OTHER.
"SEPARATE WORLDS"...
I SEE... YES, THAT'S IT...!
I ONLY SAW HER AT THE SURFACE LEVEL. I DIDN'T TRY TO UNDER-STAND WHO SHE REALLY IS ON THE INSIDE...
MUMBLE
MUMBLE
MUMBLE
MUMBLE
PERSIA?
THANKS, INUZUKA!
I'VE SEEN THE LIGHT!!
HEY, WAIT!
TOMORROW'S THE DAY WE GET TO GO TO DAHLIA TOWN...
I JUST WANTED TO ASK YOU ON A DATE...

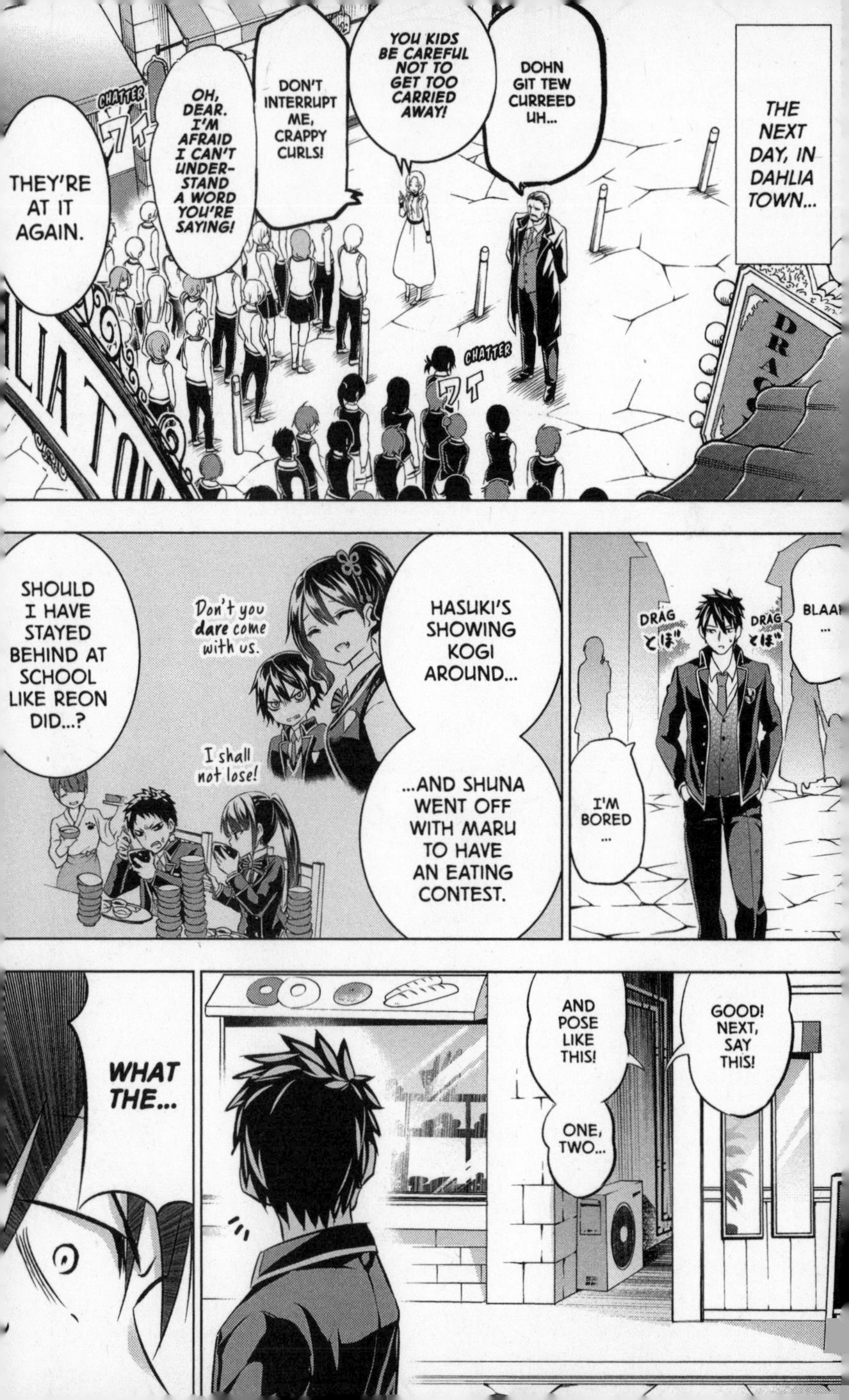
THE NEXT DAY, IN DAHLIA TOWN...
DOHN GIT TEW CURREED UH...
YOU KIDS BE CAREFUL NOT TO GET TOO CARRIED AWAY!
DON'T INTERRUPT ME, CRAPPY CURLS!
OH, DEAR. I'M AFRAID I CAN'T UNDERSTAND A WORD YOU'RE SAYING!
CHATTER
CHATTER
THEY'RE AT IT AGAIN.
DRAG
DRAG
I'M BORED...
HASUKI'S SHOWING KOGI AROUND...
...AND SHUNA WENT OFF WITH MARU TO HAVE AN EATING CONTEST.
Don't you dare come with us.
I shall not lose!
SHOULD I HAVE STAYED BEHIND AT SCHOOL LIKE REON DID...?
GOOD! NEXT, SAY THIS!
AND POSE LIKE THIS!
ONE, TWO...
WHAT THE...

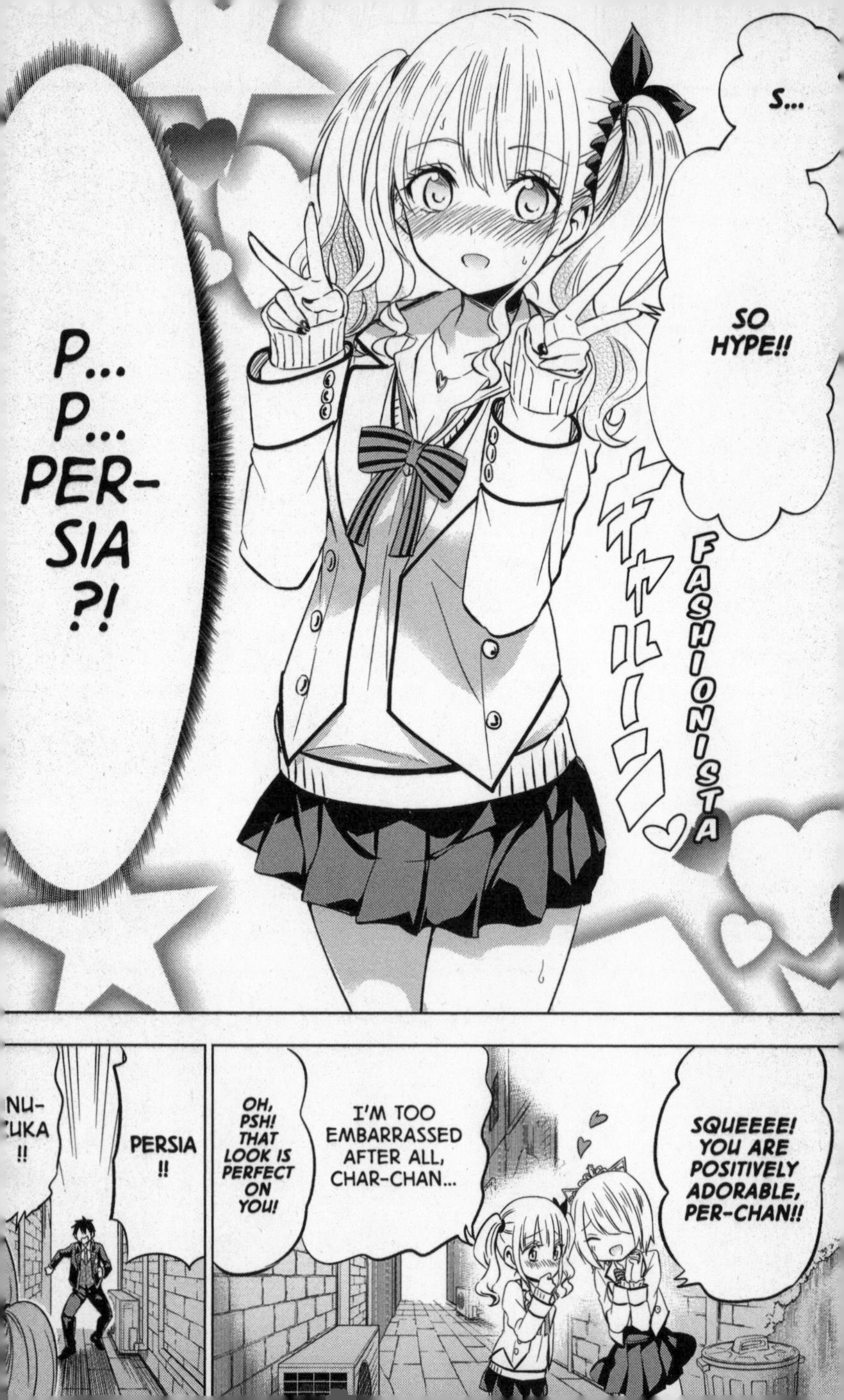
S... SO HYPE!!
キャルーン
FASHIONISTA
P... P... PER-SIA?!
SQUEEEE! YOU ARE POSITIVELY ADORABLE, PER-CHAN!!
I'M TOO EMBARRASSED AFTER ALL, CHAR-CHAN...
OH, PSH! THAT LOOK IS PERFECT ON YOU!
PERSIA!!
NU- UKA!!

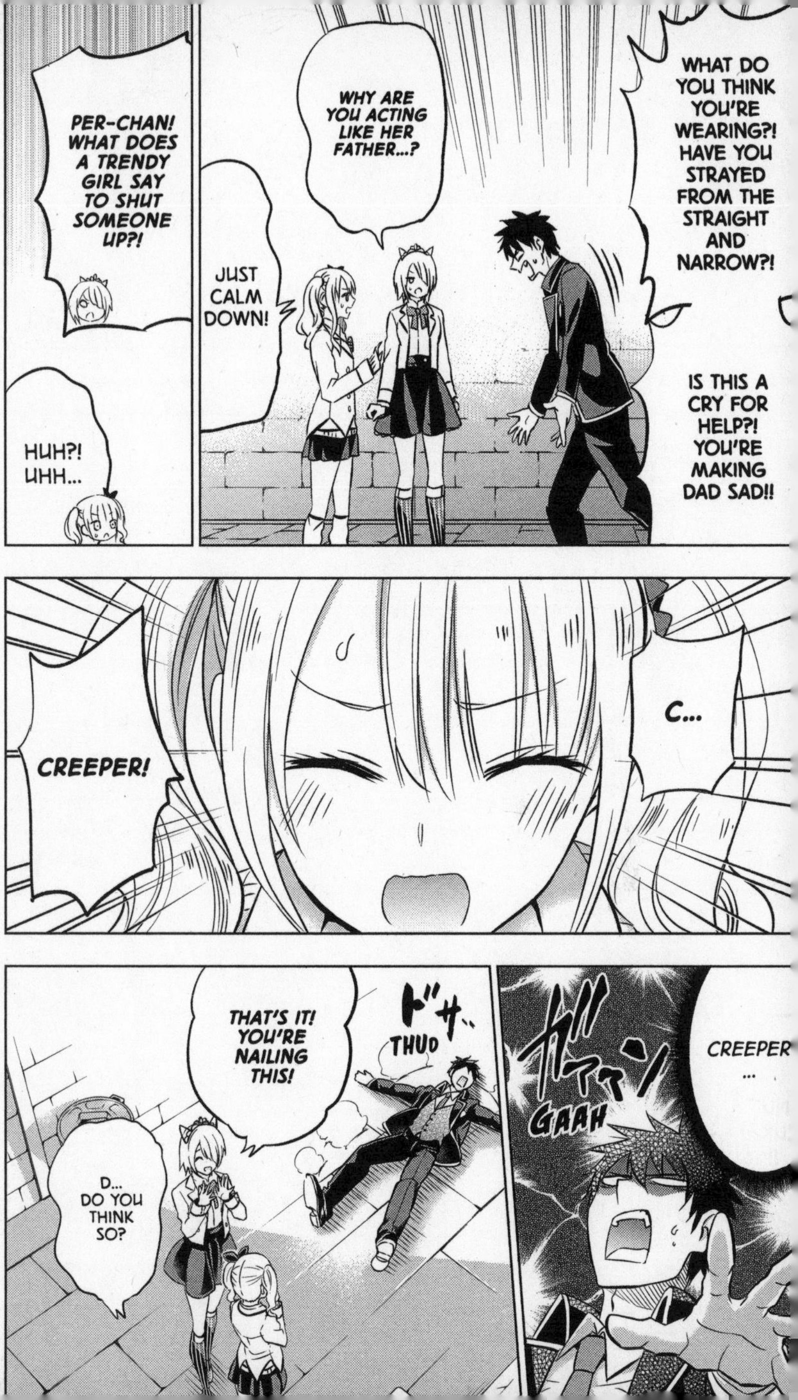
WHAT DO YOU THINK YOU'RE WEARING?! HAVE YOU STRAYED FROM THE STRAIGHT AND NARROW?!
IS THIS A CRY FOR HELP?! YOU'RE MAKING DAD SAD!!
WHY ARE YOU ACTING LIKE HER FATHER...?
JUST CALM DOWN!
PER-CHAN! WHAT DOES A TRENDY GIRL SAY TO SHUT SOMEONE UP?!
HUH?! UHH...
C...
CREEPER!
ガァン
GAAH
CREEPER ...
ドサ
THUD
THAT'S IT! YOU'RE NAILING THIS!
D... DO YOU THINK SO?

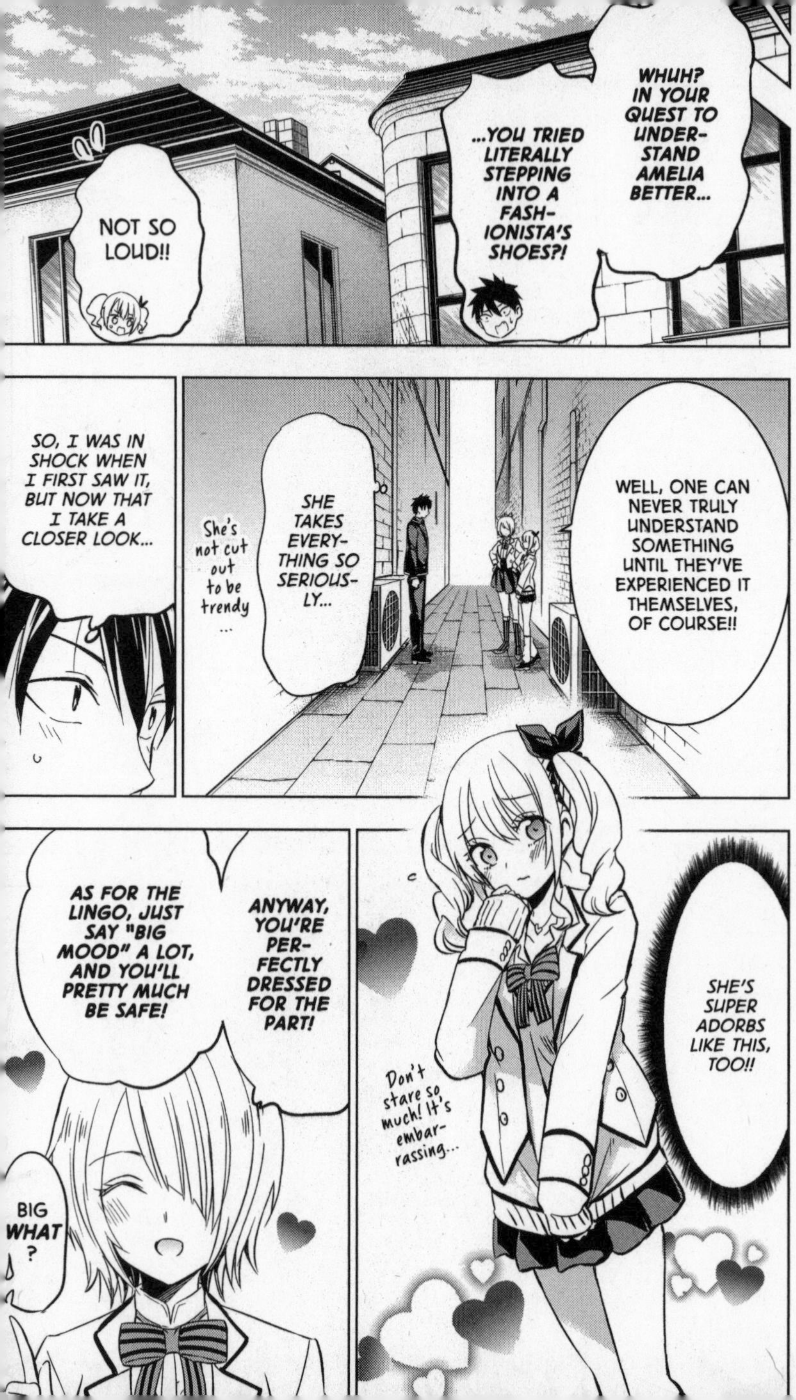
WHUH? IN YOUR QUEST TO UNDERSTAND AMELIA BETTER...
...YOU TRIED LITERALLY STEPPING INTO A FASHIONISTA'S SHOES?!
NOT SO LOUD!!
WELL, ONE CAN NEVER TRULY UNDERSTAND SOMETHING UNTIL THEY'VE EXPERIENCED IT THEMSELVES, OF COURSE!!
SHE TAKES EVERYTHING SO SERIOUSLY...
She's not cut out to be trendy...
SO, I WAS IN SHOCK WHEN I FIRST SAW IT, BUT NOW THAT I TAKE A CLOSER LOOK...
SHE'S SUPER ADORBS LIKE THIS, TOO!!
Don't stare so much! It's embarrassing...
ANYWAY, YOU'RE PERFECTLY DRESSED FOR THE PART!
AS FOR THE LINGO, JUST SAY "BIG MOOD" A LOT, AND YOU'LL PRETTY MUCH BE SAFE!
BIG WHAT?

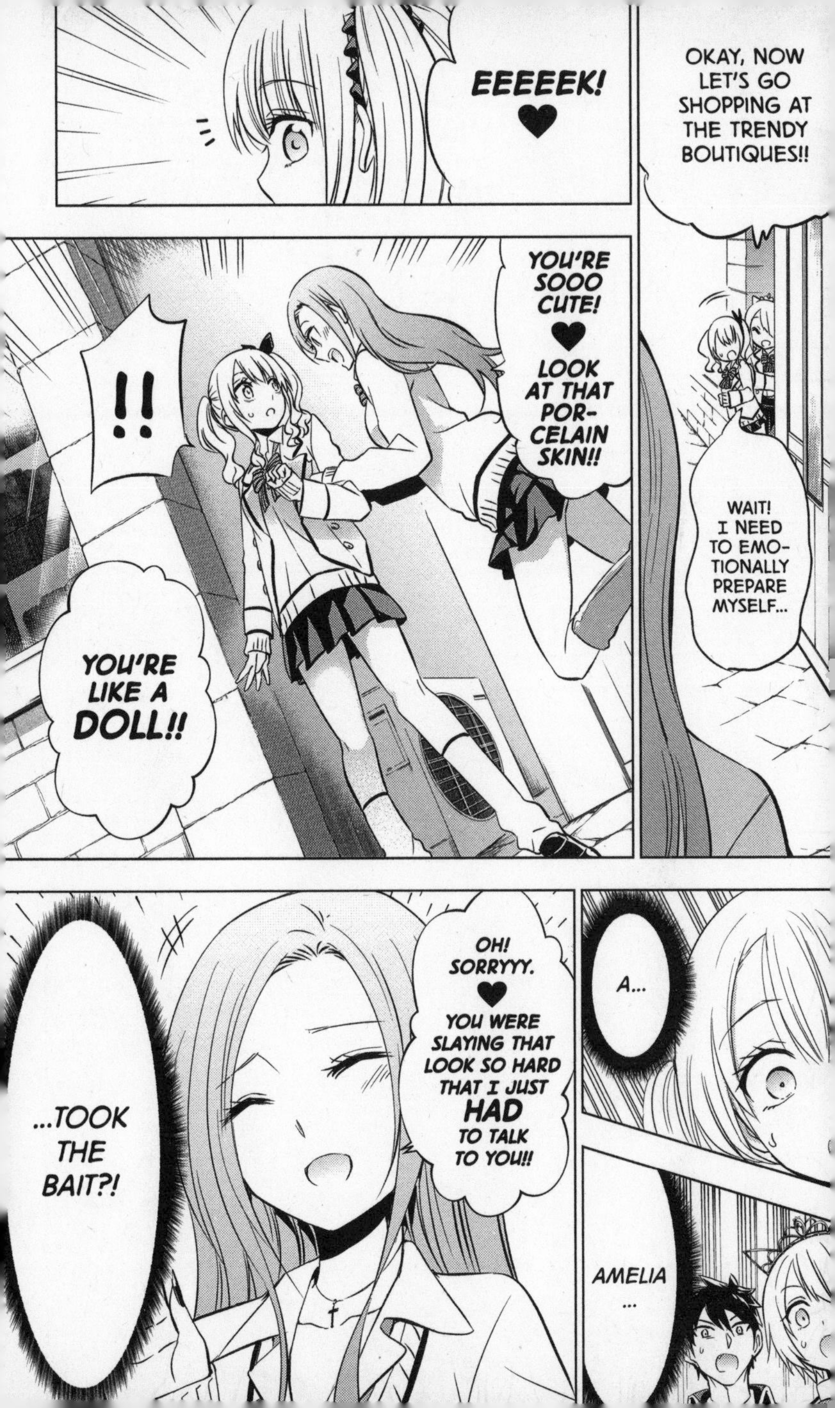
OKAY, NOW LET'S GO SHOPPING AT THE TRENDY BOUTIQUES!!
WAIT! I NEED TO EMO- TIONALLY PREPARE MYSELF...
EEEEEK! ♥
YOU'RE SOOO CUTE! ♥ LOOK AT THAT POR- CELAIN SKIN!!
!!
YOU'RE LIKE A DOLL!!
A...
AMELIA ...
OH! SORRYYY. ♥ YOU WERE SLAYING THAT LOOK SO HARD THAT I JUST HAD TO TALK TO YOU!!
...TOOK THE BAIT?!

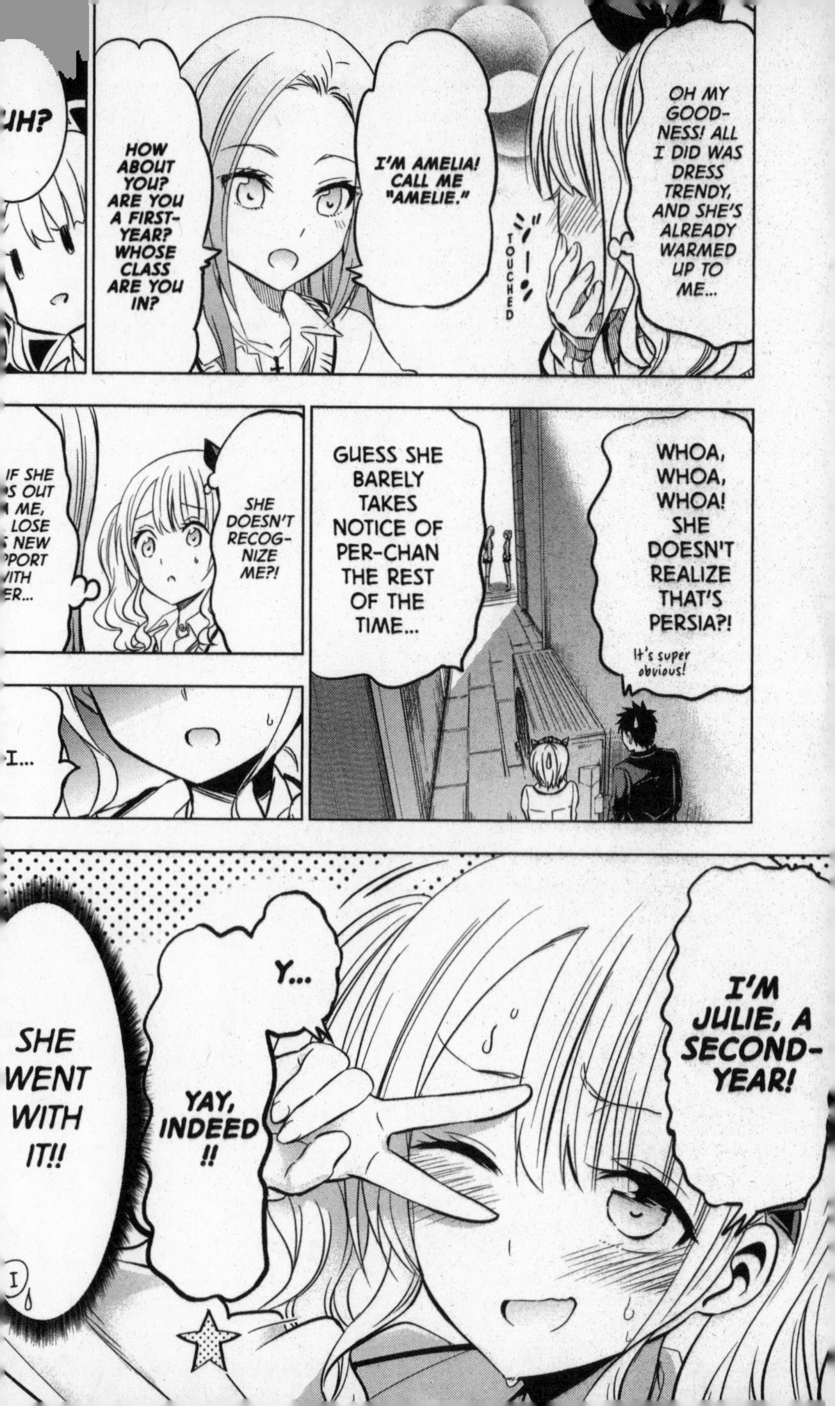
OH MY GOODNESS! ALL I DID WAS DRESS TRENDY, AND SHE'S ALREADY WARMED UP TO ME...
TOUCHED
I'M AMELIA! CALL ME "AMELIE."
HOW ABOUT YOU? ARE YOU A FIRST-YEAR? WHOSE CLASS ARE YOU IN?
UH?
WHOA, WHOA, WHOA! SHE DOESN'T REALIZE THAT'S PERSIA?!
It's super obvious!
GUESS SHE BARELY TAKES NOTICE OF PER-CHAN THE REST OF THE TIME...
SHE DOESN'T RECOGNIZE ME?!
I...
I'M JULIE, A SECOND-YEAR!
Y...
YAY, INDEED!!
SHE WENT WITH IT!!
I

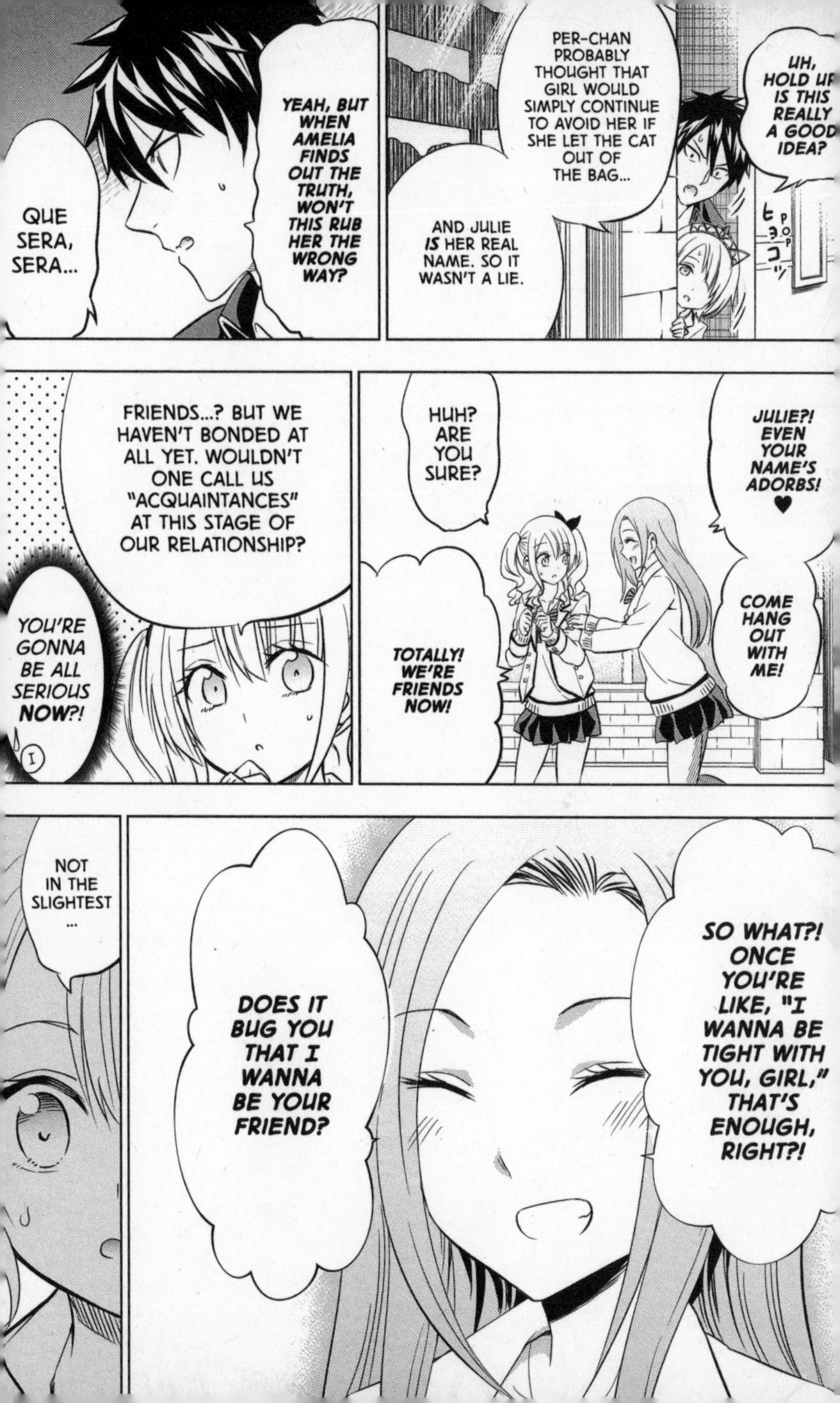
UH, HOLD UP IS THIS REALLY A GOOD IDEA?
ヒョコッ
PER-CHAN PROBABLY THOUGHT THAT GIRL WOULD SIMPLY CONTINUE TO AVOID HER IF SHE LET THE CAT OUT OF THE BAG...
AND JULIE *IS* HER REAL NAME. SO IT WASN'T A LIE.
YEAH, BUT WHEN AMELIA FINDS OUT THE TRUTH, WON'T THIS RUB HER THE WRONG WAY?
QUE SERA, SERA...
JULIE?! EVEN YOUR NAME'S ADORBS! ♥
COME HANG OUT WITH ME!
HUH? ARE YOU SURE?
TOTALLY! WE'RE FRIENDS NOW!
FRIENDS...? BUT WE HAVEN'T BONDED AT ALL YET. WOULDN'T ONE CALL US "ACQUAINTANCES" AT THIS STAGE OF OUR RELATIONSHIP?
YOU'RE GONNA BE ALL SERIOUS NOW?!
SO WHAT?! ONCE YOU'RE LIKE, "I WANNA BE TIGHT WITH YOU, GIRL," THAT'S ENOUGH, RIGHT?!
DOES IT BUG YOU THAT I WANNA BE YOUR FRIEND?
NOT IN THE SLIGHTEST...

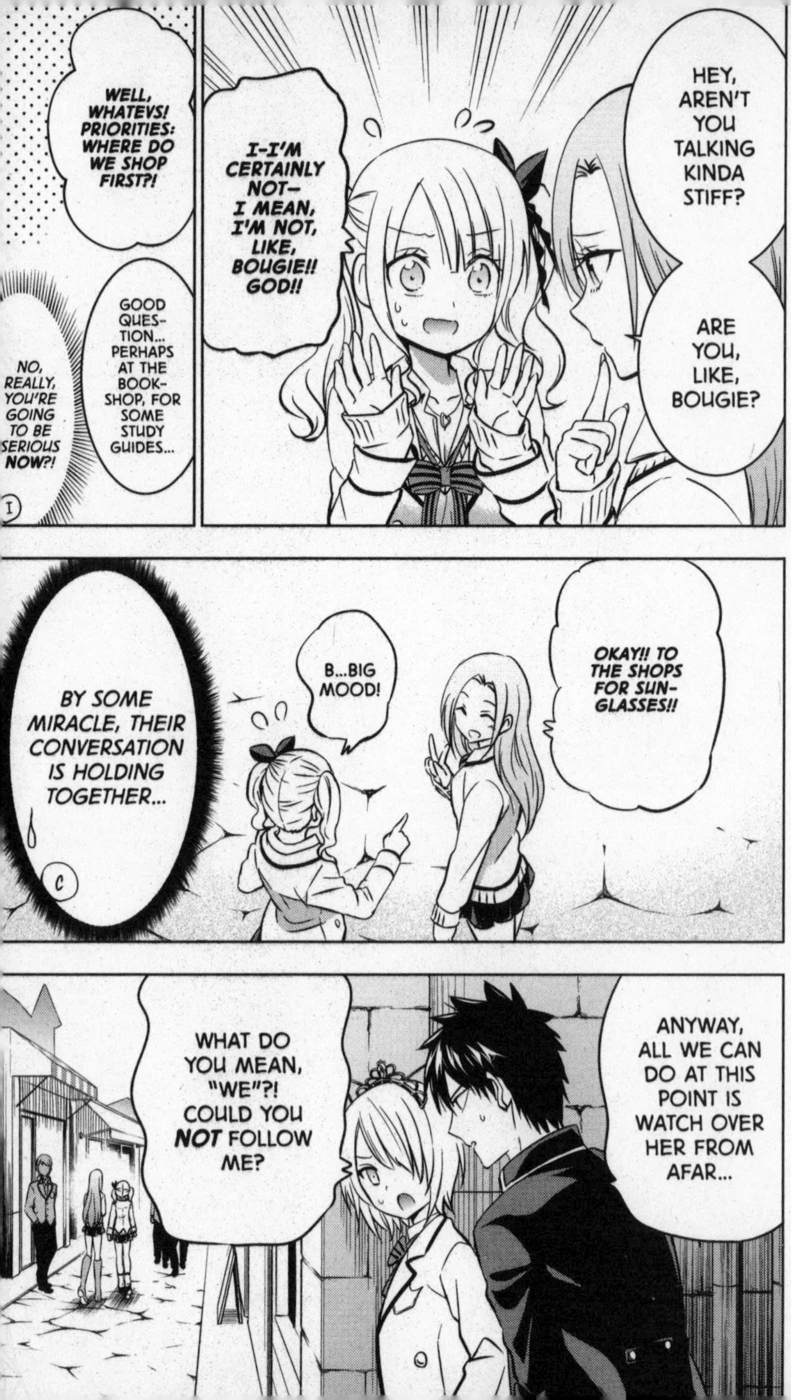
HEY, AREN'T YOU TALKING KINDA STIFF?
ARE YOU, LIKE, BOUGIE?
I-I'M CERTAINLY NOT— I MEAN, I'M NOT, LIKE, BOUGIE!! GOD!!
WELL, WHATEVS! PRIORITIES: WHERE DO WE SHOP FIRST?!
GOOD QUESTION... PERHAPS AT THE BOOKSHOP, FOR SOME STUDY GUIDES...
NO, REALLY, YOU'RE GOING TO BE SERIOUS NOW?!
OKAY!! TO THE SHOPS FOR SUNGLASSES!!
B...BIG MOOD!
BY SOME MIRACLE, THEIR CONVERSATION IS HOLDING TOGETHER...
ANYWAY, ALL WE CAN DO AT THIS POINT IS WATCH OVER HER FROM AFAR...
WHAT DO YOU MEAN, "WE"?! COULD YOU NOT FOLLOW ME?

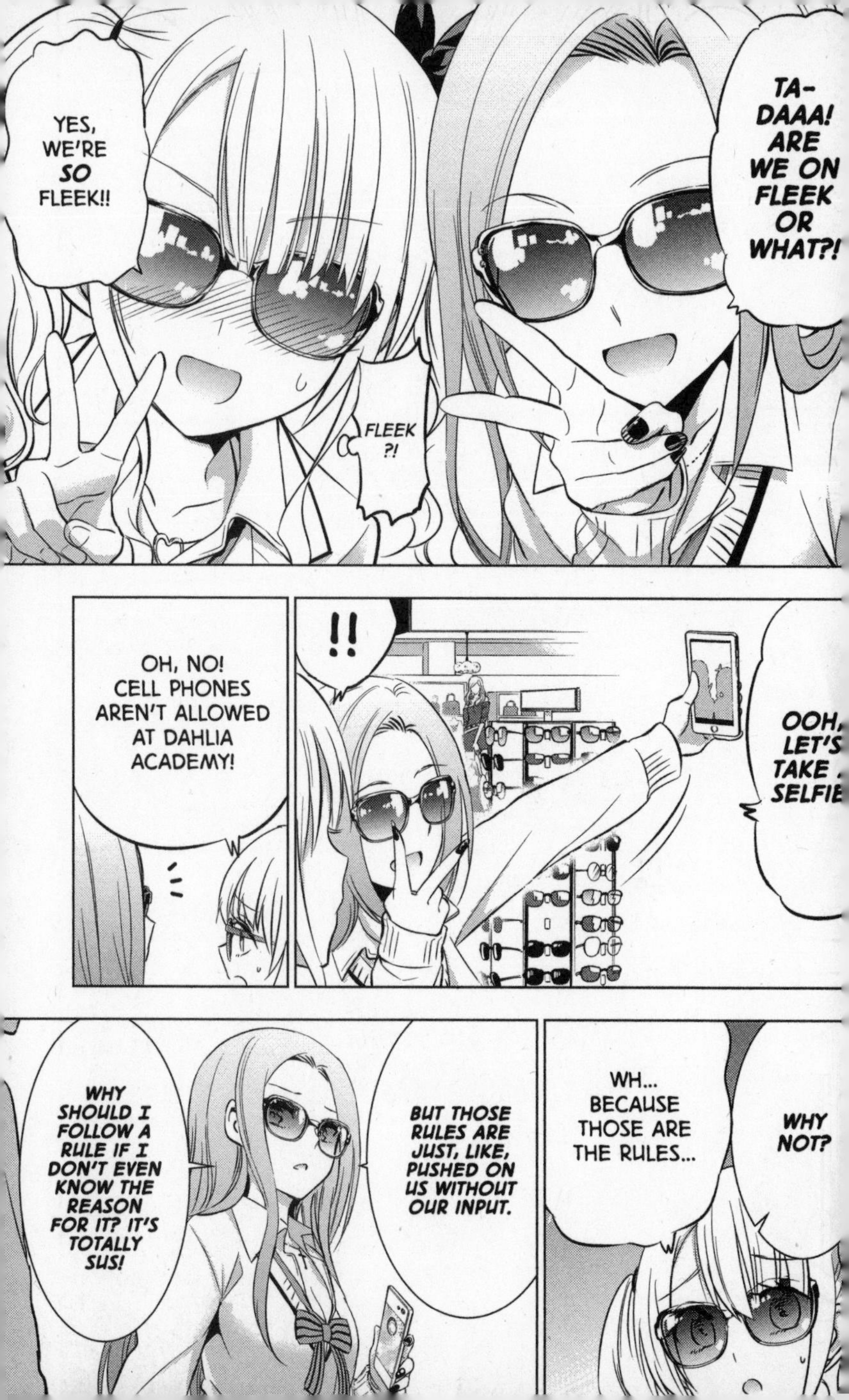
TA-DAAA! ARE WE ON FLEEK OR WHAT?!
YES, WE'RE SO FLEEK!!
FLEEK?!
OOH, LET'S TAKE SELFIE
!!
OH, NO! CELL PHONES AREN'T ALLOWED AT DAHLIA ACADEMY!
WHY NOT?
WH... BECAUSE THOSE ARE THE RULES...
BUT THOSE RULES ARE JUST, LIKE, PUSHED ON US WITHOUT OUR INPUT.
WHY SHOULD I FOLLOW A RULE IF I DON'T EVEN KNOW THE REASON FOR IT? IT'S TOTALLY SUS!

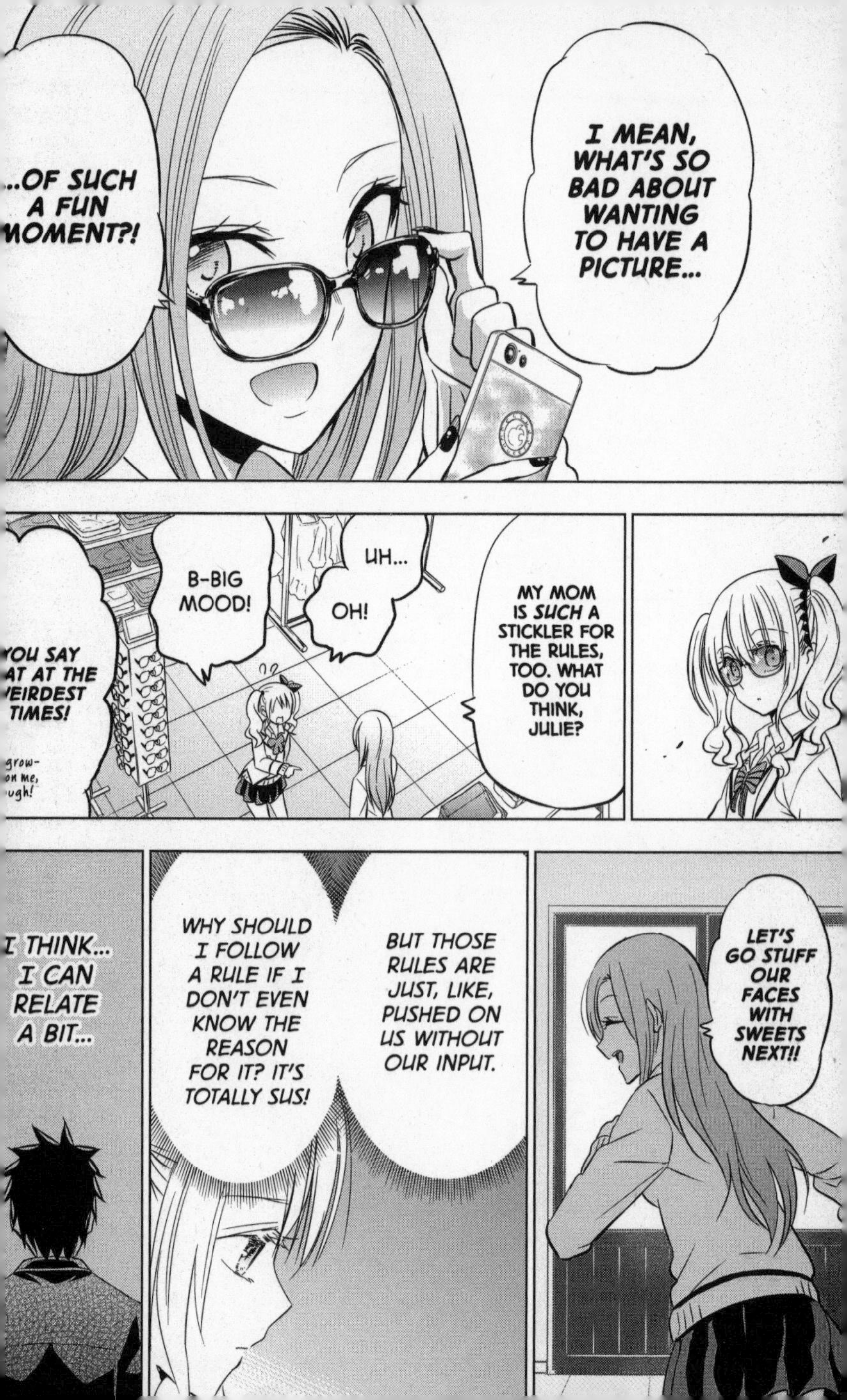

I MEAN, WHAT'S SO BAD ABOUT WANTING TO HAVE A PICTURE...
...OF SUCH A FUN MOMENT?!
MY MOM IS SUCH A STICKLER FOR THE RULES, TOO. WHAT DO YOU THINK, JULIE?
UH...
OH!
B-BIG MOOD!
OU SAY AT AT THE EIRDEST TIMES!
grow- on me, ugh!
LET'S GO STUFF OUR FACES WITH SWEETS NEXT!!
BUT THOSE RULES ARE JUST, LIKE, PUSHED ON US WITHOUT OUR INPUT.
WHY SHOULD I FOLLOW A RULE IF I DON'T EVEN KNOW THE REASON FOR IT? IT'S TOTALLY SUS!
I THINK... I CAN RELATE A BIT...

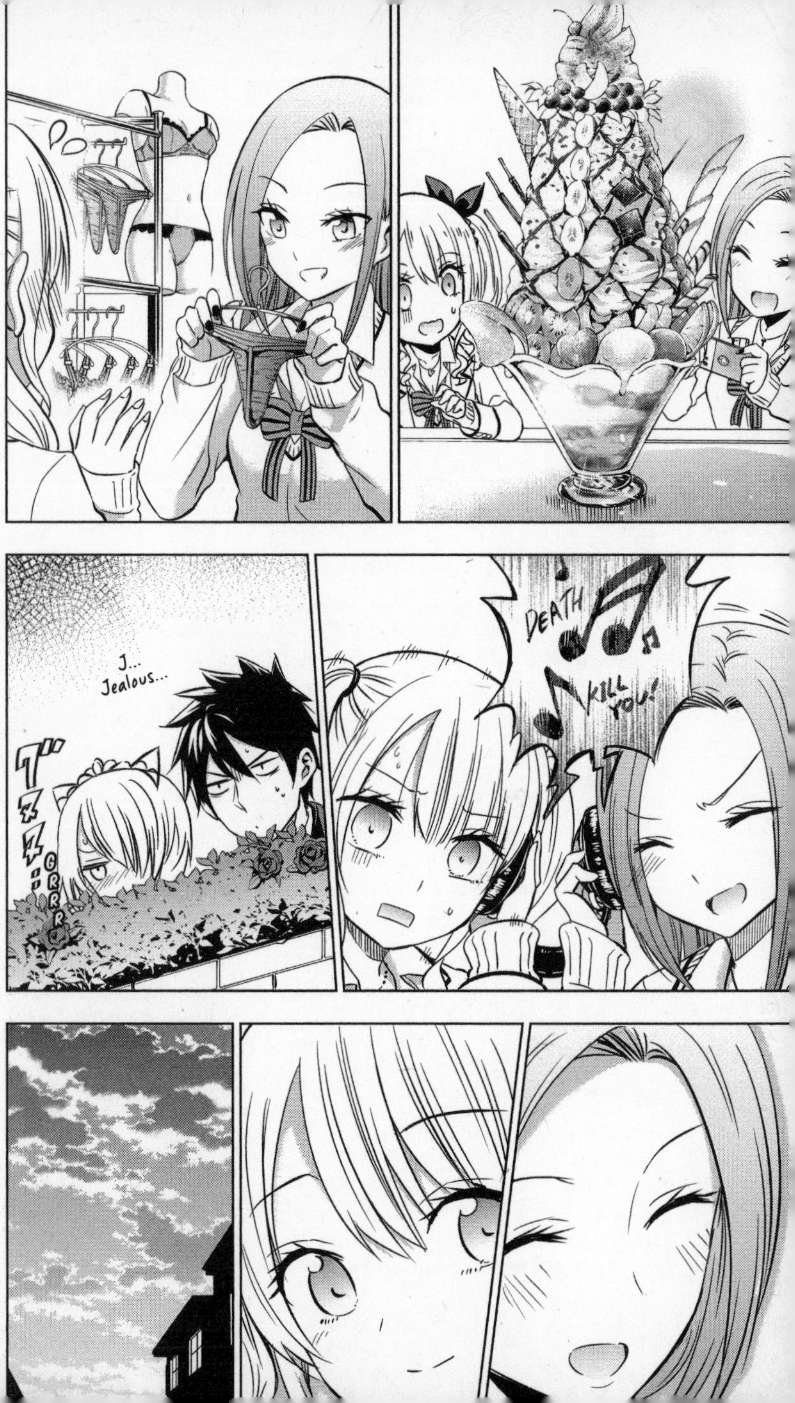
DEATH
KILL YOU!
J... Jealous...
GRRR

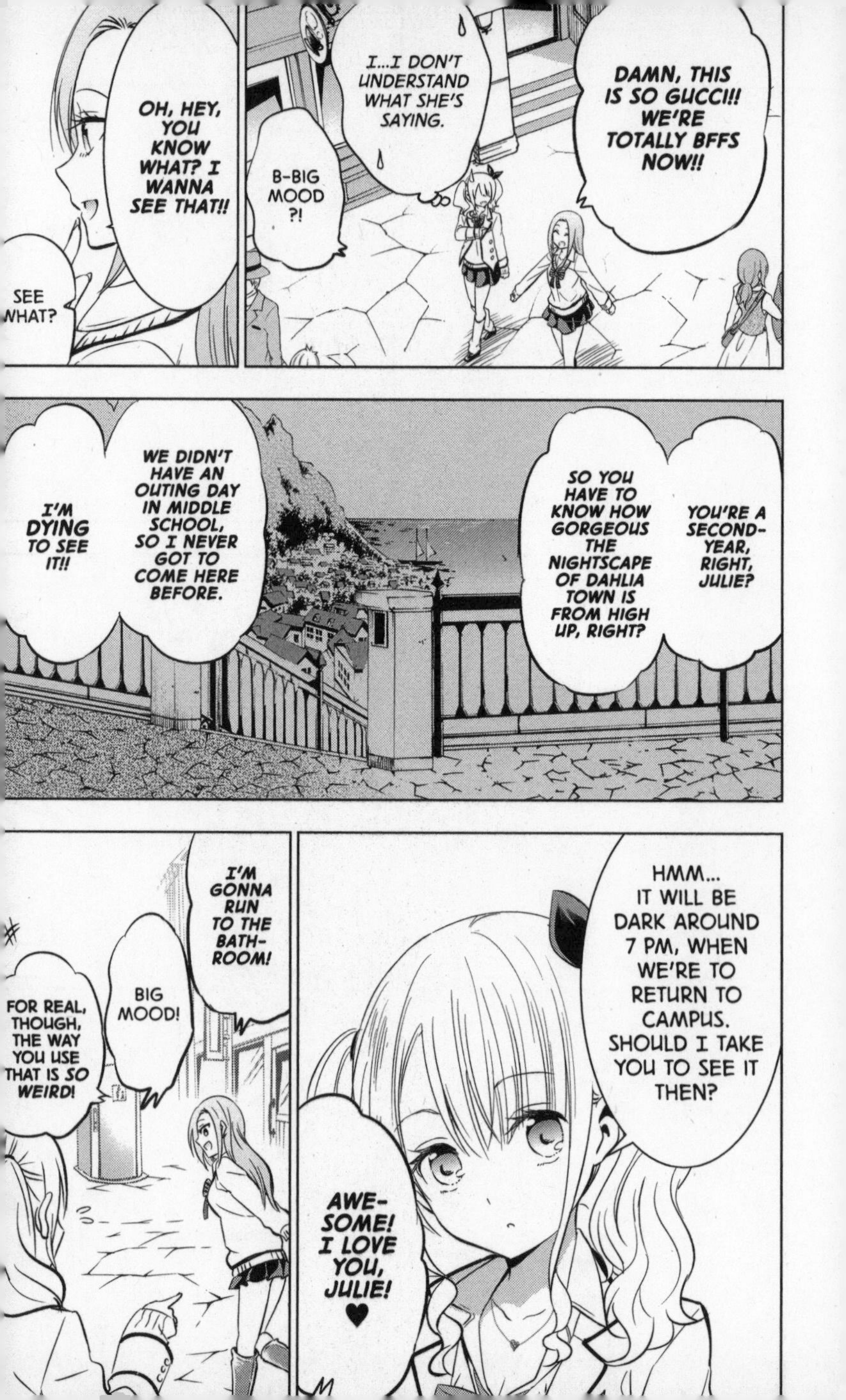
DAMN, THIS IS SO GUCCI!! WE'RE TOTALLY BFFS NOW!!
I...I DON'T UNDERSTAND WHAT SHE'S SAYING.
B-BIG MOOD ?!
OH, HEY, YOU KNOW WHAT? I WANNA SEE THAT!!
SEE WHAT?
YOU'RE A SECOND-YEAR, RIGHT, JULIE?
SO YOU HAVE TO KNOW HOW GORGEOUS THE NIGHTSCAPE OF DAHLIA TOWN IS FROM HIGH UP, RIGHT?
WE DIDN'T HAVE AN OUTING DAY IN MIDDLE SCHOOL, SO I NEVER GOT TO COME HERE BEFORE.
I'M DYING TO SEE IT!!
HMM... IT WILL BE DARK AROUND 7 PM, WHEN WE'RE TO RETURN TO CAMPUS. SHOULD I TAKE YOU TO SEE IT THEN?
AWE-SOME! I LOVE YOU, JULIE! ♥
I'M GONNA RUN TO THE BATH-ROOM!
BIG MOOD!
FOR REAL, THOUGH, THE WAY YOU USE THAT IS SO WEIRD!

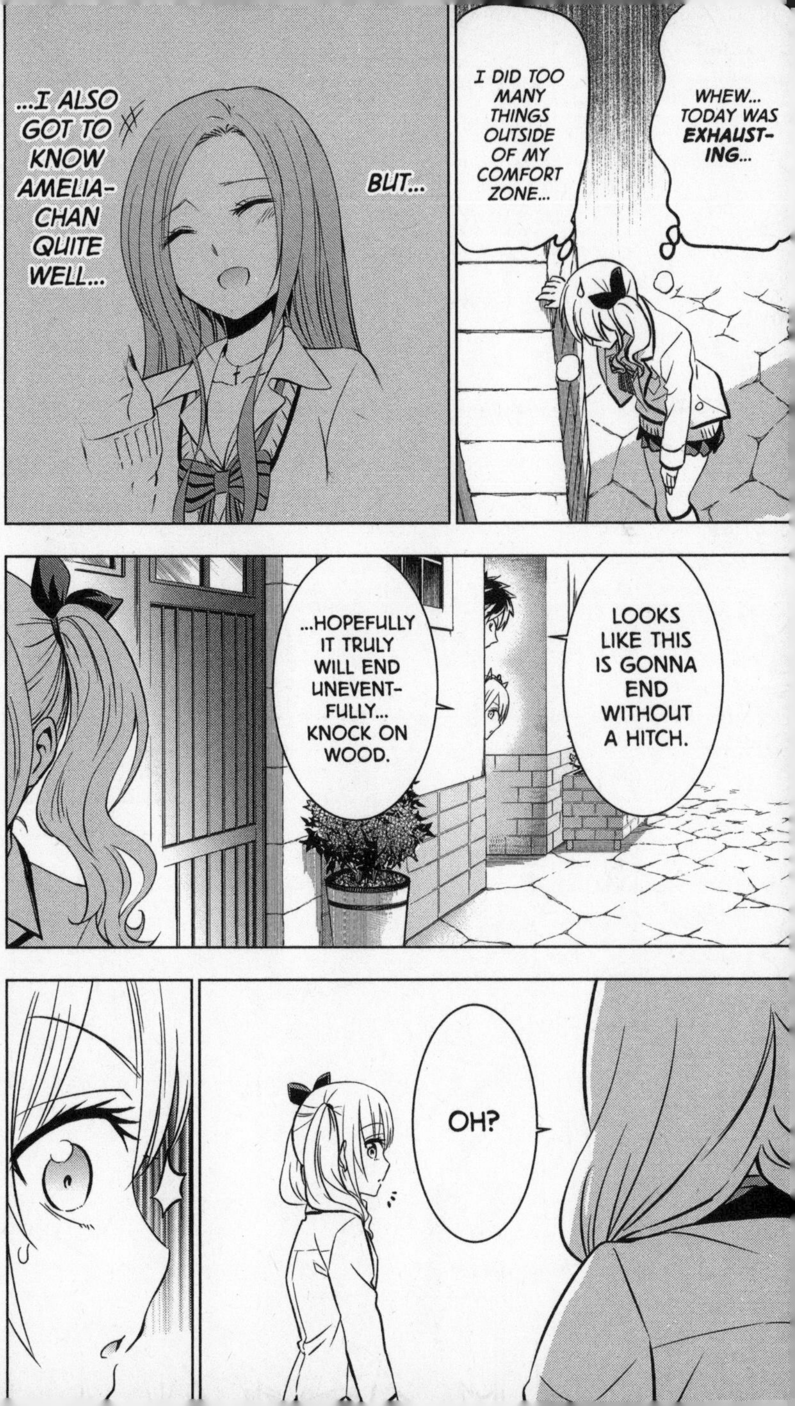
WHEW... TODAY WAS **EXHAUSTING**...
I DID TOO MANY THINGS OUTSIDE OF MY COMFORT ZONE...
BUT...
...I ALSO GOT TO KNOW AMELIA-CHAN QUITE WELL...
LOOKS LIKE THIS IS GONNA END WITHOUT A HITCH.
...HOPEFULLY IT TRULY WILL END UNEVENTFULLY... KNOCK ON WOOD.
OH?

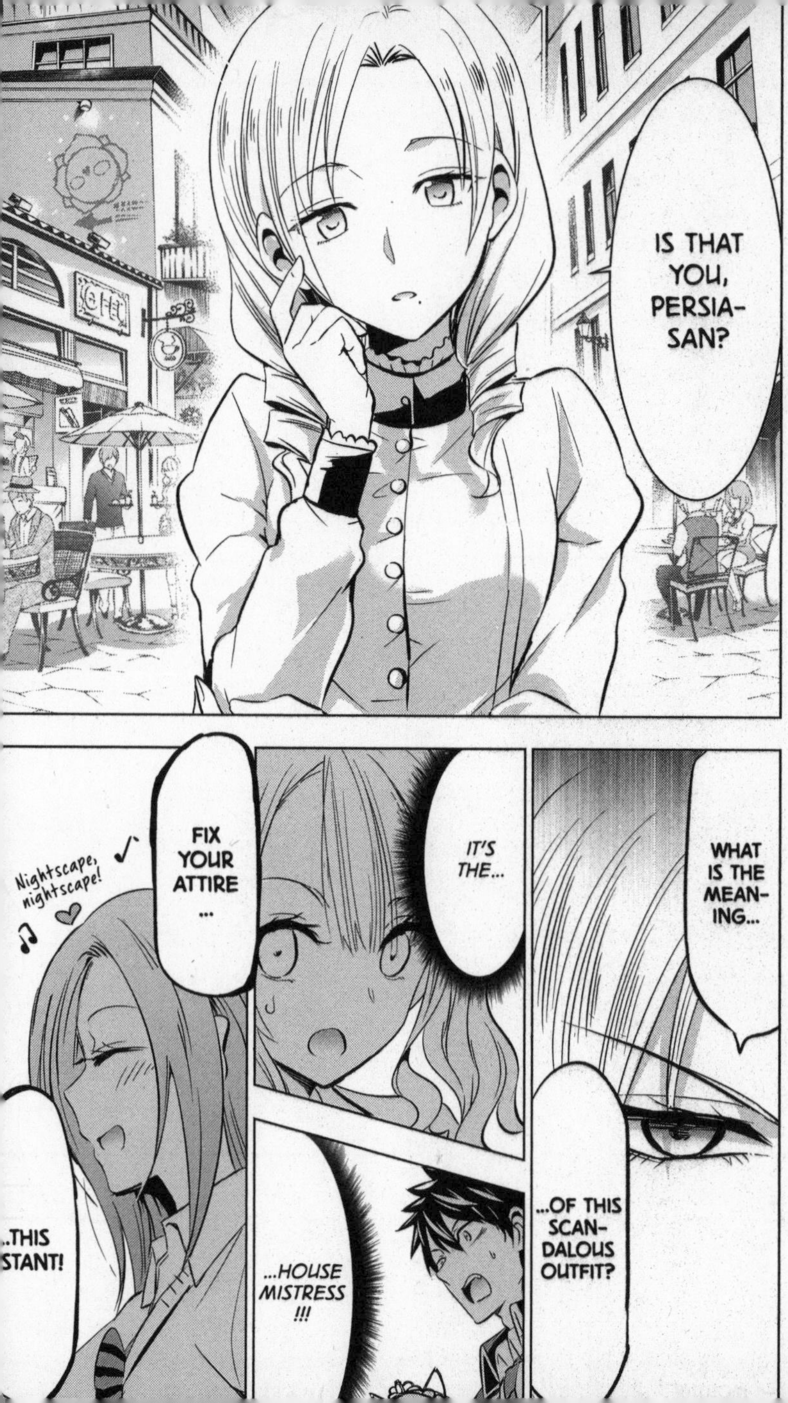
IS THAT YOU, PERSIA-SAN?
WHAT IS THE MEANING...
...OF THIS SCANDALOUS OUTFIT?
IT'S THE...
...HOUSE MISTRESS !!!
FIX YOUR ATTIRE ...
Nightscape, nightscape!
..THIS STANT!

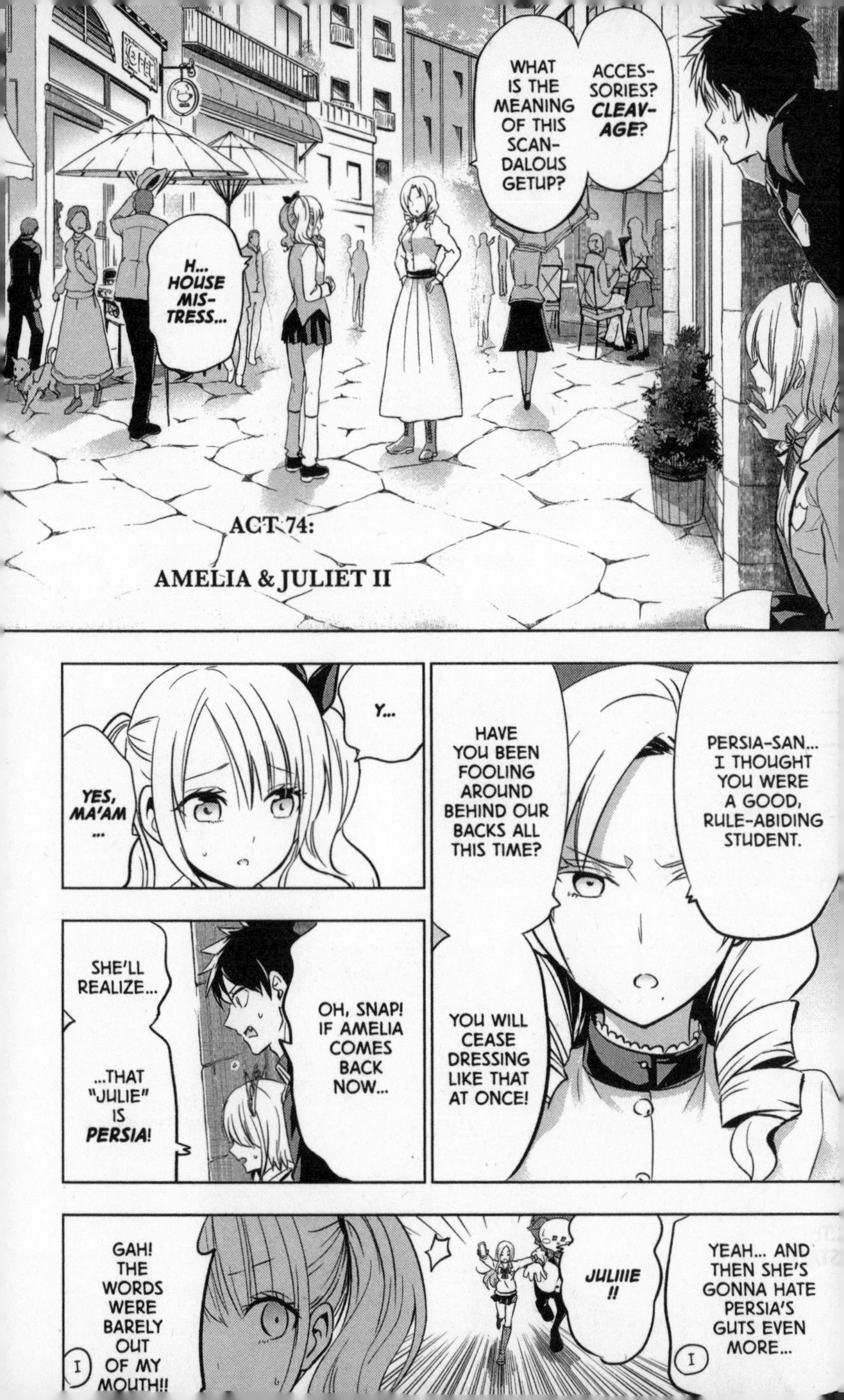
ACCESSORIES? CLEAVAGE?
WHAT IS THE MEANING OF THIS SCANDALOUS GETUP?
H... HOUSEMISTRESS...
ACT 74:
AMELIA & JULIET II
PERSIA-SAN... I THOUGHT YOU WERE A GOOD, RULE-ABIDING STUDENT.
HAVE YOU BEEN FOOLING AROUND BEHIND OUR BACKS ALL THIS TIME?
YOU WILL CEASE DRESSING LIKE THAT AT ONCE!
Y...
YES, MA'AM ...
OH, SNAP! IF AMELIA COMES BACK NOW...
SHE'LL REALIZE...
...THAT "JULIE" IS PERSIA!
YEAH... AND THEN SHE'S GONNA HATE PERSIA'S GUTS EVEN MORE...
JULIIIE !!
GAH! THE WORDS WERE BARELY OUT OF MY MOUTH!!

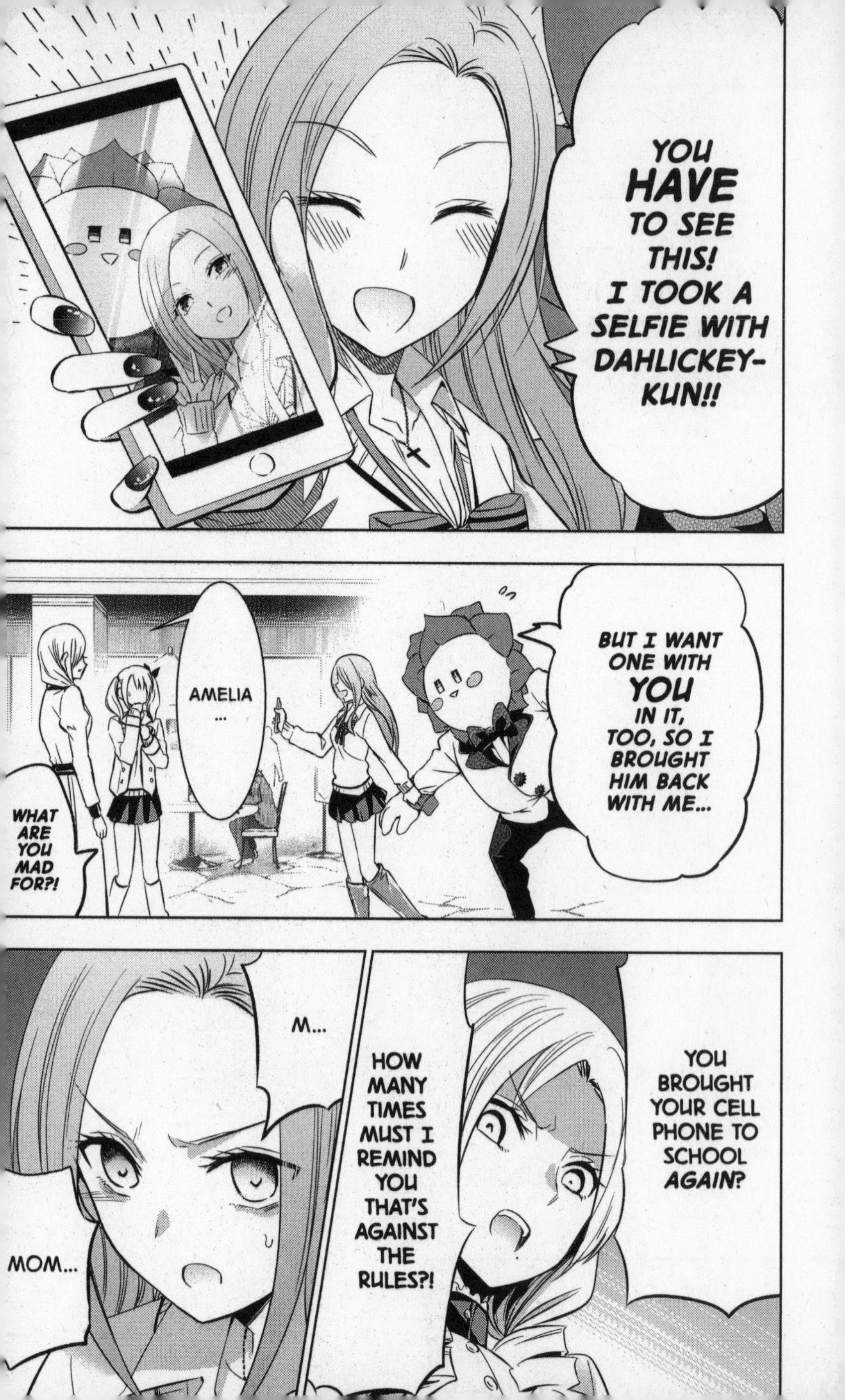
YOU HAVE TO SEE THIS! I TOOK A SELFIE WITH DAHLICKEY-KUN!!
BUT I WANT ONE WITH YOU IN IT, TOO, SO I BROUGHT HIM BACK WITH ME...
AMELIA ...
WHAT ARE YOU MAD FOR?!
YOU BROUGHT YOUR CELL PHONE TO SCHOOL AGAIN?
HOW MANY TIMES MUST I REMIND YOU THAT'S AGAINST THE RULES?!
M...
MOM...

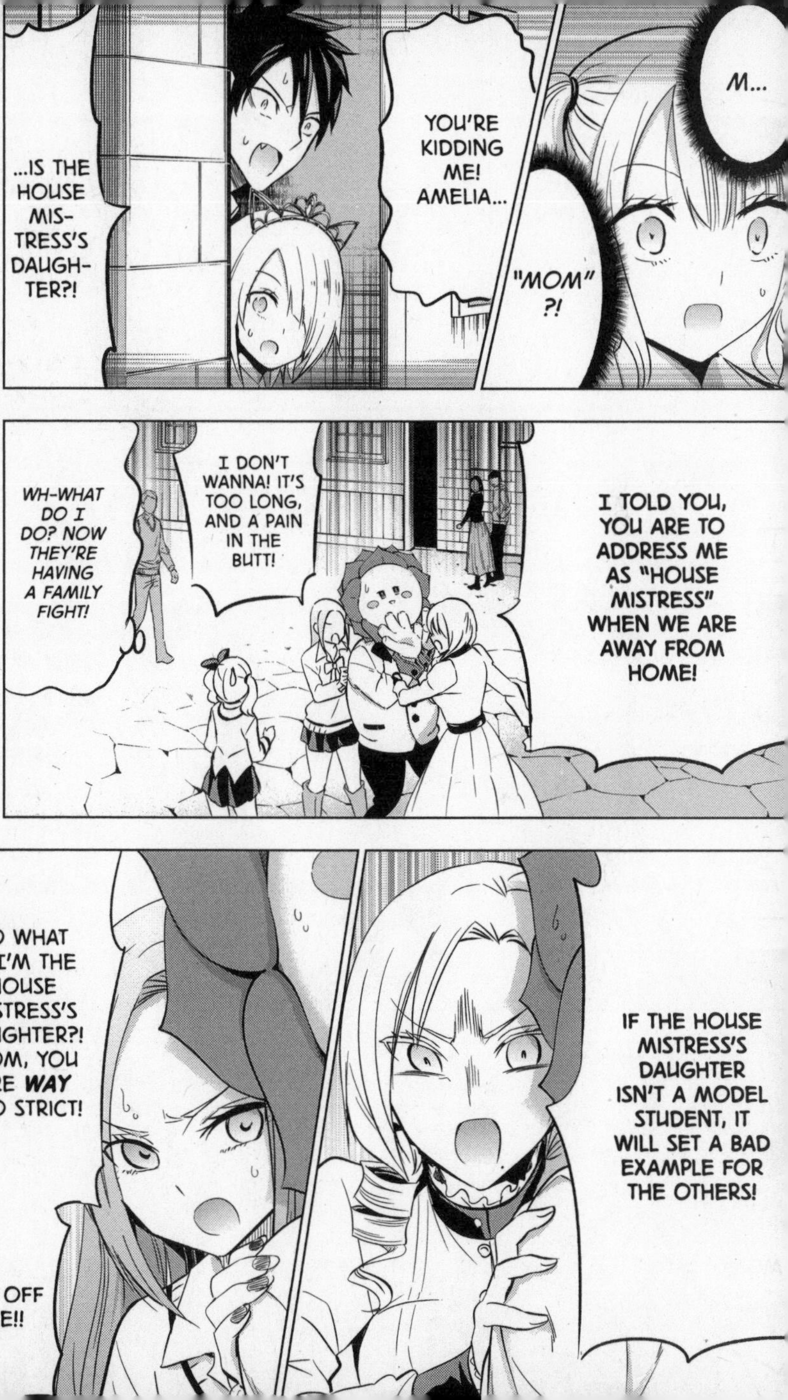
M...
"MOM" ?!
YOU'RE KIDDING ME! AMELIA...
...IS THE HOUSE MIS-TRESS'S DAUGH-TER?!
I TOLD YOU, YOU ARE TO ADDRESS ME AS "HOUSE MISTRESS" WHEN WE ARE AWAY FROM HOME!
I DON'T WANNA! IT'S TOO LONG, AND A PAIN IN THE BUTT!
WH-WHAT DO I DO? NOW THEY'RE HAVING A FAMILY FIGHT!
IF THE HOUSE MISTRESS'S DAUGHTER ISN'T A MODEL STUDENT, IT WILL SET A BAD EXAMPLE FOR THE OTHERS!
SO WHAT IF I'M THE HOUSE MISTRESS'S DAUGHTER?! MOM, YOU ARE WAY TOO STRICT!
LAY OFF ME!!

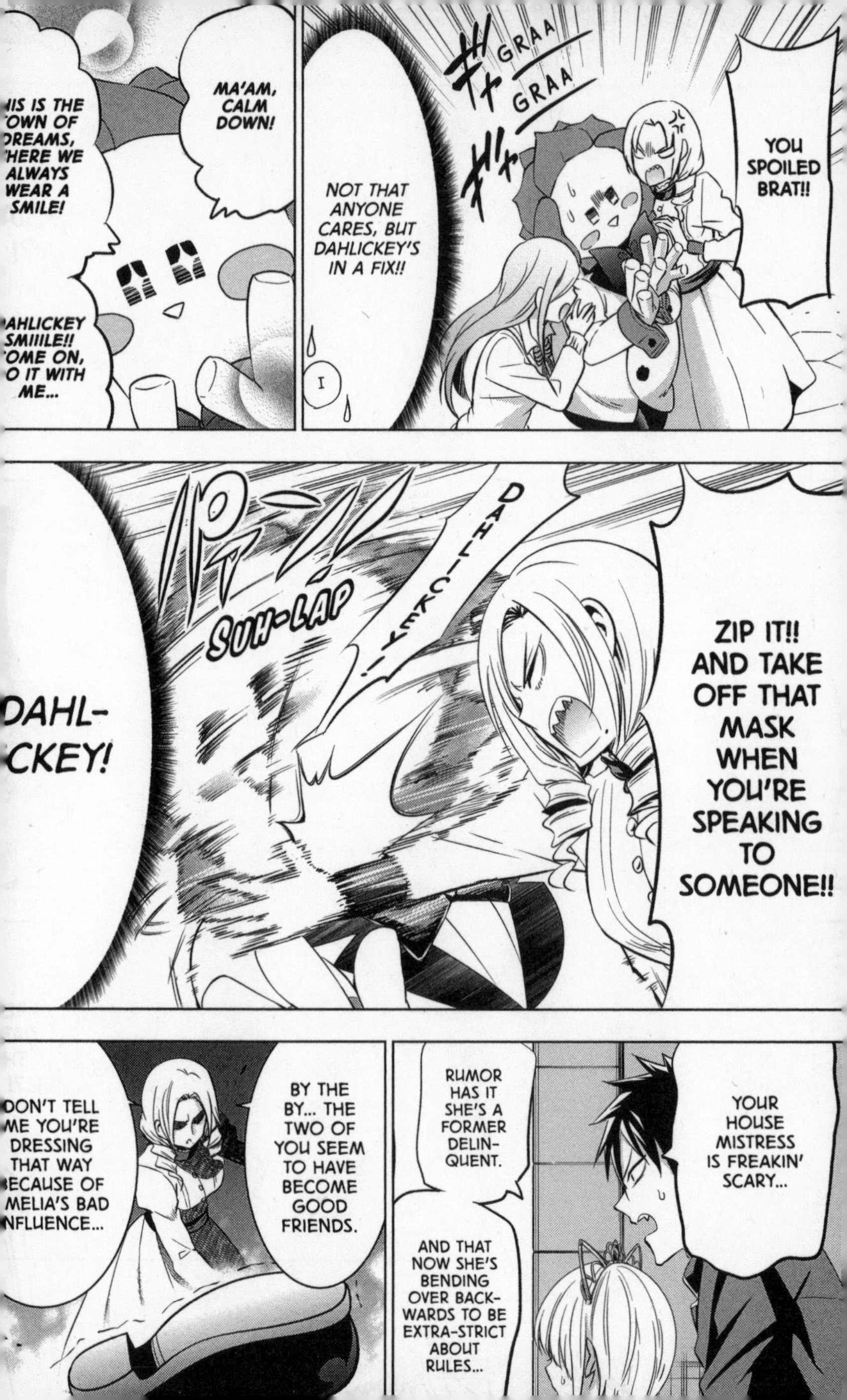
GRAA
GRAA
YOU SPOILED BRAT!!
NOT THAT ANYONE CARES, BUT DAHLICKEY'S IN A FIX!!
I
MA'AM, CALM DOWN!
IS IS THE OWN OF DREAMS, HERE WE ALWAYS WEAR A SMILE!
AHLICKEY SMIIILE!! OME ON, O IT WITH ME...
ZIP IT!! AND TAKE OFF THAT MASK WHEN YOU'RE SPEAKING TO SOMEONE!!
DAHLICKEY--!!
SUH-LAP
DAHL-CKEY!
YOUR HOUSE MISTRESS IS FREAKIN' SCARY...
RUMOR HAS IT SHE'S A FORMER DELIN-QUENT.
AND THAT NOW SHE'S BENDING OVER BACK-WARDS TO BE EXTRA-STRICT ABOUT RULES...
BY THE BY... THE TWO OF YOU SEEM TO HAVE BECOME GOOD FRIENDS.
DON'T TELL ME YOU'RE DRESSING THAT WAY ECAUSE OF MELIA'S BAD NFLUENCE...

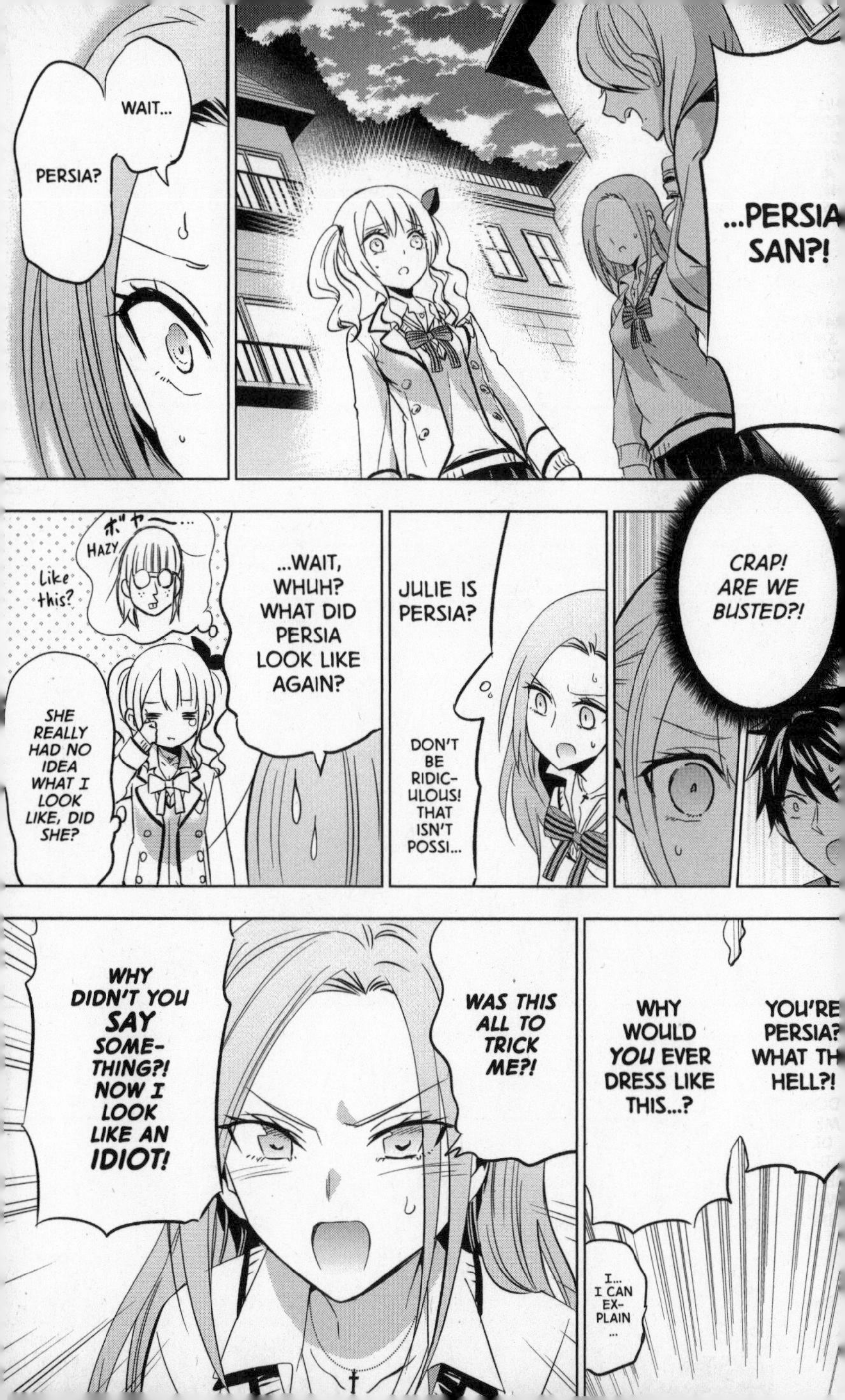
...PERSIA SAN?!
WAIT... PERSIA?
CRAP! ARE WE BUSTED?!
JULIE IS PERSIA?
DON'T BE RIDIC-ULOUS! THAT ISN'T POSSI...
...WAIT, WHUH? WHAT DID PERSIA LOOK LIKE AGAIN?
ボヤ〜…
HAZY
Like this?
SHE REALLY HAD NO IDEA WHAT I LOOK LIKE, DID SHE?
YOU'RE PERSIA? WHAT TH HELL?!
WHY WOULD YOU EVER DRESS LIKE THIS...?
I... I CAN EX-PLAIN...
WAS THIS ALL TO TRICK ME?!
WHY DIDN'T YOU SAY SOME-THING?! NOW I LOOK LIKE AN IDIOT!

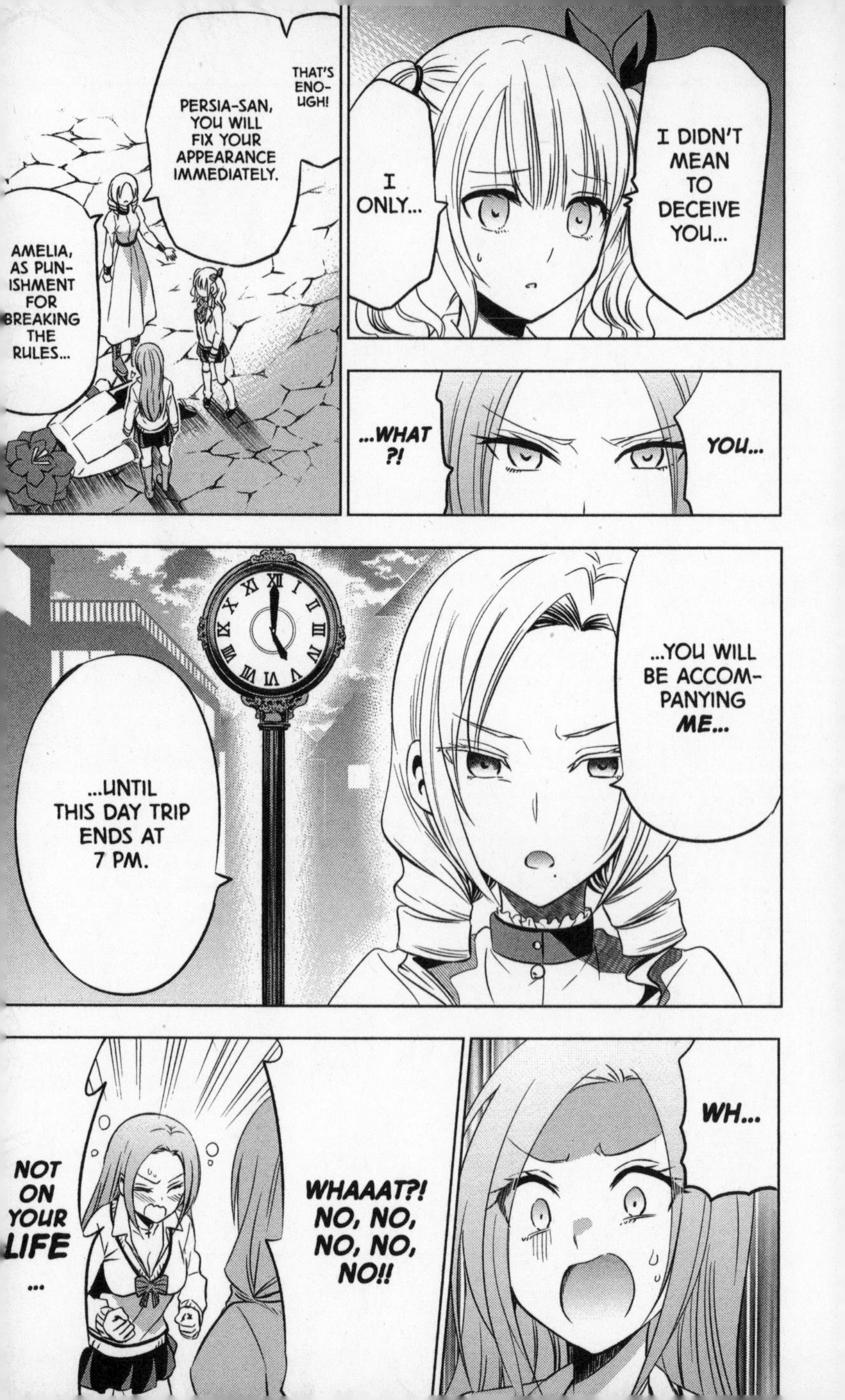
I DIDN'T MEAN TO DECEIVE YOU...
I ONLY...
YOU...
...WHAT?!
THAT'S ENOUGH!
PERSIA-SAN, YOU WILL FIX YOUR APPEARANCE IMMEDIATELY.
AMELIA, AS PUNISHMENT FOR BREAKING THE RULES...
...YOU WILL BE ACCOMPANYING ME...
...UNTIL THIS DAY TRIP ENDS AT 7 PM.
WH...
WHAAAT?! NO, NO, NO, NO, NO!!
NOT ON YOUR LIFE ...

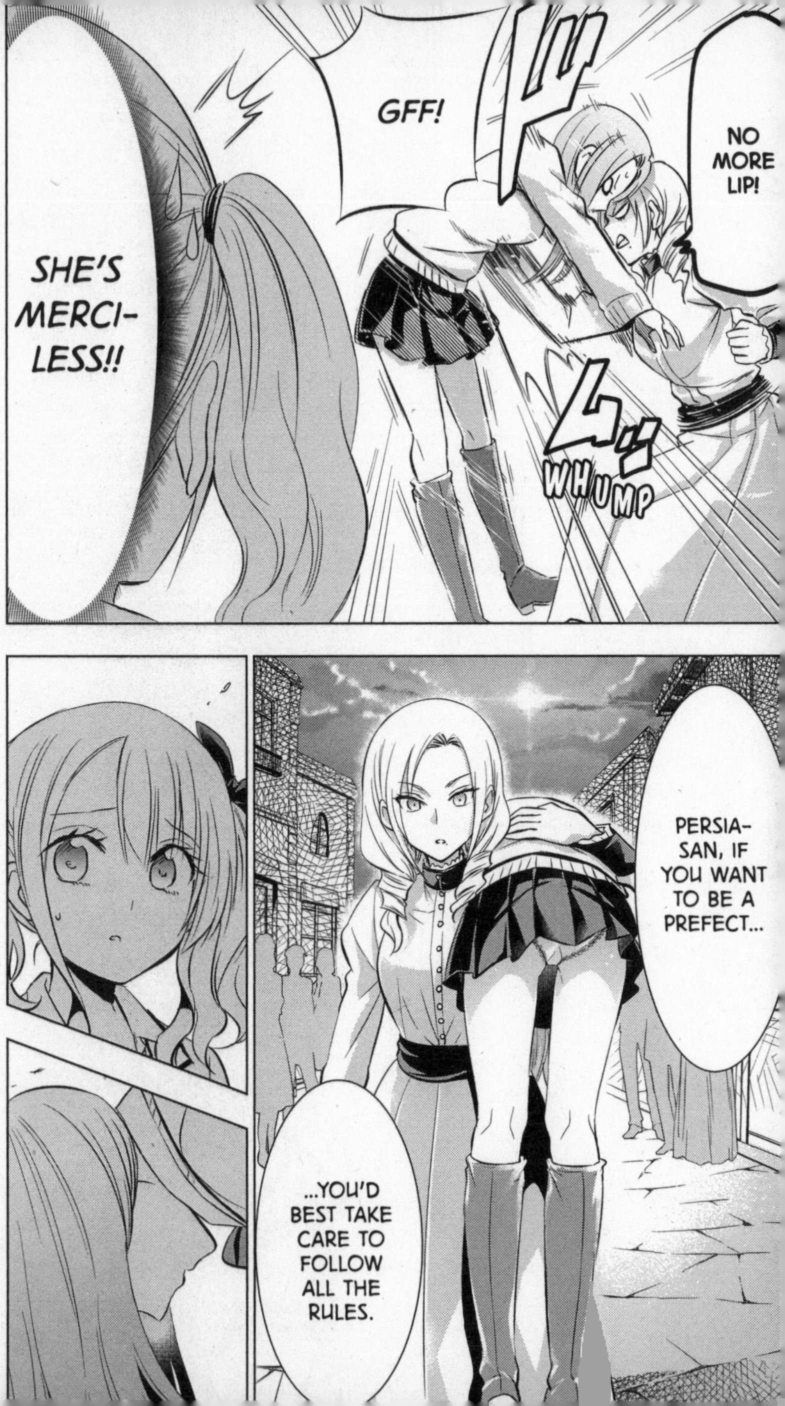
NO MORE LIP!
GFF!
WHUMP
SHE'S MERCI-LESS!!
PERSIA-SAN, IF YOU WANT TO BE A PREFECT...
...YOU'D BEST TAKE CARE TO FOLLOW ALL THE RULES.

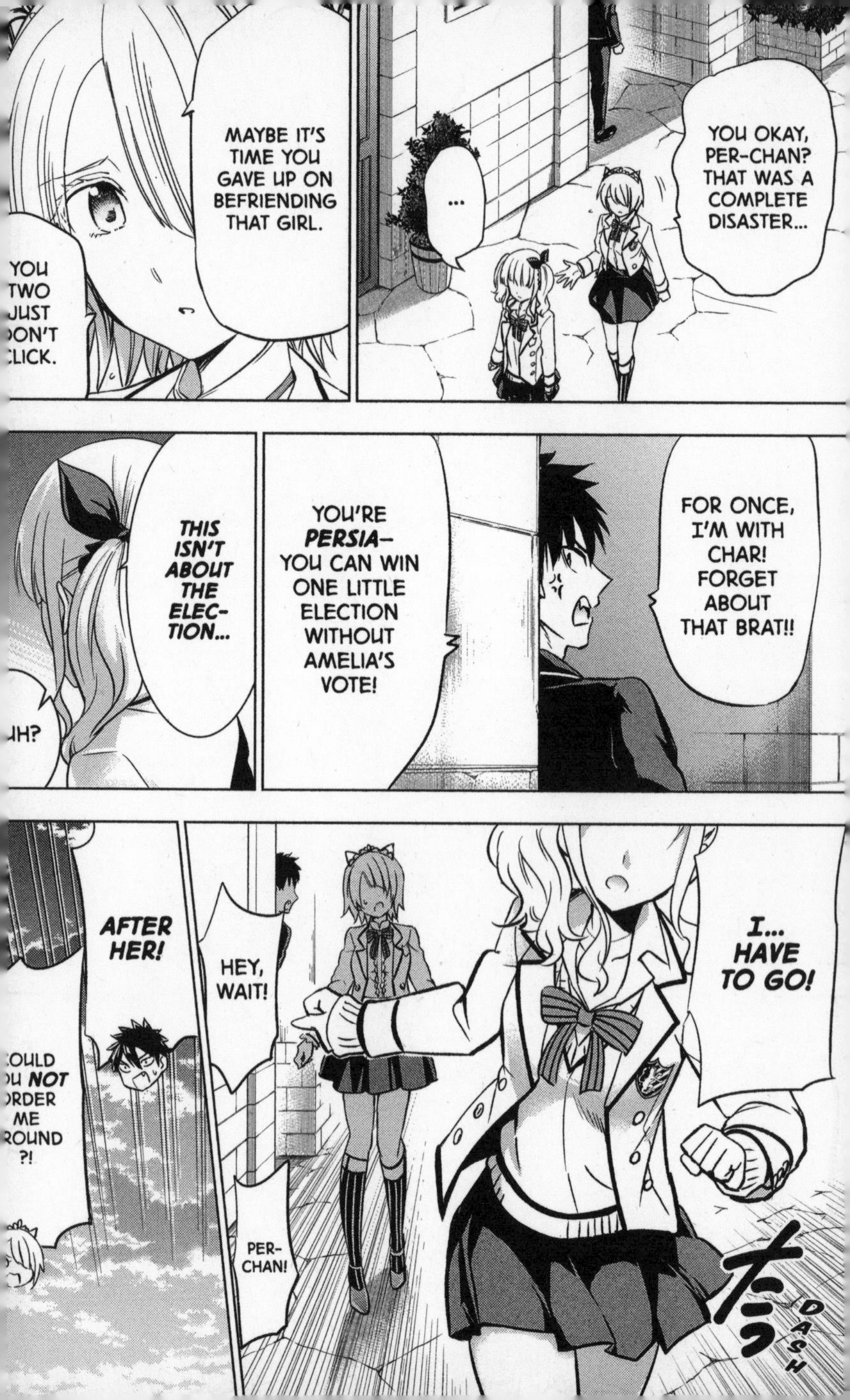
YOU OKAY, PER-CHAN? THAT WAS A COMPLETE DISASTER...
...
MAYBE IT'S TIME YOU GAVE UP ON BEFRIENDING THAT GIRL.
YOU TWO JUST DON'T CLICK.
FOR ONCE, I'M WITH CHAR! FORGET ABOUT THAT BRAT!!
YOU'RE *PERSIA*— YOU CAN WIN ONE LITTLE ELECTION WITHOUT AMELIA'S VOTE!
THIS ISN'T ABOUT THE ELEC-TION...
HUH?
I... HAVE TO GO!
DASH
HEY, WAIT!
PER-CHAN!
AFTER HER!
COULD YOU *NOT* ORDER ME AROUND?!

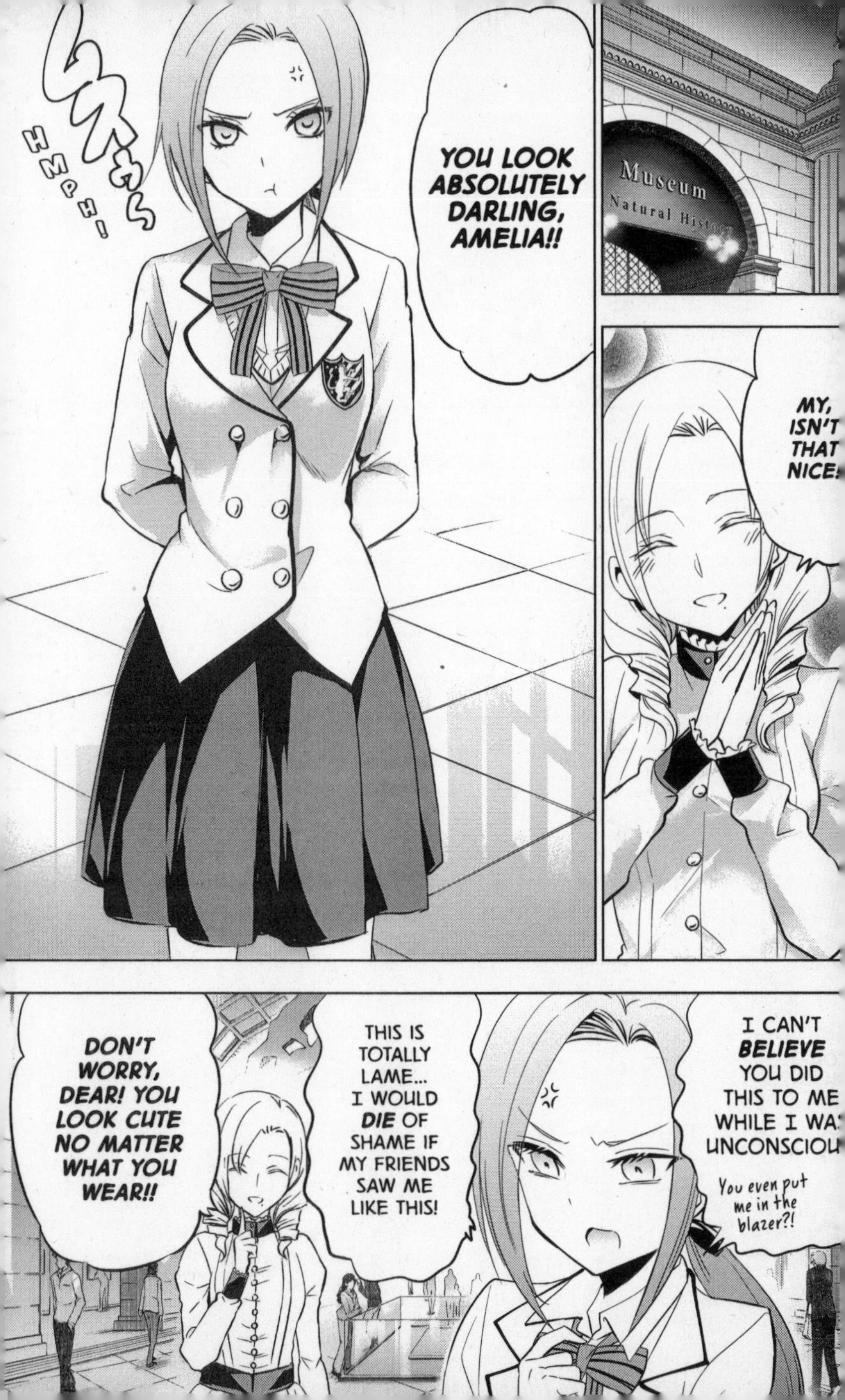

Museum
MY, ISN'T THAT NICE!
YOU LOOK ABSOLUTELY DARLING, AMELIA!!
HMPH!
I CAN'T BELIEVE YOU DID THIS TO ME WHILE I WA UNCONSCIOU
You even put me in the blazer?!
THIS IS TOTALLY LAME... I WOULD DIE OF SHAME IF MY FRIENDS SAW ME LIKE THIS!
DON'T WORRY, DEAR! YOU LOOK CUTE NO MATTER WHAT YOU WEAR!!

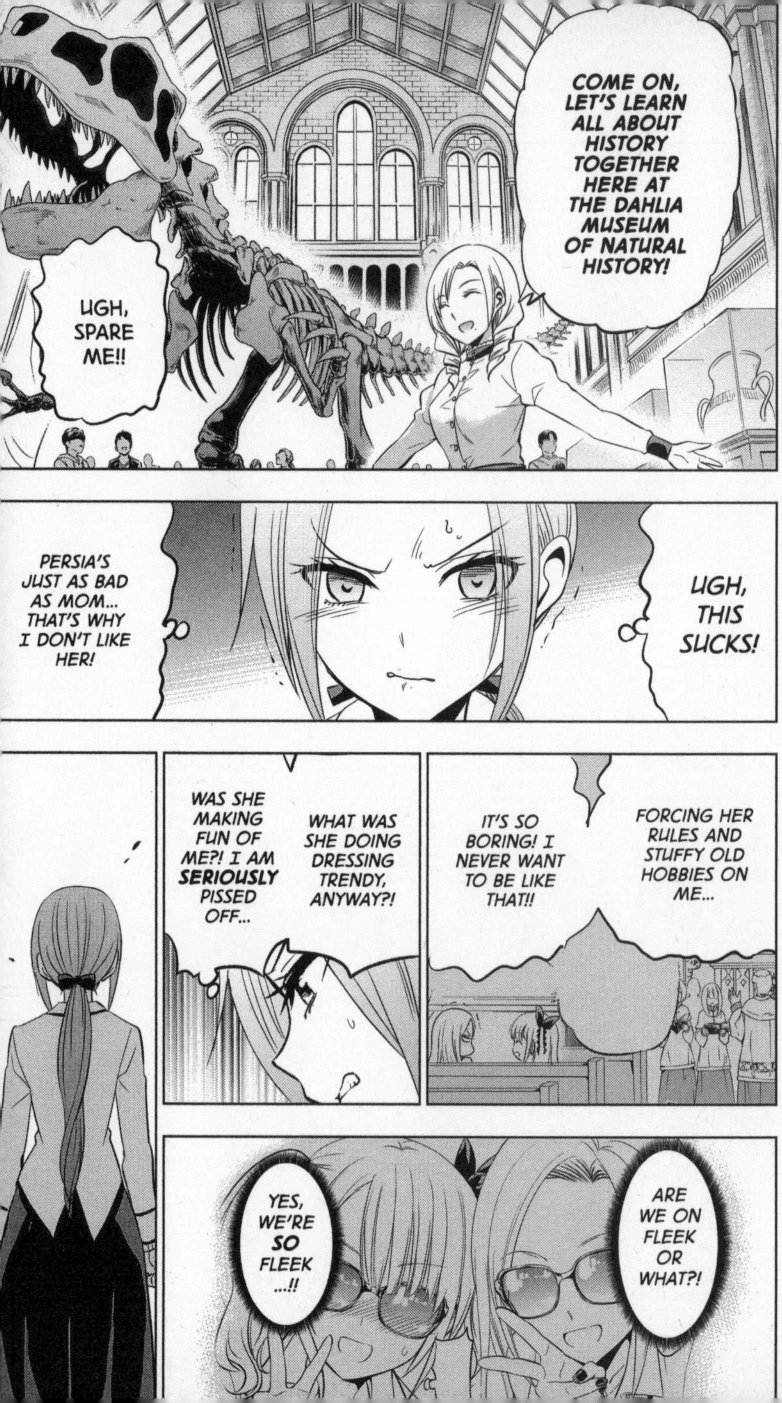
COME ON, LET'S LEARN ALL ABOUT HISTORY TOGETHER HERE AT THE DAHLIA MUSEUM OF NATURAL HISTORY!
UGH, SPARE ME!!
UGH, THIS SUCKS!
PERSIA'S JUST AS BAD AS MOM... THAT'S WHY I DON'T LIKE HER!
FORCING HER RULES AND STUFFY OLD HOBBIES ON ME...
IT'S SO BORING! I NEVER WANT TO BE LIKE THAT!!
WHAT WAS SHE DOING DRESSING TRENDY, ANYWAY?!
WAS SHE MAKING FUN OF ME?! I AM **SERIOUSLY** PISSED OFF...
ARE WE ON FLEEK OR WHAT?!
YES, WE'RE **SO** FLEEK ...!!

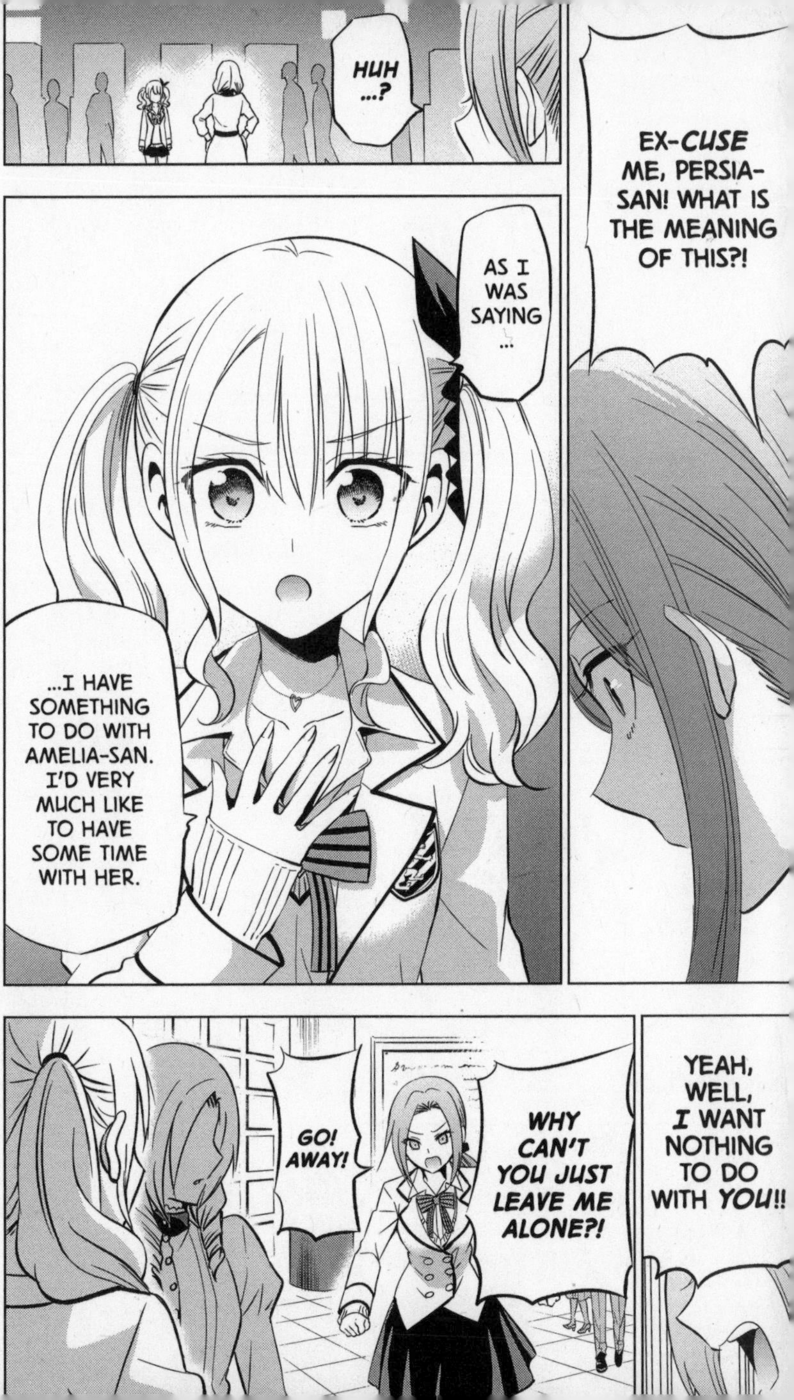
EX-*CUSE* ME, PERSIA-SAN! WHAT IS THE MEANING OF THIS?!
HUH ...?
AS I WAS SAYING ...
...I HAVE SOMETHING TO DO WITH AMELIA-SAN. I'D VERY MUCH LIKE TO HAVE SOME TIME WITH HER.
YEAH, WELL, *I* WANT NOTHING TO DO WITH *YOU*!!
WHY CAN'T YOU JUST LEAVE ME ALONE?!
GO! AWAY!

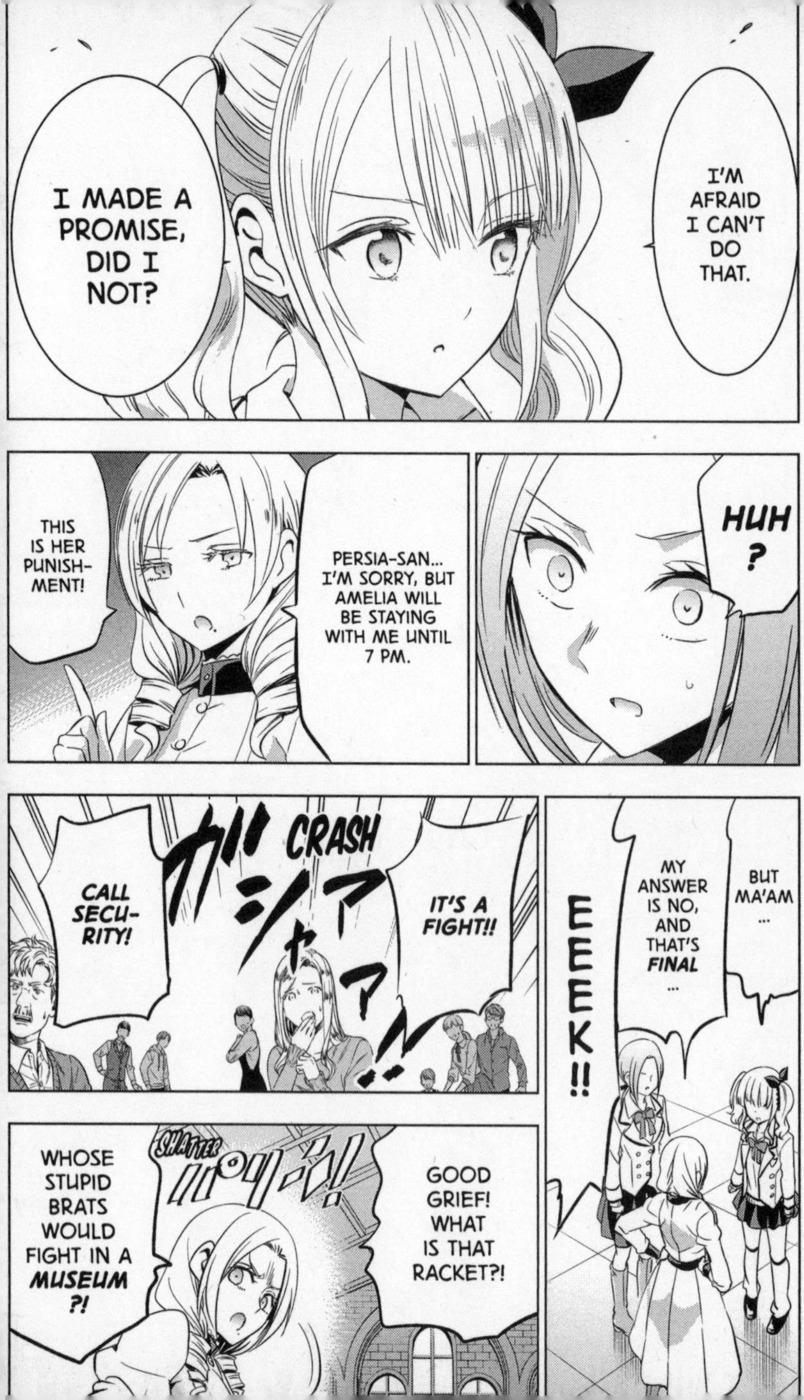
I'M AFRAID I CAN'T DO THAT.
I MADE A PROMISE, DID I NOT?
HUH?
PERSIA-SAN... I'M SORRY, BUT AMELIA WILL BE STAYING WITH ME UNTIL 7 PM.
THIS IS HER PUNISHMENT!
BUT MA'AM ...
MY ANSWER IS NO, AND THAT'S FINAL ...
EEEEK!!
CRASH
IT'S A FIGHT!!
CALL SECURITY!
SHATTER
GOOD GRIEF! WHAT IS THAT RACKET?!
WHOSE STUPID BRATS WOULD FIGHT IN A MUSEUM?!

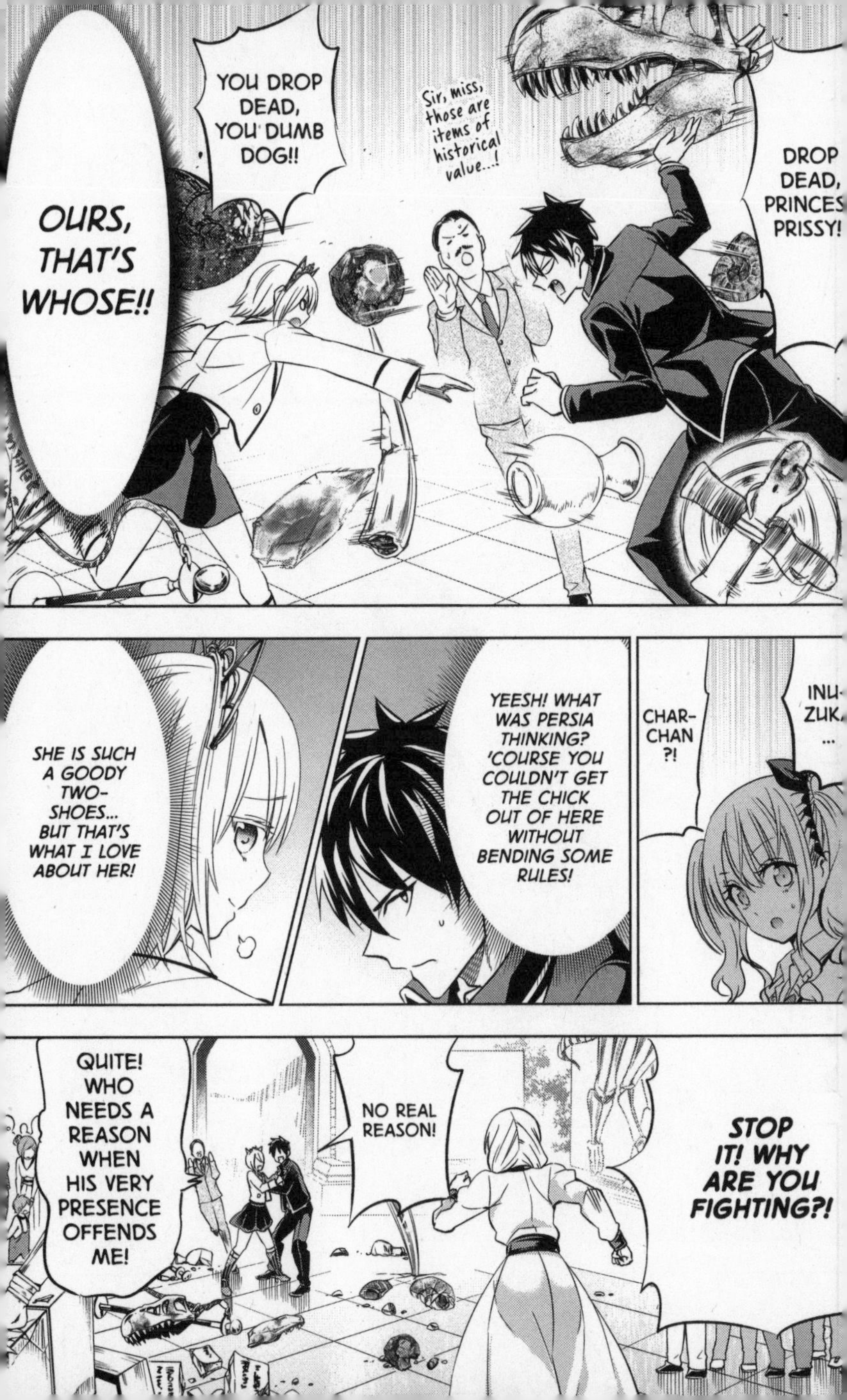
DROP DEAD, PRINCES PRISSY!
Sir, miss, those are items of historical value...!
YOU DROP DEAD, YOU DUMB DOG!!
OURS, THAT'S WHOSE!!
INU-ZUKA...
CHAR-CHAN?!
YEESH! WHAT WAS PERSIA THINKING? 'COURSE YOU COULDN'T GET THE CHICK OUT OF HERE WITHOUT BENDING SOME RULES!
SHE IS SUCH A GOODY TWO-SHOES... BUT THAT'S WHAT I LOVE ABOUT HER!
STOP IT! WHY ARE YOU FIGHTING?!
NO REAL REASON!
QUITE! WHO NEEDS A REASON WHEN HIS VERY PRESENCE OFFENDS ME!

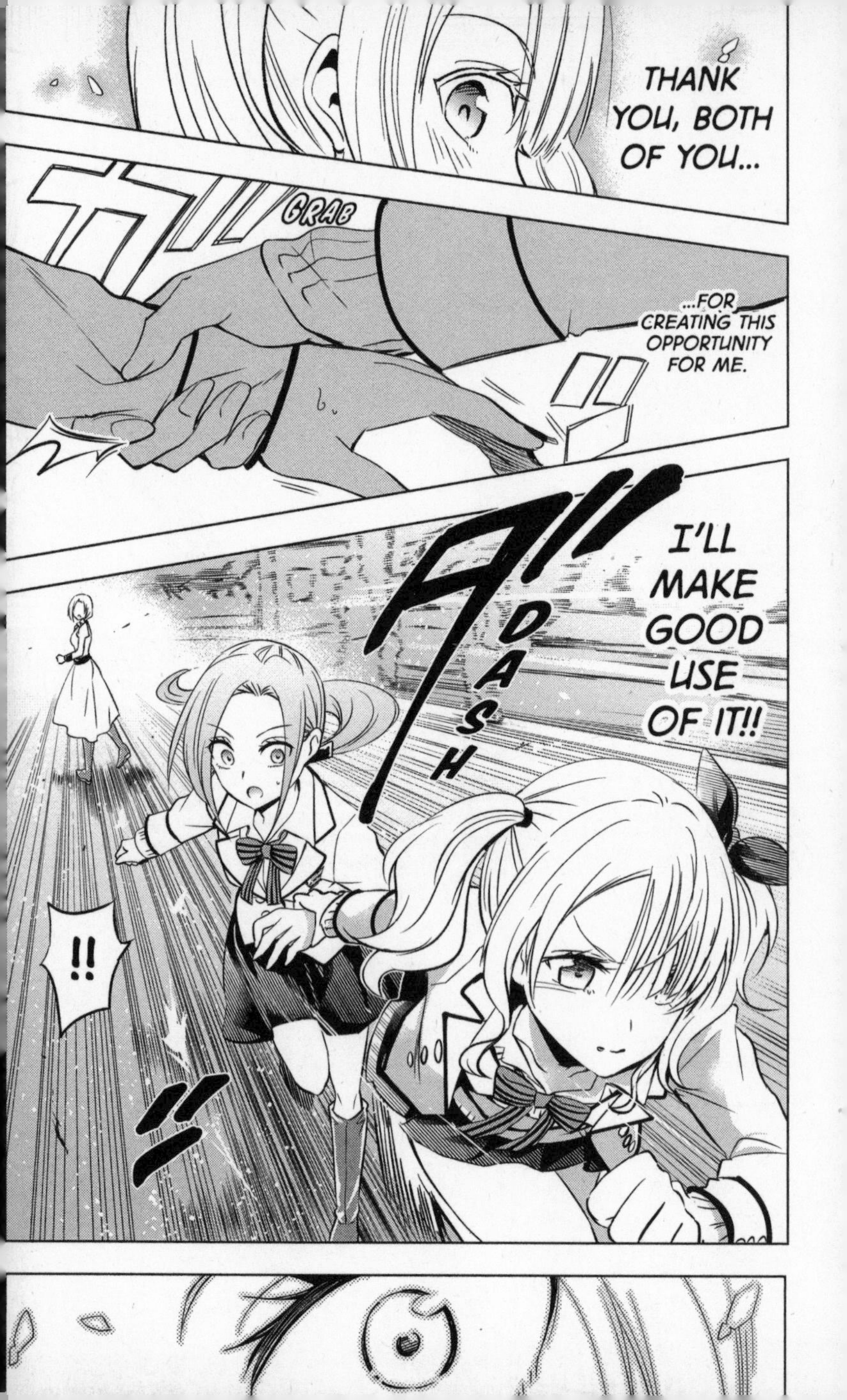
THANK YOU, BOTH OF YOU...
GRAB
...FOR CREATING THIS OPPORTUNITY FOR ME.
I'LL MAKE GOOD USE OF IT!!
DASH
!!

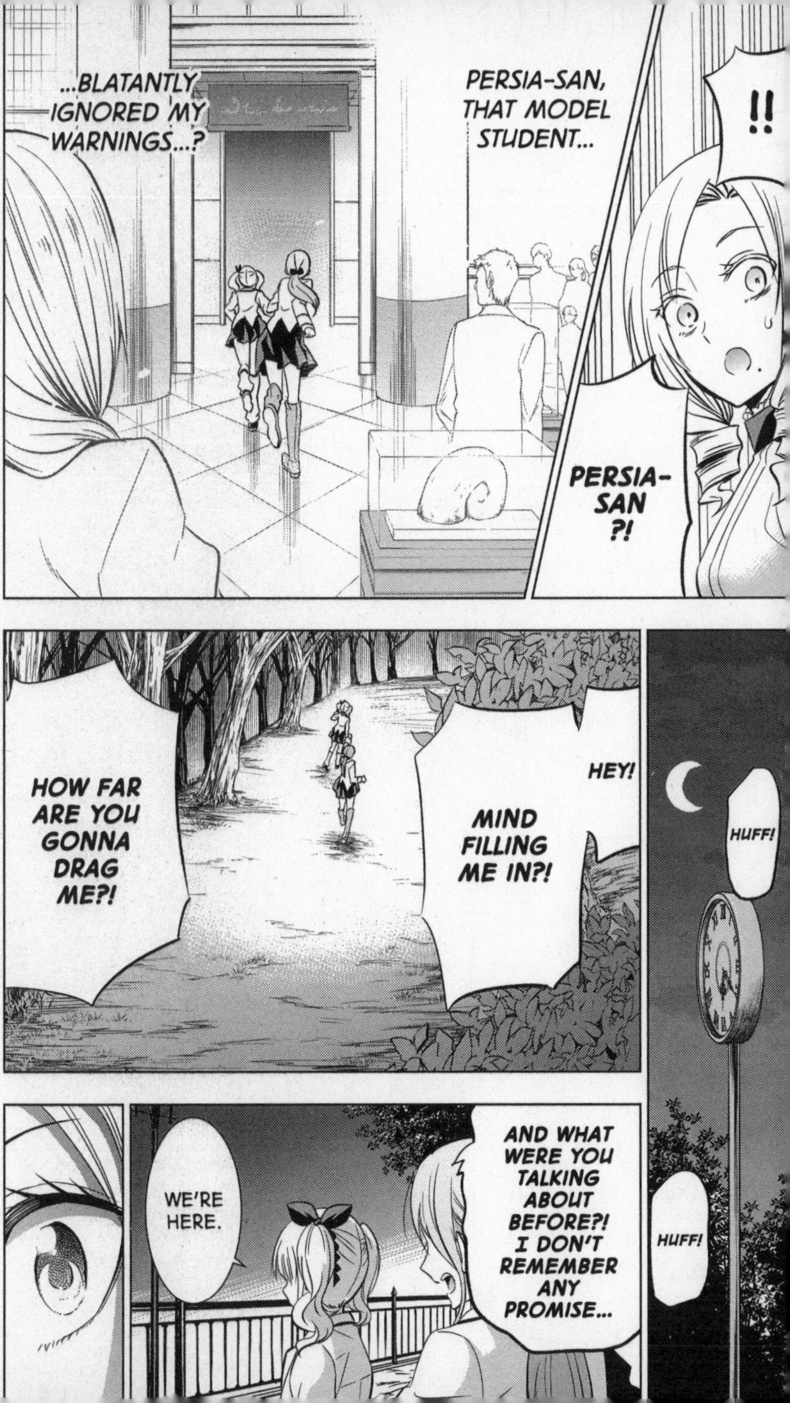
!!
PERSIA-SAN?!
PERSIA-SAN, THAT MODEL STUDENT...
...BLATANTLY IGNORED MY WARNINGS...?
HUFF!
HUFF!
HEY!
MIND FILLING ME IN?!
HOW FAR ARE YOU GONNA DRAG ME?!
AND WHAT WERE YOU TALKING ABOUT BEFORE?! I DON'T REMEMBER ANY PROMISE...
WE'RE HERE.

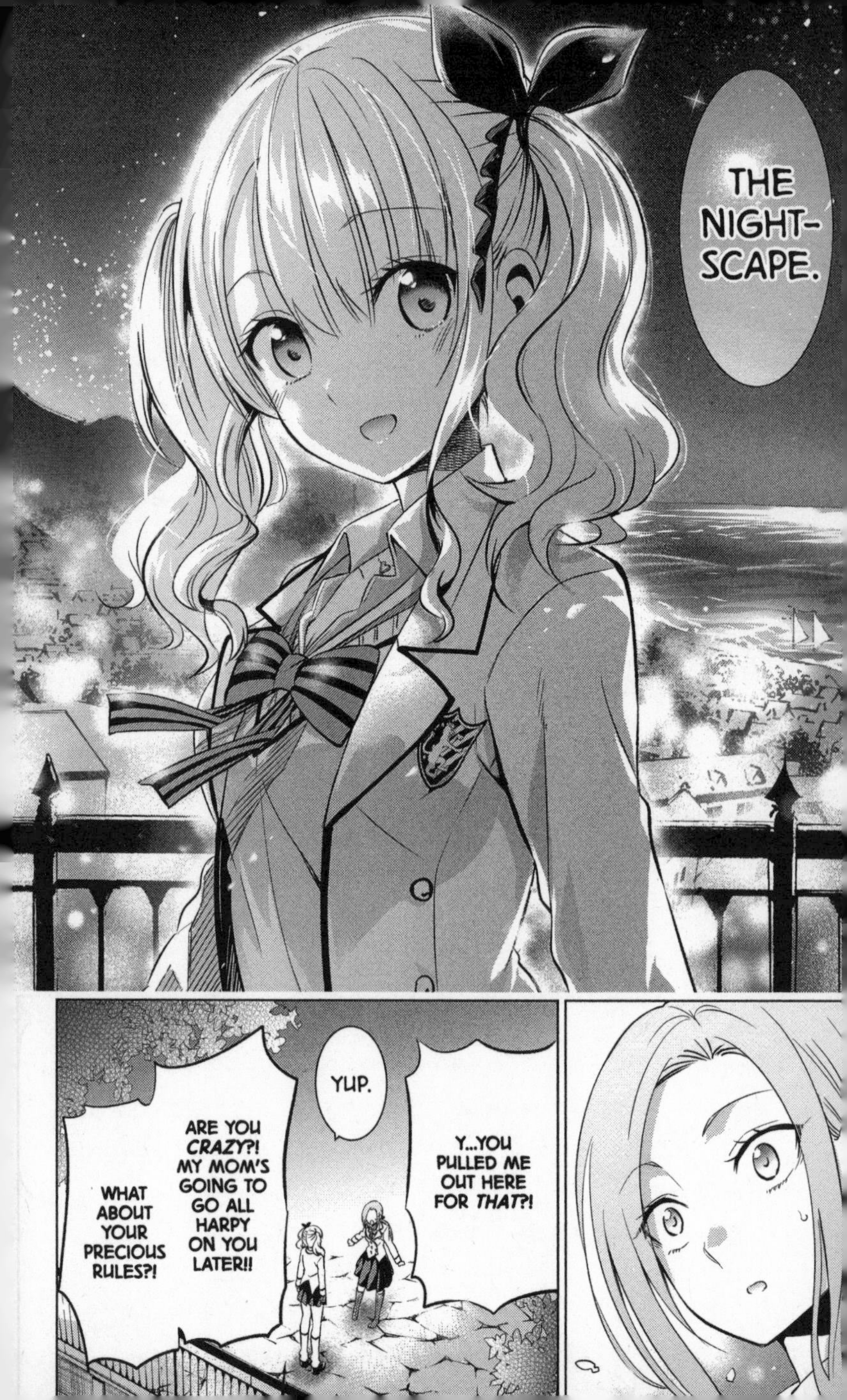
THE NIGHT-SCAPE.
Y...YOU PULLED ME OUT HERE FOR *THAT*?!
YUP.
ARE YOU *CRAZY*?! MY MOM'S GOING TO GO ALL HARPY ON YOU LATER!!
WHAT ABOUT YOUR PRECIOUS RULES?!

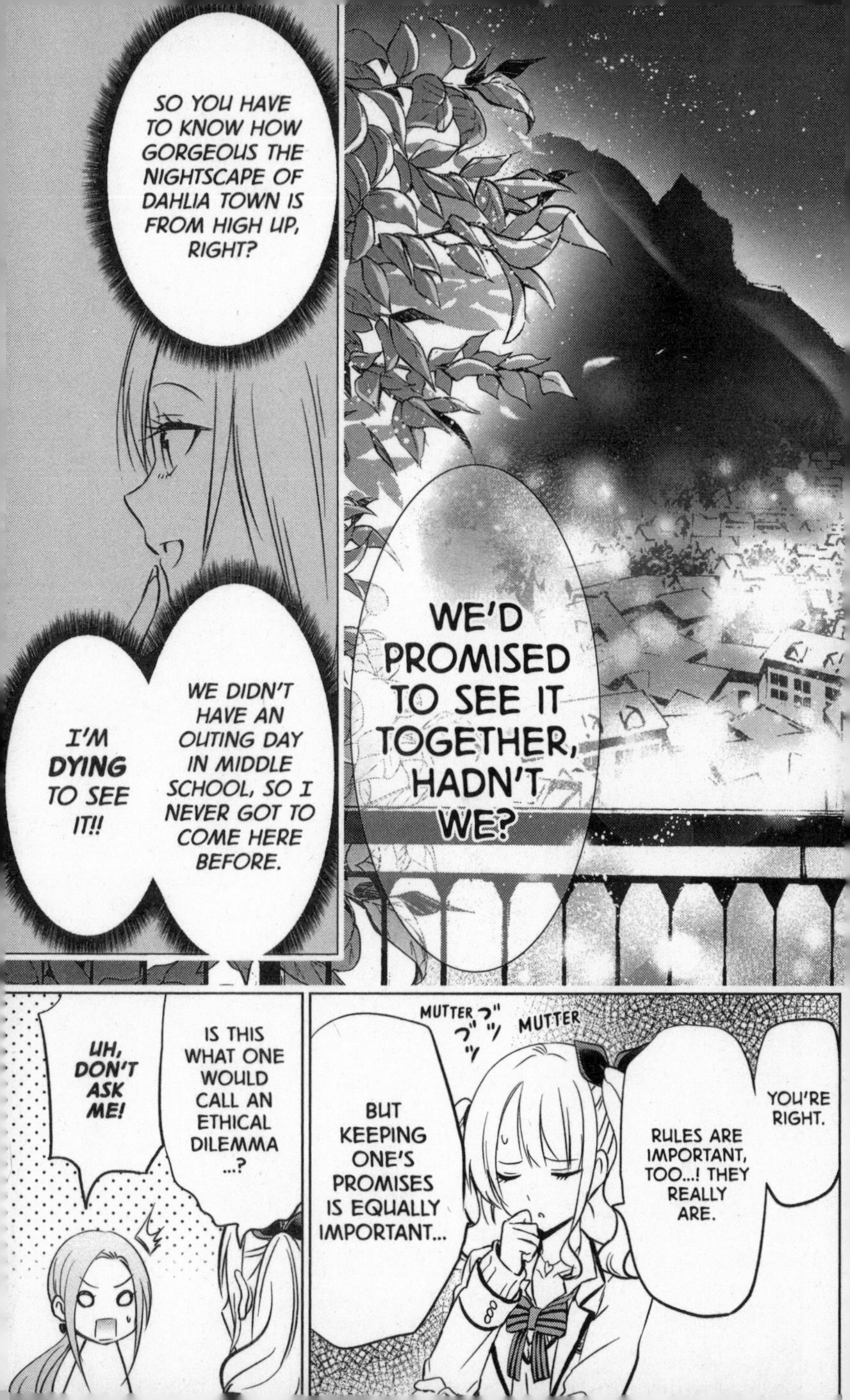
WE'D PROMISED TO SEE IT TOGETHER, HADN'T WE?
SO YOU HAVE TO KNOW HOW GORGEOUS THE NIGHTSCAPE OF DAHLIA TOWN IS FROM HIGH UP, RIGHT?
WE DIDN'T HAVE AN OUTING DAY IN MIDDLE SCHOOL, SO I NEVER GOT TO COME HERE BEFORE.
I'M **DYING** TO SEE IT!!
MUTTER
MUTTER
YOU'RE RIGHT.
RULES ARE IMPORTANT, TOO...! THEY REALLY ARE.
BUT KEEPING ONE'S PROMISES IS EQUALLY IMPORTANT...
IS THIS WHAT ONE WOULD CALL AN ETHICAL DILEMMA ...?
UH, DON'T ASK ME!

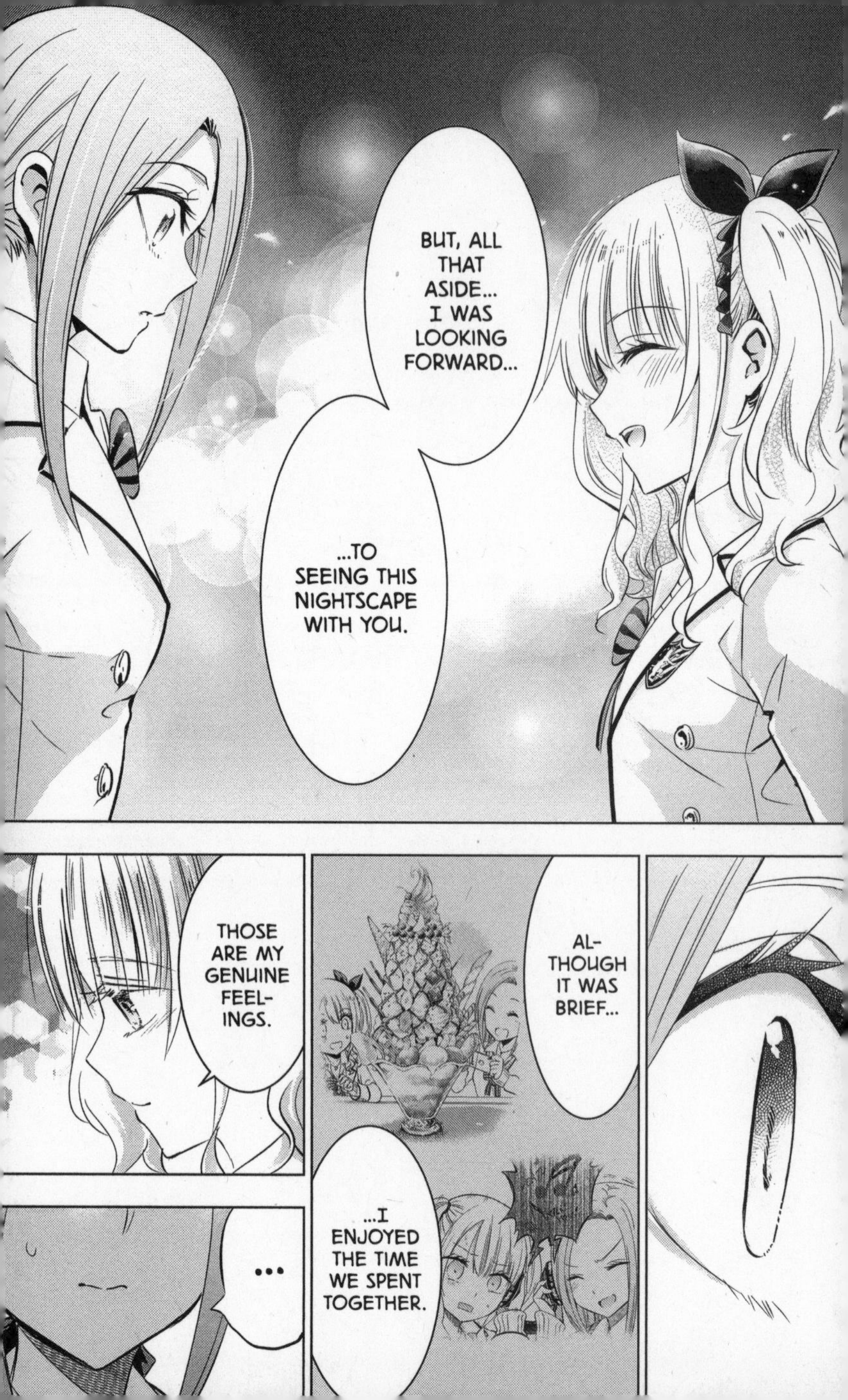
BUT, ALL THAT ASIDE... I WAS LOOKING FORWARD...
...TO SEEING THIS NIGHTSCAPE WITH YOU.
AL-THOUGH IT WAS BRIEF...
...I ENJOYED THE TIME WE SPENT TOGETHER.
THOSE ARE MY GENUINE FEEL-INGS.
...

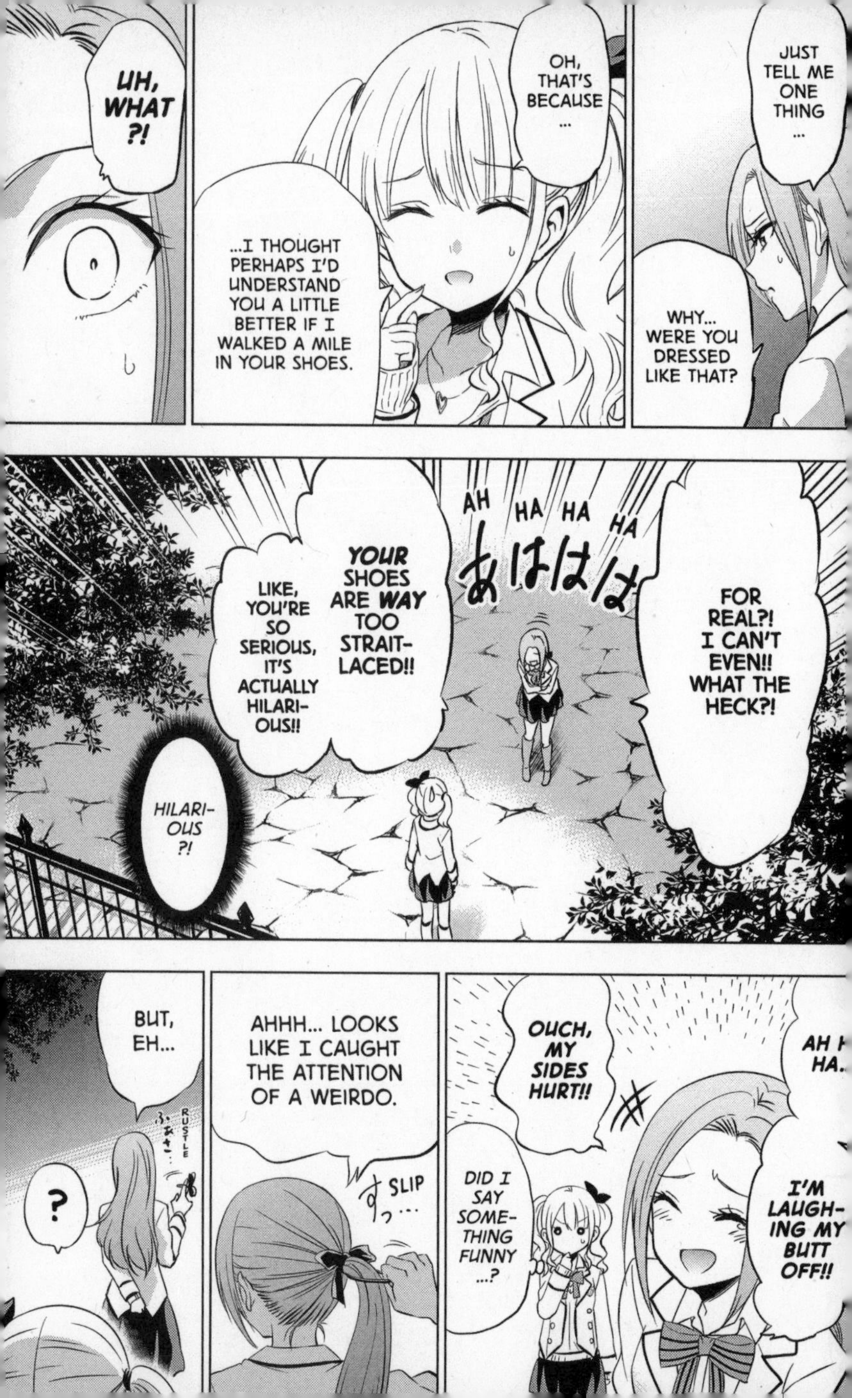
JUST TELL ME ONE THING ...
WHY... WERE YOU DRESSED LIKE THAT?
OH, THAT'S BECAUSE ...
...I THOUGHT PERHAPS I'D UNDERSTAND YOU A LITTLE BETTER IF I WALKED A MILE IN YOUR SHOES.
UH, WHAT ?!
AH HA HA HA
あははは
FOR REAL?! I CAN'T EVEN!! WHAT THE HECK?!
YOUR SHOES ARE WAY TOO STRAIT-LACED!!
LIKE, YOU'RE SO SERIOUS, IT'S ACTUALLY HILARI-OUS!!
HILARI-OUS ?!
AH H HA.
OUCH, MY SIDES HURT!!
I'M LAUGH-ING MY BUTT OFF!!
DID I SAY SOME-THING FUNNY ...?
AHHH... LOOKS LIKE I CAUGHT THE ATTENTION OF A WEIRDO.
すっ SLIP...
BUT, EH...
RUSTLE
?

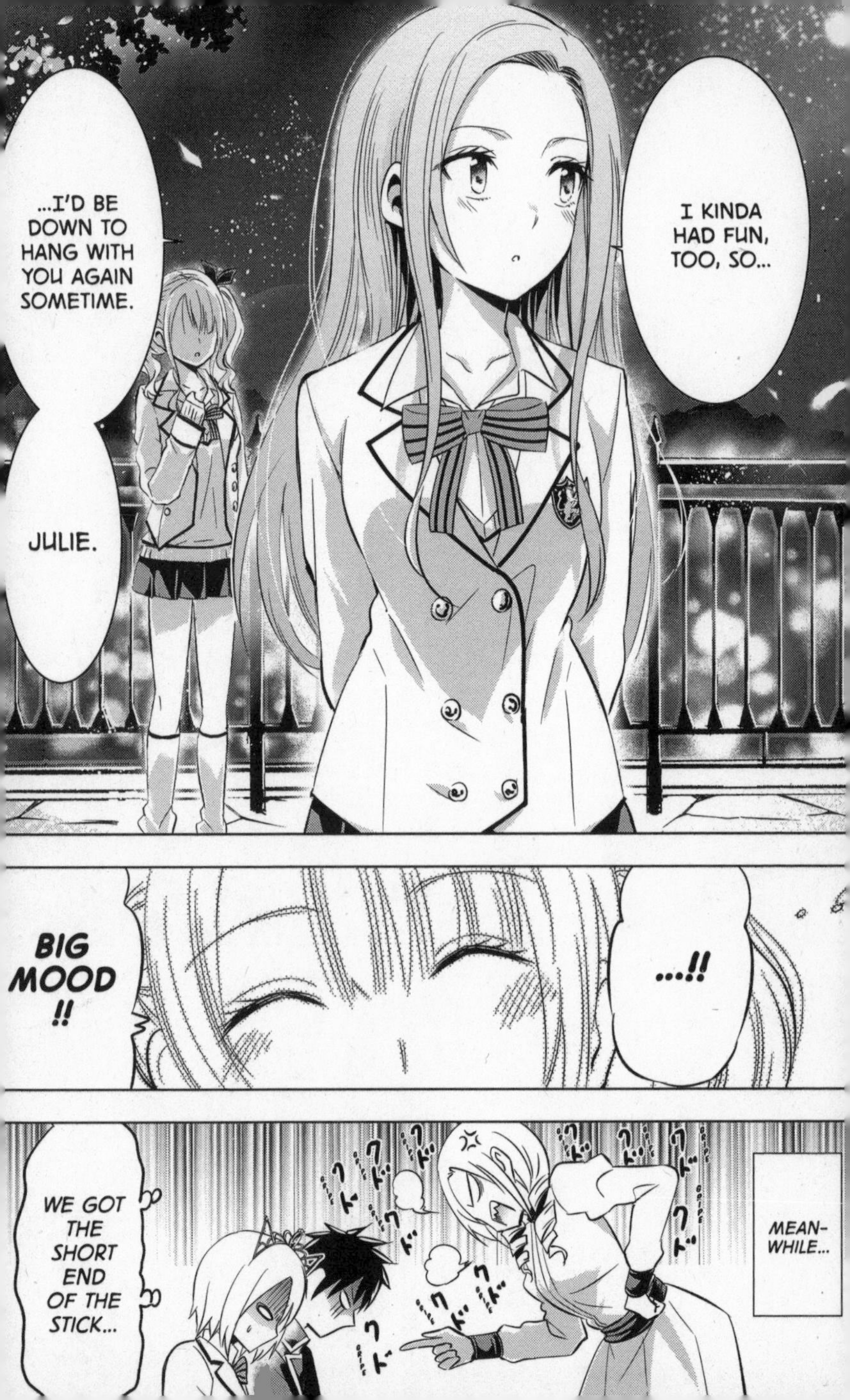
I KINDA HAD FUN, TOO, SO...
...I'D BE DOWN TO HANG WITH YOU AGAIN SOMETIME.
JULIE.
...!!
BIG MOOD !!
MEAN-WHILE...
WE GOT THE SHORT END OF THE STICK...

BOARDING SCHOOL JULIET
2,000,000+ TOTAL SALES

Very Much!

Double peace signs!

Thank You

DON'T LOOK SO SMUG!

Thank you,

thank you,

thank you,

Thank You!!

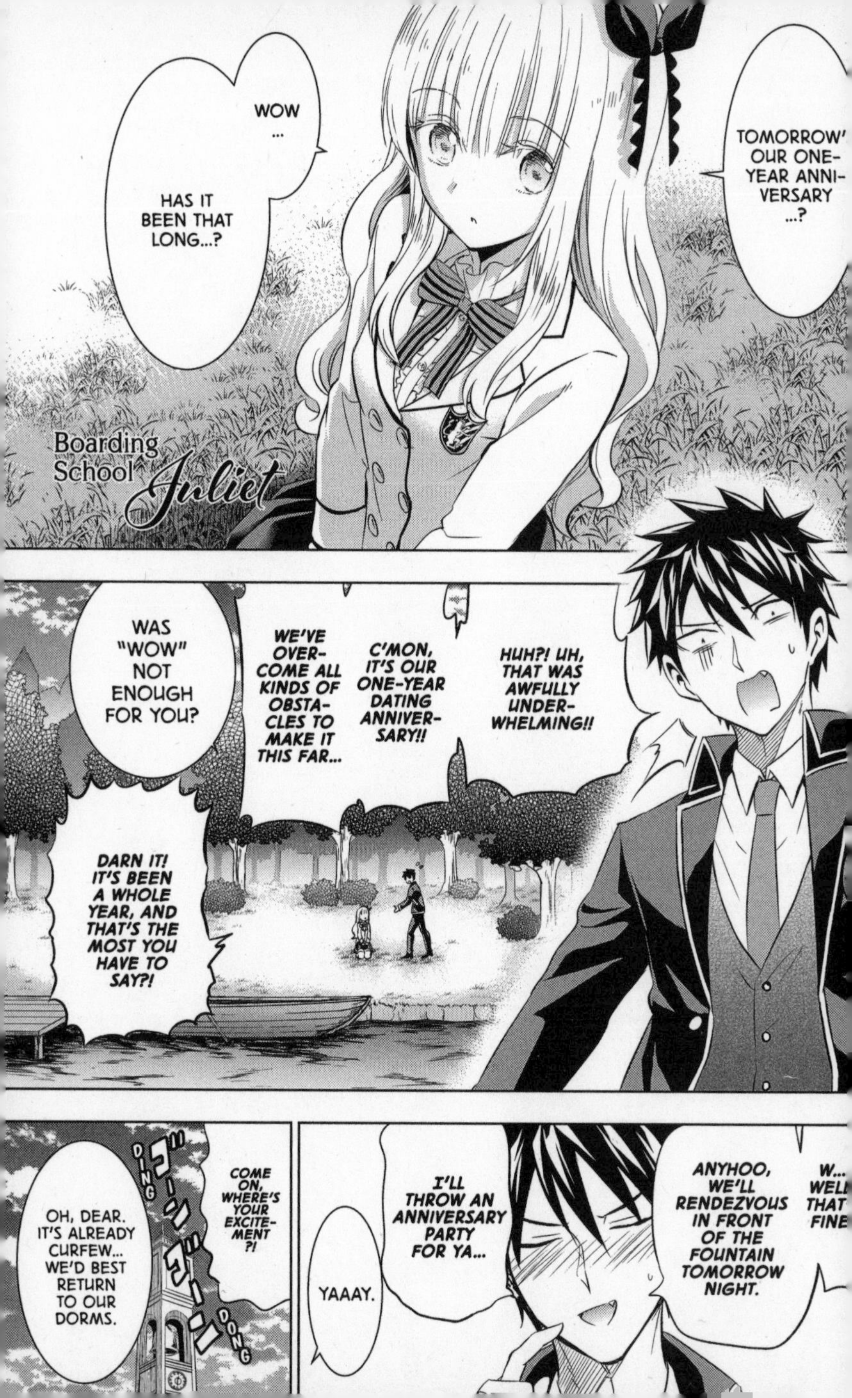
TOMORROW' OUR ONE-YEAR ANNIVERSARY ...?
WOW ...
HAS IT BEEN THAT LONG...?
Boarding School Juliet
HUH?! UH, THAT WAS AWFULLY UNDER-WHELMING!!
C'MON, IT'S OUR ONE-YEAR DATING ANNIVER-SARY!!
WE'VE OVER-COME ALL KINDS OF OBSTA-CLES TO MAKE IT THIS FAR...
WAS "WOW" NOT ENOUGH FOR YOU?
DARN IT! IT'S BEEN A WHOLE YEAR, AND THAT'S THE MOST YOU HAVE TO SAY?!
W... WELL THAT FINE
ANYHOO, WE'LL RENDEZVOUS IN FRONT OF THE FOUNTAIN TOMORROW NIGHT.
I'LL THROW AN ANNIVERSARY PARTY FOR YA...
YAAAY.
COME ON, WHERE'S YOUR EXCITE-MENT ?!
DING
DONG
OH, DEAR. IT'S ALREADY CURFEW... WE'D BEST RETURN TO OUR DORMS.

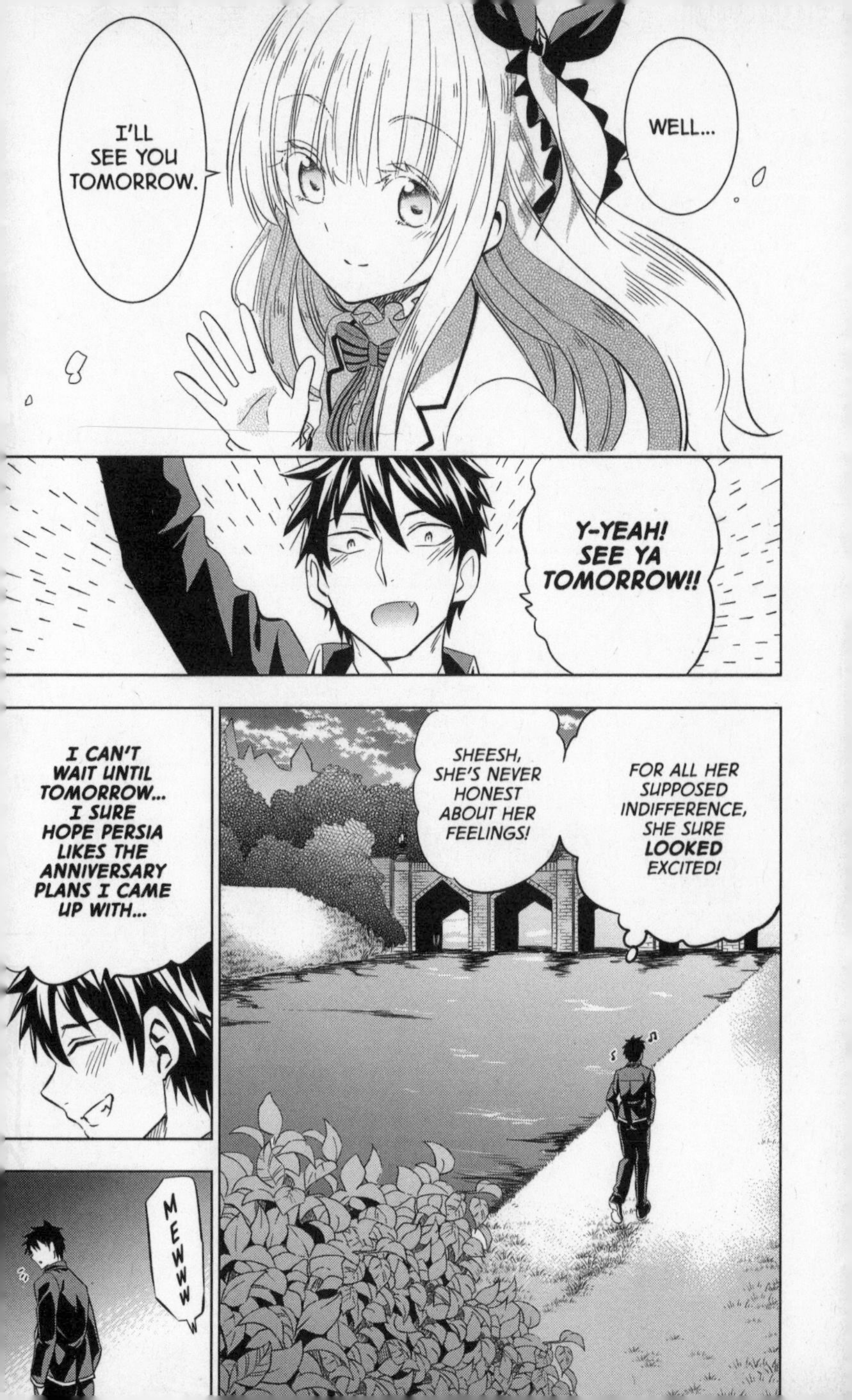
WELL...
I'LL SEE YOU TOMORROW.
Y-YEAH! SEE YA TOMORROW!!
FOR ALL HER SUPPOSED INDIFFERENCE, SHE SURE LOOKED EXCITED!
SHEESH, SHE'S NEVER HONEST ABOUT HER FEELINGS!
I CAN'T WAIT UNTIL TOMORROW... I SURE HOPE PERSIA LIKES THE ANNIVERSARY PLANS I CAME UP WITH...
MEWWW

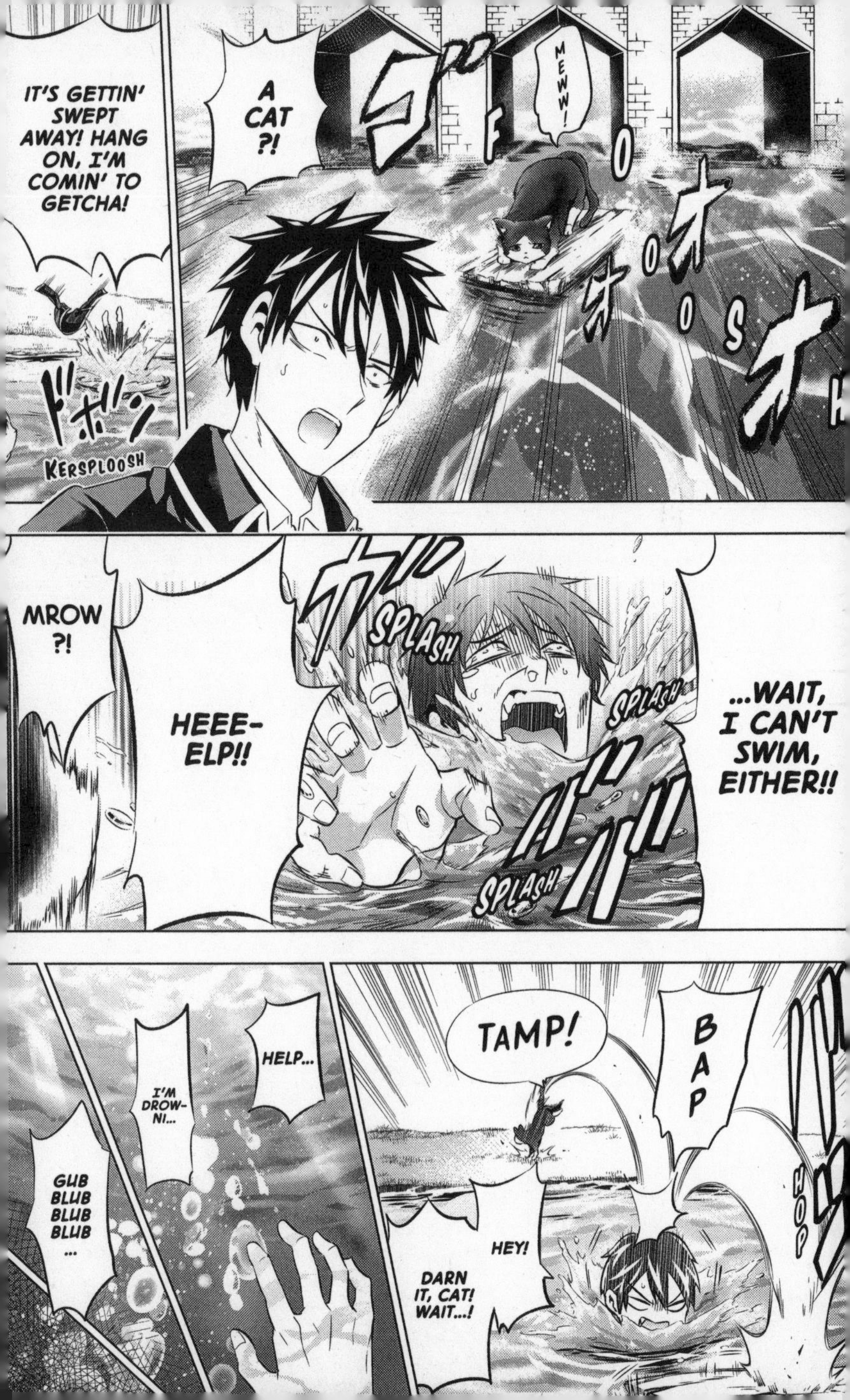
MEWW!
FOOOSH
A CAT?!
IT'S GETTIN' SWEPT AWAY! HANG ON, I'M COMIN' TO GETCHA!
KERSPLOOSH
...WAIT, I CAN'T SWIM, EITHER!!
SPLASH
SPLASH
SPLASH
HEEE-ELP!!
MROW?!
BAP
TAMP!
HOP
HEY!
DARN IT, CAT! WAIT...!
HELP...
I'M DROWNI...
GUB BLUB BLUB BLUB ...

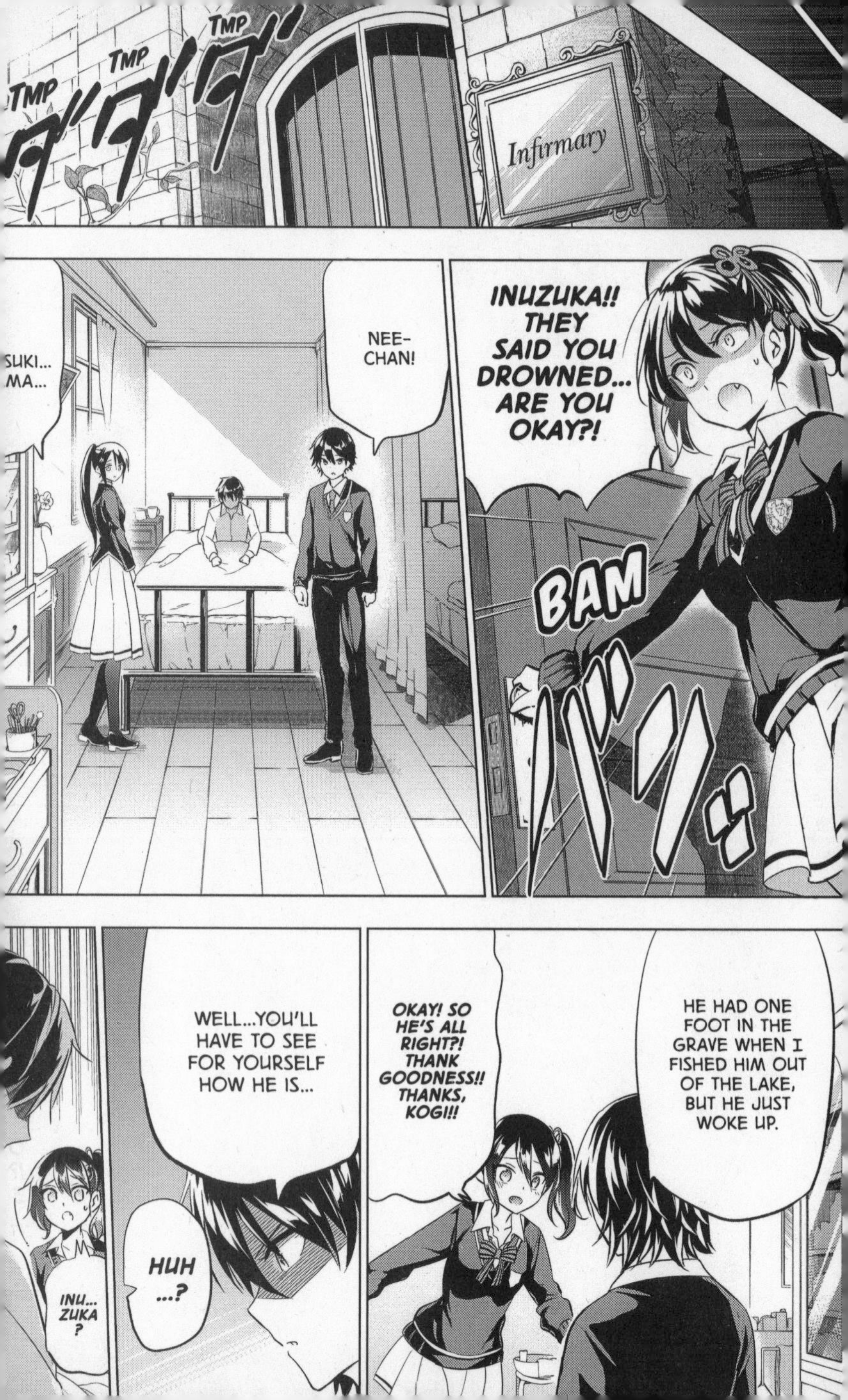
TMP
TMP
TMP
Infirmary
INUZUKA!! THEY SAID YOU DROWNED... ARE YOU OKAY?!
BAM
NEE-CHAN!
SUKI... MA...
HE HAD ONE FOOT IN THE GRAVE WHEN I FISHED HIM OUT OF THE LAKE, BUT HE JUST WOKE UP.
OKAY! SO HE'S ALL RIGHT?! THANK GOODNESS!! THANKS, KOGI!!
WELL...YOU'LL HAVE TO SEE FOR YOURSELF HOW HE IS...
HUH ...?
INU... ZUKA ?

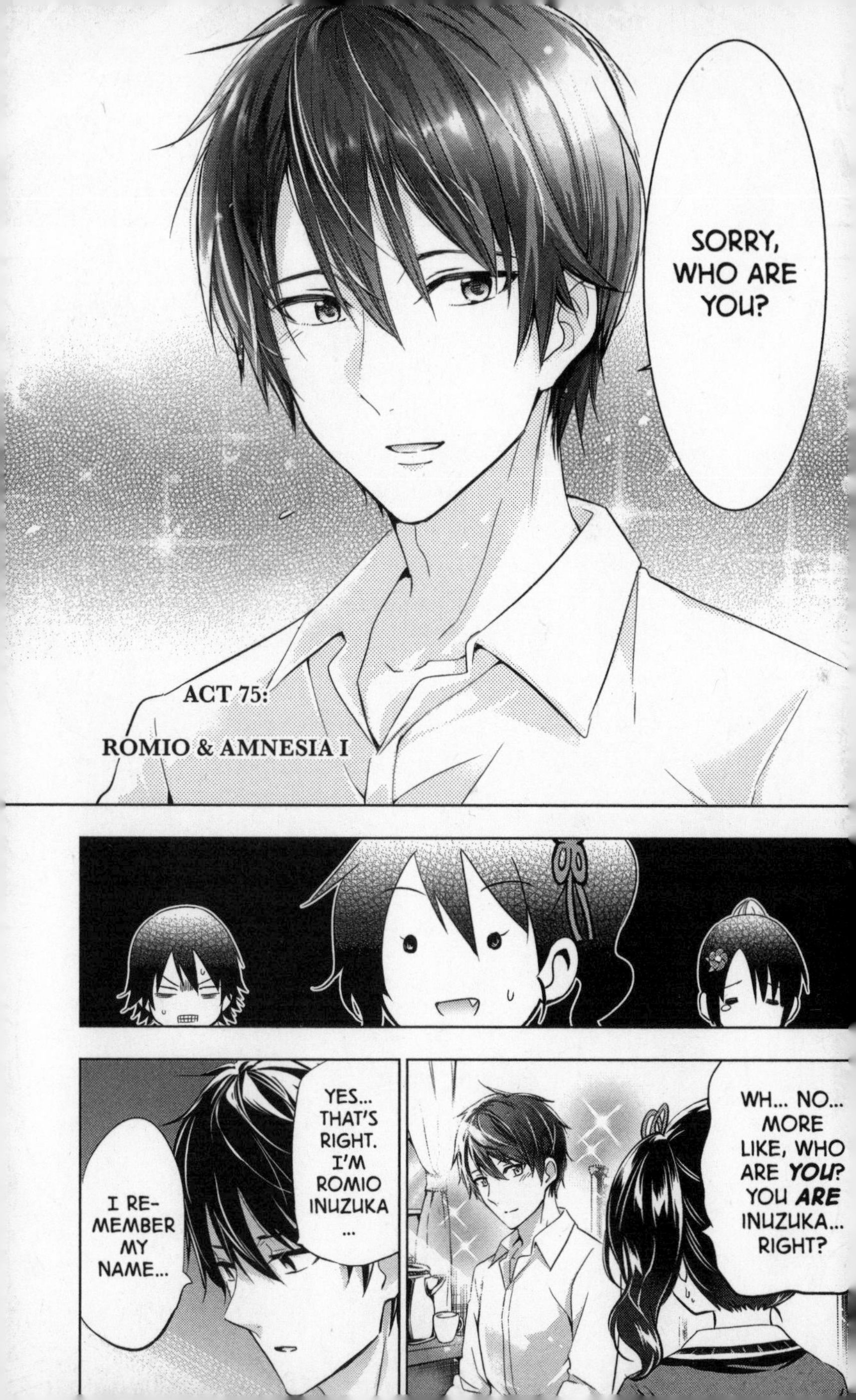
SORRY, WHO ARE YOU?
ACT 75:
ROMIO & AMNESIA I
WH... NO... MORE LIKE, WHO ARE *YOU*? YOU *ARE* INUZUKA... RIGHT?
YES... THAT'S RIGHT. I'M ROMIO INUZUKA ...
I RE-MEMBER MY NAME...

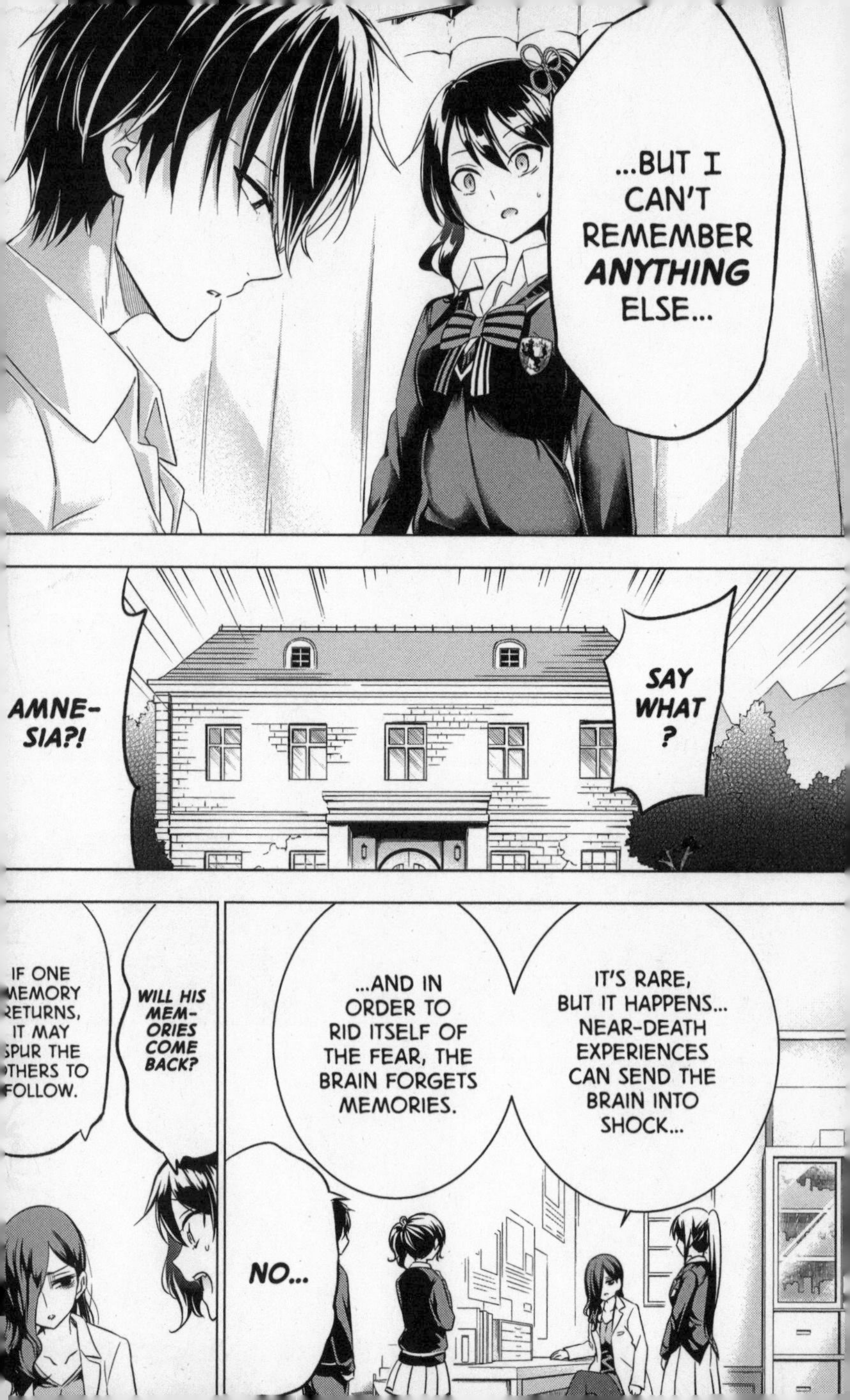
...BUT I CAN'T REMEMBER ANYTHING ELSE...
SAY WHAT?
AMNE-SIA?!
IT'S RARE, BUT IT HAPPENS... NEAR-DEATH EXPERIENCES CAN SEND THE BRAIN INTO SHOCK...
...AND IN ORDER TO RID ITSELF OF THE FEAR, THE BRAIN FORGETS MEMORIES.
NO...
WILL HIS MEM-ORIES COME BACK?
IF ONE MEMORY RETURNS, IT MAY SPUR THE OTHERS TO FOLLOW.

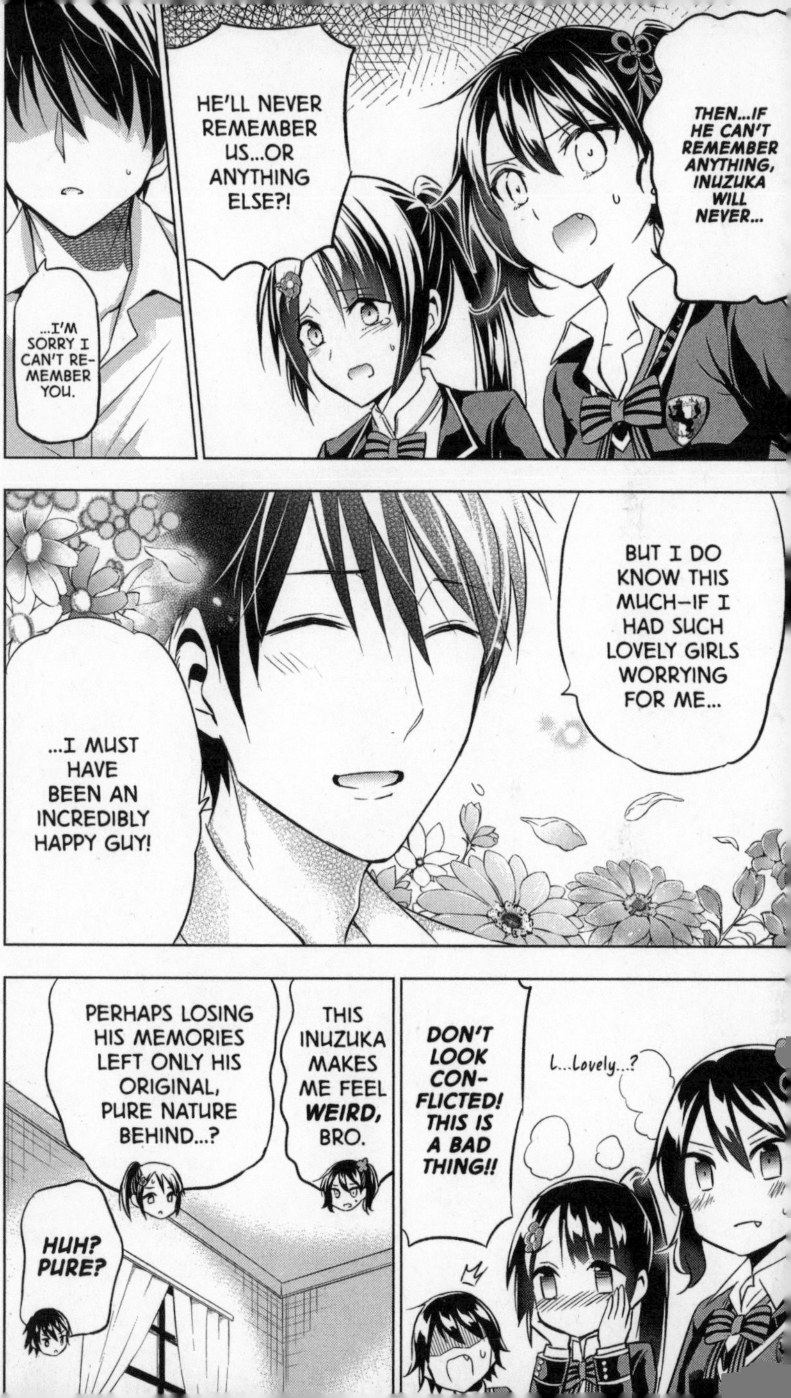
THEN...IF HE CAN'T REMEMBER ANYTHING, INUZUKA WILL NEVER...
HE'LL NEVER REMEMBER US...OR ANYTHING ELSE?!
...I'M SORRY I CAN'T RE-MEMBER YOU.
BUT I DO KNOW THIS MUCH—IF I HAD SUCH LOVELY GIRLS WORRYING FOR ME...
...I MUST HAVE BEEN AN INCREDIBLY HAPPY GUY!
L...Lovely...?
DON'T LOOK CON-FLICTED! THIS IS A BAD THING!!
THIS INUZUKA MAKES ME FEEL WEIRD, BRO.
PERHAPS LOSING HIS MEMORIES LEFT ONLY HIS ORIGINAL, PURE NATURE BEHIND...?
HUH? PURE?

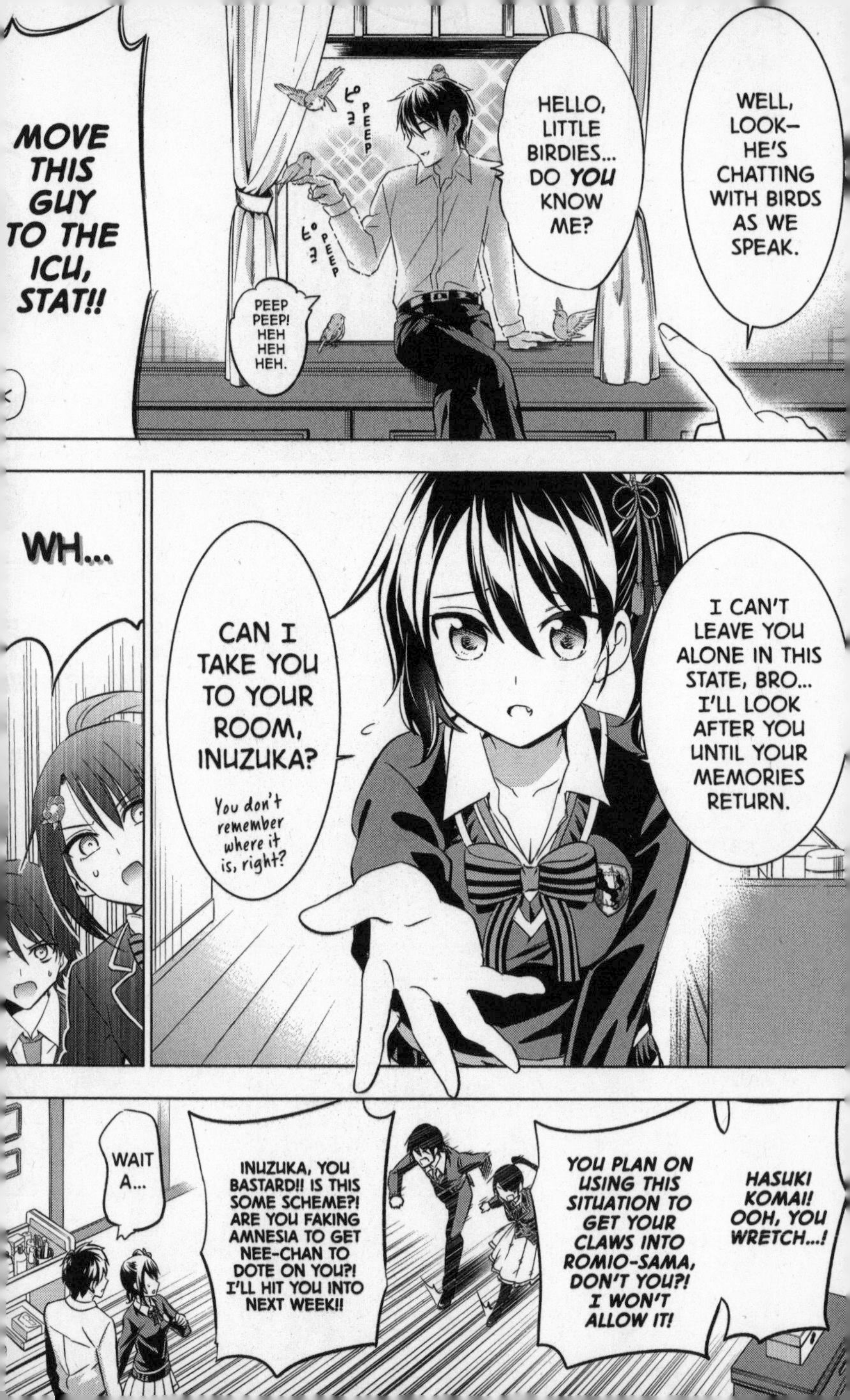
WELL, LOOK— HE'S CHATTING WITH BIRDS AS WE SPEAK.
HELLO, LITTLE BIRDIES... DO *YOU* KNOW ME?
ピヨ PEEP
ピヨ PEEP
PEEP PEEP! HEH HEH HEH.
MOVE THIS GUY TO THE ICU, STAT!!
I CAN'T LEAVE YOU ALONE IN THIS STATE, BRO... I'LL LOOK AFTER YOU UNTIL YOUR MEMORIES RETURN.
CAN I TAKE YOU TO YOUR ROOM, INUZUKA?
You don't remember where it is, right?
WH...
HASUKI KOMAI! OOH, YOU WRETCH...!
YOU PLAN ON USING THIS SITUATION TO GET YOUR CLAWS INTO ROMIO-SAMA, DON'T YOU?! I WON'T ALLOW IT!
INUZUKA, YOU BASTARD!! IS THIS SOME SCHEME?! ARE YOU FAKING AMNESIA TO GET NEE-CHAN TO DOTE ON YOU?! I'LL HIT YOU INTO NEXT WEEK!!
WAIT A...

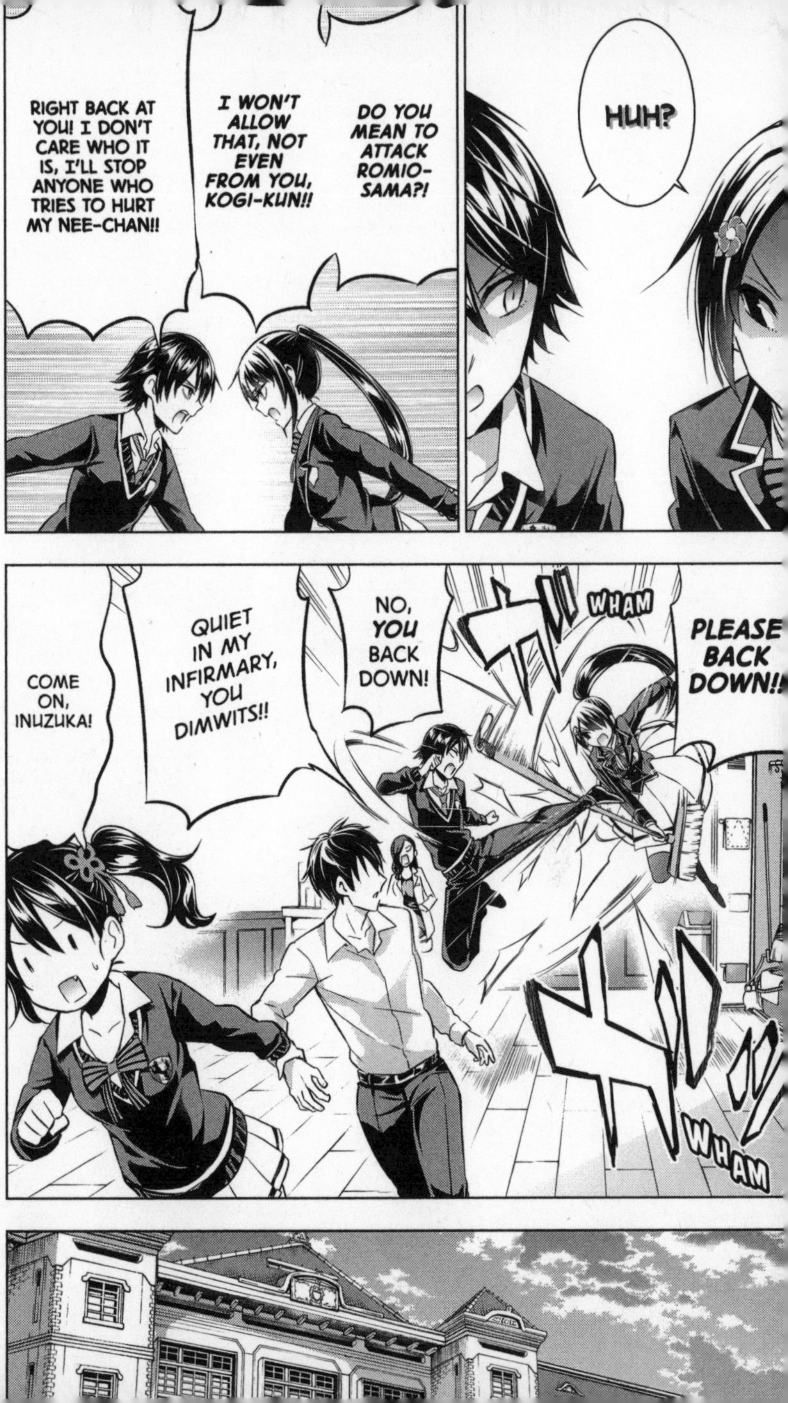
HUH?
DO YOU MEAN TO ATTACK ROMIO-SAMA?!
I WON'T ALLOW THAT, NOT EVEN FROM YOU, KOGI-KUN!!
RIGHT BACK AT YOU! I DON'T CARE WHO IT IS, I'LL STOP ANYONE WHO TRIES TO HURT MY NEE-CHAN!!
PLEASE BACK DOWN!!
WHAM
NO, YOU BACK DOWN!
QUIET IN MY INFIRMARY, YOU DIMWITS!!
COME ON, INUZUKA!
WHAM

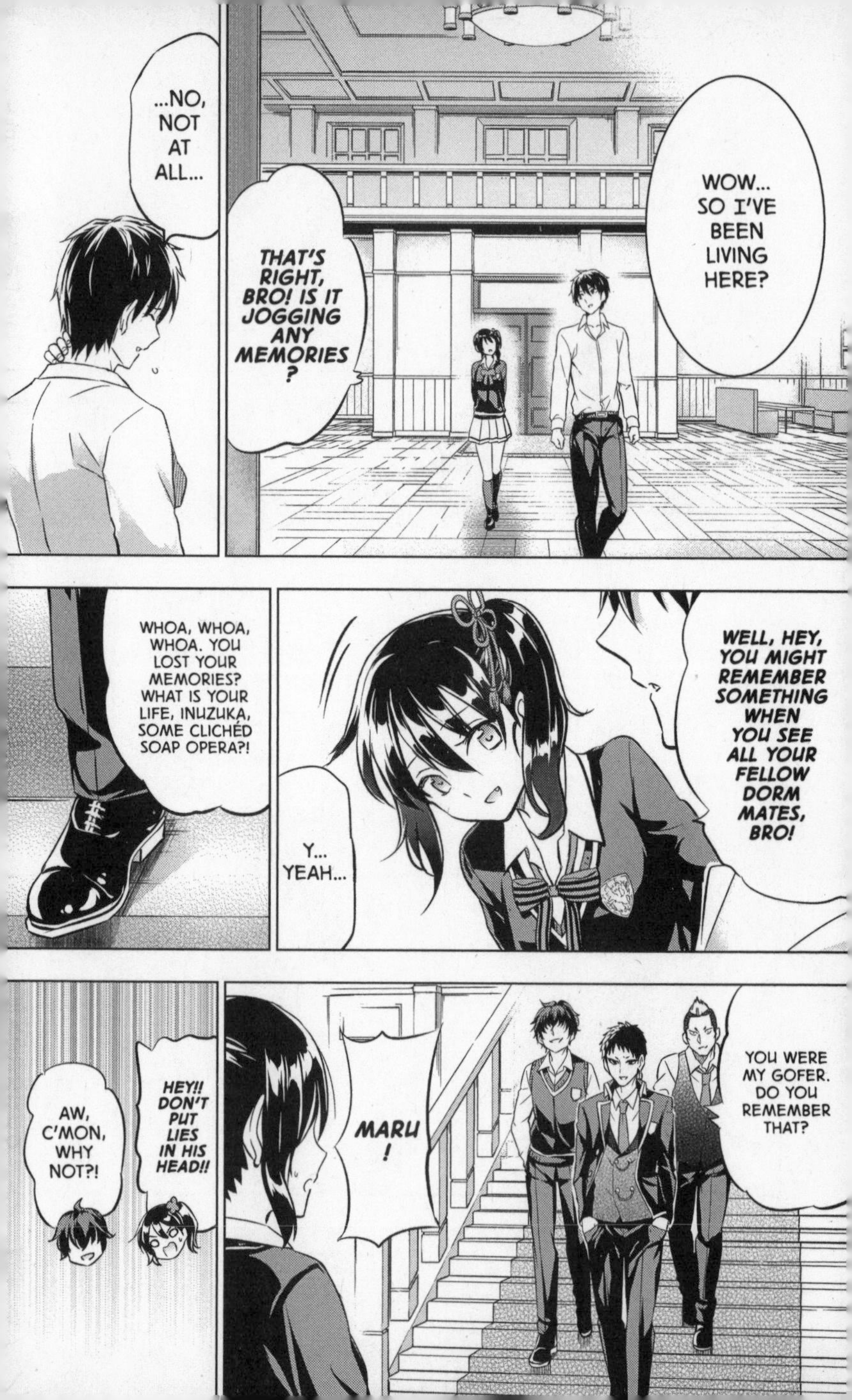

WOW... SO I'VE BEEN LIVING HERE?
THAT'S RIGHT, BRO! IS IT JOGGING ANY MEMORIES?
...NO, NOT AT ALL...
WELL, HEY, YOU MIGHT REMEMBER SOMETHING WHEN YOU SEE ALL YOUR FELLOW DORM MATES, BRO!
Y... YEAH...
WHOA, WHOA, WHOA. YOU LOST YOUR MEMORIES? WHAT IS YOUR LIFE, INUZUKA, SOME CLICHÉD SOAP OPERA?!
YOU WERE MY GOFER. DO YOU REMEMBER THAT?
MARU!
HEY!! DON'T PUT LIES IN HIS HEAD!!
AW, C'MON, WHY NOT?!

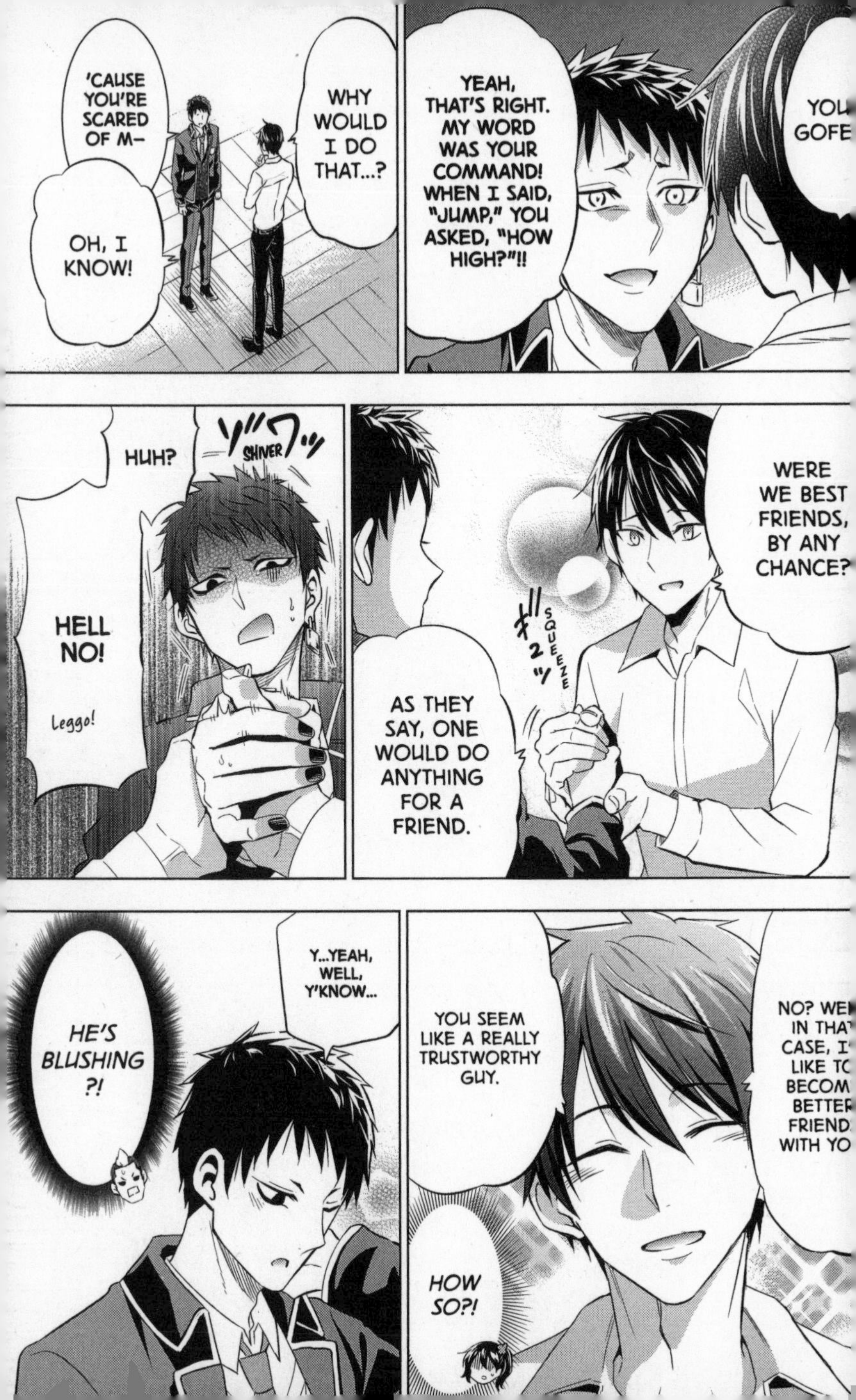
YEAH, THAT'S RIGHT. MY WORD WAS YOUR COMMAND! WHEN I SAID, "JUMP," YOU ASKED, "HOW HIGH?"!!
YOU GOFE
WHY WOULD I DO THAT...?
'CAUSE YOU'RE SCARED OF M–
OH, I KNOW!
WERE WE BEST FRIENDS, BY ANY CHANCE?
SQUEEZE
AS THEY SAY, ONE WOULD DO ANYTHING FOR A FRIEND.
SHIVER
HUH?
HELL NO!
Leggo!
NO? WE IN THAT CASE, I' LIKE TO BECOM BETTER FRIEND WITH YO
YOU SEEM LIKE A REALLY TRUSTWORTHY GUY.
HOW SO?!
Y...YEAH, WELL, Y'KNOW...
HE'S BLUSHING?!

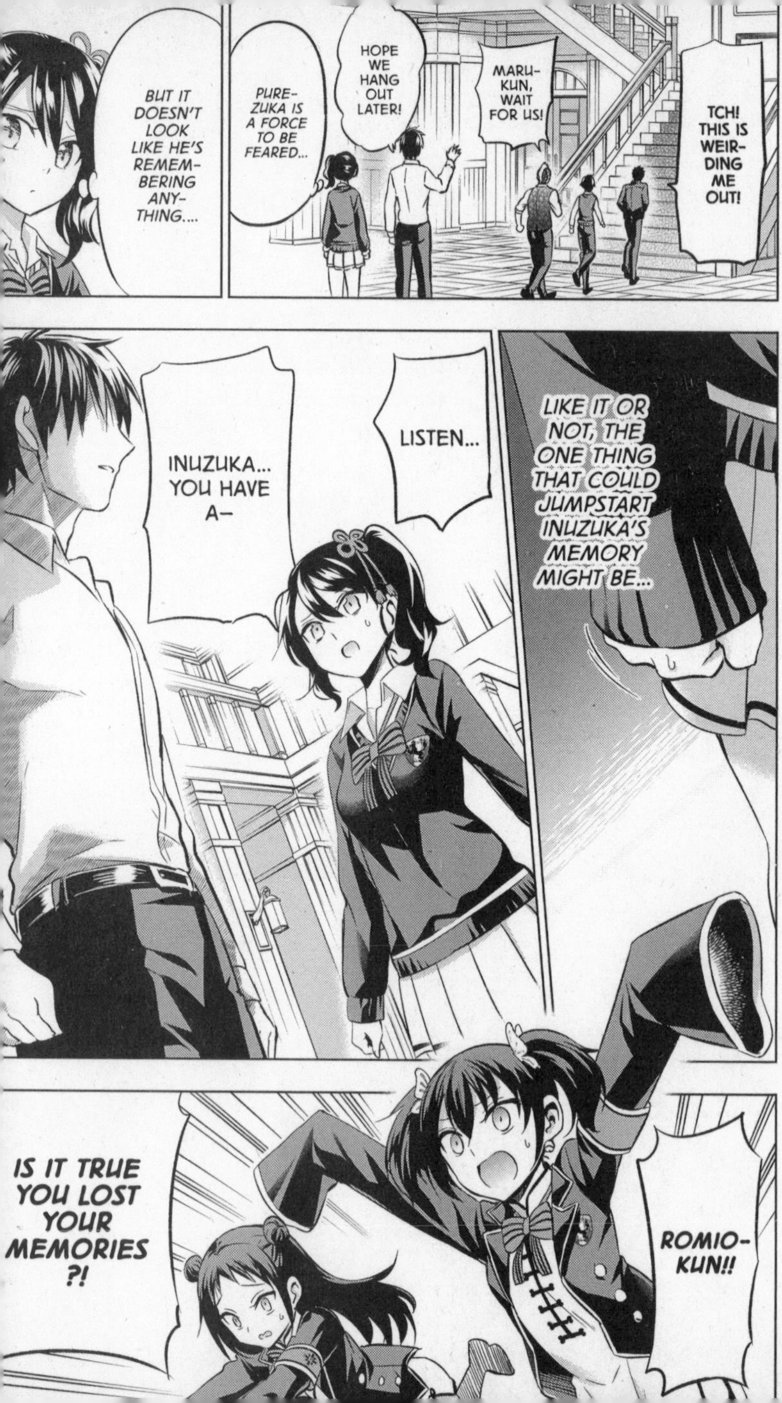
TCH! THIS IS WEIRDING ME OUT!
MARU-KUN, WAIT FOR US!
HOPE WE HANG OUT LATER!
PURE-ZUKA IS A FORCE TO BE FEARED...
BUT IT DOESN'T LOOK LIKE HE'S REMEMBERING ANYTHING....
LIKE IT OR NOT, THE ONE THING THAT COULD JUMPSTART INUZUKA'S MEMORY MIGHT BE...
LISTEN...
INUZUKA... YOU HAVE A—
ROMIO-KUN!!
IS IT TRUE YOU LOST YOUR MEMORIES?!

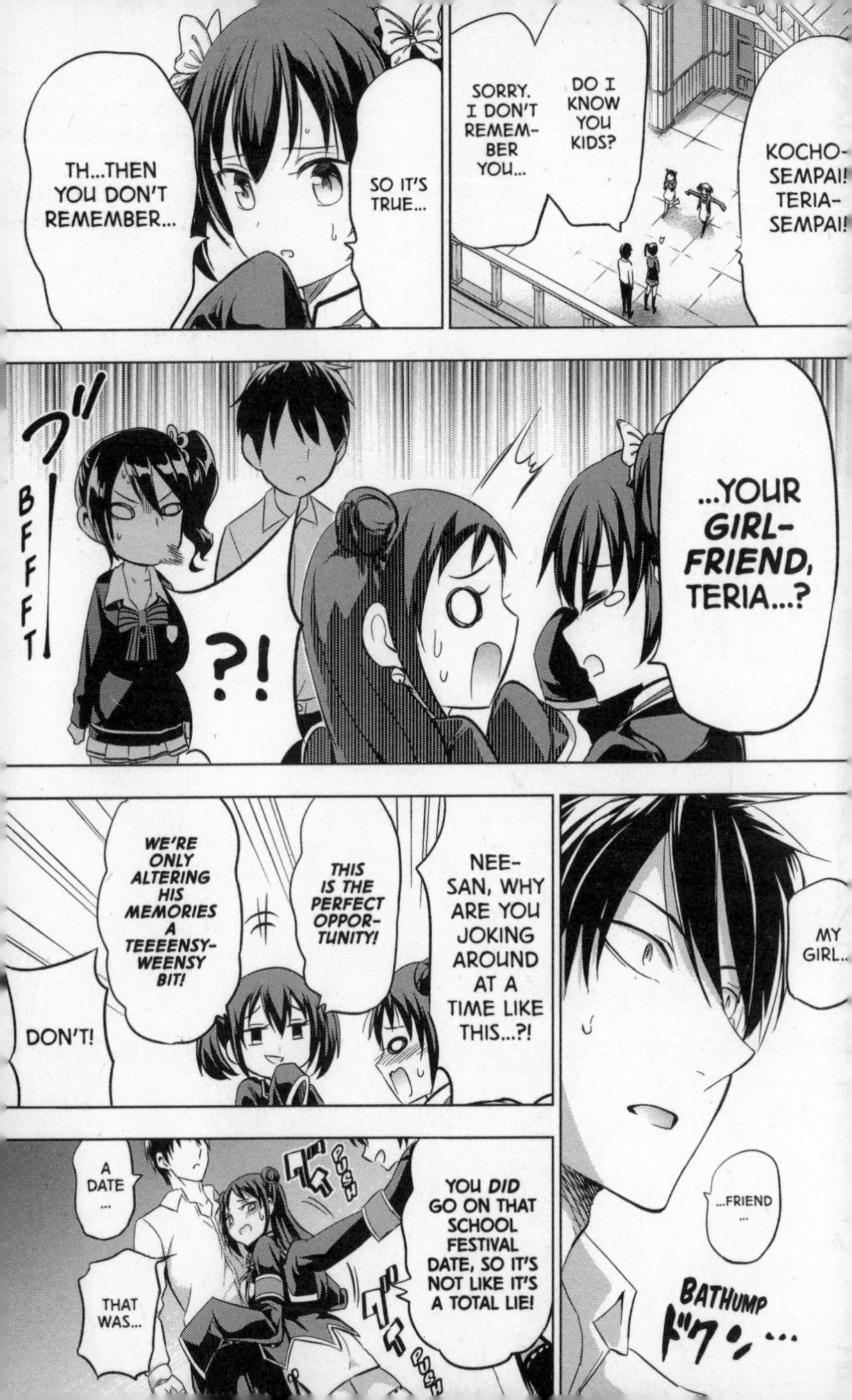
KOCHO-SEMPAI! TERIA-SEMPAI!
DO I KNOW YOU KIDS?
SORRY. I DON'T REMEM-BER YOU...
SO IT'S TRUE...
TH...THEN YOU DON'T REMEMBER...
...YOUR GIRL-FRIEND, TERIA...?
?!
BFFFT
MY GIRL...
...FRIEND...
BATHUMP
NEE-SAN, WHY ARE YOU JOKING AROUND AT A TIME LIKE THIS...?!
THIS IS THE PERFECT OPPOR-TUNITY!
WE'RE ONLY ALTERING HIS MEMORIES A TEEEENSY-WEENSY BIT!
DON'T!
YOU DID GO ON THAT SCHOOL FESTIVAL DATE, SO IT'S NOT LIKE IT'S A TOTAL LIE!
PUSH
PUSH
A DATE...
THAT WAS...

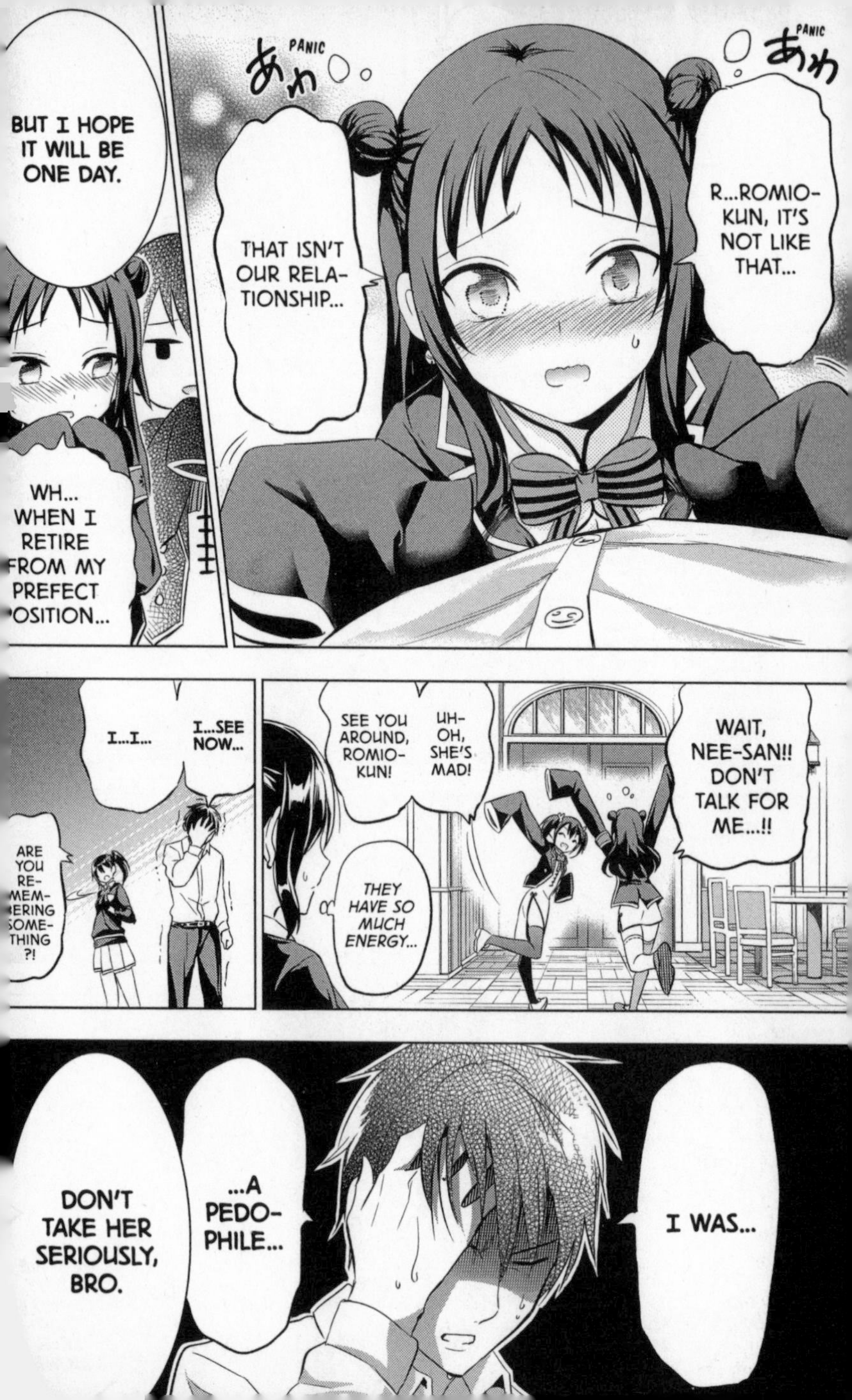

PANIC あわ
R...ROMIO-KUN, IT'S NOT LIKE THAT...
THAT ISN'T OUR RELATIONSHIP...
PANIC あわ
BUT I HOPE IT WILL BE ONE DAY.
WH... WHEN I RETIRE FROM MY PREFECT POSITION...
WAIT, NEE-SAN!! DON'T TALK FOR ME...!!
UH-OH, SHE'S MAD!
SEE YOU AROUND, ROMIO-KUN!
THEY HAVE SO MUCH ENERGY...
I...SEE NOW...
I...I...
ARE YOU REMEMBERING SOMETHING?!
I WAS...
...A PEDOPHILE...
DON'T TAKE HER SERIOUSLY, BRO.

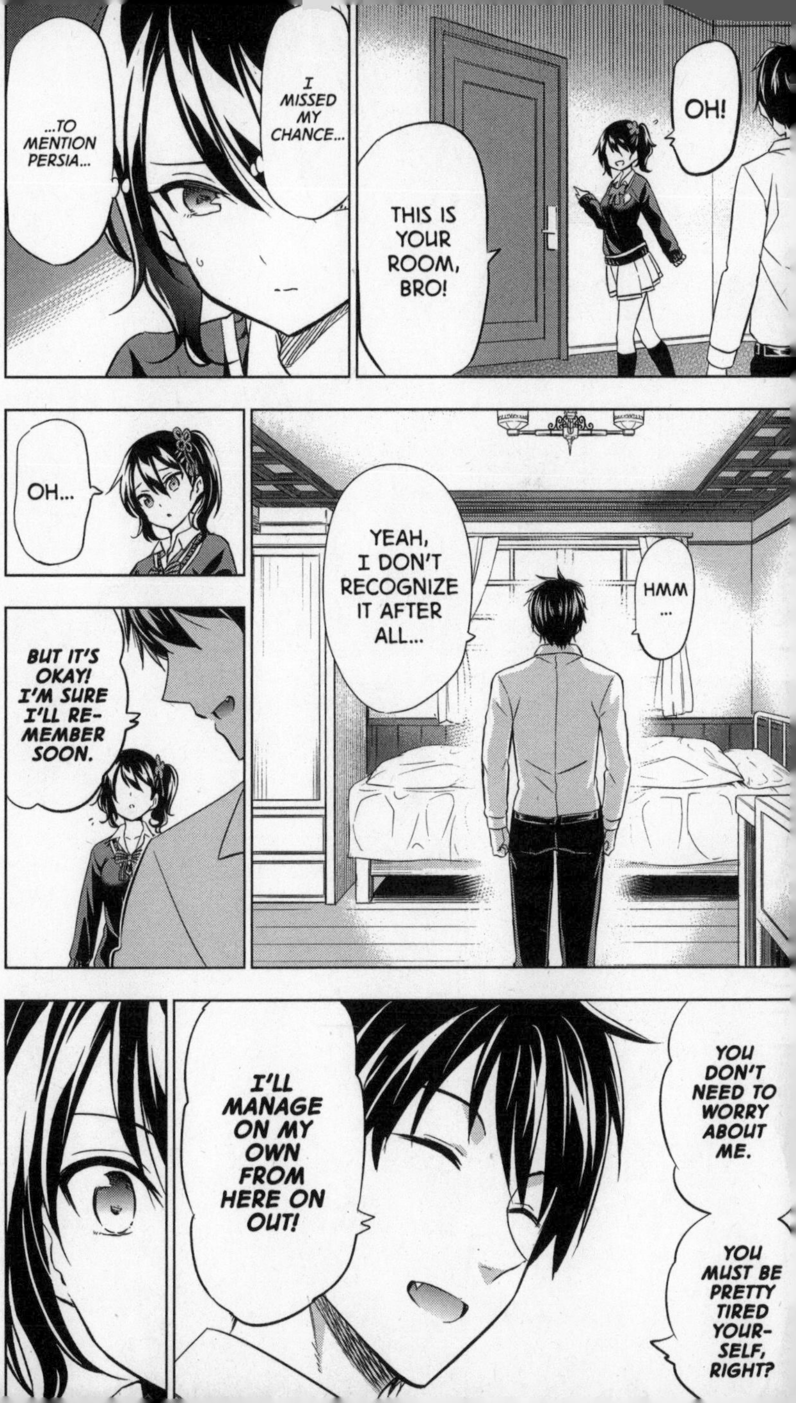
OH!
THIS IS YOUR ROOM, BRO!
I MISSED MY CHANCE...
...TO MENTION PERSIA...
HMM ...
YEAH, I DON'T RECOGNIZE IT AFTER ALL...
OH...
BUT IT'S OKAY! I'M SURE I'LL RE-MEMBER SOON.
YOU DON'T NEED TO WORRY ABOUT ME.
YOU MUST BE PRETTY TIRED YOUR-SELF, RIGHT?
I'LL MANAGE ON MY OWN FROM HERE ON OUT!

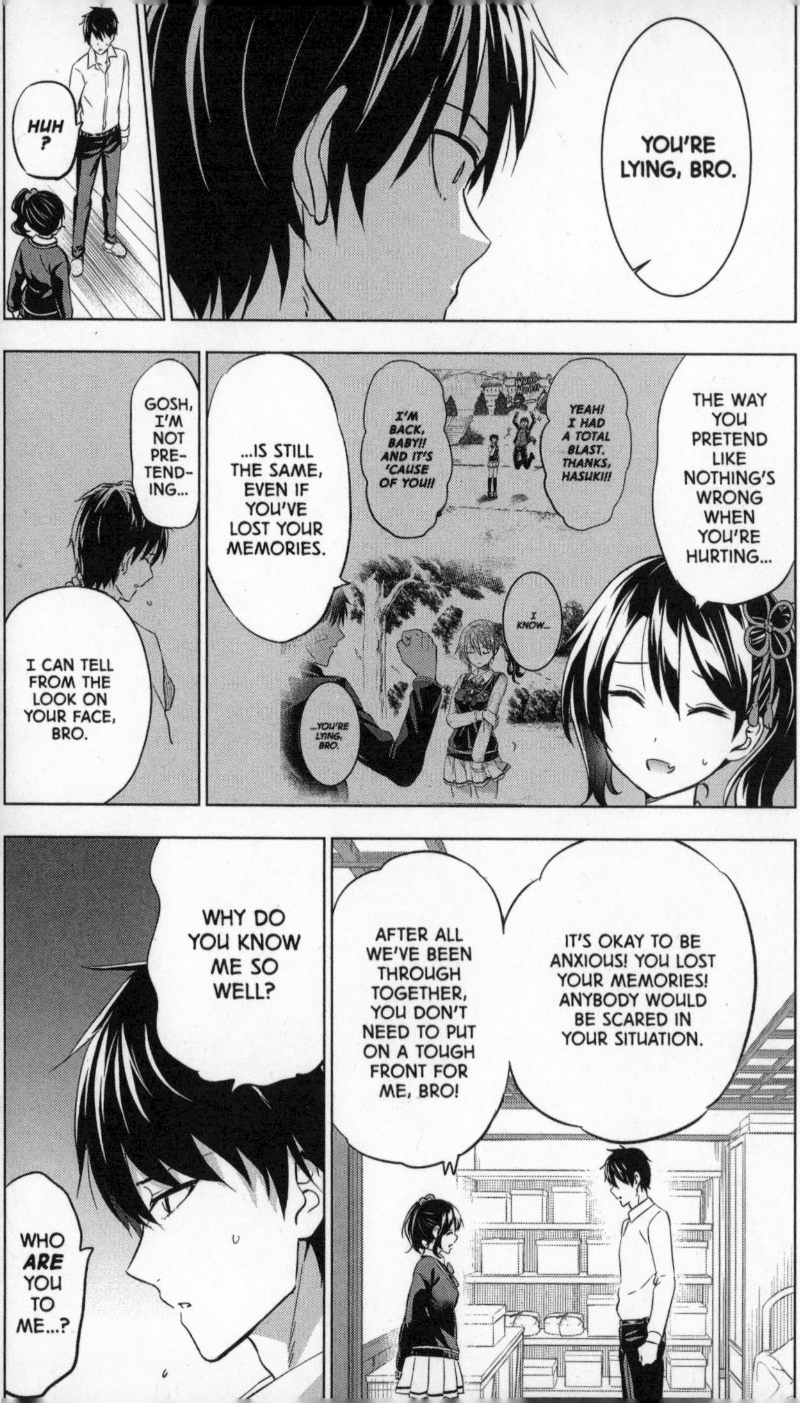
YOU'RE LYING, BRO.
HUH?
THE WAY YOU PRETEND LIKE NOTHING'S WRONG WHEN YOU'RE HURTING...
YEAH! I HAD A TOTAL BLAST. THANKS, HASUKI!!
I'M BACK, BABY!! AND IT'S 'CAUSE OF YOU!!
I KNOW...
...YOU'RE LYING, BRO.
...IS STILL THE SAME, EVEN IF YOU'VE LOST YOUR MEMORIES.
GOSH, I'M NOT PRETENDING...
I CAN TELL FROM THE LOOK ON YOUR FACE, BRO.
IT'S OKAY TO BE ANXIOUS! YOU LOST YOUR MEMORIES! ANYBODY WOULD BE SCARED IN YOUR SITUATION.
AFTER ALL WE'VE BEEN THROUGH TOGETHER, YOU DON'T NEED TO PUT ON A TOUGH FRONT FOR ME, BRO!
WHY DO YOU KNOW ME SO WELL?
WHO ARE YOU TO ME...?

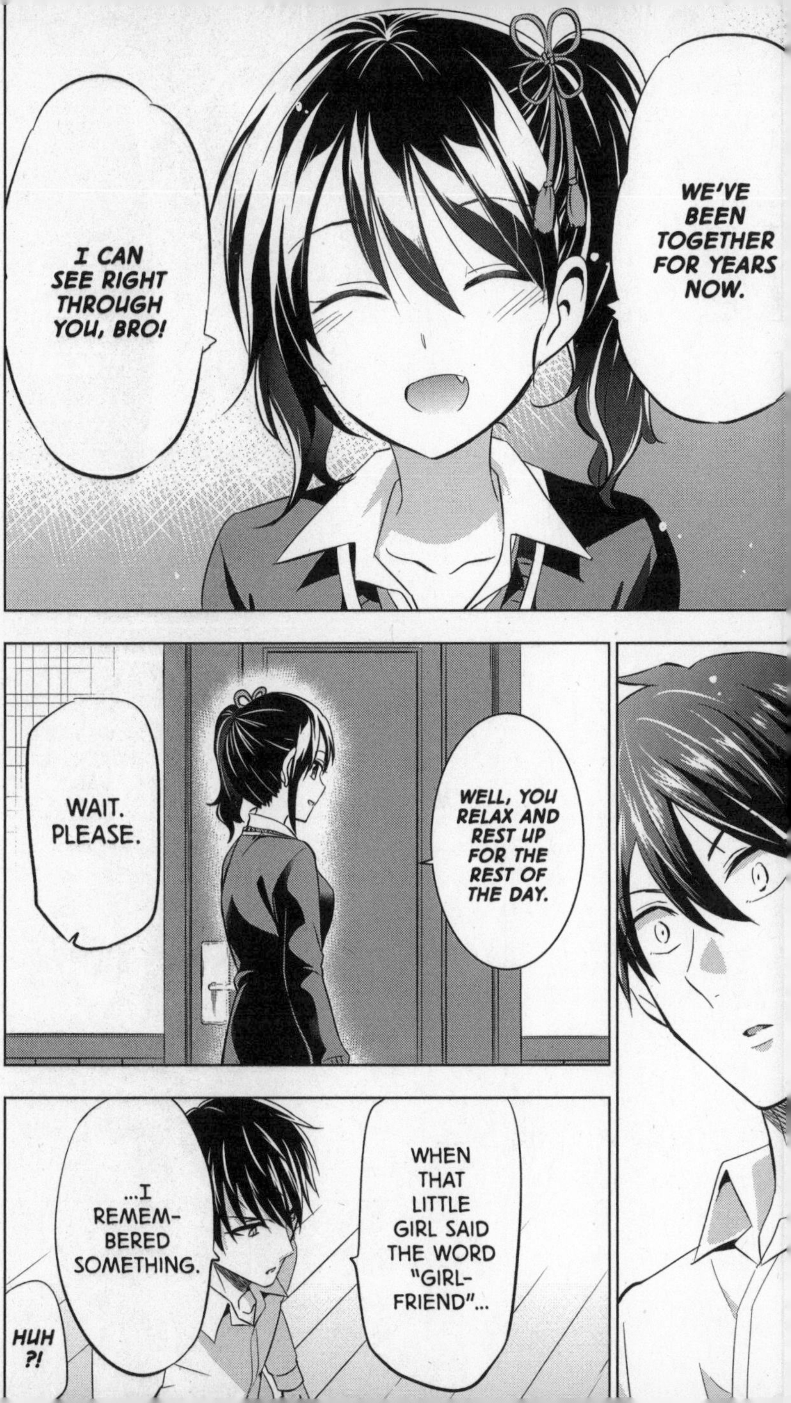
WE'VE BEEN TOGETHER FOR YEARS NOW.
I CAN SEE RIGHT THROUGH YOU, BRO!
WELL, YOU RELAX AND REST UP FOR THE REST OF THE DAY.
WAIT. PLEASE.
WHEN THAT LITTLE GIRL SAID THE WORD "GIRL-FRIEND"...
...I REMEM-BERED SOMETHING.
HUH ?!

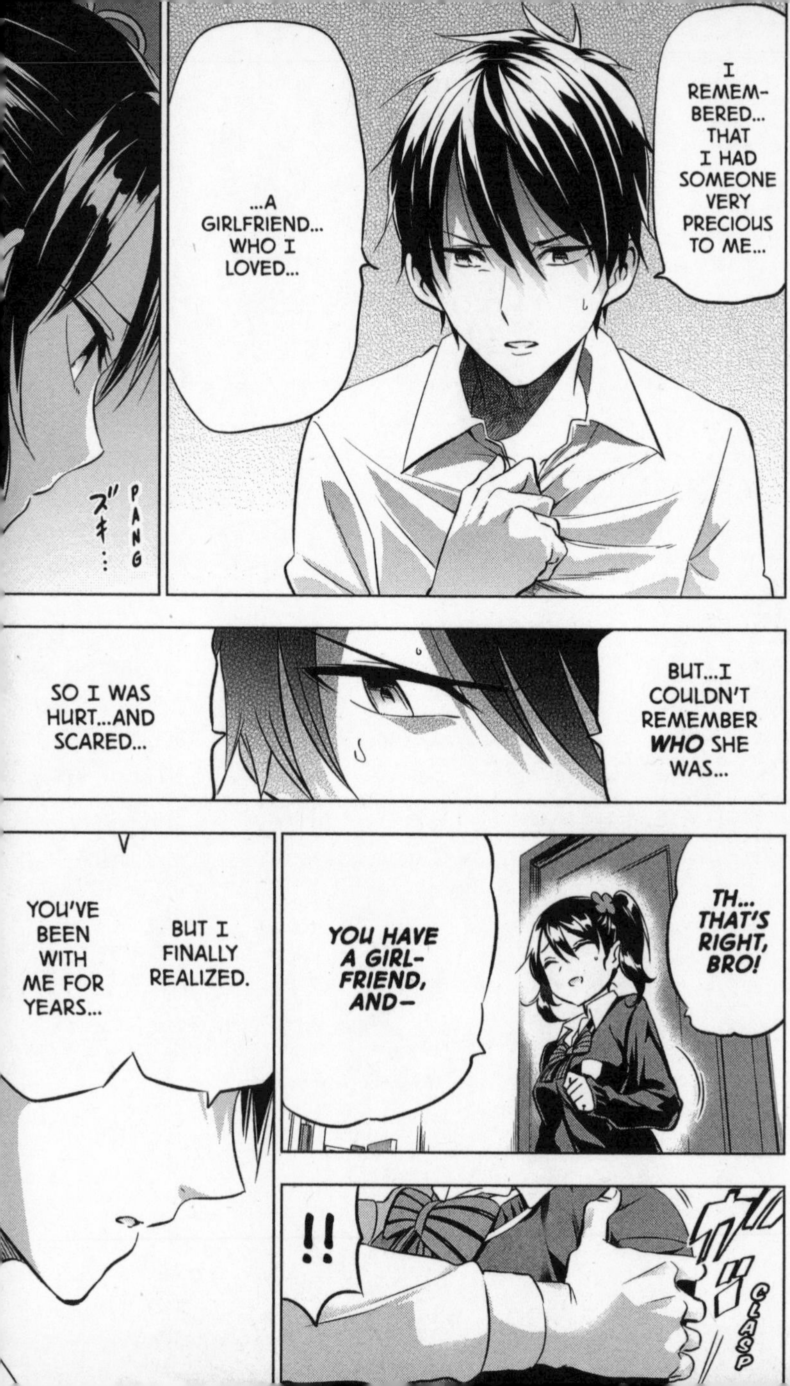
I REMEMBERED... THAT I HAD SOMEONE VERY PRECIOUS TO ME...
...A GIRLFRIEND... WHO I LOVED...
ズキ… PANG
BUT...I COULDN'T REMEMBER ***WHO*** SHE WAS...
SO I WAS HURT...AND SCARED...
TH... THAT'S RIGHT, BRO!
YOU HAVE A GIRLFRIEND, AND–
!!
CLASP
BUT I FINALLY REALIZED.
YOU'VE BEEN WITH ME FOR YEARS...

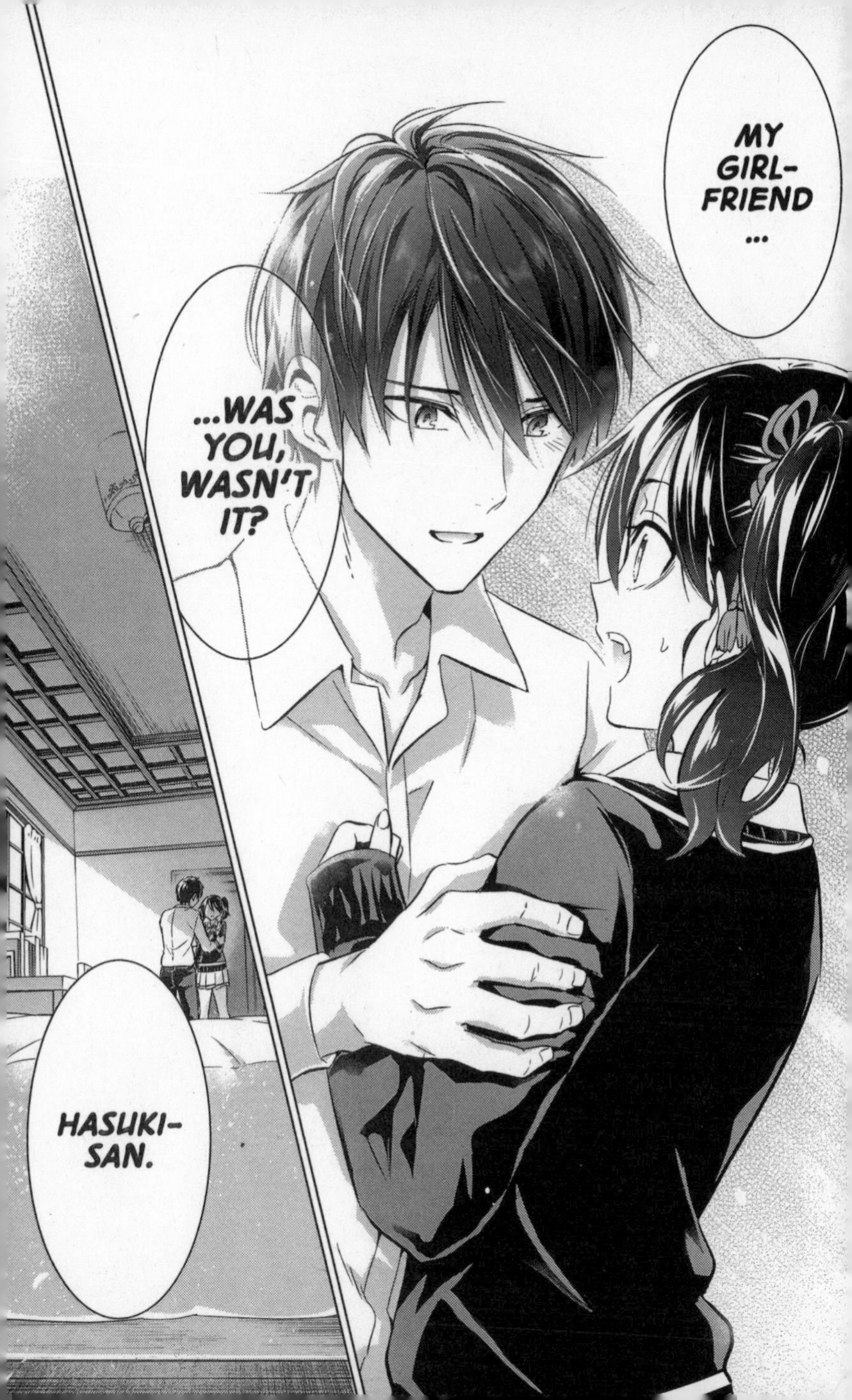
MY GIRLFRIEND...
...WAS YOU, WASN'T IT?
HASUKI-SAN.

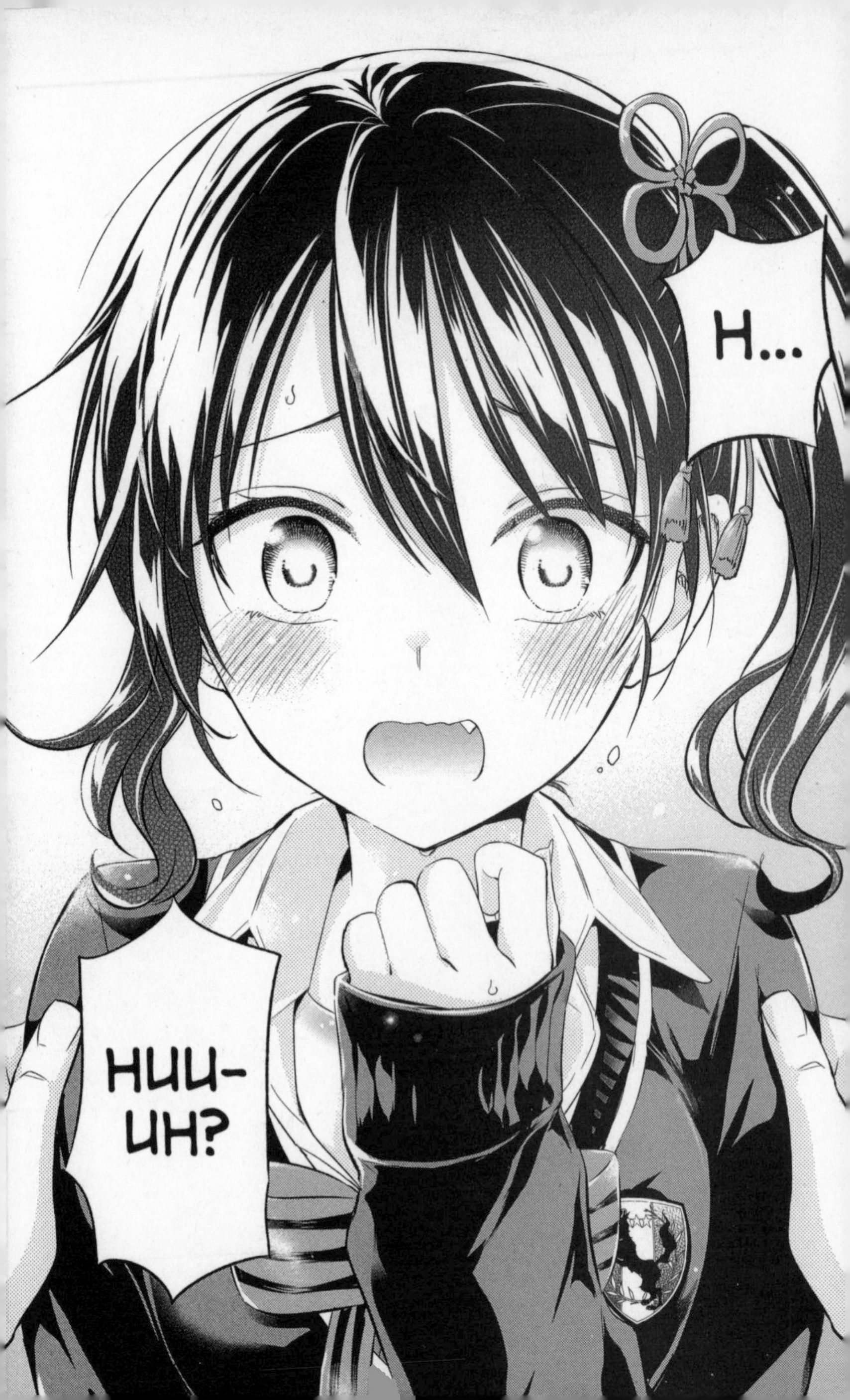
H...
HUU-UH?

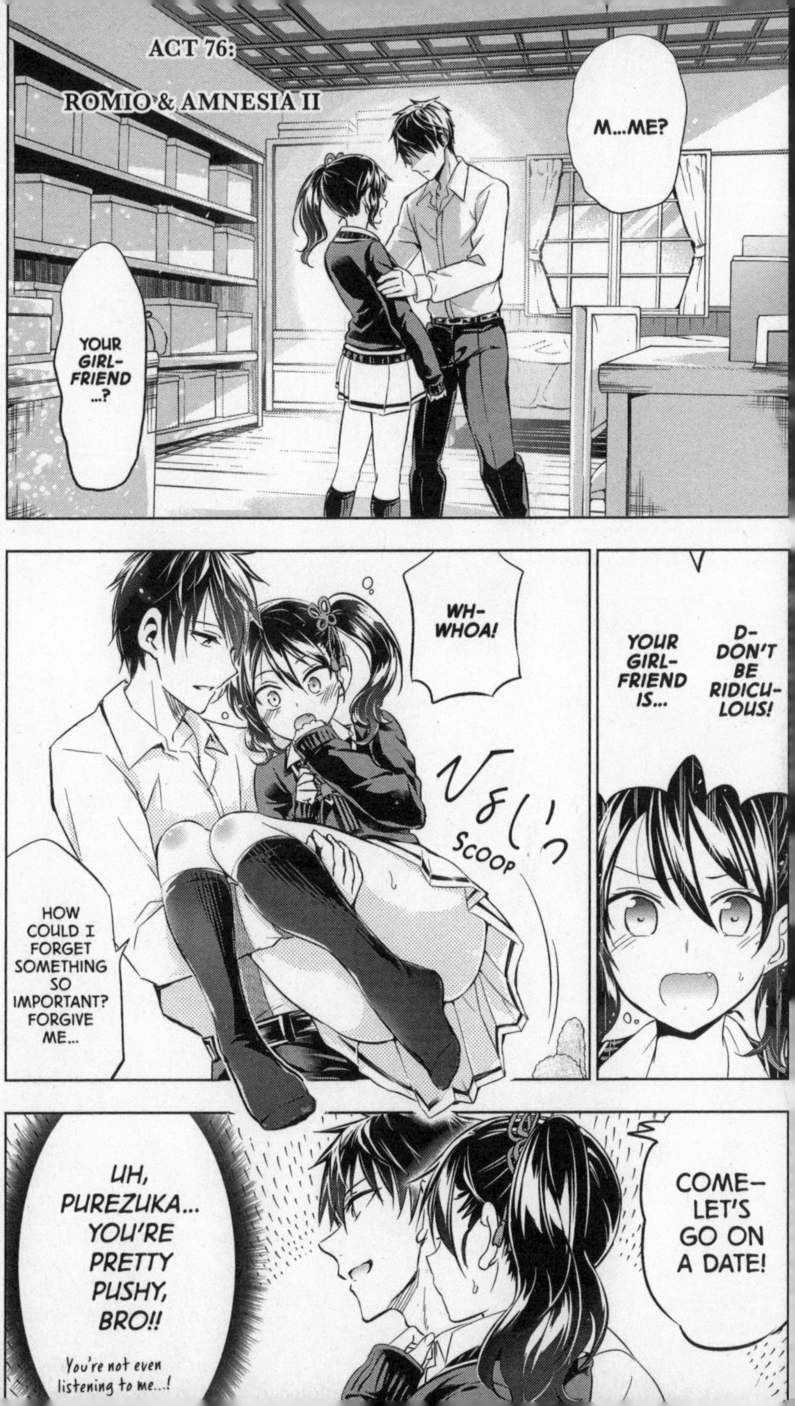
ACT 76:
ROMIO & AMNESIA II
M...ME?
YOUR GIRL-FRIEND ...?
D-DON'T BE RIDICU-LOUS!
YOUR GIRL-FRIEND IS...
WH-WHOA!
SCOOP
HOW COULD I FORGET SOMETHING SO IMPORTANT? FORGIVE ME...
COME—LET'S GO ON A DATE!
UH, PUREZUKA... YOU'RE PRETTY PUSHY, BRO!!
You're not even listening to me...!

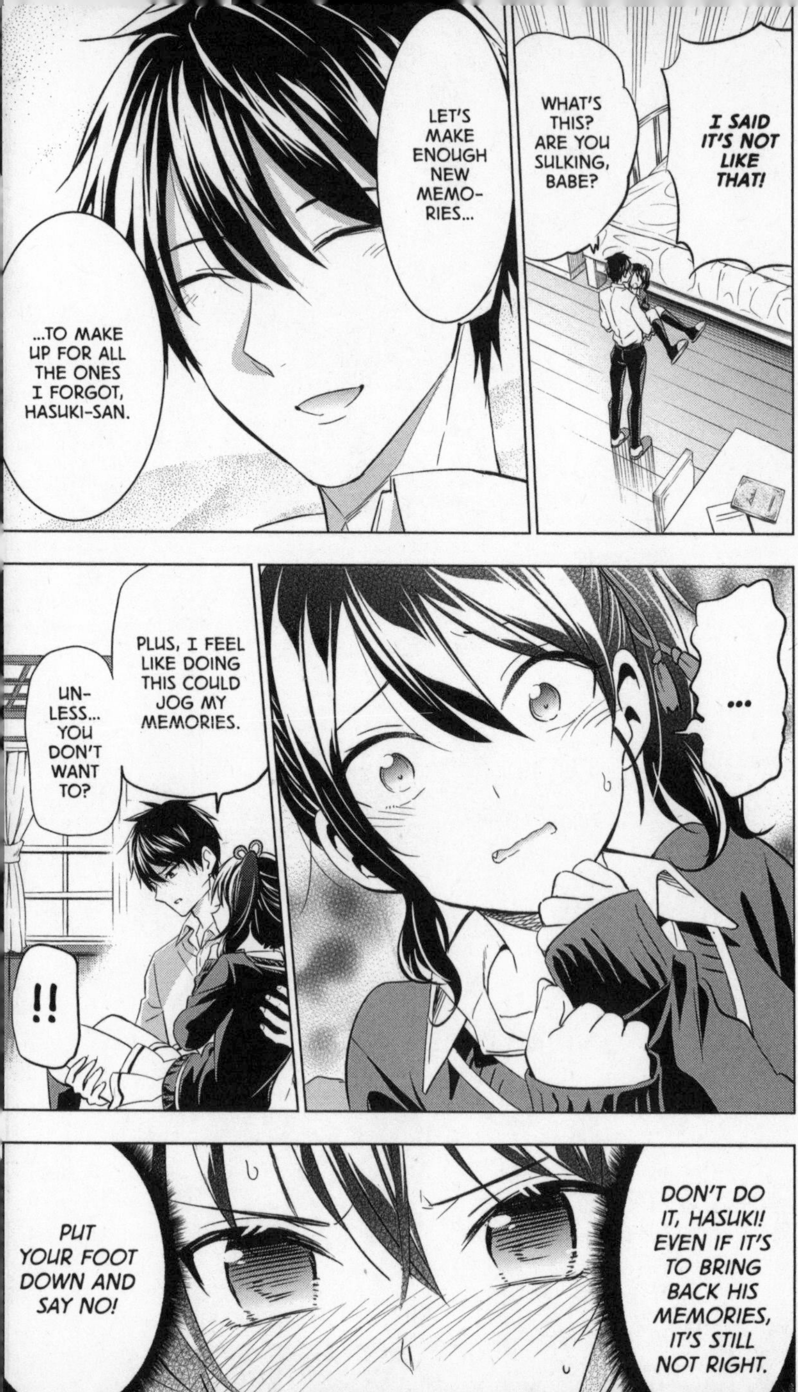
I SAID IT'S NOT LIKE THAT!
WHAT'S THIS? ARE YOU SULKING, BABE?
LET'S MAKE ENOUGH NEW MEMO-RIES...
...TO MAKE UP FOR ALL THE ONES I FORGOT, HASUKI-SAN.
...
PLUS, I FEEL LIKE DOING THIS COULD JOG MY MEMORIES.
UN-LESS... YOU DON'T WANT TO?
!!
DON'T DO IT, HASUKI! EVEN IF IT'S TO BRING BACK HIS MEMORIES, IT'S STILL NOT RIGHT.
PUT YOUR FOOT DOWN AND SAY NO!

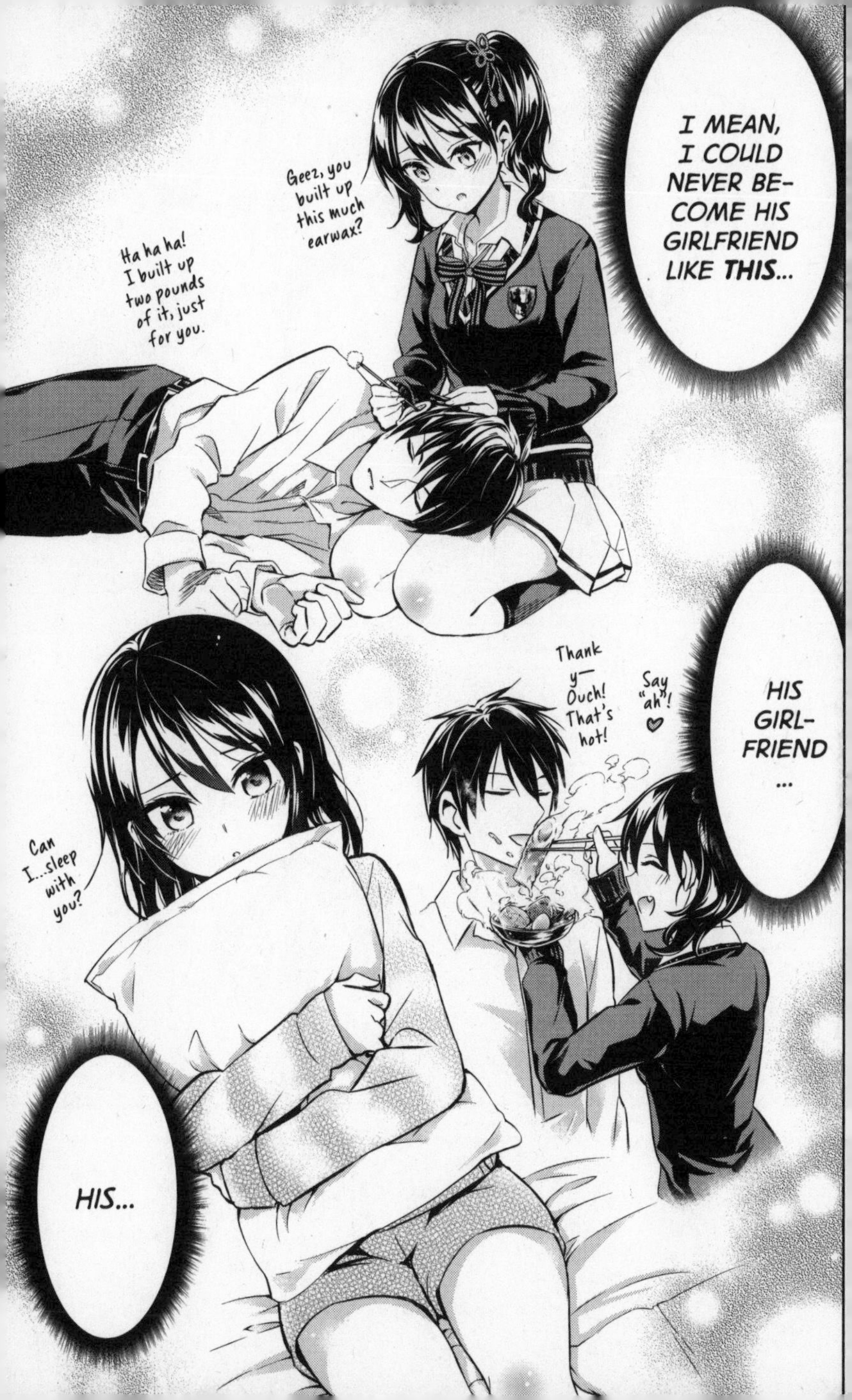
I MEAN, I COULD NEVER BE-COME HIS GIRLFRIEND LIKE **THIS**...
Geez, you built up this much earwax?
Ha ha ha! I built up two pounds of it, just for you.
HIS GIRL-FRIEND ...
Say "ah"! ♡
Thank y— Ouch! That's hot!
Can I...sleep with you?
HIS...

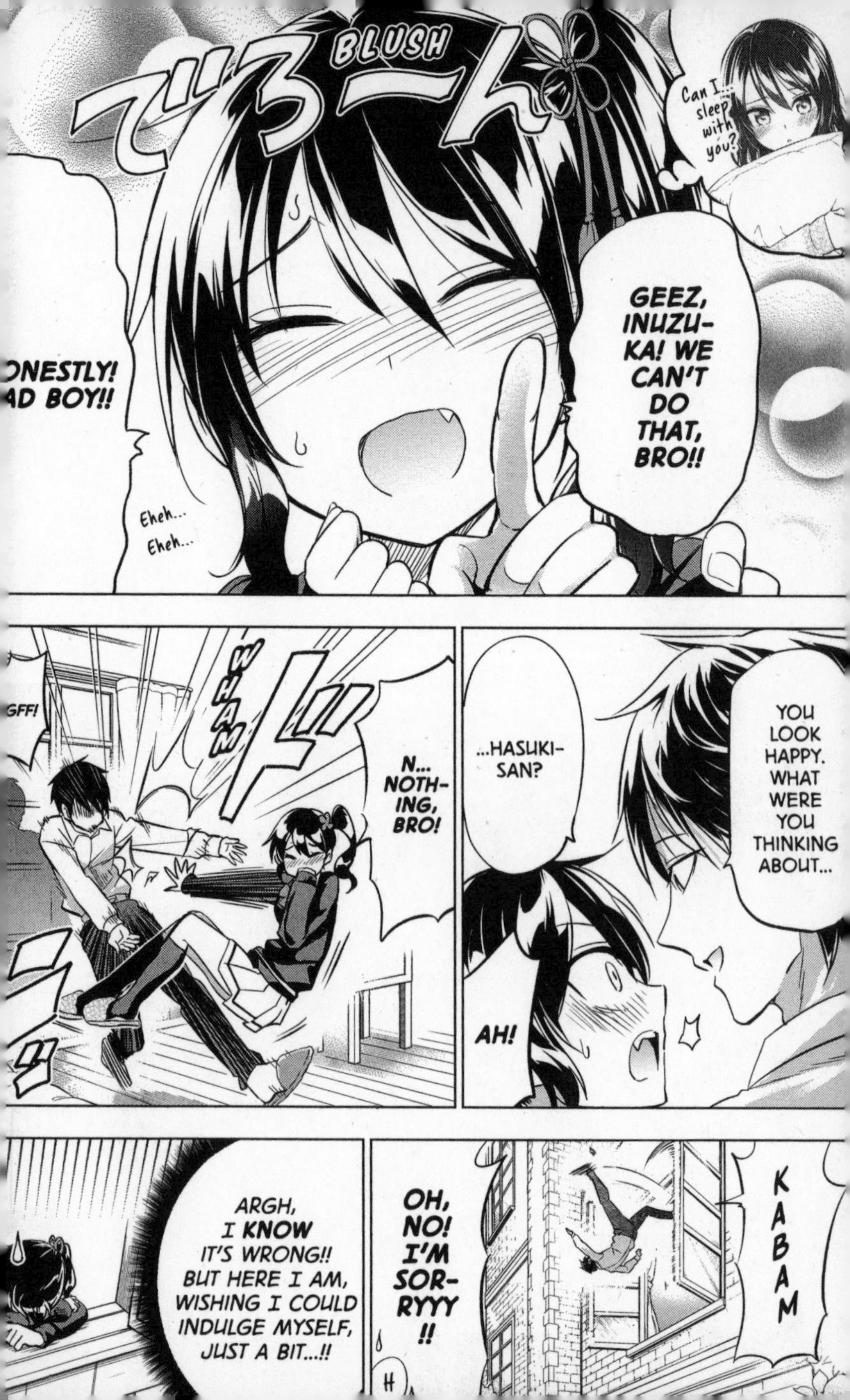

Can I... sleep with you?
でろーん
BLUSH
GEEZ, INUZUKA! WE CAN'T DO THAT, BRO!!
ONESTLY! AD BOY!!
Eheh... Eheh...
YOU LOOK HAPPY. WHAT WERE YOU THINKING ABOUT...
...HASUKI-SAN?
AH!
N... NOTHING, BRO!
WHAM
GFF!
KABAM
OH, NO! I'M SORRYYY !!
ARGH, I KNOW IT'S WRONG!! BUT HERE I AM, WISHING I COULD INDULGE MYSELF, JUST A BIT...!!

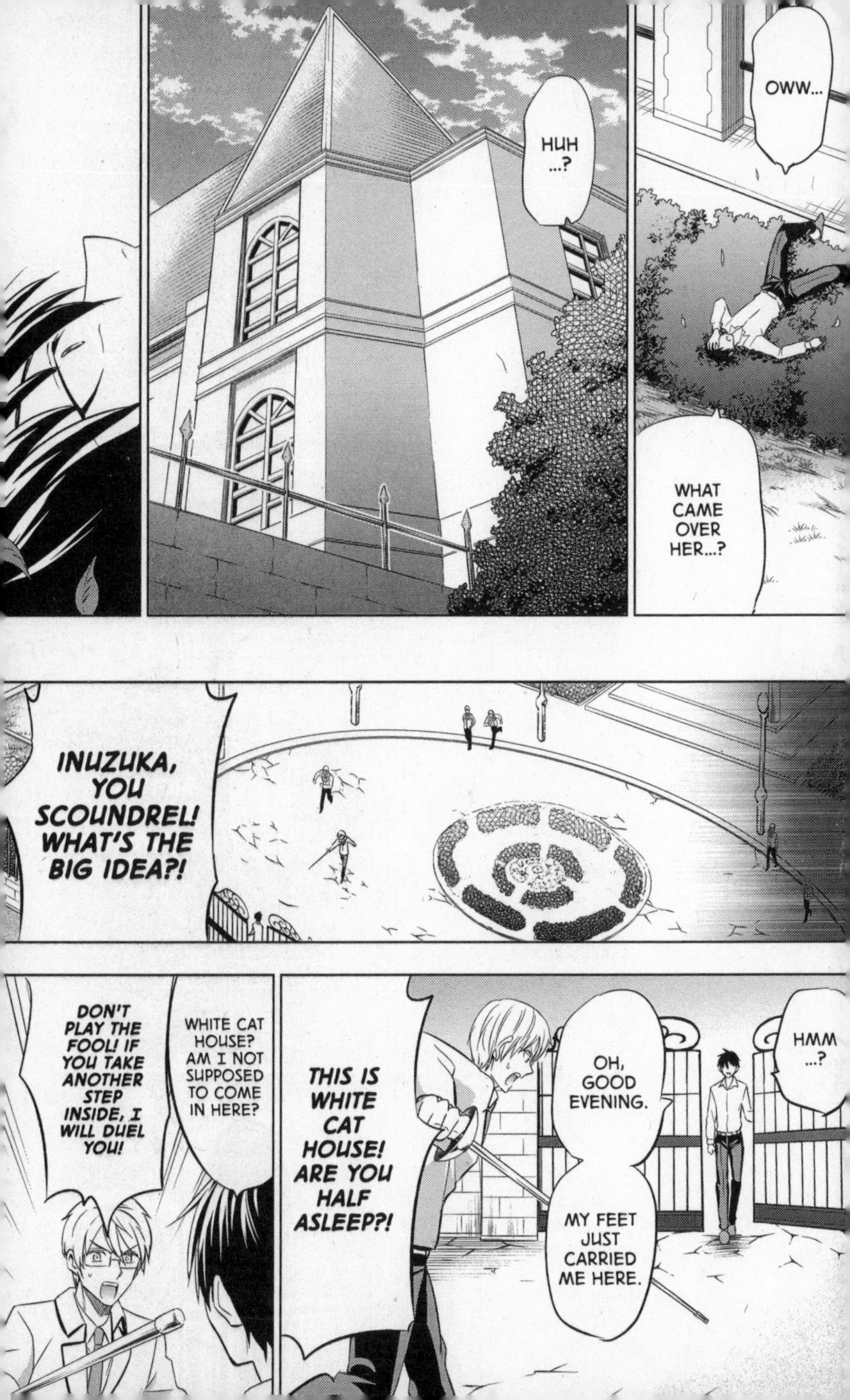
OWW...
WHAT CAME OVER HER...?
HUH ...?
INUZUKA, YOU SCOUNDREL! WHAT'S THE BIG IDEA?!
HMM ...?
OH, GOOD EVENING.
MY FEET JUST CARRIED ME HERE.
THIS IS WHITE CAT HOUSE! ARE YOU HALF ASLEEP?!
WHITE CAT HOUSE? AM I NOT SUPPOSED TO COME IN HERE?
DON'T PLAY THE FOOL! IF YOU TAKE ANOTHER STEP INSIDE, I WILL DUEL YOU!

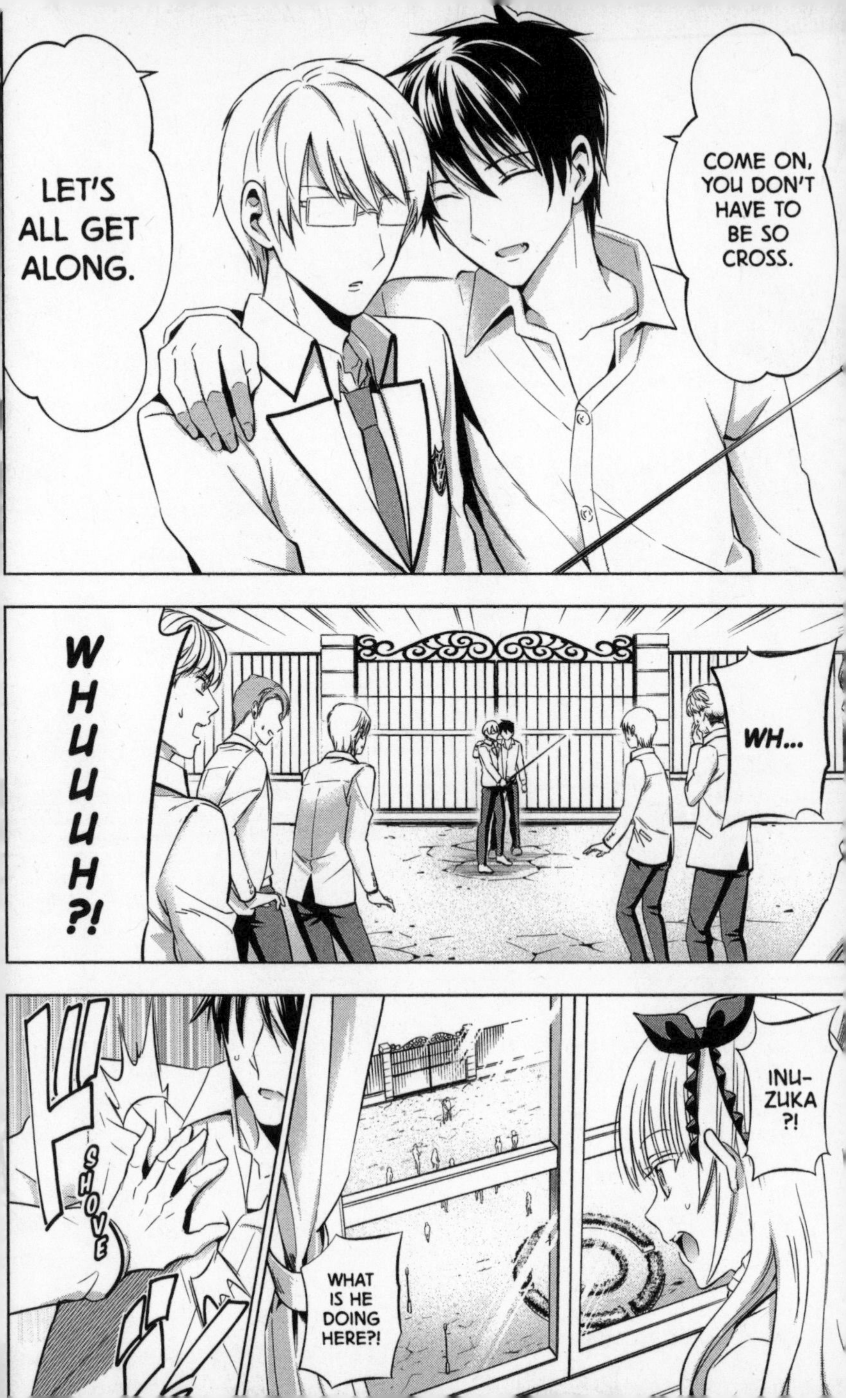
COME ON, YOU DON'T HAVE TO BE SO CROSS.
LET'S ALL GET ALONG.
WH...
WHUUUUH?!
INU-ZUKA?!
WHAT IS HE DOING HERE?!
SHOVE

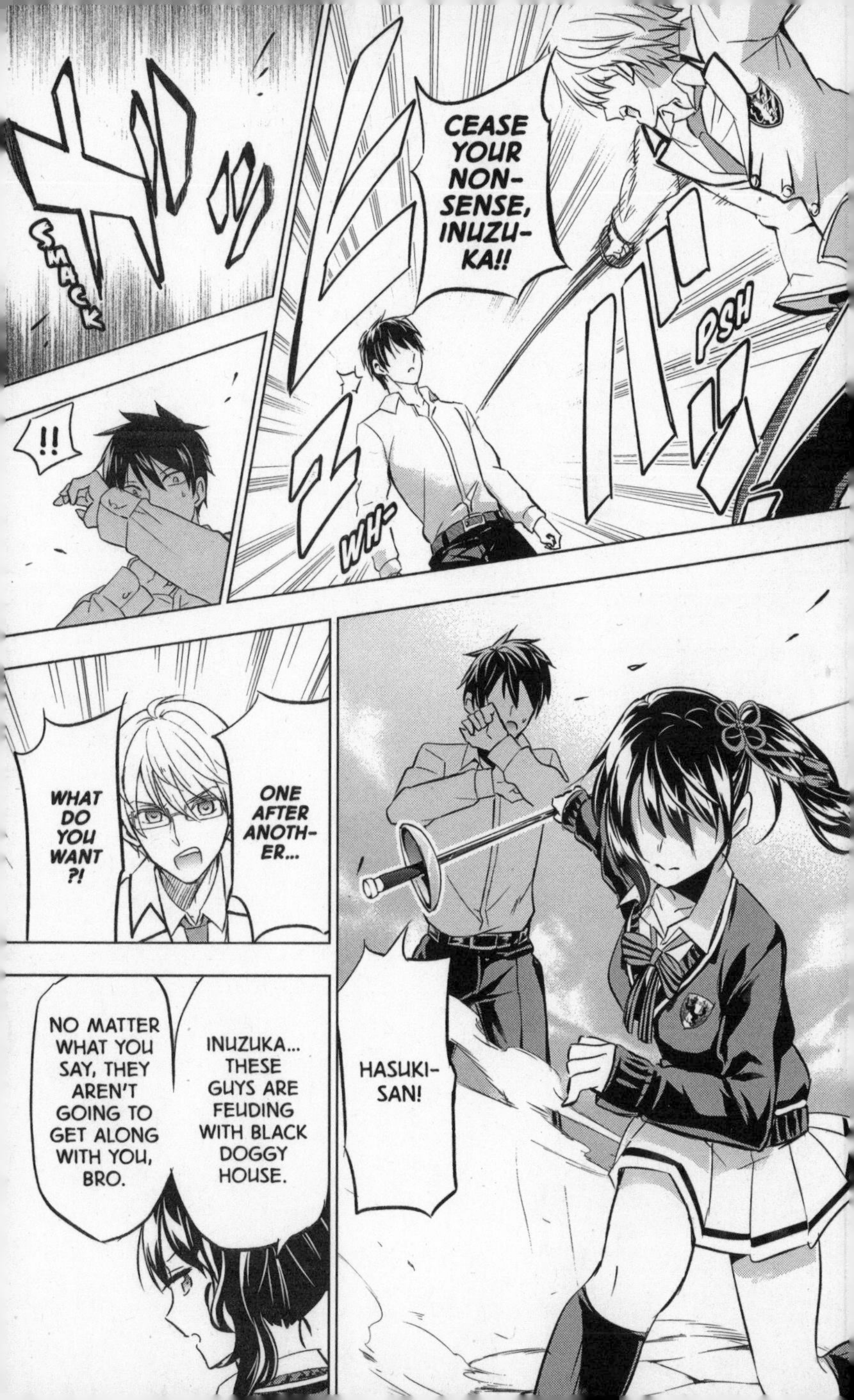
CEASE YOUR NON-SENSE, INUZUKA!!
PSH
WH-
SMACK
!!
HASUKI-SAN!
ONE AFTER ANOTH-ER...
WHAT DO YOU WANT ?!
INUZUKA... THESE GUYS ARE FEUDING WITH BLACK DOGGY HOUSE.
NO MATTER WHAT YOU SAY, THEY AREN'T GOING TO GET ALONG WITH YOU, BRO.

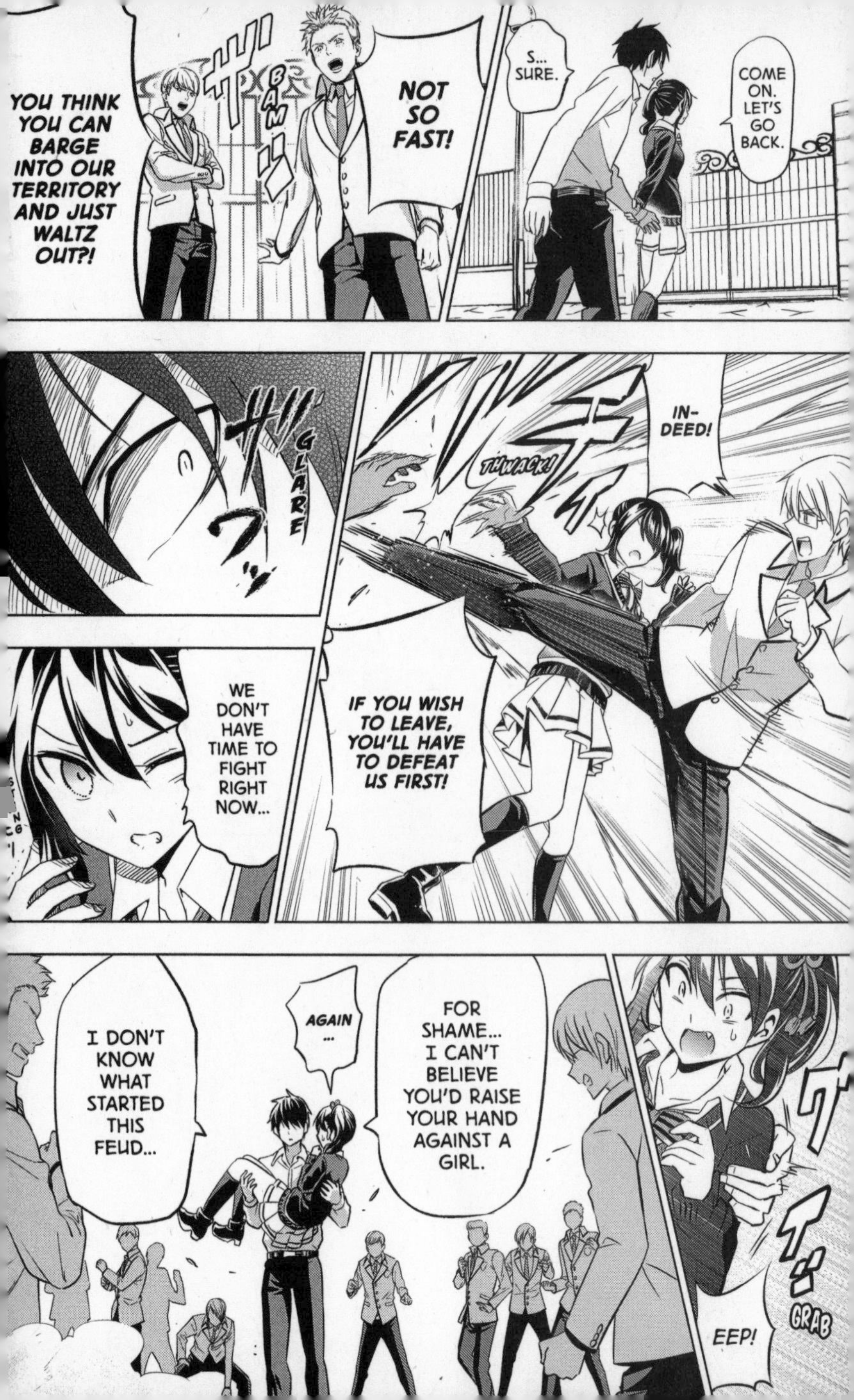
COME ON. LET'S GO BACK.
S... SURE.
NOT SO FAST!
BAM
YOU THINK YOU CAN BARGE INTO OUR TERRITORY AND JUST WALTZ OUT?!
IN-DEED!
THWACK!
IF YOU WISH TO LEAVE, YOU'LL HAVE TO DEFEAT US FIRST!
GLARE
WE DON'T HAVE TIME TO FIGHT RIGHT NOW...
GRAB
EEP!
FOR SHAME... I CAN'T BELIEVE YOU'D RAISE YOUR HAND AGAINST A GIRL.
AGAIN...
I DON'T KNOW WHAT STARTED THIS FEUD...

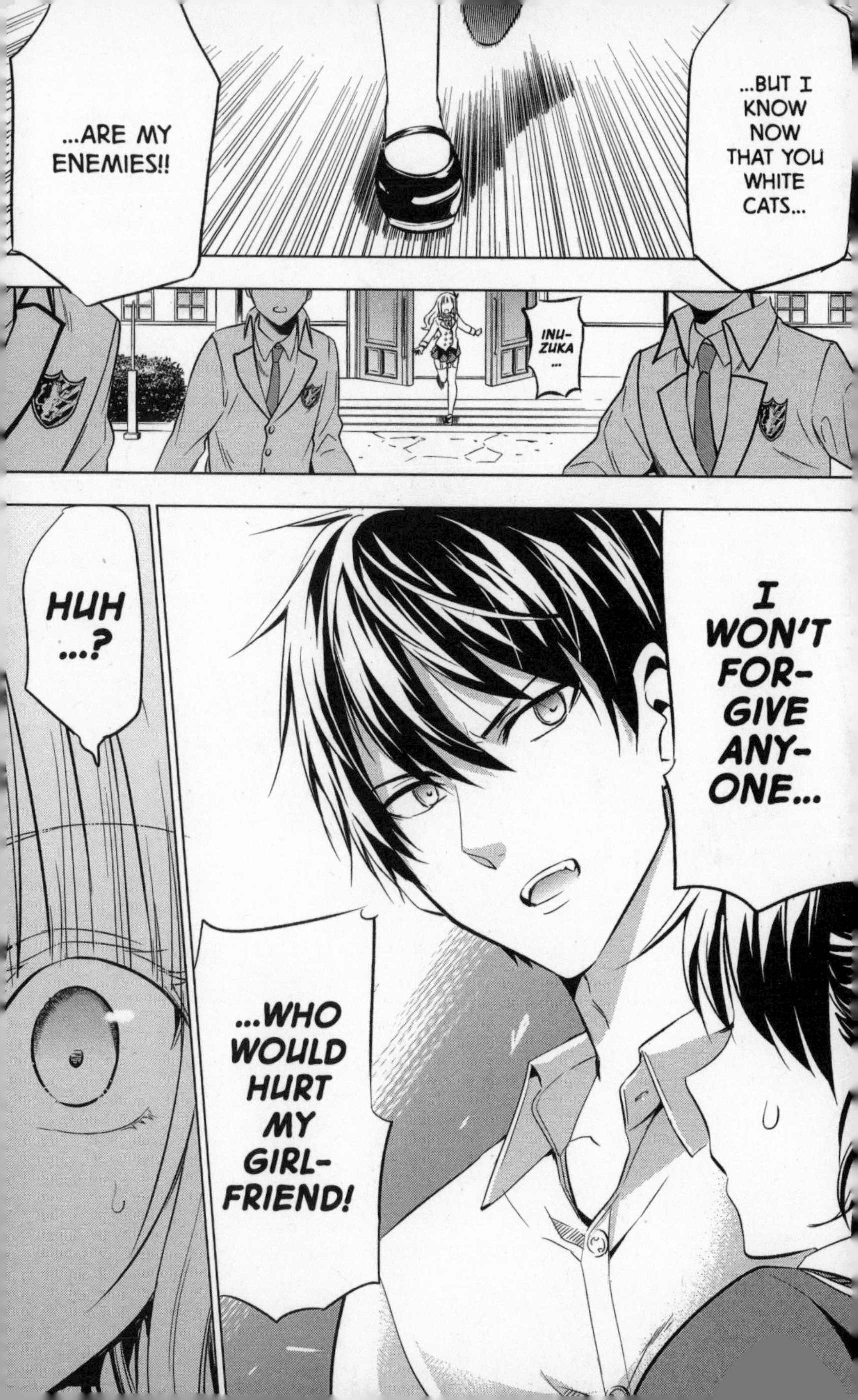
...BUT I KNOW NOW THAT YOU WHITE CATS...
...ARE MY ENEMIES!!
INU-ZUKA...
I WON'T FOR-GIVE ANY-ONE...
...WHO WOULD HURT MY GIRL-FRIEND!
HUH ...?

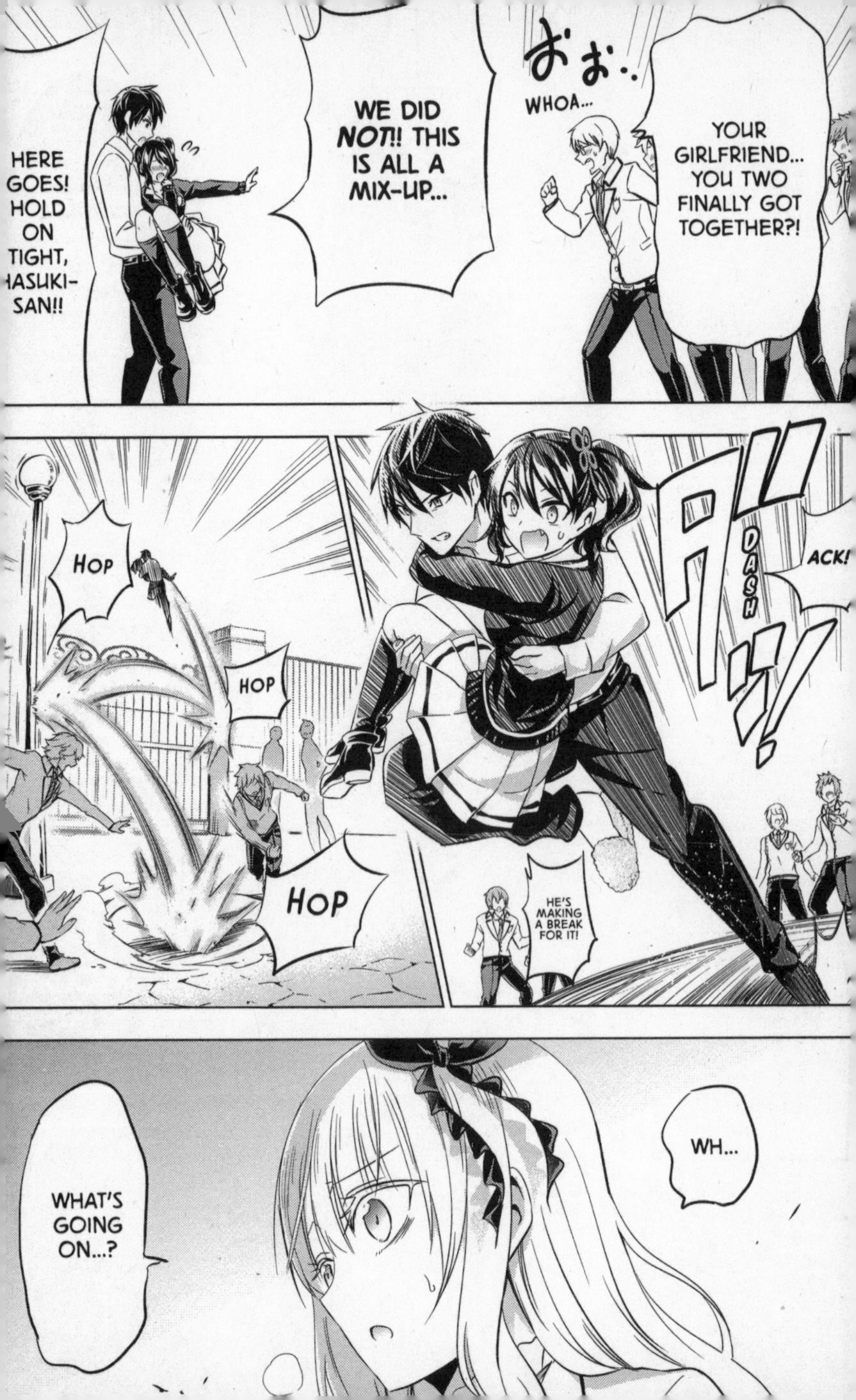
YOUR GIRLFRIEND... YOU TWO FINALLY GOT TOGETHER?!
おぉ..
WHOA...
WE DID NOT!! THIS IS ALL A MIX-UP...
HERE GOES! HOLD ON TIGHT, HASUKI-SAN!!
ダッ
DASH
ACK!
HE'S MAKING A BREAK FOR IT!
HOP
HOP
HOP
WH...
WHAT'S GOING ON...?

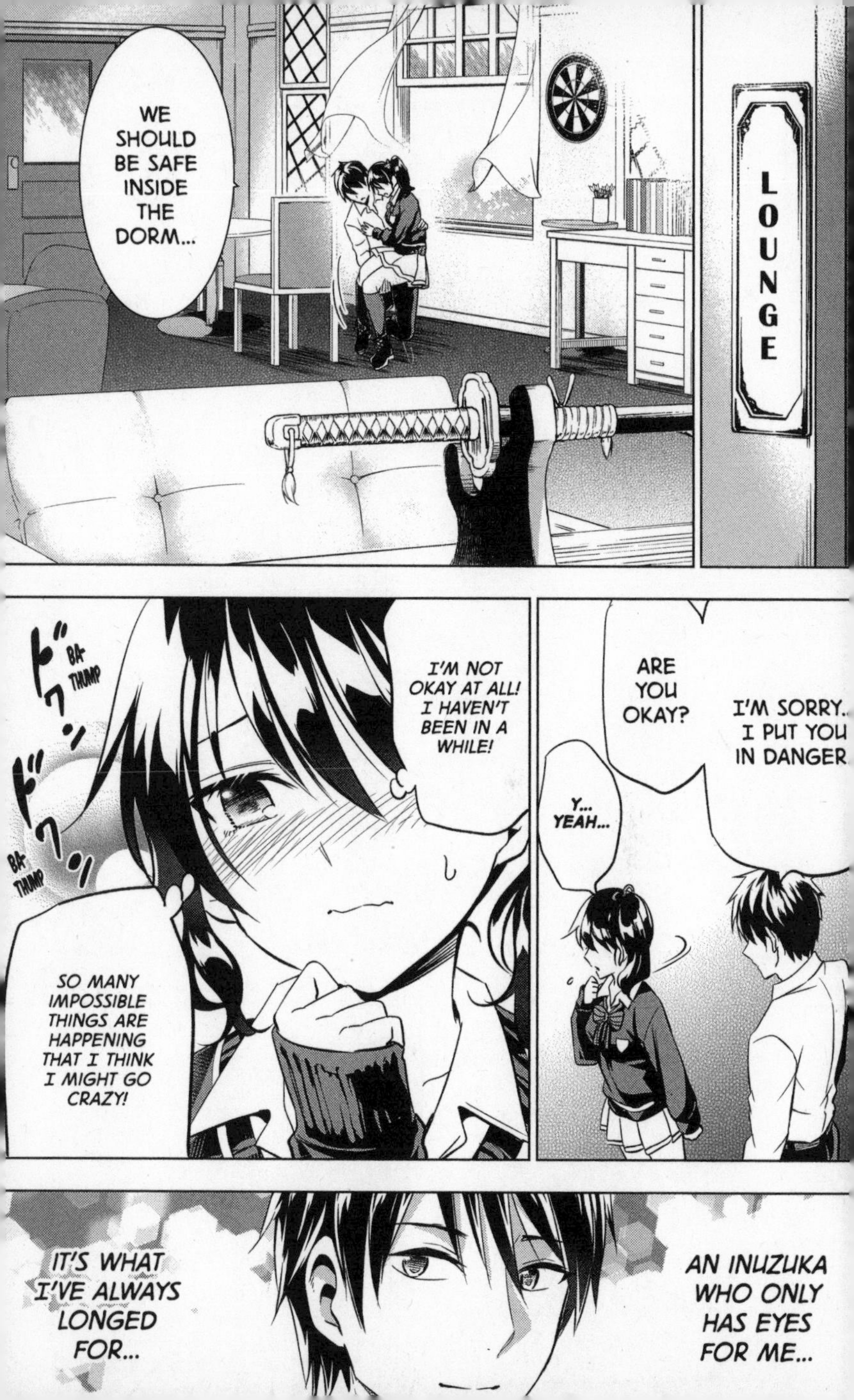
WE SHOULD BE SAFE INSIDE THE DORM...
LOUNGE
ARE YOU OKAY?
Y... YEAH...
I'M SORRY.. I PUT YOU IN DANGER
I'M NOT OKAY AT ALL! I HAVEN'T BEEN IN A WHILE!
BA-THUMP
BA-THUMP
SO MANY IMPOSSIBLE THINGS ARE HAPPENING THAT I THINK I MIGHT GO CRAZY!
AN INUZUKA WHO ONLY HAS EYES FOR ME...
IT'S WHAT I'VE ALWAYS LONGED FOR...

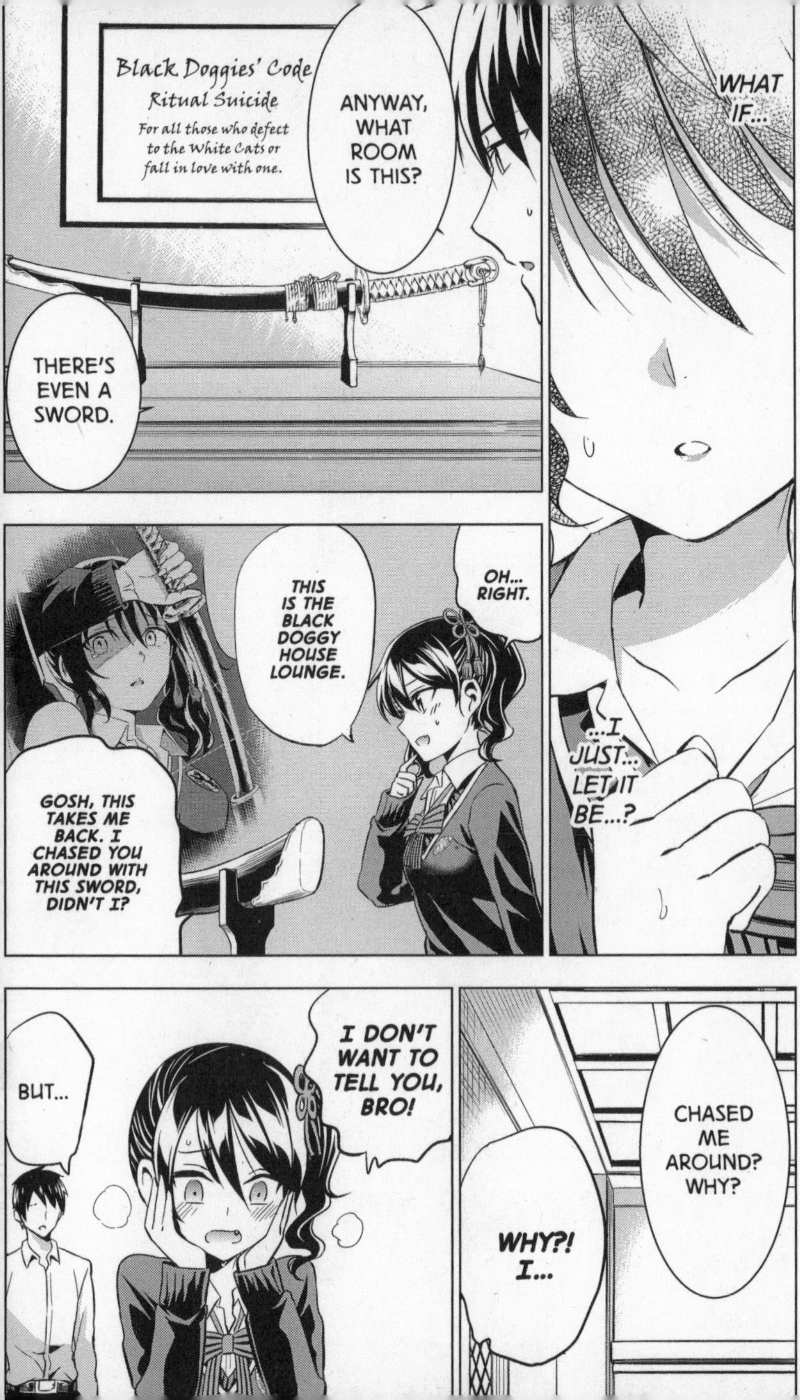
WHAT IF...
...I JUST... LET IT BE...?
ANYWAY, WHAT ROOM IS THIS?
Black Doggies' Code
Ritual Suicide
For all those who defect to the White Cats or fall in love with one.
THERE'S EVEN A SWORD.
OH... RIGHT.
THIS IS THE BLACK DOGGY HOUSE LOUNGE.
GOSH, THIS TAKES ME BACK. I CHASED YOU AROUND WITH THIS SWORD, DIDN'T I?
CHASED ME AROUND? WHY?
WHY?! I...
I DON'T WANT TO TELL YOU, BRO!
BUT...

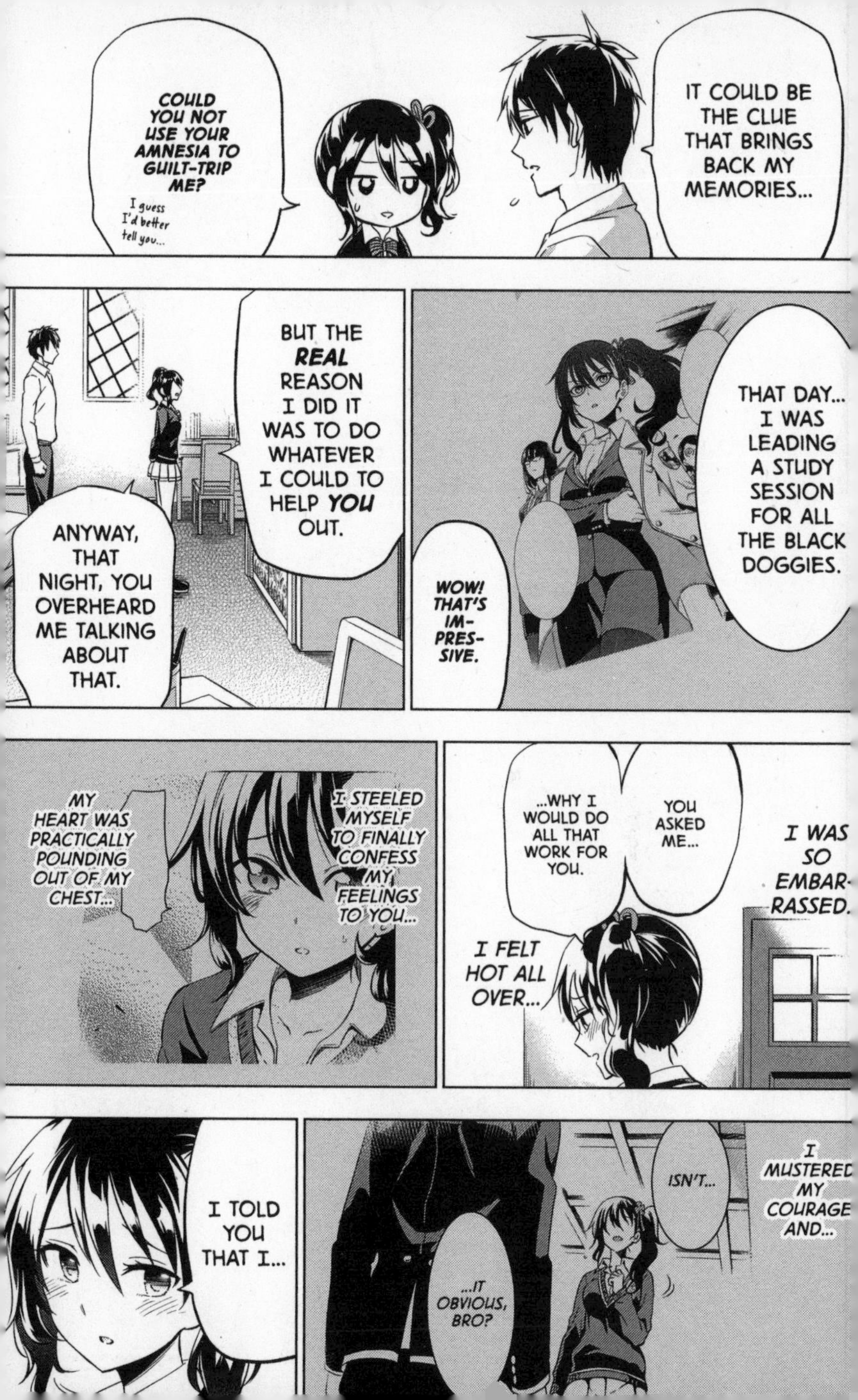
IT COULD BE THE CLUE THAT BRINGS BACK MY MEMORIES...
COULD YOU NOT USE YOUR AMNESIA TO GUILT-TRIP ME?
I guess I'd better tell you...
THAT DAY... I WAS LEADING A STUDY SESSION FOR ALL THE BLACK DOGGIES.
WOW! THAT'S IM-PRES-SIVE.
BUT THE REAL REASON I DID IT WAS TO DO WHATEVER I COULD TO HELP YOU OUT.
ANYWAY, THAT NIGHT, YOU OVERHEARD ME TALKING ABOUT THAT.
I WAS SO EMBAR-RASSED.
YOU ASKED ME...
...WHY I WOULD DO ALL THAT WORK FOR YOU.
I FELT HOT ALL OVER...
I STEELED MYSELF TO FINALLY CONFESS MY FEELINGS TO YOU...
MY HEART WAS PRACTICALLY POUNDING OUT OF MY CHEST...
I MUSTERED MY COURAGE AND...
ISN'T...
...IT OBVIOUS, BRO?
I TOLD YOU THAT I...

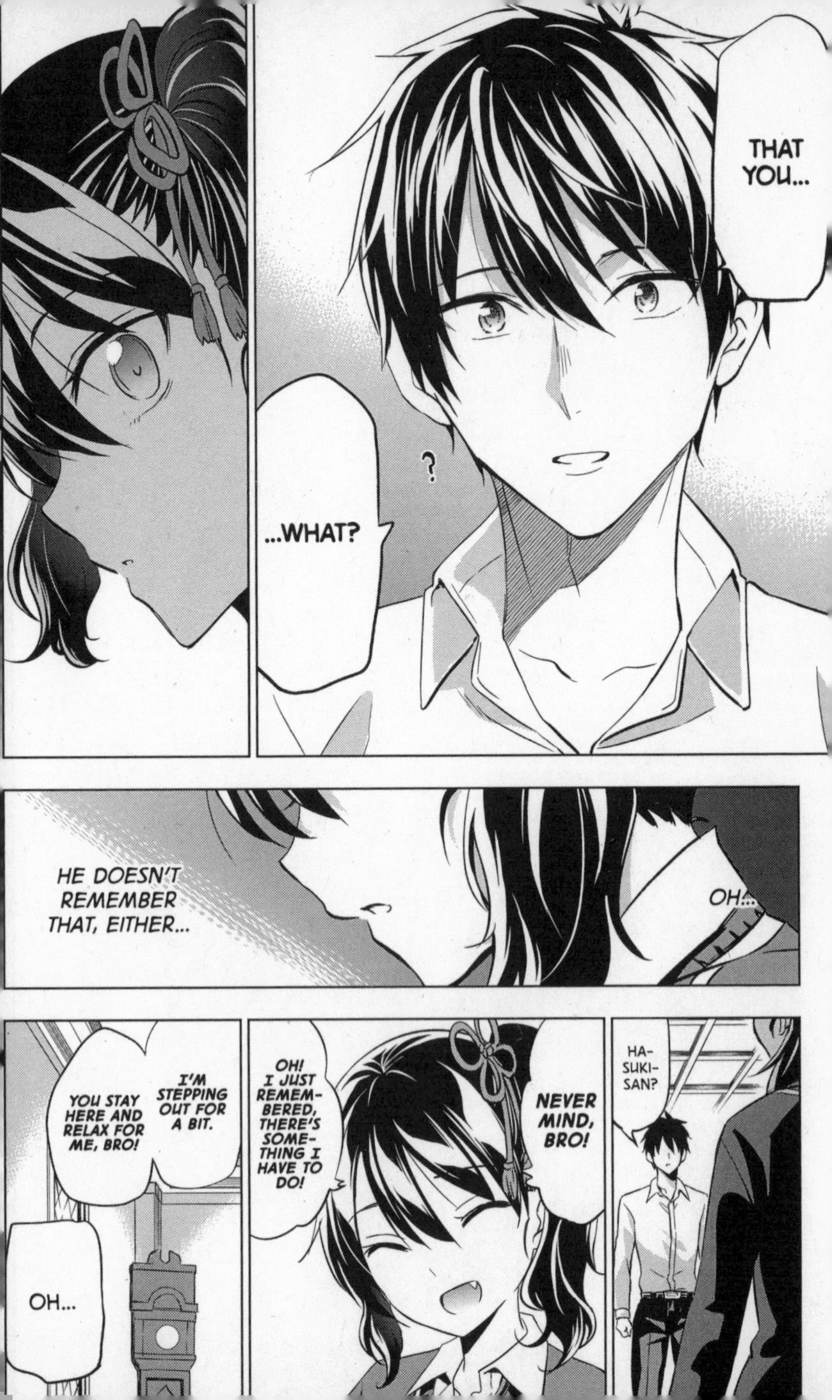
THAT YOU...
...WHAT?
OH...
HE DOESN'T REMEMBER THAT, EITHER...
HA-SUKI-SAN?
NEVER MIND, BRO!
OH! I JUST REMEMBERED, THERE'S SOMETHING I HAVE TO DO!
I'M STEPPING OUT FOR A BIT.
YOU STAY HERE AND RELAX FOR ME, BRO!
OH...

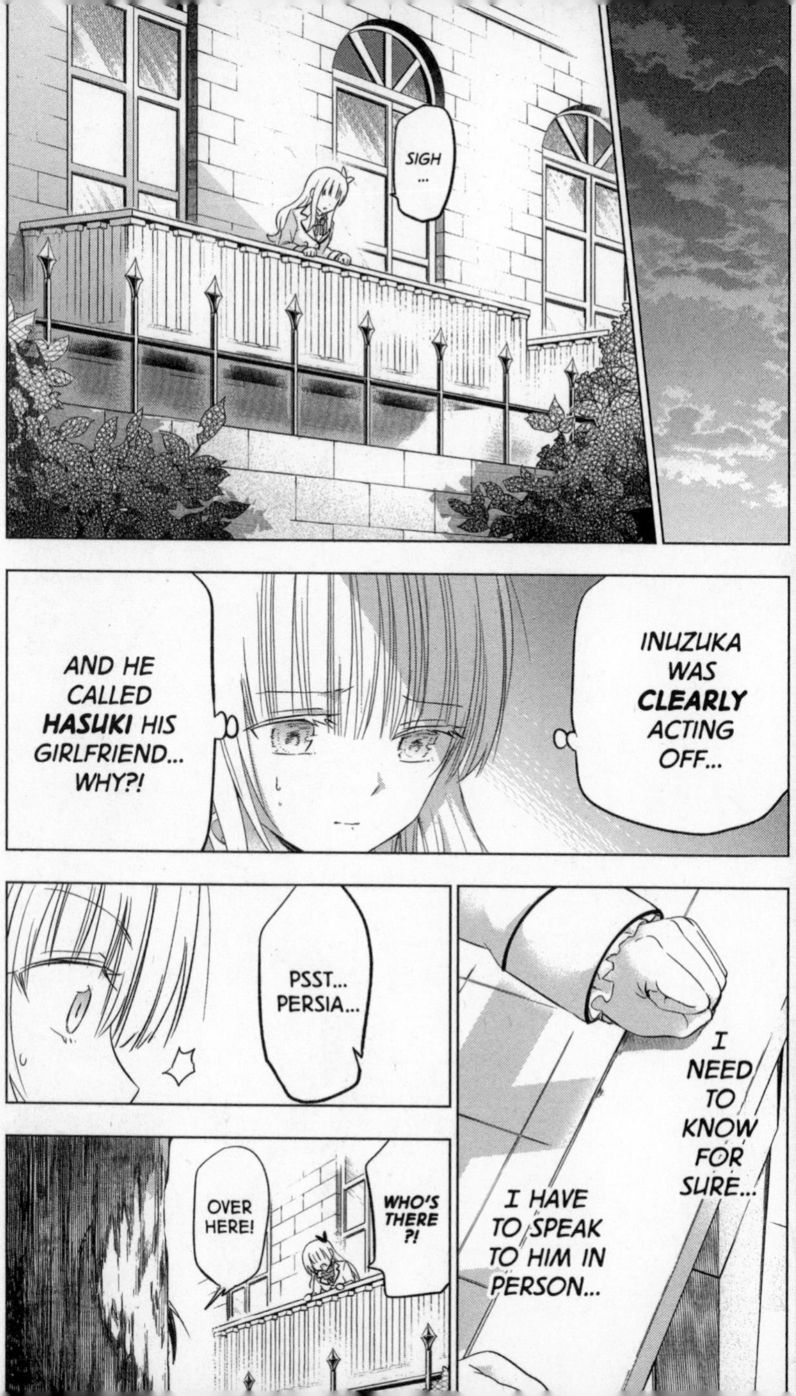
SIGH ...
INUZUKA WAS CLEARLY ACTING OFF...
AND HE CALLED HASUKI HIS GIRLFRIEND... WHY?!
I NEED TO KNOW FOR SURE...
I HAVE TO SPEAK TO HIM IN PERSON...
PSST... PERSIA...
WHO'S THERE?!
OVER HERE!

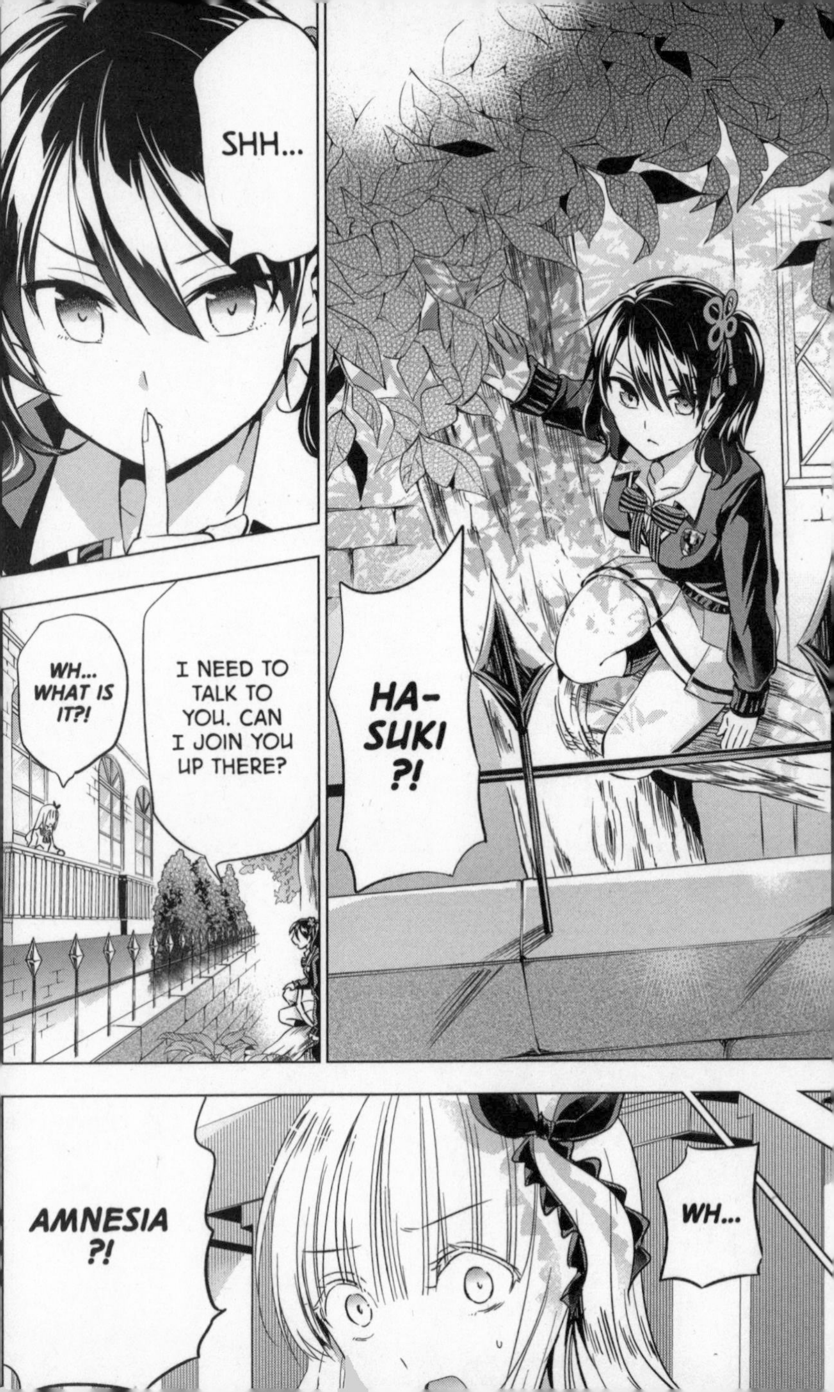
HA-SUKI?!
SHH...
I NEED TO TALK TO YOU. CAN I JOIN YOU UP THERE?
WH... WHAT IS IT?!
WH...
AMNESIA?!

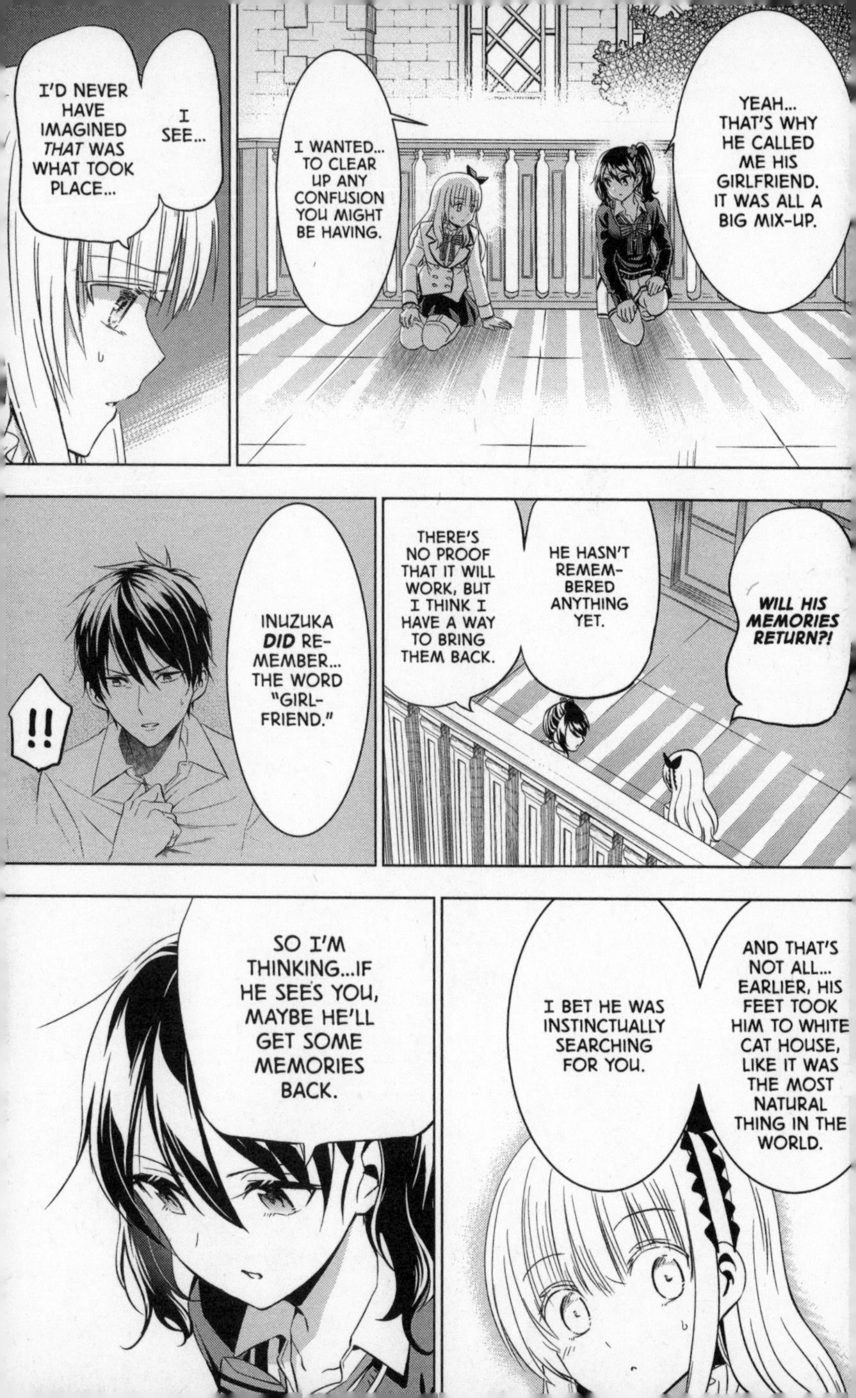
YEAH... THAT'S WHY HE CALLED ME HIS GIRLFRIEND. IT WAS ALL A BIG MIX-UP.
I WANTED... TO CLEAR UP ANY CONFUSION YOU MIGHT BE HAVING.
I SEE...
I'D NEVER HAVE IMAGINED *THAT* WAS WHAT TOOK PLACE...
WILL HIS MEMORIES RETURN?!
HE HASN'T REMEMBERED ANYTHING YET.
THERE'S NO PROOF THAT IT WILL WORK, BUT I THINK I HAVE A WAY TO BRING THEM BACK.
INUZUKA ***DID*** REMEMBER... THE WORD "GIRLFRIEND."
!!
AND THAT'S NOT ALL... EARLIER, HIS FEET TOOK HIM TO WHITE CAT HOUSE, LIKE IT WAS THE MOST NATURAL THING IN THE WORLD.
I BET HE WAS INSTINCTUALLY SEARCHING FOR YOU.
SO I'M THINKING...IF HE SEES YOU, MAYBE HE'LL GET SOME MEMORIES BACK.

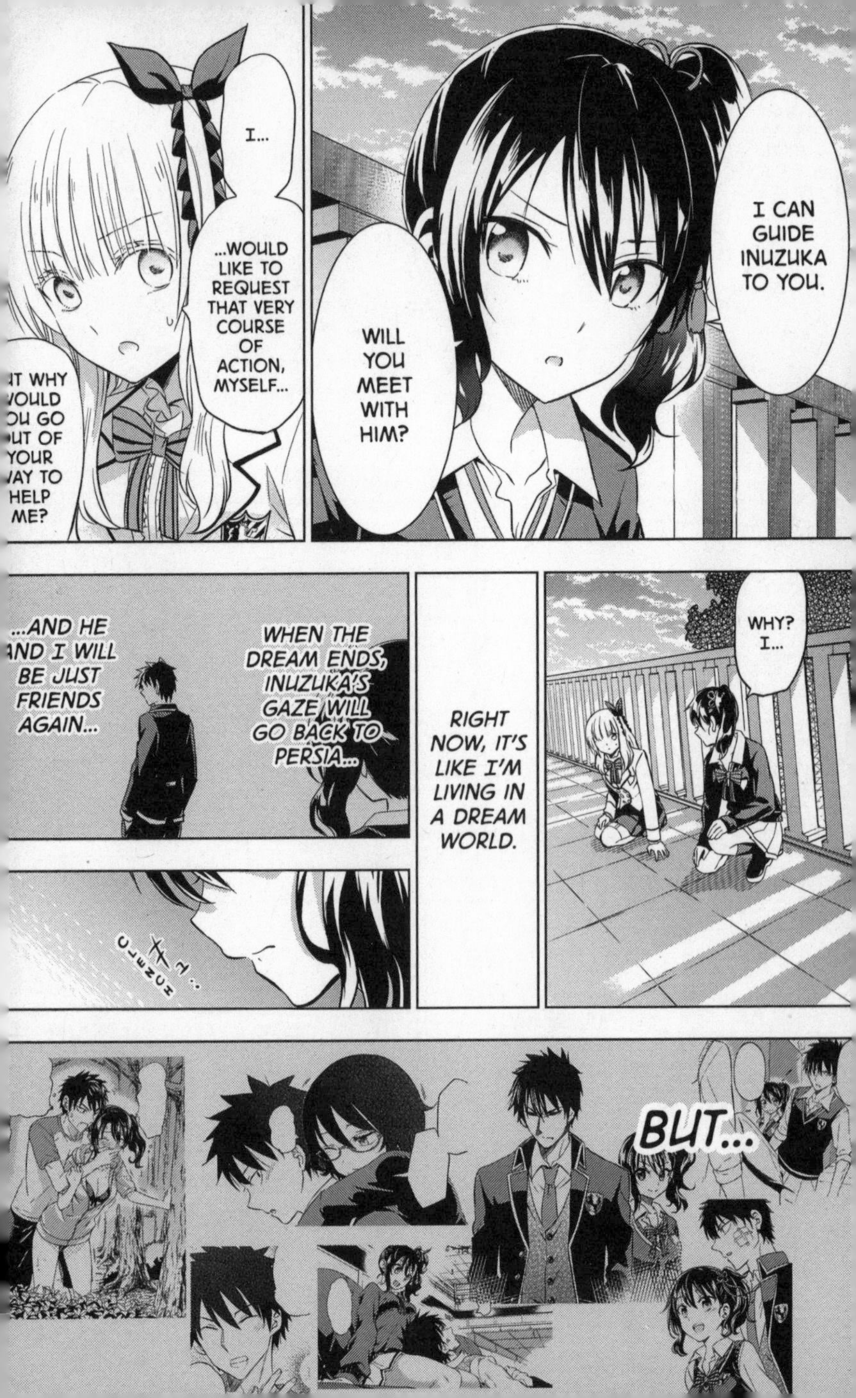
I CAN GUIDE INUZUKA TO YOU.
WILL YOU MEET WITH HIM?
I...
...WOULD LIKE TO REQUEST THAT VERY COURSE OF ACTION, MYSELF...
UT WHY OULD OU GO UT OF YOUR AY TO HELP ME?
WHY? I...
RIGHT NOW, IT'S LIKE I'M LIVING IN A DREAM WORLD.
WHEN THE DREAM ENDS, INUZUKA'S GAZE WILL GO BACK TO PERSIA...
...AND HE ND I WILL BE JUST FRIENDS AGAIN...
BUT...

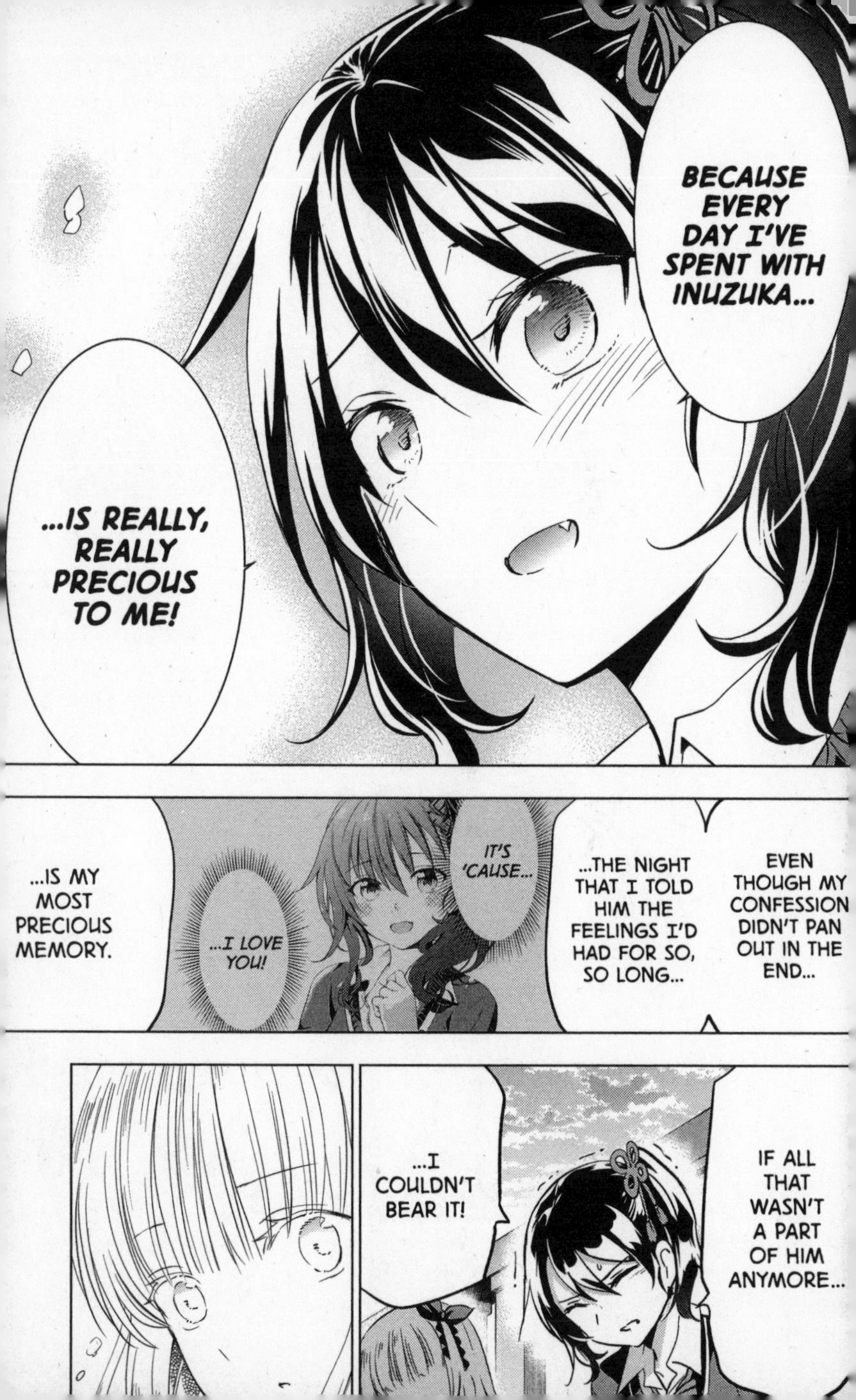
BECAUSE EVERY DAY I'VE SPENT WITH INUZUKA...
...IS REALLY, REALLY PRECIOUS TO ME!
EVEN THOUGH MY CONFESSION DIDN'T PAN OUT IN THE END...
...THE NIGHT THAT I TOLD HIM THE FEELINGS I'D HAD FOR SO, SO LONG...
IT'S 'CAUSE...
...I LOVE YOU!
...IS MY MOST PRECIOUS MEMORY.
IF ALL THAT WASN'T A PART OF HIM ANYMORE...
...I COULDN'T BEAR IT!

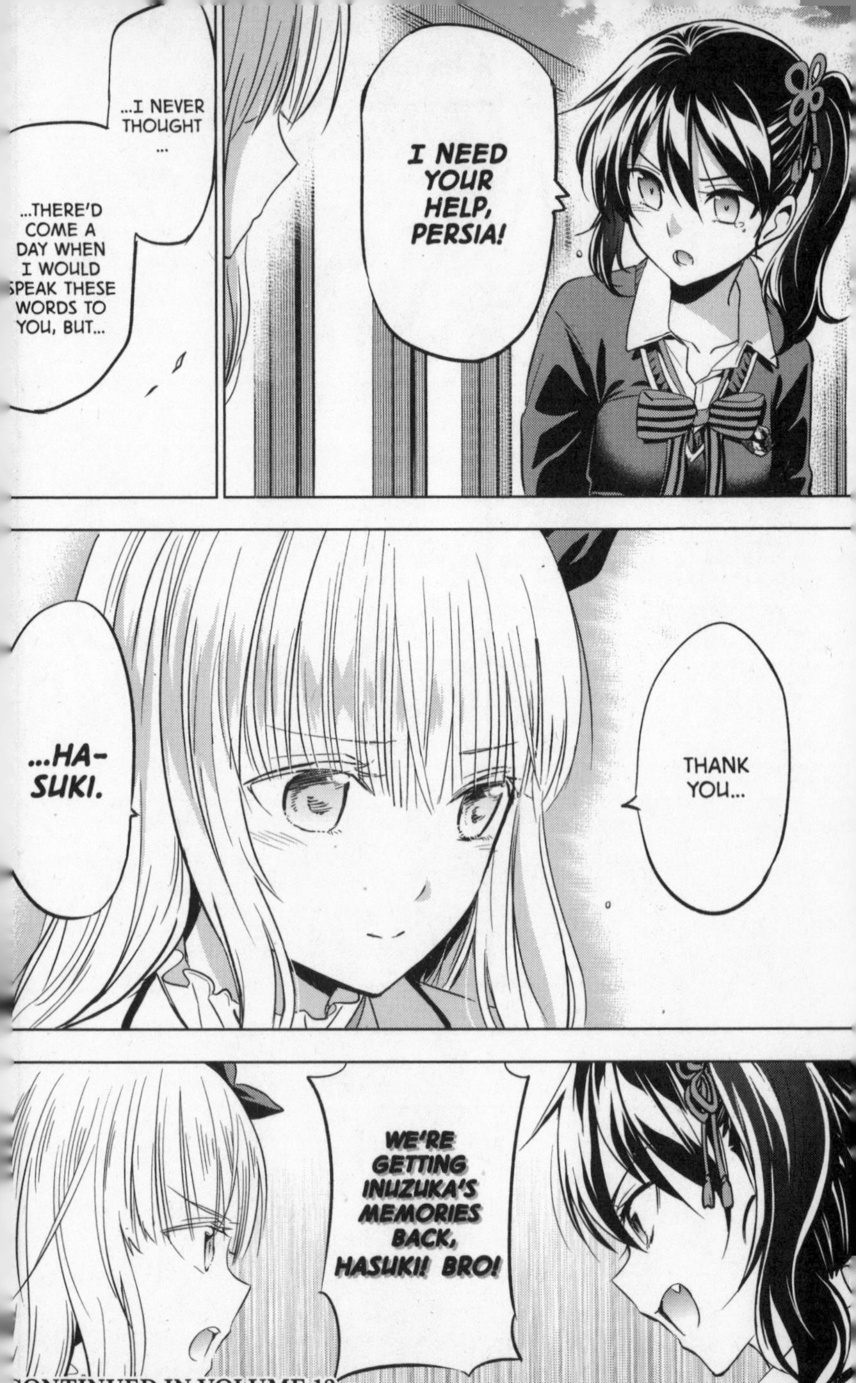
I NEED YOUR HELP, PERSIA!
...I NEVER THOUGHT ...
...THERE'D COME A DAY WHEN I WOULD SPEAK THESE WORDS TO YOU, BUT...
THANK YOU...
...HA-SUKI.
WE'RE GETTING INUZUKA'S MEMORIES BACK, HASUKI! BRO!

CONTINUED IN VOLUME 12

AFTERWORD

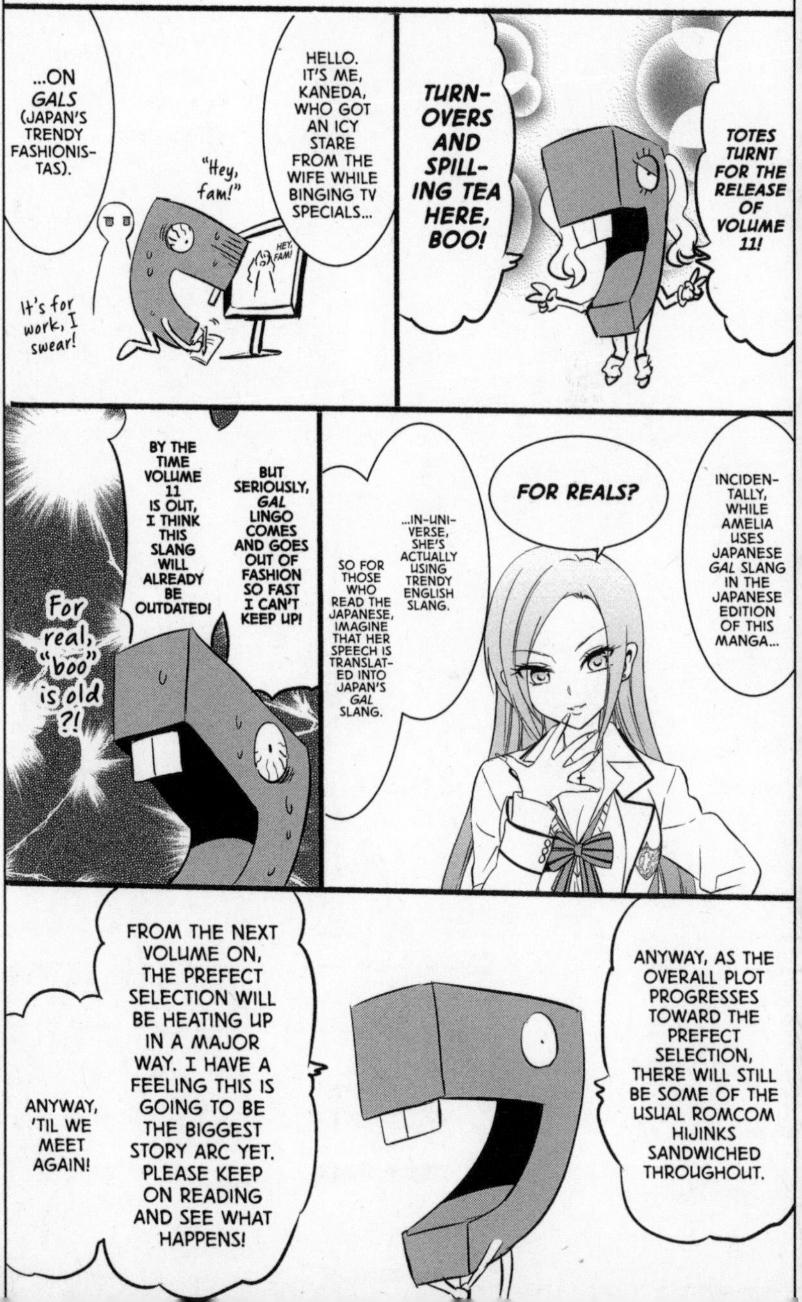
TOTES TURNT FOR THE RELEASE OF VOLUME 11!
TURN-OVERS AND SPILL-ING TEA HERE, BOO!
HELLO. IT'S ME, KANEDA, WHO GOT AN ICY STARE FROM THE WIFE WHILE BINGING TV SPECIALS...
"Hey, fam!"
HEY, FAM!
...ON *GALS* (JAPAN'S TRENDY FASHIONIS-TAS).
It's for work, I swear!
INCIDEN-TALLY, WHILE AMELIA USES JAPANESE *GAL* SLANG IN THE JAPANESE EDITION OF THIS MANGA...
FOR REALS?
...IN-UNI-VERSE, SHE'S ACTUALLY USING TRENDY ENGLISH SLANG.
SO FOR THOSE WHO READ THE JAPANESE, IMAGINE THAT HER SPEECH IS TRANSLAT-ED INTO JAPAN'S *GAL* SLANG.
BUT SERIOUSLY, *GAL* LINGO COMES AND GOES OUT OF FASHION SO FAST I CAN'T KEEP UP!
BY THE TIME VOLUME 11 IS OUT, I THINK THIS SLANG WILL ALREADY BE OUTDATED!
For real, "boo" is old?!
ANYWAY, AS THE OVERALL PLOT PROGRESSES TOWARD THE PREFECT SELECTION, THERE WILL STILL BE SOME OF THE USUAL ROMCOM HIJINKS SANDWICHED THROUGHOUT.
FROM THE NEXT VOLUME ON, THE PREFECT SELECTION WILL BE HEATING UP IN A MAJOR WAY. I HAVE A FEELING THIS IS GOING TO BE THE BIGGEST STORY ARC YET. PLEASE KEEP ON READING AND SEE WHAT HAPPENS!
ANYWAY, 'TIL WE MEET AGAIN!

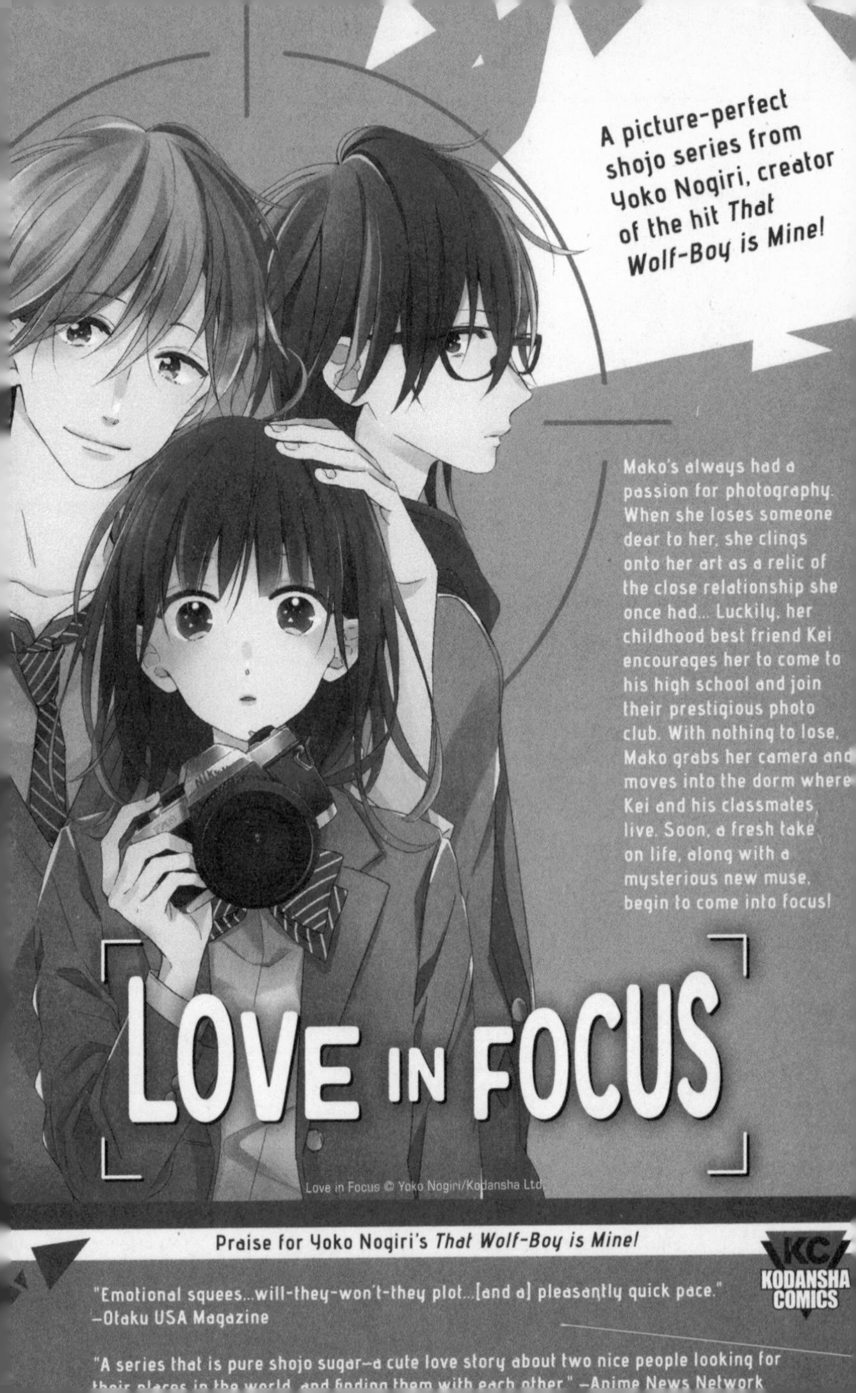
A picture-perfect shojo series from Yoko Nogiri, creator of the hit *That Wolf-Boy is Mine!*
Mako's always had a passion for photography. When she loses someone dear to her, she clings onto her art as a relic of the close relationship she once had... Luckily, her childhood best friend Kei encourages her to come to his high school and join their prestigious photo club. With nothing to lose, Mako grabs her camera and moves into the dorm where Kei and his classmates live. Soon, a fresh take on life, along with a mysterious new muse, begin to come into focus!
LOVE IN FOCUS
Love in Focus © Yoko Nogiri/Kodansha Ltd.

ANIME OUT NOW
FROM SENTAI FILMWORKS!

A BL romance between a good boy who didn't know he was waiting for a hero, and a bad boy who comes to his rescue!

Masahiro Setagawa doesn't believe in heroes but wishes he could: He's found himself in a gang of small-time street bullies, and with no prospects for a real future. But when high school teacher (and scourge of the streets) Kousuke Ohshiba comes to his rescue, he finds he may need to start believing after all... in heroes, and in his budding feelings, too.

Hitorijime My Hero

Memeco Arii

KC KODANSHA COMICS

Boarding School Juliet 11 copyright © 2018 Yousuke Kaneda
English translation copyright © 2020 Yousuke Kaneda

Published in the United States by Kodansha Comics, an imprint of Kodansha USA Publishing, LLC, New York.

Publication rights for this English edition arranged through Kodansha Ltd., Tokyo.

First published in Japan in 2018 by Kodansha Ltd., Tokyo as *Kishuku Gakkou no Jurietto*, volume 11.

ISBN 978-1-63236-905-5

Printed in the United States of America.

www.kodanshacomics.com

9 8 7 6 5 4 3 2 1
Translation: Amanda Haley
Lettering: James Dashiell
Editing: Erin Subramanian and Tiff Ferentini
Kodansha Comics edition cover design by Phil Balsman

Publisher: Kiichiro Sugawara
Managing editor: Maya Rosewood
Vice president of marketing & publicity: Naho Yamada

Director of publishing services: Ben Applegate
Associate director of operations: Stephen Pakula
Publishing services managing editor: Noelle Webster
Assistant production manager: Emi Lotto and Angela Zurlo